A GREENER FAITH

A GREENER FAITH

*Religious Environmentalism
and Our Planet's Future*

Roger S. Gottlieb

OXFORD
UNIVERSITY PRESS

OXFORD
UNIVERSITY PRESS

Oxford University Press, Inc., publishes works that further
Oxford University's objective of excellence
in research, scholarship, and education.

Oxford   New York
Auckland   Cape Town   Dar es Salaam   Hong Kong   Karachi
Kuala Lumpur   Madrid   Melbourne   Mexico City   Nairobi
New Delhi   Shanghai   Taipei   Toronto

With offices in
Argentina   Austria   Brazil   Chile   Czech Republic   France   Greece
Guatemala   Hungary   Italy   Japan   Poland   Portugal   Singapore
South Korea   Switzerland   Thailand   Turkey   Ukraine   Vietnam

Published by Oxford University Press, Inc.
198 Madison Avenue, New York, New York 10016

www.oup.com

First issued as an Oxford University Press paperback, 2009

Oxford is a registered trademark of Oxford University Press

Library of Congress Cataloging-in-Publication Data
Gottlieb, Roger S.
A greener faith : religious environmentalism and our planet's future / Roger S. Gottlieb.
p.   cm.
Includes bibliographical references and index.
ISBN 978-0-19-539620-1
1. Human ecology—Religious aspects—Christianity.   2. Environmentalism—Religious
aspects—Christianity.   3. Stewardship, Christian.   I. Title.
BT695.5.G69   2006
201'.77—dc22   2005023084

To the ponds, trees, seagulls, flowers, geese,
and breezes of Jamaica Plain;

And to the people who nourish and
protect this sacred space.

For keeping me (more or less) sane all these years,

Thank you.

Preface to the Paperback Edition

In the three years since *A Greener Faith* came out, some things have changed, and many have stayed the same. We remain in the midst of a civilization challenging environmental crisis; throughout the world a significant number of religious groups, leaders, theologians, and activists are responding to that crisis. A full-length film (*Renewal*) charts nine different religious environmental campaigns. The Green Seminaries movement lists dozens of seminaries in which ecological issues form essential parts of the curriculum. The increased commitment of generally politically conservative Evangelical Christians continues to attract attention. In large and small ways the movement described in *A Greener Faith* has continued to pick up speed.

Overall, however, most of the policies of the global society seem stuck in Business as Usual. It may indeed be the very scope of the crisis which, a little paradoxically, keeps so much of what should be changed in place. Consider, for example, the Great Pacific Garbage Patch—an area in the eastern Pacific Ocean in which a kind of stew of throwaway plastic refuse, at places just on the surface and at others as much as 300 feet deep, has been concentrated and maintained by a combination of currents. The Patch is, and I'm not making this up, approximately twice as big as the United States.

What can we do with such a "fact" but throw up our hands in despair and, if possible, change the channel? It is because of the emotional impact of such facts—along with increased awareness of the accelerating pace of global warming, larger areas affected by extreme weather events and drought, and island nations being evacuated because the sea is rising—that the greatest environmental problem remains a persistent human refusal to face the truth. And if this is the crucial problem we face, then we have an ever greater need for every possible resource to help us overcome it, especially a resource so practiced in mobilizing people for self-examination and public action as religion.

If this sounds, as some reviewers have complained, like an opportunistic use of religion for environmental purposes, then I plead guilty to hoping that religions can serve the continued flourishing of life—human and otherwise—on this planet. Despite theological attachments to a heavenly realm or to the extinction of ordinary consciousness in nirvana, the pursuit of a decent life on earth really does seem to me in line with the dominant thrust of the vast majority of the world's religions. I cannot think of any faith that would prefer the

Pacific with the Garbage Patch to what that vast ocean was 100 years ago; or which could not deeply question the moral failures (greed, selfishness, short-sightedness or pursuit of power) which brought us to this point. It is true that *my* concern is not with promoting any single version of religious truth. Yet that should not prevent anyone who is more *focused* from signing on to preserve the earth as a supportive context for human life. All this is unchanged since the book's initial publication, and is likely to remain so into the indefinite future.

What is dramatically *different* now is that the world is in the grip of a deep and frightening economic crisis, one which involves disruptions of production, consumption and physical well-being in rich and poor, developed and 'developing' nations alike. This crisis marks a deep threat to environmentalism. As the Republicans gleefully chanted "Drill baby drill" at campaign rallies, as contributions to environmental groups sharply decline, as loans for green technological innovation, or public funds for conservation, or action to save species—as all these dry up, "saving the planet" may often take a very far away back seat compared to saving our jobs, standard of living, and social services. If it is a choice between other life forms and people, typically we will choose ourselves. If it is a choice between short-term benefits and long term health and safety, we will, or at least for the most part we *have*, opted for what was right in front of our noses rather than what was coming down the pike. And as long as the immediate health effects of pollution continue to be somewhat obscure to the general public—the connection, for example, between pollution and cancer, birth defects, and infertility—environmentalism can be represented as an interest group rather than a collective need.

Yet even here there is something hopeful, which is that the book's brief discussion of the limitations of global capitalism is being writ large in bank failures, plunging stock markets, and rising unemployment. As a near universal clamor arises for governments to "do *something*" the premises which support a global system shaped by markets and unfettered corporations are questioned—as is the value of an endless growth of consumerism. Other resources—cultural over natural, human as opposed to commodified—are being recruited to help us through. Other visions of life take on a greater appeal or at least start to appear somewhat larger on the radar screen.

And this is as true of the comparatively undeveloped world as it is of the West, and in some ways more so, since less developed countries are not yet completely dependent on intense oil economies, malls, and a high consumption lifestyle. China, economic juggernaut that it is, has its profound environmental problems. By some measures virtually all of its seemingly spectacular economic growth of the last decade or so is cancelled by economic losses from environmental damage: topsoil erosion, water pollution, the financial drain of health care costs or lost labor time due to environmental illnesses. Tens of thousands of environmental demonstrations each year reflect the Chinese people's awareness that dirty rivers and unbreathable air may be too steep a price for cable TV and more cars on the roads.

In short, the economic crisis may drive us to a desperate reassertion of the primacy of industrial growth—or create serious doubts about that primacy. In those doubts could be the germ of a culturally and environmentally sustainable form of life. In the short run at least there is some definite hope to be taken from the election of Barack Obama. Throughout his remarkable candidacy he put forward the most comprehensive environmental program of any of the candidates; and received the most organized support of environmental groups. During his short presidency he has already made environmental concerns a focus of his economic stimulus effort. In many ways the missing link in a universal response to global climate change, an ecologically reoriented United States could make the difference in the activation of a coordinated, international response to global warming. That certainly would be change to believe in! Obama's candidacy was also distinct by being unafraid to be both politically liberal and also assert the value of religion for the candidate and for public life generally. Thus the coming years may be, for a variety of reasons, much more sympathetic than the past to a religiously motivated environmentalism.

Above all, the new economic crisis, combined with our ongoing awareness of ecological stresses, might lead us to refocus our attention. For, ultimately, what is most required is not another study of alternative energy use or the effects of pesticides on infertility rates. Consider, for example, what happens if we think about the effects of human action on the non-human world. What happens when we take a long, hard look? Quite often not a whole lot, for most of us do not bother to look. Or if we do what we see is an abstraction; x million animals killed in experiments, x thousands of species lost. But what if we do look, carefully, slowly, willing to accept whatever feelings arise, at—say—Polar Bears which have to cannibalize each other because global warming has melted so much ice they can no longer hunt. Look at them—magnificent creatures clad in thick white fur, superbly adapted to the frigid ice and snow, at home even in the sea. Mothers that protect their young, playful cubs, powerful hunters of seals. They are dying, not from old age or struggle with predators or competition in the herd, but because we are killing them. Through global warming. Reckless sport hunting. Human-made toxins that build up in their flesh.

The point is that it is not just the suffering of the individual polar bears that gets to us, or even the potential loss of this majestic species, it is *how hard it is to look at ourselves.* To save the Polar Bears (and the Big Cats, the Rainforest, the orphaned children who live on the garbage dumps of Rio, or the women who make pennies a day taking heavy metals out of used computers) how much would *we* have to change? How much of our economy, our culture, our family life? How many laws would we have to pass? Would we have to give up our dream of endless economic expansion so that we left some room for other species? Would we have to say that the whole human enterprise of the last 10,000 years—seeking more and more power, wealth, control, technical expertise, and shopping—should be (deeply, seriously, essentially) restrained?

But can there be a greater, a more serious, *religious* movement than to shift attention away from the "world" and onto one's own moral condition? Is this not the heart of religion, any religion? Surely it is more important to live a Christian life than to have achieved the exactly correct understanding of the mystery of the Trinity. The Torah teaches us that "we shall do and we shall hear"—that action precedes the finer points of understanding. Buddhism goes even further, often considering religious doctrine a distraction compared to other aspects of morality and spiritual practice.

For those of us on a religious path, there is no better opportunity than right now, in the face of the crises which we as humans have collectively caused, to look, and look again, at ourselves. If our environmental problems are an occasion to do this, and if the economic crisis lends added weight, it will clearly not just be that religion can serve the environmental cause, but that an expanded environmental awareness will improve our faith, our morality, and our openness to God.

PREFACE

If you're not depressed, I often joke to my students, it's only because you haven't been reading the newspaper. And indeed we do live in a frightening time, marked by fundamentalist violence, aggressive wars, ethnic conflict, starvation amid plenty, and the subject of this book: enormously pervasive environmental problems.

Yet I didn't write this book to depress us all further, but to cheer us up. I am deeply heartened by the astonishing new movement of religious environmentalism: its bold ideas, transformative effect on institutionalized religion, passionate commitment to social activism, and the way it opens our spiritual hearts. At the very least, religious environmentalism should give us all reason to hope that this oldest of human institutions can face the demands of the present and that human beings from around the world can see beyond what divides us to what we share.

The book begins by providing examples of the unique gifts religion offers to help us respond to the environmental crisis. I then describe the new green religious thought, forceful statements and commitments by religious institutions, and religious environmental activism. Because of current intense controversies over the place of faith in social life, I have included (in chapter 2) a discussion of why and how religious participation in public life, a participation that religious environmentalism requires, can be a positive force for democracy, human betterment, and a sustainable global society. There are also chapters on prayer and ritual, the personal side of the movement, and why the unique features of secular environmentalism make it a natural ally of religion. After all this good news, the book concludes with a sobering assessment of the major forces that obstruct religious environmentalism, as well as some reflections on how those forces might be overcome.

Trying to make this book accessible to that mythical being, the "general reader," I have confined a good deal of reference material, as well as some extended discussions of particular points, to the notes. There the "nongeneral reader" will find sources and quotations that reinforce the points made in the text and provide a basis for further study. One indication of the scope of religious environmentalism is that even after 130,000 words I have not touched on a plethora of books, articles, public statements, activist groups, and public projects. The movement is now much too large to be covered completely by any one book. Because I consider myself a participant in religious environmentalism as well as its chronicler and occasional critic, this is, I believe, a very good thing.

⌒

I offer here a brief note on terminology.

To some extent, we all know what "religion" is and what it means to be "spiritual." Yet, because these familiar words may be known in different ways, it may be useful to clarify how I use them in this book. For me, religions are systems of belief, ritual, institutional life, spiritual aspiration, and ethical orientation that view human beings as more than simply their social or physical selves. Teachings are "religious" when they assert (as in Judaism, Christianity, and Islam) that there exists a Supreme Being whose moral commands and ultimate power supersedes even the grandest of earthly political authorities. Alternatively, even without a Supreme Being, Buddhism offers a religious insight when it teaches that we can achieve a state of consciousness that transcends the attachments and passions of our ordinary social egos. To be religious, in this sense, is to be aware that some things have "ultimate significance"—in the sense of being supremely fitting to who we really are.

As religious beings, we move between the holy and the secular, between our spiritual aspirations and our conventional lives, reaching toward God or Ultimate Truth and just hanging out. In this complex and demanding dance, religions prescribe norms of conduct to root our everyday relationships in truths about our essential identity. God, Truth, Buddha Nature, or our responsibility to the Spirits of Nature can be expressed in the way we marry, do business, raise our children, and deal with rush-hour traffic. To make these ideas vital presences in the world, church schools teach the young and buildings are maintained for collective gatherings. Special holidays provide concentrated arenas of religious energy. Ritual acts of prayerful worship, meditation, collective contrition, or celebration awaken and reinforce personal and communal connections to Ultimate Truth(s), train the personality to reflect certain values in daily life, and provide emotional outlets during life-cycle events such as marriage, birth, and death.

Finally, religions invite us to cultivate a sense of awe and mystery. This need not be a blind attachment to a confusing creed or a dogmatic attachment to making endless moral judgments about others. It can simply reflect a sense that both the universe as a whole and human existence within it are more beautiful and profound than we can ever fully realize.

"Spiritual" is a term often used to suggest something different from—but closely related to—religion. "I'm not religious at all," people will frequently say, "but I do have a pretty active spiritual life." Spiritual aspirations, I believe, are in fact a *kind* of religious perspective, sharing the emphasis on a reality distinct from one's conventional social position and on values that dissent from the social order. These values often take the form of virtues—gratitude, patience, humility, serenity—that serve the happiness of both the person who manifests them and everyone around that person. Yet it is a kind of religiosity that accentuates personal experience, theological tolerance, and lifelong pursuit of spiritual growth rather than attachment to an established religious normality. People who say they are "spiritual" but not "religious" often mean that they pick and choose among different traditions and practices, that they are not part of a formal religious congregation, and that they are more concerned with enhancing their own virtues than with judging the religious orthodoxy of anyone else. For my purposes, then, the term "spirituality" is not opposed to religion, but simply emphasizes a certain way of being religious.

The word "nature" may be as contested as "religion," and because I will frequently talk of nature in what follows, it may be helpful to explain what I mean by it. The term is confusing because on the one hand familiar ways of talking make a clear distinction between human beings and nature: we have "natural" foods (grown with as little human interference as possible), "nature" preserves (areas where human development is forbidden), vacations in "nature" (not, to be sure, in the city!). There are books with titles like *The End of Nature* and *The Death of Nature*. Used this way, "nature" stands for that part of the universe that is *not* created, affected, or determined by people. Nature in this sense is opposed to history, language, high-level thinking processes, technology, formal systems of morality, and politics.

On the other hand, however, there is a nearly equally widespread understanding in which humans and nature are inseparable. Surely my body, no less than my desk, will obey the laws of physics if it is thrown off the roof. Surely humans developed their biological human *nature* (notice the term that easily comes to mind) the same way apes, squirrels, and eels did—through the mechanism of evolution. The chemicals that make up my cells are no different than those that make up a clam, and the atoms in my body, like the atoms in everything else, were present at the Big Bang.

How are we to deal with the contradictions between the two ways in which the term is used?

For the most part in what follows, I will mean by "nature" the earth's system of living beings and the support systems for them. Thus the fish and the ocean, the elk and the tundra, the butterflies and the flowers are all part of nature. When I talk about the human relation to nature, I will take for granted that humans are as biologically, chemically, and physically as natural as anything else. But humans, among other species, are unique in three ways. First, we seem to have a unique ability to destabilize environments and destroy other species. Second, we seem to have a unique ability to integrate technology into our "natural" bodies. Third, we seem to have a unique ability to ask ourselves questions about our behaviors: to create and argue about morality, what is right, and what we should (or should not) be doing. A phrase like "humanity's treatment of nature," then, is not meant to imply that humans are not natural, but rather focuses attention on how human beings affect the rest of life on earth.

Finally, disagreements about the meaning of "God" have occasioned the spilling of much ink—and far too much blood. My own beliefs about this matter are not particularly relevant here, except to say that I am quite certain that if God can be male, God can also be female. For that reason, and because exclusively male God references are experienced as patriarchal and marginalizing by many people, I use both masculine and feminine pronouns for God.

ACKNOWLEDGMENTS

It is a real pleasure to acknowledge the help I've received, all of which has made this a better book.

Worcester Polytechnic Institute, my academic home for twenty-five years, helped start the project off with a sabbatical leave. David Barnhill, once again, read the whole thing and provided detailed corrections and searching questions. Tom Shannon, once again, helped me understand Christianity and commented on drafts of several chapters. Michelle Ephraim and Miriam Greenspan helped make chapter 7 more believable and readable. John Sanbonmatsu, Peter Amato, Mark Wallace, and Seamus Carey gave me important and supportive feedback.

The book's basic ideas were developed in some of my courses at WPI and in talks at many places, including Thiel College, College of the Holy Cross, Tufts University, Episcopal Divinity School, Boston Theological Institute, the American Philosophical Association, the American Academy of Religion, the Boston Social Forum, Colorado College, Hampshire County Interfaith Council, General Assembly of Unitarian Universalists, and the BioDevastation 2000 Conference. I am grateful for critical encouragement from all these sources.

As "Reading Spirit" columnist for *Tikkun* magazine, I wrote review essays that helped form part of passages in chapter 2 (on religion and political life) and chapter 8 (on globalization).

For over a decade I've been blessed to be part of the Religion and Ecology group of the American Academy of Religion. Their knowledge, commitment, and fellowship have been an unfailing source of strength.

Cynthia Read, religion editor at Oxford University Press, provided constant support, judicious suggestions, and a sense that the book mattered. She is a great editor. Judith Hoover did a splendid job of copyediting.

Dozens of busy people were kind enough to take the time to answer my questions or participate in lengthy interviews about their work. Much of this book's value comes from their words.

Finally, and most important, throughout the world men and women are joining hands to try to steer our global civilization in a new direction: one less determined by lust for power and greed and more in harmony with Life and Spirit. Their work is the subject of this book, and its inspiration.

CONTENTS

A Greener Faith

INTRODUCTION

RELIGION AND THE HUMAN MEANING OF ENVIRONMENTAL CRISIS

> Humans are damaging the planet at an unprecedented rate and raising
> risks of abrupt collapses in nature that could spur disease, deforestation,
> or "dead zones" in the seas, an international report said yesterday.
>
> —Alister Doyle, "Strain on Planet Worsening,
> Report Warns," *Boston Globe*, March 31, 2005

> God loves the earth fully. By loving one another and every sentient
> being—even the rocks who cry out—we love God. In this love we are
> called to resist the poisoning of peoples and the earth.
>
> —Karen Baker-Fletcher, *Sisters of Dust,
> Sisters of Spirit: Womanist Wording on God and Creation*

With each breath and each mouthful of food, whenever we make love, witness the miracle of birth, or bury a loved one, our spirits engage with our physical selves. Every time we stick our head out the window to scrutinize the weather, thrill to the sudden glimpse of a cardinal's scarlet plumage, or throw ourselves with gleeful abandon into the ocean's stinging immensity, we engage with that encompassing reality that we may think of as nature, the earth, or the environment.

To begin with, then, the environmental crisis betokens a deep and frightening shift in our relations to both our physical selves and to nature. Haunting the exquisiteness of nature—the cascading colors of a summer sunset, the exuberant rushing waters of an untamed river, the brilliant ferocity of a leopard—are gloomy, nagging questions. How much of the intensity of that particular sunset's colors is caused by air pollution? Does the river contain invisible toxins that make it unsafe for swimming or fishing? How many leopards are left, and will our grandchildren even believe that such marvelous creatures ever existed outside of zoos or picture books? These questions, multiplied by our scrutiny of the chemicals in our food, by every half-suppressed, vaguely anxious thought about what will happen if the global warming predictions are true or if the hole in the ozone layer expands, darken our sense of nature's majesty, peacefulness, and promise.

Such uncertainties are not limited to our sense of the "outside," but are as intimate as an upcoming mammogram or a nagging asthmatic cough. For we have come to see that the environmental crisis is not only written on the land and water and air, but also permeates our own bodies. We know that our breasts, our prostates, our lungs, and our bloodstream are no longer what they were, and that just as we have put dioxins in the river and imperiled the last of the leopards, so a mother's breast milk may be too polluted for her baby to drink, and cancer rates, deeply influenced by environmental pollution, continue to climb.[1]

In our anxiety over what may be happening to us, in our deep grief when the possible becomes actual in our own lives, and in our aching sense of violation when we see a favorite bit of forest turned into a mall or notice how many fewer songbirds there are in the spring, these perils affect us personally. They are also a profound collective challenge. It is our nation's health care system that must pay for the environmentally induced illnesses, our water treatment system that must take over the purifying functions of the now eliminated wetlands, and our land that suffers as chemical fertilizers degrade the topsoil. Beyond anyone's national boundaries, comparable problems afflict the planet as a whole, taking particular forms in each locale and constituting a collective predicament without historical precedent. Industrial civilization, despite (or because of!) its technological brilliance, has created a grave threat unlike anything humanity has ever done before. No tyrant, emperor, or czar could have eliminated so much of the rain forests, raised the earth's temperature, extinguished 150 species each day, or caused children's lungs, as they do in certain highly polluted sections of Los Angeles, to grow abnormally small.

❧

Besides the physical threat and the physical loss, the increase in illness and the decrease in biodiversity, there are more diffuse, harder to identify, but equally threatening dimensions of the crisis. For the environmental crisis is not only a danger to our physical and economic well-being, but a unique challenge to our fundamental sense of what it means to be human. It requires that we rethink our most important beliefs about who we are and how we ought to live.

For a start, the environmental crisis creates real doubts about our sense of human worth. When we see a sign warning us "Do not under *any* circumstances fish in this stream because of pollution!!!" or realize that genetic engineering is threatening the monarch butterfly or that oil development in

Nigeria has devastated the local tribes, we may feel a deep sense of shame, both for our whole species and for our individual selves as well. Is this really the best that corporations, governments, and communities can do? And what of our own actions? We know, even if the knowledge is suppressed most of the time, that all those long drives, all those appliances, all that stuff we've bought play some part. In response to this pained awareness, once again nagging questions arise, this time undermining our prevailing species smugness: What is the worth of human beings if this is what we do? How can we believe that we are the "crown of creation" when we engage in a collective and unthinking ruin of the creatures that surround us? What kinds of lives are we living if we continue to shop, drive our cars, fly ozone-destroying jets, and act as if nothing really critical is taking place?

Shame and guilt for the present give rise to deep fears about the future. We wonder, in what might be called a perennial state of environmental anxiety, how much worse it will be for our children. A sense that the future is bright, that the next decade will be better than the previous one, gives way to a kind of chronic low-level despair, a sense that it's only going to get worse. We know that each generation will have less wilderness with which to engage and be increasingly dependent on ever more ambitious cancer treatments. Few things will become cleaner, fresher, more pure; most will become a little bit more polluted or diminished. We have moved, as Frederic Buell tells us, from thinking of the environmental crisis as some kind of apocalypse to resignedly accepting it as a way of life.[2]

As we recognize our present moral failings and despair over the future, we must confront grim questions about our collective goals and limits. For hundreds of years we have envisioned human life as a continuous pattern of development: better machines to go along with better social values, more sophisticated science to go along with greater personal freedom. Anything we *could* do, we thought, we *should* do: What else is the human mind for if not to plumb the depths of knowledge and create new things? What purpose does the market have other than to satisfy our desires and stimulate new ones? Now, however, we wonder if in some ways we have gone too far. The explosive proliferation of industrial chemicals, the endless stream of pesticides, the unforeseen consequences surrounding genetically modified organisms—these cause us to think, and think again, about placing some restraints on our scientific and technological innovation. Further, when we see how much stuff we have, and what that stuff costs the earth, we ask if there might also be a limit to our own entitlement to consume. We come to see, if only quite dimly, that everything has a price in more than money: the nifty air conditioners in our cars depleted the ozone layer and made us more susceptible to skin cancer and blindness; the chemicals that kill mosquitoes may make us sterile; the high-powered fertilizers producing this year's crops diminish the soil's fertility for next year's seeds.

Finally, the environmental crisis darkens our sense of the presence of the sacred in our daily lives. For those of us who do not see visions or hear voices, outside of scripture God's presence on earth resides in the beauties of creation. Thus, for generations, many Christians believed that (as in the words of Psalm 19) the heavens declared "the glory of God."[3] Even those who do not believe in anything like the traditional God of Western monotheism often find a special kind of value in nature. It is in nature, many say, that they feel taken out of themselves, soothed, and brought into contact with the sacred. The range of all these feelings was beautifully expressed by Anne Frank, as she hid for almost two years in an Amsterdam attic to evade the Nazis: "The best remedy for those who are afraid, lonely, or unhappy is to go outside, somewhere where they can be quite alone with the heavens, nature, and God. Because only then does one feel that all is as it should be and that God wishes to see people happy, amidst the simple beauty of nature. As long as this exists, and it certainly always will, I know that then there will always be comfort for every storm."[4]

What happens to Frank's certainty if we try to be "alone with the heavens, nature, and God" and find that we cannot do so because there are cars whizzing by and planes buzzing overhead and that the simple "beauty of nature" we had thought to find has just been "developed" into a ski resort with trailside condos? Can people who are "spiritual but not religious" find comfort from nature when a casual stroll in a pine forest is jolted by a strange smell that turns out to be illegal dumping of toxic material in a nearby pond? Might not a meditative moment on the beach turn to shock as used syringes and human waste wash in on the tide? If nature has ended, as Bill McKibben suggests, because the impact of human beings is everywhere, then this will surely, and tragically, diminish our sense of the sacred as found in nature. We will look to nature for comfort and find broken beer bottles on mountaintops or sea birds choking on plastic bags; we will find, that is, only ourselves. As the Raji people, forest dwellers facing extreme deforestation on the Nepal–India border, put it, "Before, we knew where the gods were. They were in the trees. Now there are no more trees."[5]

Thus, the environmental crisis challenges us not just to save our skins, but to discern anew what we are doing with our lives. If human beings are so important, blessed by a uniquely valuable ability to reason, why have we behaved so irrationally? If the purpose of life is wealth, ease, and technological innovation, why has our culture's achievements in these areas made such a mess of things? If we really love our children, why are we bringing them into a world in which so many environmental indicators are worsening year by year? If we are as moral as we say we are, how can we support—through what we buy and sell, how we work and seek pleasure—a system that has disproportionately painful effects on our own poor and on the developing nations? If God is, as many say, everywhere, how do we recognize Him in the toxic waste dumps, the dead lakes, and the coral bleached white by warming oceans?

～

When our hopes are called into question and our self-worth has become doubtful, when despair lurks close by and we sense the need for some deep changes in our lives, some would say we should turn to faith—for it is the job of religion to lend a hand precisely when things seem darkest. Religion offers hope of miracles: the Hebrew slaves liberated from Egypt, Jesus resurrected from the dead, the exuberantly impossible Buddhist ideal in which every single being is freed from suffering. On the personal side, as inspirational Christian writer C. S. Lewis told us, suffering is God's wake-up call, and we may well respond to that call by seeking out religious wisdom.[6] Much of religion is, after all, geared to help us in need. It can both morally instruct and comfort us, providing rituals in which we acknowledge our sins and receive forgiveness. Religion reassures us that a change of heart is always possible, for if God can act for us, we can also act for ourselves. As well, religion also offers a fresh perspective on the meaning of life: stressing obedience to God rather than worship of emperors, the pursuit of sacred rather than monetary goals, and love of moral virtue over social standing. Most important, religion has said in no uncertain terms that we can find God in solidarity with the afflicted and the vulnerable, that wisdom begins with compassion, and that God was willing to take on a whole world's suffering in hopes of releasing us from it.

Indeed, I have written this book in part because I believe quite strongly that religion has profound contributions to make to our collective response to the environmental crisis. As we shall see, many in the world's faith communities have taken up the challenges posed by the environmental crisis and responded with passionate commitment. Religions have become part of the all too scarce good news on the environmental front—one more element in a worldwide environmental movement.

This is, of course, not equally true for every religion or every religious person. In a world as diverse as ours, every daunting historical concern—the pursuit of women's equality, war with Iraq, acceptance of homosexuality—will occasion a wide variety of responses. And the environmental crisis in particular raises deeply controversial issues, ranging from the true value of nature to our conception of a just economy. Yet, if religion's commitment to environmentalism is not absolute, it is extremely powerful and widespread.

Clearly, this was not always the case. Although in many cases, religions are now part of the solution to our environmental problems, it is also true that for a very long time they were part of the cause. Many assumed that human beings were of inestimable value and had an unquestioned right to use the earth to fulfill their desires and needs; and most acted that way in practice even if their doctrines said something different. Although we might be subject to Original Sin and be dependent on God for salvation, we are also the only living creature made in God's image, a little lower than the gels, and possessed of an immortal soul the eventual fate of which is a matter of cosmic importance. We alone are able to succeed or fail at being part of God's plan, while the rest of the earth is essentially a theater for the great drama of the human struggle to realize a divine destiny. For the most part, religious teachings conferred a moral value on us and on nothing else on earth. As a conservative American Protestant minister puts it, "Yes, the pollution and wanton exploitation and destruction of the environment are foolish and wrong. But the folly and evil of worshiping Mother Earth and treating each species as sacred and having the same rights as humans is even more wrong."[7]

It is true that a few religious voices were not so sure that only human beings are important to God, or that nature has no meaning of its own. St. Francis, who eight hundred years later would be proposed as the patron saint of modern Christian ecology, talked of "Brother Son and Sister Moon." Maimonides, perhaps the most important Jewish thinker of the past one thousand years, cautioned people not to believe "that all the beings exist for the sake of the existence of humanity. On the contrary, all the other beings too have been intended for their own sakes, and not for the sake of something else."[8] And the Qur'an (40:57) states with surprising directness that "assuredly the creation of the heavens and the earth is greater than the creation of humankind; Yet most people understand not." St. Francis was honored for piety, humility, and austerity, but the full implications of his attitude toward nature were generally ignored. Maimonides' statement, similarly, was treated as an odd exception to the prevailing Jewish attitude which held that although natural resources should not be wasted (because ultimately they belonged to God, not humans), they were devoid of sacred meaning in their own right. And few Muslims read that particular passage of the Qur'an with much seriousness at all.

More recently, institutionalized religions typically held favorable attitudes toward the rise of industrial civilization. Initial conflicts with modern science gave way to comparatively insignificant quarrels about the theory of evolution. Most religious leaders took it for granted that economic development and technological progress, as long as their fruits were distributed with a modicum of fairness, were good things. When doubts arose, they had to do with the effects of technological society on people's consciousness, not on what it was doing to the earth. Before the 1960s, searching questions about the ultimate fate of a world in which mechanized mass production was transforming both people and nature were much more likely to come from eccentric loners, marginal philosophers, or leftist social critics.[9] Correspondingly, the first wave of modern environmentalism, in which the movement turned away from conserving land and toward a focus on pollution and global warming, had little to do with organized religion. It came from naturalists like Rachel Carson, secular politicians like Gaylord Nelson (organizer of the first Earth Day), and focused environmental organizations from the Sierra Club to the Audubon Society.

∾

The central argument of this book is that all this has changed. Religion is now a leading voice telling us to respect the earth, love our nonhuman as well as our human neighbors, and think deeply about our social policies and economic priorities. Religions now offer Earth Day prayers, critical comments on the environmental effects of World Bank loans, cautions about the dangers of genetic engineering, and Sunday School lessons about how Christians should respond to environmentally induced asthma.

The full scope of religious environmentalism is the subject of this book. I provide an account of how religious thinking has changed, how religious institutions have committed themselves to environmental causes, and of the distinct and crucially important partnership between people of faith and the secular environmental community.[10]

As a prelude, let me offer a glimpse of the comfort and support religion can offer as we face the emotional and moral demands, the human meaning, of the environmental crisis.

First, there is the question of just grappling with the reality of our enormous carelessness and destructiveness. Is there something from theology in particular or the culture of religion in general that can both soothe our spirits and rouse our energies?

We can begin to answer this question by noting that even before we can respond to the environmental crisis, we need to be aware of just what it is. Its scope and frightening content make that awareness difficult to come by. Our collective inability to pay attention to what is going on long enough to take in the crucial information is a kind of "problem before the problem." This denial and avoidance make any rational and heartfelt response to environmental problems all too rare. Our eyes glimpse a story in the newspaper on radioactive wastes, global warming–induced droughts in the Midwest, or cancer clusters on Long Island, and without missing a beat we shift to another part of the page. Increasingly shrill environmental pleas about dying forests or depleted fish stocks are, after all, a real drag. Better to think about something, anything, else.[11]

Here we can remember that virtually all religious traditions demand the ability to attend, focus the mind, and concentrate. If we are to pray or meditate, to reflect on our own faults or study scripture, our committed intention is an essential ingredient. Further, the objects of religious attention are often far from comforting or pleasant. Serious religious life demands that we look at stuff most of us would prefer not to. Buddhists must spend long hours thinking about their own mortality, for instance, what their bodies will look like long after death. Catholics must regularly confess their sins, a practice that can be trivialized but that is quite demanding if taken seriously. Judaism asks us to wrestle with the ethical challenge of Abraham's being willing to sacrifice his son, and Christianity puts forth the mysterious idea of a Trinity. In such instances (and many more that could be described), religious life forbids the easy shift of attention, the quick channel change or mouse click. It says "Look at this—and don't look away even if what you see is very disturbing."

In response to the environmental crisis, religious teachers and leaders are now directing us not to look away from something that is indeed very, very disturbing. In doing so, they serve as a powerful resource to help us over our environmental avoidance and denial. This can be seen, for example, in the work of Joanna Macy, a widely known teacher and activist who combines Buddhism and deep ecology, integrating traditional forms of meditation with environmental concern. It is essential, Macy tells us, that we learn to "sustain the gaze," to focus on the full reality of ecological dangers without avoidance or denial. If we wish to progress spiritually, we will have to open our hearts to the suffering of the world, examine the morality (or immorality) of our collective conduct, and immerse ourselves in awareness of our own grief, fear, and gloom. Macy is clear that meditative techniques used for thousands of years to promote compassion and quiet the mind now face something historically unprecedented: "We are barraged by data that render questionable the survival of our culture, our species, and even our planet as a viable home for conscious life. Despair, in this context . . . is the loss of the assumption that the species will inevitably pull through."[12] A contemporary Buddhist, she explains, will face this despair as directly and honestly as he or she faces any more familiar Buddhist concern. In particular, through participation in the Nuclear Guardianship Project, Macy has proposed that Buddhist meditation centers be built on the grounds of storage facilities for nuclear waste so that focused attention might be brought to bear on the world's most dangerous toxic material, so that we could see this stuff for what it truly is and learn the lessons it has to teach.[13]

Similar encouragement for attention can be found when our treatment of the earth is the subject of a Christian Earth Day service, a phenomenon that has become increasingly widespread over the past decade. Although participating in such a service guarantees nothing, I believe it is harder to turn away from a sustained prayer than from a newspaper headline or a story on the evening news. The National Council of Churches, an umbrella organization whose member churches represent more than 50 million Americans in 140,000 congregations, offers the following prayer as part of an Earth Day service: "On this Earth Sabbath we open our minds to learn about ecological threats to the health of present and future generations and to the whole community of life. . . . God of mercy, we confess that we are damaging the earth, the home that you have given us. We buy and use products that pollute our air, land, and water, harming wildlife and endangering human health. Forgive us, O God, and inspire us to change."[14] Of course, this prayer, like those that instruct us to care for the poor or practice humility, may be ignored. We can lift our voices in rousing earth anthems and then drive home in our SUVs! As in all human affairs, people will have to choose wisdom over folly, good over evil, love over thoughtlessness. But religion, here as elsewhere, can offer one more reason to do the right thing.[15]

The next gift of religious environmentalism is to provide us with the proper language with which to express what we think and feel about what we've attended to. As we take in the extent of ecological devastation, we cannot be content simply with complaints that it threatens our health, blights the landscape, or makes a day at the (polluted) beach a lot less pleasurable. The anguish we feel for what has been lost tells us we are concerned for more than our own fate. Something else is at stake, something that may best be expressed in religious language. When the Evangelical Lutheran Church says that "sin" is one of the roots of the environmental crisis and that being made in the image of God is not a license to "dominate and exploit," or calls environmental destruction the product of the sins of "self-serving bias" and "infinite greed rather than finite need," then something new and profound has entered the discussion.[16]

The language of sin may indeed be alienating to many, especially as it seems to come so easily from the mouths of religious conservatives who are often eager to cast the first stone. Yet, when spoken with a self-reflective humility that includes the person speaking, it invokes a kind of moral seriousness that seems particularly appropriate in this context. We are not talking about simple mistakes, inconveniences easily rectified, or strategic errors. We are confronting a profound and wide-ranging failing of virtually every aspect of modern society. Speaking of this failing as a sin indicates (at least) how seriously it should be taken. When we see a clear-cut forest or realize that the local air pollution index has been stuck on "dangerous—don't go outside" for days, we sense that how we treat nature is not simply a matter of human convenience, pleasure, or usefulness. As Sallie Bingham, Episcopal environmental leader, says, "God's purpose for us is to love and to live in harmony with all that He made. All of creation and all generations to come are our neighbors."[17] These are neighbors, it is clear, that we have been loving very poorly indeed.

Often, religion helps us articulate the full measure of the pain we feel over the environmental crisis more effectively than the language of secular politics. As well as political, economic, and technological, our plight is *spiritual*: it involves our deepest concerns about what is of truly lasting importance in our lives. I remember reading a compelling account of environmental devastation in the Philippines—with its graphic descriptions of hillsides denuded by timber companies, urban children poisoned by leaded gasoline in old taxis, and coral reefs destroyed by human waste—and feeling that an enormous sacrilege had been committed, a sacrilege of which I, as a beneficiary of modern technological society, was partly guilty.[18] I was not afraid for my own health, nor was a polluted Philippines going to affect my daily life, but nevertheless I felt a deep apprehension for what I would like to call my soul.

Part of this concern involved my own moral responsibility—and, to be blunt about it, my own guilt. In the case of the environmental crisis, this is of particular importance, for certainly the vast majority of people who read this book, as citizens of the United States or some other highly developed economy, will be participants in causing environmental problems even if they also wish to solve them.

Religion is well practiced in matters of guilt and repentance. Its mechanisms of self-examination, public acknowledgment of moral error, and contrition are, I believe, of great value. Integrating our environmental concern into a religious framework, uttering prayers in which we confess that we are damaging the earth (as in the Earth Day service quoted earlier) enables us to face the seriousness of what is going on in a way that simply saying some industrial policy is in error does not. Once again, of course, there is no assurance that we will really take our guilt to heart and change our ways. Real moral transformation remains something of a mystery, and thus no certainty that it will occur is ever possible. My point is simply that collective spiritual processing of our moral errors will help us confront what we have been doing.

However, our shared complicity in the environmental crisis means that environmentalism is no place for either self-righteousness or politically correct moral arrogance. Here again religion can be a help, even if distasteful tendencies in that direction are part of the worst of what religion has to offer. For unlike most secular political movements, religions have taught the virtue of humility, and religious social activists from Gandhi and Martin Luther King to Burma's Aung San Suu Kyi and the Dalai Lama have modeled how to combine principled political struggle with recognition of one's own personal limitations. Gandhi, for example, often said that one source of his absolute commitment to nonviolence was his firm belief that he, like everyone else, was a sinner.

Finally, many religious teachings reassure us that though we should face up to our moral failings, we need not be paralyzed by the scope of what lies before us. We will not be able to fix everything, for the only one responsible for "everything" is God. Nevertheless, it is up to us to do our part.

✺

These brief reflections indicate some of the distinct and important roles religion can play in helping us face and respond to the environmental crisis. Next we must ask about the central goals of human existence. If life's main purposes are not ceaseless "progress" and more stuff all around, what are they? Here again religion has a distinct role to play, because, despite its frequent support for the social status quo, it has also affirmed critical alternative values.

In fact, part of the religious vision has always run counter to the "common sense" of its time. Its hallmark is not realism or conformism but a prophetic challenge to conventional social standards. Isaiah was passionate in his denunciation of formalistic and inauthentic Judaism. Christianity has taught that the poor and the peacemakers, not the rich and powerful, are most favored by God. In Buddhism, the common sense that says the goal of life is to get more, have more, and "be" more is rejected as simply false. Now our task is to find alternatives to our culture's ever more deadly environmental style and to determine what we are to live for in place of thoughtless technological innovation and compulsive consumerism.

It is particularly important to turn to religious environmentalists on this issue, for they offer a comprehensive vision in which care for the earth and care for people go hand in hand. This vision is not simply about what is wrong but about what can be right, not just about "living with less" but about living an authentic and ultimately much more satisfying form of life. This positive dimension is particularly important for environmental politics, for if we have learned anything, it is that threatening people with doom and scolding them for waste and pollution are not terribly effective ways to rally the masses to the cause.

Far more than most versions of secular liberalism, religious traditions can offer comprehensive, large-scale understandings of what human beings are and what should be of ultimate value to us. When religious environmentalists offer such perspectives (as I argue throughout this book), they should not be thought of as importing religion into a placidly secular and otherwise efficient and rational social order. Religious environmentalism does not *introduce* a moral vision where none exists. It offers an *alternative* to the ones that dominate society now. The mall, the medical school, and (certainly) Wall Street all have their sense of what is valuable and what is not, what we should live for and what isn't worth the trouble. Describing the drive to globalization, which has accelerated ecological destruction throughout the world, a third world Christian theologian tells us that global development "has its God: profit and money . . . its high priests: GATT, WTO, IMF-WB . . . its doctrines and dogmas: import liberalization, deregulation . . . its temples: the super megamalls. It has its victims on the altar of sacrifice: the majority of the world— the excluded and marginalized poor."[19] In fact, virtually every large-scale social decision invokes a vision of what is best for society as a whole. It is the task of religious environmentalism to set itself against the reigning social vision, putting forward values that will ultimately serve people and the earth far better than the ones currently in place.

Although few people will respond to appeals for austerity, at least some will be moved if we can offer a comprehensive plan in which something of value takes the place of what we are going to lose. Jewish philosopher Aryeh Carmel spells out the choice clearly: "The truth is that the goal of unlimited physical growth is no longer tenable. The only way out of the human predicament of our time lies in a complete and radical change, not of *methods* but of *goals*. . . .There is only one way to avert the disaster which threatens to overwhelm mankind. *Material goals must be replaced by spiritual goals.*"[20]

This imperative may seem initially appealing. Even a casual glance at the gridlocked cars spewing carbon dioxide, your local multiplex offering endless advertisements for passionless sex and pointless violence, and the steady erosion of basic morality from the corporate boardroom to cheating high school students might well give you the feeling that something pretty basic is out of whack around here. And when we juxtapose the conspicuous consumption of the United States or Western Europe with the crushingly unnecessary poverty of Bangladesh or Guatemala, we sense that a good part of what is out of whack is that our addictive attachments to wealth, power, and gadgets have led us astray. It is not surprising that many would like to see Carmel's "spiritual goals" brought into such a world.

At this point, however, the Voice of Reason will probably appear. "To begin with," the Voice will caution, "all this talk about 'spiritual values' is a little vague (to say the least). What does it mean when we have to run an economy, an educational system, hospitals, and airports? Besides, spiritual goals vary from person to person and community to community. Do spiritual values mean traditional social roles for women? Biblical bans on homosexuality? Priests and mullahs running the government? Watch out that we don't replace our materialism and ecological problems with the irrational fanaticisms of people who are all too eager to stuff their spiritual values down your throat, whether you like them or not. All these rather distasteful possibilities show why spiritual values, religious beliefs, and all that, whoever they belong to, are private matters that should be kept separate from political, social, and, yes, ecological matters. Let the religious types soothe their souls any way they want, and let the sober, down-to-earth, practical engineers, politicians, and corporations take care of production, consumption, trade, energy supply, and dealing with whatever environmental problems we have."

Not surprisingly, religious environmentalists disagree. Beginning from something like Carmel's position—that a solution to the environmental crisis requires a fundamental shift in our basic values—they soon assert that religious values are most definitely not purely private matters. The National Religious Partnership for the Environment, founded in 1993 by representatives of Judaism, Catholicism, the National Churches of Christ, and the Evangelical Environmental Network, defines its mission thus: "To weave care for God's creation throughout religious life in such a way as to provide inspiration, moral vision, and commitment to social justice for all efforts to protect habitat and human well-being within it." Among the multiple resources it calls on are "Judeo-Christian teachings and traditions from scripture, theology, ethics, and education" and "social thought to amplify a vision of environmental sustainability and justice with religious and moral perspectives, in addition to those of science and economics."[21] In other words, to frame its specific recommendations, the Partnership will draw on political theory and scripture, intelligent science and inspired morality. In practice, this has meant initiating conferences on ecotheology, leading interfaith campaigns on global warming, and facilitating exchanges among corporate CEOs, labor unions, scientific associations, environmental groups, *and* religious leaders to discuss possible responses to climate change. What could be more "practical"?

To take another example to show how religiously inspired environmental visions can lead to hard-nosed social policy, consider *Tikkun* magazine editor and author Rabbi Michael Lerner's call for a "new bottom line" throughout the global economy. Lerner proposes that society partly evaluate corporations by how well they serve the community, care for their workers, and respect the environment. Lerner would tie the renewal of corporate legal charters to community, worker, and investor evaluation of corporate fulfillment of this new standard. Because corporations are in many ways legally and economically dependent on special legal status and government protection, it is only fair, Lerner argues, that they be appraised for their effects on our society as a whole, not just by their earnings. For Lerner, "Productivity and efficiency must no longer be judged solely by the degree to which any corporation or institution maximizes profits or power, but also by the degree to which it supports ethical, spiritual, and ecological health." We want, he tells us, "all of our economic and social institutions to be judged successful to the extent that they foster caring and respect for all peoples and for the planet."[22] Thus, instead of simply admonishing "don't pollute," Lerner is proposing a collective moral evaluation of our economic system, one that would promise a better life for society as a whole, not just one with less consumption.[23] This change would require new laws to go along with new "spiritual goals"—and a practical commitment to take the environment seriously in all aspects of our economic life. Thus, Lerner's proposal, in a form typical of religious environmentalists, combines universal values grounded in a religious vision of the ultimate worth of life with detailed proposals for deep-seated societal reform.

Once again the Voice of Reason chimes in: "Are you kidding? Totally impractical! This naïve idea just shows that religious values, even if well intentioned, have no place in the real world." Such a worldly wise response makes perfect sense—until, that is, we remember occasions when similarly "naïve" and "impractical" religious ideas took leading roles in profound social transformation. I am thinking, for a start, of passionate preachers who denounced an entrenched economic arrangement called slavery some forty years before slavery was outlawed; of an introspective African American minister named Martin Luther King who combined religious nonviolence with a deep faith in democracy, helping to alter forever southern society and American politics; and of the religious presence in the antinuclear movement of the 1980s, a movement that played a significant role in galvanizing American support for a nuclear test ban treaty. If we look carefully, we can find religious voices in the fall of apartheid and the collapse of tyrannical communism, in the brave spirit of democracy in Burma and of reconciliation in Cambodia, in the movement to end the Vietnam War, and even, surprisingly, in the movement for women's equality. Lerner's particular vision of a new bottom line, along with religious environmentalists' proposals for fundamental changes in the way we produce, allocate, and utilize our economic wealth and social power, take their place in a long line of religious contributions to seemingly impossible social change.[24]

Despite their rejections of the Voice of Reason's insistence on the necessarily private or impractical nature of religious values, religious environmentalists do share a concern with repressive religion. I believe, and this belief is, I suspect, shared widely in the religious environmentalist community, that the great task of religion in our era is to maintain its public presence in harmony with the great secular accomplishments of democracy and human rights. Such is the hallmark of eminent progressive religious social activists from King and Gandhi to the present. And such is the hallmark of religious environmentalism generally. Yet this problem, ironically, affects all who would reform social life. How are any of us to walk the line between simply accepting the current social order and dictatorially forcing a change on others? Antislavery groups, women suffragists, and supporters of gay marriage have all been criticized for trying to impose their minority views on everyone else. Whether our values come from the Bible or intuitions about human rights, conflicts between "what most of us think" and "what is right" are endemic to any nontotalitarian society in which there are basic disagreements about justice and the good life.

∾

The question of how to feel God's presence despite the magnitude of unjustified suffering is at least as old as Job. Because of our era's ever larger capacity for destruction, the anguish that attends the search for God has only increased. We have asked, "Where is God when millions died in the trenches in WWI, when the bombs hit Hiroshima and Nagasaki, or in Auschwitz?" And now we ask, "Where is God when the rain forest is burning, when the water is not safe to drink, when another friend calls with bad news about breast cancer?" Ironically, despite all our technological "advances," we are like the Raji: when we seek God's presence in nature, we are no longer sure where He (or She) can be found.

The religious struggle with suffering is not principally about the ancient question of theodicy, of how an all-powerful, all-wise, all-good God can coexist with the immense scope of the present destruction. The familiar solutions to what is often called the Problem of Evil will succeed or fail for the environmental crisis as they have succeeded or failed for the Holocaust, world poverty, and even the untimely loss of a beloved family member. We will chalk up the suffering to human free will or cling to the belief that "all is for the best" even though we just can't see why at the moment.

Rather, our present dilemma is more personal, experiential, and subjective. The question is not How we can we *believe* in God? but How are we to *feel* God's presence, or a truly spiritual joy, in the face of what is going on? Theologically, we can attribute all of this mess to mistaken human choices, to selfishness or sin, but such a theology doesn't do much to ease my deep sadness when I confront a dead lake or otters drenched in spilled oil. How am I to feel joy in existence when existence is such a mess? And if I cannot feel that, all in all, this world—despite everything—is holy, then what kind of religious life will I be left with?

Clearly, the full answer to this question requires (at least!) a book in its own right.[25] Here I will simply note some of the kinds of answers that have been offered.

For a start, notice that if we truly give up denial and avoidance, then our sense of the sacred on the earth will have to include pain and loss. When Aldo Leopold, a key figure in the creation of modern environmental ethics, said that "to have an ecological education is to walk alone in a world of wounds,"[26] he was saying something of profound importance about religious life as well as about the natural world.

Yet the presence of pain does not mean the absence of God, at least not if God is (among other things) that force in the universe that creates and sustains transformation, healing, and wholeness. Or if, we might say, God is the name for the power that brings something out of nothing, more out of less, and love out of torment. Despite the horrors that surround us, then, we can at least find God in the human capacity to face these horrors, take them in emotionally, and act to resist them. God is, we might say, the source of our strength to resist, and in the actions of the worldwide environmental movement we can find (even if most environmentalists wouldn't put it this way) the sacred.[27]

The willingness to resist requires a kind of faith that one's actions make a difference, even if it is hard to see what that difference is. We also find God, then, in the faith to act, a faith that reflects a passionate choice rather than a reasoned account of current social forces and trends. We will believe that one species saved from extinction, one poor community protected from toxic wastes, one carcinogen taken off the market registers in some cosmic accounting. Surely this faith reflects a sense of the holiness of life, and thus of Whoever or Whatever creates and sustains life.

Also, despite everything that has been lost, there is still much beauty and wonder in the world. Even if countless trees are dying from acid rain, the ones that are not are as wondrous as ever—branches reaching to the sky, roots clinging to the earth, leaves brilliant in the sunshine.[28] If we will seek God on earth, She may be a little harder to locate, but Her presence can be found. We can celebrate that Presence, even if we must do so while we are crying for what has been irretrievably lost.

Finally, we can find God in our appreciation of the simple mystery of existence. What is the purpose of our own lives and that of the rest of the earth? Is this really a cosmic testing ground for the afterlife, or a biological fluke? Do humans truly have an immeasurably important destiny, or are we a minuscule episode in the universe story? Religious life is often identified with giving answers to these questions. I believe religion is found in our acceptance of the fact that we will never truly settle them. To see life as a mystery—strange, intriguing, surprising—is at least halfway to seeing it as holy, for in the face of mystery we open our eyes and hearts and allow ourselves to be touched and transformed. Or at least we might.

CHAPTER 1

RELIGION, NATURE, ENVIRONMENT

The anthropocentrism of ecclesial titles like "People of God" is appalling....What about the four-legged people? The cloud people? The tree people? The winged and finned people? Are they not also integral to the love of the Creator?

—Matthew Fox, "How the Environment Can Assist Us to
Deconstruct and Reconstruct Theology and Religion,"
Friends of Creation Spirituality

I don't think God is going to ask us how he created the earth, but he will ask us what we did with what he created.

—Reverend Rich Cizik, vice president of the National Association of
Evangelicals, *New York Times*, March 10, 2005

Like the rise of natural science or the terrors of the Holocaust, the environmental crisis requires a profound shift in religion's understanding of human existence. The world has changed forever, and the new ecotheology is an attempt to come to grips with that change from the standpoint of faith, the divine, and spiritual truth. As a response to this change, monotheistic traditions will ask about God, creation, and moral values. Faiths not centered on a single divine Being must rethink their use of nature as a symbol of enlightenment or source of refuge, and about the possibilities of any kind of personal illumination at a time of collective destruction. The pressure to change may affect even the most familiar and comforting of religious rituals. Can communion wine really be the blood of Christ if it contains poisonous pesticide residues? Is the age-old Buddhist meditation practice of attending to the breath rendered suspect when we are breathing polluted air?

The new ecotheologies—accounts of God, ultimate meaning, human responsibility, and ethical life—typically begin with the pained recognition of just how bad things have become. Ecotheologians write about our situation with a passion born of grief, fear, and at times profound anger.[1] These feelings are tied to an understanding of the basic features of the crisis that eco-theologians share with scientists, secular environmentalists, and informed members of the public. Thus, Catholic ethicist Daniel Maguire expresses a widely held sentiment when he grieves that "for the first time, our power to destroy outstrips the earth's power to restore."[2] Overviews of the bleak facts typically follow such dire generalizations, as in the beginning of a book by a contemporary Protestant theologian: "Global warming, holes in the ozone layer, toxic wastes, oil spills, acid rain, drinking water contamination, over-flowing landfills, top-soil erosion, species extinction, destruction of the rain forests, leakage of nuclear waste, lead poisoning, desertification, smog [are the] bald-faced reality of contemporary life in the world today."[3] It is quite interesting and not a little ironic that the new ecotheologies often start not by discussing God, faith, tradition, or the holy, but with references to infor-mation provided by biologists, chemists, and ecologists. The findings of sci-ence are leading theologians to reexamine some of the most fundamental tenets of their faith.

Alongside recognition of the severity of the crisis there is a passionate concern that religion help stop it or, at the very least, cease causing it. In 1988 Catholic priest Thomas Berry lamented, "After dealing with suicide, homicide, and genocide, our Western Christian moral code collapses com-pletely: it cannot deal with biocide. . . . Nor have church authorities made any sustained protest against the violence being done to the planet."[4] Some com-mentators have even suggested that the particular attitude of Protestantism toward the Bible—that it is the *literal* word of God—removed the symbolic meanings that had previously infused the natural world and paved the way for science's disenchantment of the world and for environmental excess: "Those who believed that the Deity had imposed a particular order on the cosmos moved their attention away from the symbolic function of objects and focused instead on the ways in which the things of nature might play some practical role in human welfare."[5] Thus, Protestantism, the common faith of the leading figures and nations of the Industrial Revolution and the growth of modern economies, may have had a particular affinity for environ-mental unconcern.

With representatives from the full spectrum of the world's faiths, not every ecotheologian sees religion at the center of our ecological predicament. Some agree with Berry; others argue (as we will see) that traditional texts in fact contain powerful ecological messages, or at least provide some important resources to help improve our relation to nature. Many say the problem is that their faith's teachings have not been followed widely enough; others want to take marginalized elements of the past and give them new power and presence today.

Despite their differences, one thing is constant for virtually all the thinkers represented here: the belief that whatever religion's past responsibility, it must now marshal all its resources to respond to the crisis. These resources may include neglected parts of tradition, reinterpretation of the familiar, the adaptation of the old to the unprecedented demands of the present, or radical innovation.

Why do we need ecotheology? Simply because before we can act, we must think, and before religion can act in response to the environmental crisis, it must learn to think religiously about it. Thus, the task of the new ecotheology is to think about the environmental crisis, and our human response to it, in religious terms. In a sense, then, ecotheology is one long response to Berry's claim that "religion cannot deal with biocide." We will see, I believe, that if this was true in the mid-1980s, when Berry's work was being done, it is not true now. Later chapters show what this means in terms of institutional commitment, political action, and liturgy. Here we will examine ecotheology's profound contributions to our understanding of the world, God, and the sacred.

Of course, human destructiveness of the natural world, with dire consequences for nature and people alike, is hardly unprecedented. The ancient Babylonians decimated their fields by overirrigation. In the *Critias*, Plato described nine thousand years of poor farming practices, which turned once thriving agricultural land into barren wastes and ravines. Native Americans overhunted many large mammal species to extinction. And even a biblical prophet criticized those "who join house to house, / who add field to field, / until there is room for no one but you" (Isa. 5:18).[6] What *is* new, however, is the unprecedented scope of the crisis. For example, no previous society could take part in the greatest mass species extinction in 70 million years.

Yet, even as the environmental crisis demands that we think in new terms, we will also have to draw on some of the theological, ethical, and political resources of the past. We can repair the boat of human culture—which carries us, as it were, on the sea of life—only as we are sailing it. There is no dry land—no life without culture—on which to switch to a totally different boat.[7] We will have to engage our past wisdom as well as respond in ways that could not have been conceived of generations ago. Ecotheologians face the delicate task of helping us make new religious sense of the environmental crisis while drawing on existing religious sensibilities.

∾

Protected by rights in our secular democracies or obeying the enforced imperatives of dictatorships, assured of our cosmic importance by our churches and our car salesmen, busily pursuing goals set by our bank accounts or our egos, and ceaselessly increasing our technological prowess, humans have come to see themselves as surrounded by beings who lack moral standing, subjectivity, purpose, or meaning. For the most part, the industrialized world views nature as a resource to be exploited: a mass of animals and plants, minerals and water, whose purpose is to serve humanity. This fundamentally human-centered, or anthropocentric, perspective on nature, many theologians believe, is at the core of the crisis.[8] It justifies thoughtless devastation of anything that gets in our way or looks like it might come in handy.

What can religion offer in its place?

Ecotheology offers an enormous range of answers to this question, reflecting a breathtaking diversity of traditional viewpoints and contemporary responses. What is shared by virtually all these approaches is a commitment to take nature seriously in at least two basic ways. First, nature has, in and of itself, value. Second, one reason it has value is that nature is closer to us, more like us, more connected to us, than we have realized or admitted.

Because of its centrality to Western history, I will begin to explain these general claims by focusing on the Bible, perhaps the single most important text that needs to be reinterpreted in light of ecological problems. Is the Bible green? Or can it, without doing violence to its basic intent, become so? Given its role in a Western and capitalist culture that has been the source of environmentally destructive industrialization, this is a key question.

For some people, the answer is an unambiguous no. Historian Lynn White helped initiate the debate about religion's environmental responsibility in a groundbreaking 1967 article in which he argued that Judaism and Christianity paved the way for the environmental crisis by "desacrilizing nature." Once the world is viewed as the product of a transcendent, immaterial "sky God," White wrote, once holiness is removed from our surroundings and transferred without residue to their Source, the way is paved for using those surroundings any way we wish. God's command to Adam in Genesis 1:28—"Fill the earth and master it"—becomes a religious license for humans to dominate, to exploit, and (whether this was intended or not) to ruin.[9] White's criticism is echoed in an even wider generalization by Steven Rockefeller: "The social and moral traditions that have been dominant in the West . . . have not involved the idea that animals, trees, or the land in their own right, as distinct from their owners or their Creator, have moral standing. Only a few saints and reformers have taught that people have direct moral responsibilities to nonhuman creatures."[10]

The common theme of commentators like White and Rockefeller is that by removing God(s) from the earth and making the creation of the world itself a distinctly unnatural act (where in nature, after all, do we find beings coming into existence simply because someone says something?), the Bible has also removed moral value from nature. Unlike creation myths of many other cultures, which frequently center on oversized but familiar natural processes of birth, egg laying, or rainfall, Judaism and Christianity embrace a narrative that distinguishes divinely creative processes from natural ones. Further, the many biblical passages in which humans in general or the Israelites in particular are separated from the natural world—given "dominion," allowed to name, encouraged to multiply, given special responsibilities and covenants—create a profound sense of alienation between humans and the natural world. The Bible, it is argued, simply does not direct us to respect the earth or love its creatures.

Although ecological critics of the Bible have been many, it has also had its defenders, who argue that antinature readings seriously obscure both the complexity of the Bible and its many positive resources for environmentalism. To begin with, the idea that the earth was given to humans by God can be a basis for valuing it and offers a vitally important obstacle to unrestrained ecological exploitation. "Viewed in terms of the popular scientific under-standing," Norman Wirzba tells us, "nature is simply matter in motion guided by impersonal laws. Viewed economically, nature is a resource ready for us to be appropriated at will. Viewed religiously nature is an expression of God's joy and love."[11] This idea of the divine origins of the physical world is central to Western religion. Taken seriously, it could be a guide to a much more sustainable form of life. For in the biblical view, nature is *creation*, a sublime gift made for us to use but that ultimately still belongs to God.

Jewish ecotheologians have in fact made much of this last point, placing great emphasis on the biblical injunction "Do not destroy" (Deut. 20:19–20), which, as Daniel Swartz summarizes, was initially meant to restrict ecological destruction as a tactic of war: "Do not cut down trees even to prevent ambush or to build siege engines; do not foul waters or burn crops even to cause an enemy's submission." And if one is not to cause unnecessary harm to the environment in war, Swartz points out, how much the more so "during the ordinary course of life."[12] Indeed, this scriptural passage gave rise to Talmudic laws governing personal and economic life. Although these laws (forbidding, for instance, wanton razing of buildings or tearing of clothes) would hardly match the scope of our current problems, adherence to the notion of not destroying (and thus not wasting) would require profound changes in our current mode of life.[13] Those who waste, warned the Talmud, are on their way to idol worship, because wasting indicates a profound loss of self-control. If we examine contemporary consumer society, or the devastated landscapes that surround open-pit mines, we immediately see the wisdom of this point.[14]

I do not believe there is a single "correct" resolution to this disagreement between those who do and those who do not find environmentalism in the Bible. That is because there is always a tension between what the Bible *says*, its literal words, and what the Bible has *meant*. Like virtually all other tra-ditional scriptures, the Bible consists of a confusing and often contradictory array of narratives, values, and commands, allowing different generations to define its meaning in ways shaped by their own creativity. In the face of the environmental crisis, ecotheologians of all types are showing that whatever meaning their texts had *in the past*, for religious environmentalism they must have a different meaning *now*. These thinkers are finding environmentalism in the Bible because they have been pressured to do so by the environmental crisis.[15] Yet the need to innovate is not an invitation to violate. The sense of

the earth as creation, the warning not to waste—these are *in the scriptures.*
In the past, however, such key passages were not used for environmental
purposes. Hence the old words must be read anew.

As an example of this new reading, let us consider what is perhaps the
most ecologically problematic passage of the Hebrew Bible:

> Then God said, "Let us make man in our image, in our likeness, and let them
> rule over the fish of the sea and the birds of the air, over the livestock, over all
> the earth, and over all the creatures that move along the ground." So God
> created man in his own image, in the image of God he created him; male and
> female he created them. God blessed them and said to them, "Be fruitful and
> increase in number; fill the earth and subdue it. Rule over the fish of the sea
> and the birds of the air and over every living creature that moves on the
> ground." (Gen. 1:26–28)

Many have said the text clearly provides a license for ecological unconcern
by establishing human difference from and dominion over the natural world.
Yet, on closer examination, things might not be so simple. For example, some
scholars tell us that for long periods of time, "the earth" was read symbolically
to stand for unruly human desires, and thus the command to "rule" over
earthly creatures promoted moral development and not ecological policy.[16]
Jeremy Cohen, perhaps the leading scholar of the history of how this passage
has been taken, admits that "mastery" can sometimes mean domination but
cites other interpretations in which ascribing dominion is really only a reference to human uniqueness. Such uniqueness might confer the right to
exploit, or it might, as in one traditional Jewish interpretation, refer to our
distinctive capacity to recognize moral rules and face moral choices.[17] Similarly, several contemporary Christian theologians have stressed that humanity's uniqueness resides in the special responsibility that follows our special
gifts, not in special privileges.[18] We have dominion not because we are enabled to indulge ourselves in thoughtless excess, but because we are expected
to be God's representatives on earth. Such a reading can be justified in the
text, for a close analysis of the Hebrew phrase translated as "created in the
image of God" shows that it alludes to the way images of kings were stamped
on coins or used to legitimate a subordinate's social authority.[19] Read in this
way, the passage suggests that it is people's duty to represent God on earth,
to be the bearers of God's intentions in the earthly realm. The passage recognizes that humans have potentially greater power than any other living
being but does not tell us how that power is to be exercised—for it does not
specify what God's intentions are.

Given this range of possibilities, the decisive meaning of "fill the earth and
subdue it" may well be determined not by this passage alone but by which
other verses we read along with it, for there are many other biblical passages
in which humans are described as being fully part of, and even as having

responsibilities to, the rest of creation.[20] In the second version of human origins in Genesis 2, for example, the first person is made *from the earth* (actually, the Hebrew name Adam is closely related to the word for earth, *adamah*) and will after death return to the earth. This earthy being is not sharply set apart from other animals, and in fact at times in Genesis the same phrase, "chayyim nefesh," is used to refer to all living beings.[21] The man's task in the garden, we are told, was "to work it and take care of it" (Gen. 2:15). Because "take care" has also been translated as "keep" and even "serve," we find a sense of deep connection to nature in the text.[22]

We might also consider history's first recorded endangered species act, the story of Noah, who was given the task of saving *all* the beasts of the earth, not just those useful to people. After the flood, God makes a covenant— before making one with Abraham later in Genesis—with creation as a whole: "Behold, I establish my covenant with you and your descendants after you ... and with every living creature that is with you. ... Never again shall all flesh be cut off by the waters of a flood, and never again shall there be a flood to destroy the earth. ... I will remember my covenant which is between me and you and every living creature of all flesh; and the waters shall never again become a flood to destroy all flesh" (Gen. 9:9–15).

The rainbow—based, we are told, on the sign of a bow (that is, a weapon) turned into a sign of compact and peace—is extended to every living thing on earth. If God is committed to preserving the world, religious environmentalists ask, can humans, as least humans who take the Bible seriously, have the arrogance to destroy it? Clearly, it is argued, whatever was intended by the words "dominion" and "mastery," these other writings suggest definite and significant limits to legitimate human power.

Support for taking nature seriously and responsibly can also be found in what the Bible teaches us about what will happen if we fail to care for it. The Israelites were offered a gift of good land, land God cares for (Deut. 11: 12). However, the gift was not absolute, but conditional: the people were to act wisely toward it, to be grateful to God for it, and to treat each other and strangers morally.[23] Indeed, the Bible repeatedly makes it clear that the Promised Land ultimately belongs only to God and that humans will suffer both divine displeasure and failures of the land if they forget this elementary truth.

Thus, the Bible endorses, at the very least, a set of cautionary general principles that far exceed the simple prudence of "not wasting" and that teach human beings to recognize the value of the earth and act accordingly. At least three other biblical themes push these general principles further and suggest the outlines of a seriously ecological vision.

First, we are instructed in very particular ways to exercise regard for other creatures. The ox cannot be muzzled when he threshes the grain, but must be allowed to eat as he works. The mother bird must not be taken along with her eggs. Fruit trees must be valued even in a siege. As humans pursue legitimate purposes—threshing grain, finding food, making war—there are limits to how we can treat other living things in pursuit of our ends.[24] Our right to use other life forms is not an unlimited right. Our "dominion" and "mastery" go so far, and no further. These restrictions on our use of animals and the promise of their redemption remind us of some of the earliest passages in Genesis, those in which God proclaims the work of Creation "good" and Creation as a whole "very good." In light of this judgment, says animal rights theologian Andrew Linzey, "Animals are valuable *in themselves* by virtue of their creation by God."[25] Thus, it should not surprise us that vegetarianism, hinted at in the Torah in the limitations and rules of meat consumption, is at times part of prophetic images of the reign of the messiah: " 'The wolf and the lamb will feed together, and the lion will eat straw like the ox, but dust will be the serpent's food. They will neither harm nor destroy on all my holy mountain,' says the Lord" (Isa. 65:25). This idea is expanded further in Christian scriptures, where it is all of nature, and not only humans, which is to be redeemed. Jesus, we are told, has come to save *everything*, not just people.[26]

Second, the weekly Sabbath and the sabbatical (once every seven years) and jubilee (once every five decades) years place explicit limits on both the labor we perform and the property we accumulate (e.g., Exod. 23:10, Lev. 25: 3–7). In appreciation for Creation and remembrance of God's rest, humans, too, must rest each week. Work, even legitimate, nonwasteful, nonpolluting work, cannot go on all the time—not for us, our servants, or even our animals. The fruits of labor are limited as well. In the jubilee year, all loans are forgiven and all large holdings broken up. And while our fields lay fallow during the sabbatical, what comes spontaneously out of the earth is left for both the human poor and the "wild beasts" (that is, those that don't serve human needs; Exod. 23:11). The Bible, in short, directs us to consider the needs of the land and the other creatures as well as our own.

Finally, many passages in the Bible take nature seriously as an aid to understanding and worshipping God. Here nature is clearly not depicted as some kind of inert collection of objects designed only to help humans achieve whatever they want. Rather, the physical universe gleams with a kind of ecstatic light that invites us to see all of Creation as joined with us in the divine drama of existence. In the Psalms, "The heavens declare the glory of God . . . and their voice goes out into all the earth" (19:1, 4) and the "sea and everything in it" can sing God's praises (96:11). Psalm 104 sees God's presence in the ecological balance of the water cycle (10–13) and reminds us that all things are made in God's wisdom (24). The Song of Songs, declared by Jewish sage Hillel to be the crowning achievement of scripture, uses erotic poetry and the beauties of the Mediterranean spring as symbols of the relationship between God and human beings. In the book of Job, the majesties of creation are described as signs of God's greatness. In all these biblical passages, and many more that could be listed, we do not stand out *against* a background of nature, but stand *with it* in the light of God.

This brief account of some of the new ecotheological readings of the Bible indicates that scripturally based forms of Judaism or Christianity need not feel that environmentalism is alien to their tradition. If the Bible has been used in support of antiecological positions, as it so often has in the past several centuries, it can also be used to help us value nature and see ourselves as deeply connected to it.

No less than the Bible itself, the ensuing Jewish and Christian traditions are multifaceted in regard to environmental issues. Given the length of time and the variety of historical and cultural settings in which the world's major religions have existed, this is hardly surprising. Christianity spread over an enormous territory, in the process mixing with and being influenced by a host of local cultures.

On what is for religious environmentalists the positive side, there have always been voices in the tradition that connected religious sensibility to the nature-honoring and human-limiting elements of the Bible. St. Francis is singled out by Lynn White as the patron saint of Christian environmentalism, a designation formally reinforced by a proclamation of Pope John Paul II in 1980. Francis celebrated all living things, from the worms that he would carry out of the road to save from being crushed, to wild plants he had planted around human-designed gardens. He would preach (as do certain Buddhist monks) to flowers and invite them to praise God.[27] Numerous other monks, mystics, and theologians—from little-known "desert fathers" to luminaries such as Augustine, Calvin, and John Wesley—manifest what H. Paul Santmire calls an "ecological motif," that is, a sensitivity to and concern for nature that can be extremely valuable for the attempt to root contemporary ecology in elements of traditional Christianity.[28] Up through the Middle Ages, and even beyond, it was a familiar practice for common people to bring animals into churches for a blessing, to see them as companions and even teachers of saints and hermits, and even to invest them with a semidivine status themselves.[29] The point of all this is not that Judaism or Christianity were "really" quite ecologically minded, and that somehow this fact has been missed not only by contemporary critics but also by most of the adherents of these religions during the past several centuries. Rather, the point is that these resources do exist in the tradition—and if they have been generally marginalized up to now, they need be so no longer.[30]

∾

What Jewish and Christian ecotheologians have done with the Bible and some key later voices, Buddhists have done with Buddhism. Their first resources are some of Buddhism's essential precepts, for example, its rejection of individualism.[31] The "Jewel Net of Indra," the classic Buddhist image for universal interdependence, depicts a net of infinite size covered in jewels, each one of which reflects all the others.[32] This image signals the reality of interdependence that gives the lie to the idea that I can be taken care of while everything around me gets trashed. "Strictly speaking, delusion begins when man thinks he is separable from his world or his environment, when he wants only some kind of private 'peace of mind.' "[33] This basic teaching indicates why the attachment to individualism is for Buddhism a cardinal "sin," which in Buddhist terms means a fundamental misunderstanding that produces fundamental unhappiness. The insight can easily be adapted to ecological practices that presume that the fate of people can be separated from the fate of their environment.

The rejection of individualism goes hand in hand with Buddhism's critical treatment of desires to possess, own, or consume. In Buddhist terms, such desires are the very centerpiece of human misery. Thinking constantly about "I, me, and mine" not only reflects a delusory idea of separateness, but leads to great suffering. It is only when we renounce our desire to control the world and detach from our desires rather than compulsively try to satisfy them that lasting contentment is possible. This elementary aspect of Buddhist theology is thus a direct negation of the consumerist compulsions of twenty-first-century market society.

Finally, there is basic Buddhist moral teaching, which typically stresses nonviolence and a wide-ranging compassion that wishes an end to the misery of all beings. Buddhist morality is, at least in general intention, at odds with the destruction of ecosystems. Although the abstract goal of universal happiness may be just a little daunting as a practical goal, it nevertheless can serve as a basic orientation when relating to nature as well as to other people.[34]

These features of Buddhism make a form of mystical and emotional engagement with the natural world easy for many Buddhists.[35] Not surprisingly, then, there are numerous places where Buddhists confer a kind of essential spiritual status on nature, talking of—and to—it in terms similar to human communication. Myoe, a twelfth-century Japanese monk, wrote a letter to an island, asking after its health and offering his respects. He wrote that "since the nature of physical form is identical to wisdom, there is nothing that is not enlightened. . . . The underlying principle of the universe is identical to the world of ordinary beings."[36] In thirteenth-century Buddhist monk Dogen's famous "River and Mountain" sutra, we find this surprising declaration: "The mountains and rivers of this moment are the actualization of the way of the ancient Buddha's. Each, abiding in its own phenomenal expression, realizes completeness. . . . Because they have been the self since before form arose, they are liberated and realized. . . . Blue Mountains are neither sentient nor insentient. You are neither sentient nor insentient. At this moment, you cannot doubt the Blue Mountains walking."[37] In other examples, we find the numerous and widely read moral instructions of the "Jataka" tales of the earlier lives of the Buddha in which he either took the form of an animal or sacrificed his own life to defend the lives of animals.[38]

Scholar William LaFleur calls these ideas examples of Buddhism's distinct "galloping universalism."[39] In this perspective, common distinctions between sentient and nonsentient, human and nonhuman, rational and instinctive are questioned and ultimately dismissed. The very mental habit of dwelling on them is a product of the ego-based mind of desire and attachments, the mind that, Buddhism always insists, is very far from wisdom or real happiness.

These Buddhist images may seem strange at first, yet they reflect a kind of interpenetration of the human and the natural that can be found in other religious traditions as well. How many times, after all, does the Bible refer to people as sheep and God as a shepherd? Is this so different from Buddhists (and Hindus) speaking of humans, when meditating, as sitting in the "lotus posture" (after the lotus flowers that float in ponds)? If you and I are like lotus flowers when we meditate, or the Lord is our shepherd, why can't mountains be "enlightened"? These images offer the ultimate rejection of an anthropocentrism that sees religious identity, moral value, or inherent worth possible only for people. The result is a worldview in which the critical distinctions between people and the rest of the beings in the universe—precisely those distinctions that so clearly support the destructive environmental practices of the present—are denied.[40]

Like Judaism, Christianity, and Buddhism, the Islamic tradition, too, has been mined for its environmental resources. And as in these other traditions, some writers believe that one need only return to the texts to find an early and authentic environmental message, whereas others search for comparatively marginalized elements and see the need for genuine theological creativity. The Qur'an, a Pakistani geographer and early ecotheologian tells us, makes it "abundantly clear that God has created the earth for the service of man, but at the same time man is also constantly reminded that the earth ...belongs to Almighty Allah."[41] Ibrahim Ozdemir argues that any serious reading of the Qur'an reveals a perspective in which the earth is a gift from God with its own independent value, and in which people, as God's "vice-regents" on earth, have the responsibility to care for the rest of life and make their own patterns of desire and consumption temperate.[42] Numerous passages from Islamic scripture reveal how compatible its theology is with Judaism and Christianity in this regard, from the idea of the earth belonging to God to descriptions of nature celebrating its Creator: "The seven heavens and the earth, and all beings therein," says the Qur'an (17:46), sounding exactly like Psalm 19, "declare His glory."

Although an Islamic ethic of environmental responsibility toward God's creation can be rooted in extensive quotations from the Qur'an and other important sources, Islam, no less than Christianity or Judaism, faces the dilemma that such sources have been, for the most part, neglected. Like Christianity, Islam has been predominantly anthropocentric in practice, and thus, many contemporary Islamic writers tell us, requires at the very least a reorientation toward its own founding texts.

⚬

A good deal of what has been described so far, especially in the Western religious idea of nature as creation, and the consequent human responsibility to and limitations in regard to nature, has been described as a "stewardship" model of environmental concern. We have dominion over God's property and must treat it—like a priceless set of tools given to us by a loving Father—with respect and care. Widespread adoption of this perspective could lead to a vast improvement over current practice, but it still leaves open the question of what constitutes reasonable and moral uses of this gift.[43] How much exploitation is responsible and how much is excessive? What makes sense and what is just, well, *too much*? And is this gift like a priceless violin, or like a handy throwaway camera? It is not clear that anything in the idea of stewardship *alone* will answer such questions, especially when they are pointedly applied to, for a start, suburban sprawl, automobile use, pesticides, genetic engineering, or commercial fishing. And this is not to mention what responsible stewardship means in relation to population, especially now that we have pretty clearly "filled the earth" already!

In a clear example of this problem, many nineteenth-century Protestant industrialists saw the vast American wilderness as both a sign of God's greatness and as something to be developed for human ends. Such a dual perspective can be deeply contradictory: after a while, we will see that the more there is of the development, the less there will be of the sign. Eventually, environmental stewardship and unrestrained economic growth will appear as conflicting alternatives.

The problem is not restricted to stewardship models, in which nature has a transcendent creator. Even if we say that nature has its own value and that we should not exalt ourselves above it, we still must use, consume, and exploit it to sustain ourselves. To put the matter in nontheistic, Buddhist terms: the Blue Mountains may be as sentient as we are, but does that mean we shouldn't mine them or turn them into ski resorts? How about a little sustainable logging or sport hunting? And if we protect the Blue Mountains as wilderness areas, what about the less impressive woods nearby, the ocean fish, the land cleared for agriculture? What can we use, consume, displace—and what not?

Answers to these difficult questions, as we shall see, turn not only on continually more detailed and sophisticated accounts of the human-nature relationship, but on moral teachings about wealth and poverty, justice and oppression, temperance and greed, and the connection between moral values and material ones. Our relations with nature are not just about penguins and brooks, but about ourselves. Getting a rational and moral sense of what is responsible treatment of the earth depends on our getting a responsible and moral sense of what it means to be human and of how we ought to treat each other as well as the rest of the earth.

Yet, even on their own terms, and even as a beginning rather than an end to the conversation, these new readings of ancient religious texts are very important. Human culture does not make decisive changes easily, and no change as profound as that necessary to deal with the environmental crisis can be envisaged without using resources from past cultural traditions. Blanket condemnation of religion as *the* source of environmental problems would leave many people with a painful and ultimately untenable choice between environmentalism and faith. Religious environmentalists deny the necessity of such a choice. You can be, these writers have taught us, sound, believing Christians, devoted Jews, committed Buddhists, devout Muslims, and *also* be serious, devoted, committed, and devout environmentalists.

∾

Alongside the labor of recovery, religious environmentalists also offer direct and unflinching criticism. Such criticism does not stem from hostility, but from the belief that religions are ongoing, human-made traditions that require continual revision to remain vital and spiritually authentic. Even the most profound of revelations must be interpreted, made sense of, and applied to the concrete realities of our own situation. This was true of every religion at its origins and has been true ever since. As "theologians," which is ultimately just a fancy word for people who try to say what a religious tradition should mean, we are continuing the work begun by others, and we fully expect others to revise, perhaps very deeply, what we do now. We are able to criticize respectfully because we employ resources we have learned from our forbears. If we see farther than they, it is often because we stand on their shoulders. It is given to each generation to push the work of religion further, always acknowledging that we did not begin it and will not end it.

In the present context, the absolute necessity for criticism and change stems from the fact that what was once "nature" or "creation" has become, in a sense that is often bleak, "the environment." Even if age-old religious traditions do have wonderful resources for dealing with the former, they really can have little sense of the latter. The basic intuition that the earth exceeds our understanding and our power, as Bill McKibben decisively showed in *The End of Nature*, has been lost forever.[44] Whatever may be true about the rest of the universe, it is now clear that humans can decisively alter the web of life on earth. Changing the climate and atmosphere, eliminating species, creating new life by combining genes from wildly different organisms—these and many other activities indicate that the nature that we used to face with awe and fear has become something we can now treat with disdain. The biblical injunction to "tend and serve" the garden was never as salient as it is right now—and never as ignored. And it is in that spirit of care that ecotheologians take a critical stance toward their own traditions.

For Western religions, perhaps the most important of these criticisms focuses on a fundamental mind-body or soul-body dualism that has haunted Christianity in particular, but can be found in other traditions as well. Such dualism means that in Western traditions, the differences between humanity and nature, even when accompanied by a stewardship ideal, can slide all too easily toward an unthinking and unprincipled anthropocentrism in which only human beings have any moral value. "Ongoing repentance," writes Protestant theologian and social activist James Nash, "is warranted. . . . For most theologians . . . the theological focus has been on sin and salvation, the fall and redemption, the divine-human relationship *over against* the biophysical world as a whole. The focus has been overwhelmingly on human history to the neglect of natural history."[45]

Once again its centrality to Western culture in general and capitalist industrialism in particular requires us to examine Christianity in some detail. Over the centuries, the dominant interpretation of Christianity developed an increasingly disdainful attitude toward human physical existence and, as a consequence, toward the sheer physicality of the rest of nature as well. Summarizing basic Christian doctrine, Anna Peterson writes, "The soul that all other animals lack both defines humans and gives them transcendent value. In the end, the image of God implanted in the human creature returns to God. This means, crucially, that humanity's real home does not lie among the rest of creation, but rather with God in heaven."[46] The soul was thought of as a distinct nonphysical substance, rather than as an aspect or dimension of our corporeal being, something separate from the world rather than a way of being in the world. A picture of the universe emerged in which a "great chain of being" stretched from the perfection of God at the top through the angels and down to human beings (men, of course, above women), and then to sentient animals, plants, and the earth itself. The key to this image was a clear sense of *hierarchy*: it was crucial to know of any given entity how important, vital, and valuable it was, how close—or distant—from God.[47]

Privileging a nonmaterial soul over the physical body reinforces the special value of humans. If the soul is nonmaterial and possessed only by humans, then clearly only humans matter. Even if we should be careful not to waste what God has given us, we are still given leave to do whatever is within our reasonable interests. In this way, the *difference* between humans and the rest of nature—celebrated in religious texts, whether as dominion or stewardship—became the foundation for a simple and global sense of human *superiority*. Leonard Boff, one of the most important of Latin America's liberation theologians, sums up the anthropocentrism of traditional Christianity: "Everything is centered on human beings: salvation is for them; they alone have a future."[48] This anthropocentrism, which, as we have seen, emerged from a more mixed biblical and cultural base, increasingly dominated Christian thought. In the theology of colonial conquerors or the religious code of industrial capitalists, the fate of the earth was given practically no attention. In the mid-fifteenth century, Pope Nicolas granted Portugal's King Alfonso the right to "take possession of the new world," a possession that included the right to use (non-Christian!) people and the rest of nature without limit.[49] As the centuries unfolded, writes historian Mark Stoll, Christians "of all creeds" joined in the process of development and colonization: "Clearing land, introducing foreign plants and animals, expanding agriculture, developing trade, and conquering, converting, expelling or exterminating aborigines—in sum, the wholesale transformation of entire ecosystems—all received blessing as God's work."[50]

Christianity was thus keyed to a kind of detachment from the rest of nature, and thus necessarily to a fundamental lack of preparedness to defend it when, under the onslaught of the Industrial Revolution, humans begin to affect it in ways for which no one had been prepared. The complexities and scope of nature might have been taken as a sign of God's existence, a "natural theology" whose importance grew as revealed scripture and tradition lost their hold on ever larger numbers of people. Yet few of the faithful asked what it meant for belief in God the Designer if His design was being clear-cut, paved over, or rendered extinct by the fur trade. Most important, despite the prominence of natural theology in the pulpit and popular books, it had—outside of the first efforts to conserve a few of the more dramatically beautiful places in the United States—comparatively little effect on the way people behaved.

Somewhat ironically, the religious strain in Christianity in which value resided in God and people but not nature seemed to reach its furthest extremity in modern science. At least as commonly understood, science implied that material reality could be truly known only through the mathematical language of physics. For a worldview in which only numbers are real, the actual beauty and wonder of nature become subjective and sentimental, "written off as poetry."[51] The banishing of the spirits from nature that White had complained of in the Bible thus came to be the common sense of the secular West as well. Over the centuries, we went from a "primitive" mentality in which we could have reciprocal relations with nature, to the idea that the truly sacred is removed from nature but designs and controls it. This led to the belief that God can be known—or at least we can have knowledge like God's—if we come to know (through science) how the world works. Eventually, however, an increasingly abstract account of God freed matter from any connection to the sacred whatsoever, and the pursuit of knowledge turned into the goal of total control and management. No longer something with which we had a reciprocal relationship, or a sign of Divine power, nature became simply a "standing reserve" for human interests.[52] If anything, the Divine became identified with our own *human* subjectivity—with what we thought, felt, and wanted.[53]

A few nineteenth-century voices—most famously Emerson, Thoreau, and Muir—proclaimed the moral value of wilderness and the spiritual wisdom of nature, but at best, most conservation aimed only at the rational management of resources. A "religious" attitude toward nature, in all the senses of the term, was rare and was almost never a guiding source of public policy. Whatever the outlook of *individual* conservationists, even important ones, organized religious *institutions* for the most part ignored the subject entirely. They had not noticed the change from nature to environment and still thought of nature as (at best) God's immutable handiwork or as resources to be developed, rather than a fragile balance increasingly threatened by humans.[54]

The West went from a largely agrarian and technologically rather primitive society to an industrial juggernaut, which transformed its own lands and spread throughout the world. Some self-consciously Protestant industrialists might donate a few dollars to conservation causes, and nineteenth-century liberal Protestantism might see the need to manage wilderness resources wisely so that future generations could enjoy them, but the dominant message of virtually all of Christianity was that industrialization, providing its fruits were distributed with a certain amount of justice, was a fine thing. Industrialization meant progress, and progress was measured solely in terms of its effects on human beings.[55] What industrialization was doing to the natural world, and what nature's fate at the hands of humanity meant about humanity's own moral status, did not really figure into the accounting Christianity made of itself. The rise of a scientific worldview, the conflict between aristocracy and democracy, tensions within Christianity itself, the diminishing role of religion in society, the militant atheism of socialist and communist movements—these were the crucial issues. Speaking of the church's most authoritative attitudes as late as the 1960s, Catholic environmental theologian John Hart describes "a hierarchically structured pyramid with humanity atop as its ruler in God's image, exercising dominion over Earth and being the ultimate and appropriate beneficiary of Earth's goods, which were provided by the Creator to serve humanity." For the church, the right to human dominion, Hart tells us, was limited only by concern with other humans.[56] John Cobb puts the matter precisely, with special attention to his own tradition, asserting that with regard to anthropocentrism, "as a Protestant Christian I am impelled to move quickly to acknowledge that Protestant theology has been an extreme case."[57]

∾

Outside the Western context, religions played a different role in environmental problems (when, that is, the impact of colonialism did not lead local elites to simply abandon tradition in favor of Western attitudes toward nature, technological progress, and consumption). In Buddhism, for instance, neither the body nor the mind has inherent reality: both are constantly changing, and the reality of each depends on the reality of the other. The distinction is, at best, an occasionally convenient way to approach a particular situation, not something to make a big deal about. That is one reason why, as we have seen, Buddhism's distinction between humans and nature is much less charged, and can even be dismissed completely. Any suggestion of superiority ("dominion") over nature would be taken as a manifestation of precisely the kind of self-consciousness and selfishness that Buddhism is designed to eradicate.

However, another kind of dualism permeated Buddhism, one perhaps less pronounced in certain forms of Buddhism *in theory*, but that was widespread throughout the Buddhist world *in practice*. This was the dualism between *samsara*, the world of desire, frustration, and illusion, and *nirvana*, that of enlightenment. Even though the Mahayana school (which emerged about three centuries after the Buddha's death and came to prominence in China, Tibet, and Japan) theoretically denied any categorical distinction between the two, its extensive system of monasteries focused attention on a life of spiritual self-absorption and detachment from the wider world. Involvement with social issues—and thus necessarily with the ecological consequences of human social actions—was extremely hard to come by in most Buddhist traditions. In this way, Buddhism is representative of Hinduism and Taoism (though not Confucianism) as well as the mirror image of Judaism, Christianity, and Islam. These Western traditions are much more committed to the relationship between religion and social justice, but also more committed to an anthropocentric theology. In the East, the distinctions between humans and nature are much less rigid and pronounced, but connections between religion and social justice—the prophetic call so essential to the West—are more muted.

That is why contemporary Buddhist concern with ecology arises as an aspect of "engaged Buddhism," which, says founder Thich Nhat Hanh, includes a sense of the essential interconnections between the individual Buddhist and social institutions.[58] When engaged Buddhism emerged from Vietnam, Sri Lanka, and Thailand, its concerns with social life were often rejected by traditional monks as being peripheral to monastic discipline. The battle of Buddhist ecotheologians is not with their religion's theology of nature, but with its deep-seated social quietism. Like the soul-body dualism of Christianity and its idea that true fulfillment lies in a heavenly realm, traditional Buddhism's pursuit of Enlightenment led away from awareness of the actual condition of all the beings with whom Buddhism claimed each person was interrelated.

As contemporary Jewish writers apply Bal Taschit, or Muslims use scattered Qur'anic verses concerning how all the other animals have communities just as humans do, so ecologically minded Buddhists now employ doctrines of interdependence and compassion to extend concern to nature and to engage with society's devastating environmental practices. Hindus face a comparable theological challenge.[59]

❧

Along with reinterpretation and criticism, ecotheology offers vital new contributions to religion's ongoing evolution. Fashioned at a time when technology was limited and human effects on nature worked very slowly, it is not
surprising that Talmudic rules or models of Christian virtues are not adequate
to what we face, and what we are doing, now. As the fall of the Second
Temple required a new kind of Judaism, and the encounter with a world of
different faiths deeply affected Christianity, so the environmental crisis calls
for critical theological creativity. As Norman C. Habel puts it for Christianity,
but in terms that can be extended to every other tradition, along with saving
souls and liberating oppressed communities, "Christians now face a third
mission: healing earth."[60]

Consider, for instance, the simple but profound idea of "eco-kosher," as
proposed by social activist Rabbi Arthur Waskow and Jewish scholar Art
Green. The traditional Jewish laws of *kashrut* were based on biblical dietary
regulations. Certain animals (pigs, shellfish) are outlawed entirely, certain
foods that can be eaten separately cannot be eaten together (meat and milk),
and certain foods cannot be eaten at certain times (leavened bread during
the eight days of Passover). The driving idea behind this is that all aspects
of life must be ordered according to God's will, the intake of food no less
than prayer, family, and social relationships. What Green and Waskow have
done is *extend* this concept to environmental matters. Waskow asks, "Is it
'kosher' to drive an SUV? What would happen if our rabbis said in sermons
that an SUV is no more kosher than a ham sandwich, and a lot more destructive to the earth and humankind? Would people storm out—or
change?"[61] He expands his challenging question to tomatoes drenched in pesticides, windows that waste heat, and banks that invest in polluting companies, thereby redefining "kosher" to signify a "good practice" based on "the
deep well-springs of Jewish wisdom about protecting the Earth."[62]

Art Green has suggested that vegetarianism may be a "kashrut for our
age," for which there are reasons *"just as compelling ... as the reason for the
selective taboos against certain animals must have been when the Community
of Israel came to accept these as the word of God."* For Green, these reasons
include factory farming's disastrous ecological consequences, inherent cru-
elty, and effects on human health. His response is also rooted in the Jewish
experience of the Holocaust, in which Jews were "treated as cattle rather than
human beings." "A vegetarian Judaism," he tells us, "would be more whole
in its ability to embrace the presence of God in all of Creation."[63]

Protestant theologian and past president of the American Academy of
Religion Sallie McFague has explored new ground for Christian thinking in
an ecological age. One of her most thought-provoking ideas is the simple but
profound suggestion that we look on the earth as the "body of God." McFague
begins by turning to the long-lost "organic" tradition in Christianity, which

viewed the church as the "body of Christ" and saw this body firmly rooted in the earth. Building on the organic model, McFague proposes a more relational, less hierarchical image in which all the parts are valued and humans do not get special place. The holiness of the earth, she argues, derives from basic Christian doctrine: if God can become flesh, there is no reason that flesh—and by extension all of life—cannot become Godly. Further, if God is not "in the world," how could we ever have a relationship with Her? Where else would God be? Yet God's presence, for McFague, is less a matter of initial design, like a clever craftsman who makes a beautiful watch and then retires to observe it from a distance, than of an active and permeating spirit. God is the "aliveness" of creation, including "the breath that enlivens and energizes it."[64] This perspective actually resonates with many biblical passages that depict God as an ever present force rather than a remote Designer: "You make the grass grow for the cattle, and herbage for man's labor . . . the trees of the Lord drink their fill. . . . When you send back Your breath, they are created, and you renew the face of the earth" (Ps. 104:14, 16, 30). Protestant theologian Mark Wallace stresses the biblical descriptions of the Holy Spirit as a natural presence: as bird, fire, and wind. "All things," insists Wallace, "are made of Spirit *and* are part of the continuous biological flow patterns that constitute life on our planet."[65] We may note that thinkers like McFague and Wallace are enlarging the range of ways God can be experienced. For them, the aloof, commanding, patriarchal Father figure of tradition or the distant Designer of later periods are not the only, and certainly not necessarily the best, models of God on which to hang our spiritual hats. We can seek God deeply and passionately, yet need not be limited to such images.

When God is seen as in and of the earth as well as a transcendent sprit, McFague and other Christian theologians point out, we come into a powerful emotional relationship with the suffering of the earth. As the Trinity offers an image of God Who is both transcendent and immanent, both infinitely powerful and capable of enormous suffering, so an ecological Christianity sees both the awesomeness of the earth and the way life on earth is being, we might say, crucified. The animals tortured by factory farming and frivolous laboratory uses, the soil made lifeless by chemicals, the species extinguished carry the face of Jesus no less than the human poor ignored by the rich.[66]

∞

It is not only the Bible or the Sutras that religious environmentalists read, but also the book of nature itself, a book that is revealed to them in great measure by science. For centuries, religious thinkers saw science as a great enemy, yet ecotheologians find that the accomplishments of modern science do not purge the world of God, but confirm Her presence.[67] The history of the universe and accounts of the detailed interconnections of ecosystems can serve a *religious* function. That is, they have become "mythic": accounts of the world that provide meaning and morality, frames through which our lives are understood and our actions directed.[68]

Thomas Berry, one of the earliest and most influential ecotheologians, believes that to face the horrors of the environmental crisis, we desperately need a new "universe story" that can help us understand where we have come from and surmount our "autism" in regard to the rest of life. For Berry, the preferred version of this story is not the poetry of Genesis, but the reigning scientific account. It begins with the Big Bang and traces 14 billion years in which the galaxies formed, our solar system emerged, life appeared, and humans evolved. Cosmic and biological evolution has led toward increasingly complex life forms, marvelously interdependent ecosystems, increasing intelligence, and subjective experience. This story as a whole, Berry believes, reveals that the universe *itself* is for us the "primary mode of God's presence."[69] Drawing on Thomas Aquinas, Berry makes it clear that the unit of value here is the *whole*, not just humans. Divine goodness, wrote Aquinas, "could not be adequately represented by one creature alone, He produced many and diverse creatures. For goodness, which in God is simple and uniform, in creatures is manifold and divided; and hence the whole universe together participates in the divine goodness more perfectly and represents it better than any single creature whatever."[70] Ultimately, if every natural being is a revelation of some aspect of God, if God's presence is known *through* the complexity, interdependence, and increasing self-consciousness of what is manifest in the universe, then the more life we destroy, the less we are able to know—and to worship—God.

Berry's perspective may remind us of natural theology's use of the scope and complexity of the universe as evidence of a Transcendent Designer. Yet the cultural contexts of natural theology and of ecotheology are very different. The former sought to defend religion from being seen as irrational in comparison to science and necessarily stressed how much grander the universe was than anything humans could create. Now ecotheologians seek to invest religion with a scientific understanding of—and *hence a reverence for*—nature. Ironically, this reversal seems called for not only because of our vastly increased knowledge, but also because of what we now know about the fragility of nature itself. It is just because humans can exterminate species and destabilize the climate that we need to think of nature in a dramatically different way.

Yet, despite science's contribution to ecology, it cannot stand alone. The deep flaw in Western religions and Western secular culture both, Berry argues, is the failure to appreciate the wonder of this universe story. Treating nature cavalierly, religions, particularly his own, have reserved reverence for books, buildings, people, and human institutions. Similarly, much of the scientific establishment and an even more scientistic culture have seized on the "facts" but left out a sense of awe and mystery. Neither religion nor science has been seriously "concerned with the integral functioning of the earth community,"[71] and thus neither has been an adequate resource to resist the environmental crisis.

In a sense, what Berry proposes is a marriage of religion's capacity for reverence with science's capacity to describe reality. If this is somewhat of an arranged marriage, driven by a desperate need to find some new cultural resources to respond to the environmental crisis, that doesn't mean it can't develop into a serious and productive relationship.

For ecotheology, this relationship leads to the widespread assertion that we are neither so different nor so separate from the earth community as many traditional religions have taught. Furthermore, we are the product of an amazing history and integral parts of breathtakingly complex webs of life. The intricacy of ecosystems, the mutual dependence of vastly different species, and the stunning ingenuity of the forms and functions of this nearly infinite array of beings naturally lead us into the kind of awe that can only be called "spiritual," if not downright religious. Once we begin to really take in the scope of the universe, the earth, and life, the proper moral and spiritual response will not be far behind.[72]

To take one illuminating example: when animal researcher Mark Bekoff describes some marvelous instances of animal cognition, ingenuity, loving bonds, and emotion, his work can have serious implications not only for animal rights but for religion as well.[73] If God permeates the cosmos, Jay McDaniel asks in response to Bekoff's research, is not our knowledge of the cosmos a kind of knowledge of God? If

all things live and move and have their being in God, then when we try to imagine what it is like to be inside a coyote or penguin, a bluejay or a small child we are, in our way, exploring the very mind of God. And when scientists try—as for instance serious students of animal consciousness do—to comprehend what it is like to be inside the skin of other living beings, they too are praying. Of course they would not call it prayer. They would call it understanding. But in their way they are reaching out to ask: "What is it like to be you, who are different from me? And how are things for you?" When we find ourselves entering into imaginative empathy, we are simultaneously entering a space where science and religion meet. We are reaching out to something beyond ourselves, trustful that there is a greater whole in which all living beings are small but included.[74]

Continuing this line of thought, Holmes Rolston suggests that our proper understanding of evolution, far from eliminating a place for God, can have the opposite effect. There is, Rolston points out, a fascinating convergence between science and religion as knowledgeable scientists themselves hold a respect for nature that borders on—and sometimes crosses over into—wonder and reverence. Rolston quotes famed biologist Ernst Mayr: "Virtually all biologists are religious in the deeper sense of the word. . . . The unknown and maybe unknowable instills in us a sense of humility and awe."[75] If this is something of an overstatement, it is at least partially true, and indicates how scientific knowledge and reverence for life need not exclude one another.

This new harmony between religion and science is of great importance. Yet, as much as I am in sympathy with these reflections on the implications of scientific knowledge, I think a cautionary word is in order, for sometimes ecotheologians write as if knowledge of the complexities of life or the marvelous interdependence of ecosystems *guarantees* profound new environmental attitudes. This, I believe, is a mistake. We could, after all, look at the 14 billion–year universe story or the intricacies of life that so enthrall Berry, McFague, Mary Evelyn Tucker, Larry Rasmussen, and many others and instead respond with a Camus-like shrug that sees only "benign indifference," not a sacred story calling for reverence. As the character Orestes in Jean-Paul Sartre's play *The Flies* showed his distinctly human freedom by rejecting God's demand for obedience, so people are always able to react to what they see around them in a wide variety of ways. The point is not that the facts of ecology *compel* reverence of the earth, but that such reverence is *at least as justified* as the positivist notion that physical existence carries no meaning whatsoever, or as some religious views that place sacred meaning only in the nonmaterial. All of these frameworks fit "the facts." The only mistake is to think that any of them is the only rational response.

This point can be underscored if we examine Lisa Sideris's criticism of many widely read ecotheologians for their inability to deal with the biological realities of pain, predation, parasitism, and death.[76] In seeing only cooperation, beauty, and wonder, she argues, these thinkers project human values and perspectives onto the rest of the universe. Although they claim to love and respect nature, what they see *as* nature is too often a fantasy of ecological stability and harmony. Yet nature, Sideris reminds us, is not pretty. In the long run, countless species appear and die off, even without human intervention; in the short run, sustenance for any creature often means the death of another, at times in a gruesome manner. If we look at nature and see harmony, we are not seeing clearly.

To some extent, Sideris's criticisms are well taken. In nature, as we know, the lion doesn't lie down with the lamb (or if he does, only one of them gets up afterward). Drawing moral principles from ecological balance is a chancy business, as such balance requires nonstop rending, tearing, and chewing.[77]

Still, although there is clearly death in nature, there is also birth; if species eat each other, they also feed each other. No scientific account will tell us what all this means, or whether one of the pair is more "real" than the other. Facts do not have any religious or moral meanings by themselves, but only because humans perceive, interpret, and respond to them. Just as earlier members of our species had to fashion responses to the power of thunderstorms, the regularity of the seasons, and the inevitability of death, so we have to decide what to do with all the scientific knowledge we now possess. Evolution, which creates and eliminates species by the million, can be seen as murderous competition and profligate waste *or*, as Gary Snyder puts it, as a process in which different forms of energy call other beings into existence. The berries call the bear, the salmon call the orcas, and "the whole show calls us."[78] Is it an infinite dance, or an endless slaughter? If anything, it is both. Thus, at its best, ecotheology will recognize that scientific knowledge does not reveal a pristine perfection but a miraculous totality that requires that we affirm the pain and the loss along with the grandeur.

With such an attitude, rather than any ecological whitewashing, can indeed come some moral lessons. Rejecting the notion that because of our highly developed intelligence and capacity for choice we are so different from other species that our moral lives have nothing to learn from them, Rosemary Radford Ruether suggests that we "must reshape our basic sense of self in relation to the life cycle." Learning from nature's "cycle of growth and disintegration," we should be conscious of—and stop denying—our own mortality. "Humans are also finite organisms, centers of experience in a life cycle that must disintegrate back into the nexus of life and arise again in new forms."[79]

My own view is that in some respects, we can also use nature as a kind of model for the spiritually developed person. In the modern world, for example, our social conventions direct us to compete, achieve, be better than our neighbor, rise to the top, and stay at number one. The net result is a small number of successful people and a huge number who feel like failures. Ecosystems, by contrast, can work only if each species plays its distinct function. The tiny phytoplankton at the bottom of the ocean's food chain is as important as the mighty whale, the nitrogen-fixing bacteria as essential as the redwoods. Everything has its place—and knows it. Would that each of us felt the same way! And that we could realize that our own distinct contribution, given with love and care, matters as much as (and no more than) everyone else's.

Paradoxically, the living dynamic of nature can even encompass as seemingly *unnatural* a theological concept as immortality. Rachel Carson wrote, "Every living thing of the ocean, plant and animal alike, returns to the water at the end of its own life span the materials which had been temporarily assembled to form its body. Thus, individual elements are lost to view, only to reappear again and again in different incarnation in a kind of material immortality."[80]

∾

This survey of ecotheological writings reveals a wide variety of descriptions of nature's value and our relationships with it:

- Nature is a gift from God, and should be treasured as such.
- Nature's majesty testifies to the grandeur of God, and its behavior is a celebration of God.[81]
- Nature is permeated by a Divine Spirit.
- Because we have emerged from, depend on, and are so much like nature, we must extend our sense of moral value to it. We have responsibilities to nature and so must "tend the garden." Nature is the stranger and the poor for whom we are called on to care.
- Nature awes us with its scope and complexity. It is marvelous and calls forth a respect bordering on reverence.
- The interdependence and selflessness that mark the holistic character of ecosystems contain moral lessons.
- The environment has rights, deserves compassion, and can suffer (is "cruciform").
- Other animals have self-awareness, can communicate, and have family structures—and therefore deserve moral concern.
- Distinguishing between ourselves and nature reflects a self-centered arrogance that will make spiritual growth impossible.

These ideas, I believe, provide the foundation for a worldview and a moral code—and they also invite us to a distinctive kind of personal transformation. It is not the same old self who is going to acquire new beliefs about the importance of nature or start a recycling program at the church. It is, rather, that thinking—and acting—ecologically requires a new sense of who we are. Like traditional Judaism (which Rabbi Dovid Gottlieb characterizes as aimed at the basic transformation of personality)[82] or Christianity (which invites us to be "born again" in Christ), ecotheology calls us to realize an "ecological self" at the center of our spiritual lives.

This ecological self is first and foremost capable of a kind of intimate connection with (in David Abram's wonderful phrase) the "more-than-human."[83] The experience that we get in any form of collective religious practice—the group recitation of sins by Jews on Yom Kippur, the solemn joy of the Eucharist, the brilliant silence of the Buddhist meditation hall—is to be extended to a glimpse of new flowers in spring, the sound of ice cracking on a bitter winter night, the magic of birdsong. Enlarging our powers of imagination, insight, and vibrant feeling enables us to see God in places where for too long She was absent. And so the community of persons, of Beings That Matter, gets expanded and enriched. When we write letters to islands, let the ox eat some of the grain he is threshing, and hear the mountains praising God, we broaden our sense of kinship and divinity.

The particular principles the new ecotheology insists on will, I suspect, make little sense—or have much practical effect—if we are not directed back to these primordial experiences of the world. What we *make* of such experiences will vary in different traditions. We may say that nature is a Gift from God or "the body of God," or that everything in nature is "also a community like yours" (Qur'an 6:28), or that the Blue Mountains are walking. We may even be told, as a Jewish Midrash teaches, that nature follows its Torah as we are to follow ours.[84] From these different vocabularies a common message emerges: Seek out, recognize, and celebrate that which we have been ignoring, consuming, and destroying.

Yet birds do not pray in words as we do, nor rivers affirm that they are part of our faith communities. Other species won't argue about the rightness of a creed, choose one plan for living out of range of possible choices, or construct stories about what life means. If we are to welcome nature as one of our own, to celebrate our communion with it, we must do more than view *it* differently, we also have to take very seriously some other part of *ourselves* than that which we usually stress so much. If rivers and whales have inherent value without arguing for themselves in the public square, claiming their rights, or asking—in words—for recognition, then to truly recognize their moral contours we have to see that there is part of us that has value beyond our self-representing, self-interested ego, our repeated expressions of what we think is "right" and "wrong," our endless claims, demands, and beliefs. Metaphors of walking mountains, hills proclaiming God's glory, or the "Torah of the Earth" suggest that those without, no less than those with, an ego are "created in the image of God." How is this possible?

Running through ecotheology is the sense that we live *communally* with nature, that we can *communicate* with it, and that therefore *communion* with it is possible. Clearly, however, it is not the normal ego, at least the normal ego of the industrialized world, that hears trees or learns from rivers. Usually the best we can do is know when to feed the dog. Thinking of religious value as extending only to people and moral rights as belonging to the human alone goes with our inability to talk—and listen—to nature. This is perhaps the fundamental difference between the modern world and that of shamans and indigenous peoples.[85]

To commune with nature we must find something within ourselves that is not tied to our social identity or rooted in complicated verbal self-description. And this we cannot do as doctors or plumbers, Republicans or New Yorkers. We must do it, at least, as beings that breathe and eat, sense the sun, feel the wind and rain, and experience love, fear, and pleasure in their bodies. If the trees root to the earth, so do—in rather more mobile ways—our own legs. If the earth's surface is 80 percent ocean, so is our own body. Human children frolicking in the grass can surely remind us of kittens playing, and ten thousand ants working together are not, seen in a certain light, all that different from workers headed for a day at the office. As the trees breathe out, we breathe in—and vice versa. Our eyes have evolved to see this landscape, our ears to hear these birds and rustling leaves, our

tongues to taste the food that grows here. Trying to cut ourselves loose from
the earth is as foolish as denying that we were formed by our families and
our native cultures.

We may have forgotten all this, but surely we can, if we choose, remember.
To do so, we will have to move out of our normal egos—a move, interestingly,
that religion has always asked us to make. Whether it is the state beyond
attachment of Buddhism or Islam's complete submission to God, faiths teach
us that we must go a little crazy if we are to become truly sane. We must
transform ourselves: literally uproot our physical body (as when Abraham
had to leave the land of his father) and our social position (as when Jesus
told the rich man to give his wealth to the poor).

It is also true that in most religious narratives we can experience life
beyond the ego only after, and in part because of, some kind of crisis. Jesus
must die before he can fully realize his Divinity; the Jews have to suffer slavery
and wander in the wilderness before they can fully embrace the Torah; fledg-
ling Buddhists spend thousands of frustrating and lonely hours on the meditation mat wrestling with their egos. What those events and processes were
to traditional religion, the environmental crisis is to religion now. Sensing
the gravity of our situation, bereft for all our losses, knowing that the future
may hold much worse, a fundamental ground is being removed from under
our feet and a sheltering canopy taken from above our heads. Our need to
sense a communion with the earth is not just about how grand the universe
is and how complex and marvelous ecosystems are. It is also about the cry
of the earth and the cry of other human beings who are suffering. This cry
will either provoke a new sense of self, or humanity will choke on its own
wastes.

Perhaps, as Paul Shepard recommends, it will become easier to do this if
we remember that our senses and social organization were formed by hunting, or, in Joanna Macy's words, if we think of ourselves as beings every atom
of whose bodies were formed by the great fireball of the Big Bang 14 billion
years ago. It may be cultivated by growing organic food, long hours of watching birds build nests, walking silently in a forest, or getting to know thirty
native plants that grow within a mile of your house.[86] It could require that
we sit with one tree a few minutes each day—for years. It may be helped by
learning some of the more amazing scientific facts about the natural world:
that trees communicate with each other or that an adult rat will raise orphaned rabbits. When we see impalas grooming each other, mongooses sharing babysitting, or elephants weeping for their dead mates, we know that our
own feelings and acts of love and compassion resonate with the realm of
nature from which we emerged.[87] Given the structure of modern life, it will
probably take creativity, serious attention, and a real willingness to change.
Doubtless there will be many ways of achieving this communion, and it is
essential that ecotheology not only assert the need for such communion, but
also direct us toward ways of achieving it.[88]

∾

David Brower, one of America's most important environmentalists, was once referred to as an "Archdruid," as someone, that is, who would cheerfully sacrifice people to trees.[89] At times, both secular and religious environmentalism are targeted by similar disparagement. Such criticism may occasionally be justified, but for the most part, it is an (often willful) distortion of what religious environmentalism actually teaches. From the earliest work of John Cobb and Rosemary Ruether[90] in the 1970s to the plethora of contemporary writings, religious environmentalists (like most secular ones) have joined concern for the earth with concern for people. If we love redwoods and dolphins because they are kin, that does not mean we should cease to love our human kin as well. The entire "earth community," as Larry Rasmussen put it, is the focus of our work. The reasons for valuing nature—as creations of God, as interdependent parts of a system of life, as subjects of their own lives, as unique products of an evolutionary history—apply to people as well.

One reason these concerns go together, many believe, is that it is the same misguided ideas and unjust social structures that destroy species, unbalance ecosystems, *and* oppress human beings. With this perspective, ecotheology moves from reforming religious traditions to challenging beliefs and institutions throughout society as a whole. In this development it moves toward what is often called "ecojustice": a prophetic vision of a social order in which both nature and people are treated with respect and care. When it takes the form of ecojustice, ecotheology overlaps with secular environmentalism and progressive political movements generally. If ecojustice is ultimately *rooted* in a vision of the Sermon on the Mount or God's command "Justice, justice shall you pursue" (Deut. 16:20; also Qur'an 16:90), many of its *goals* are indistinguishable from those of the Sierra Club, neighborhood activists, or antiglobalization protestors at the World Social Forum. When theologians James Martin-Schramm and Robert Stivers offer principles to guide a specifically Christian ethic of ecological justice, for example, they offer "justice," "sustainability," "participation" (a broad democracy), "sufficiency" (modesty in consumption), and solidarity with all of life.[91] Comparable values are stressed by representatives of virtually every world religion when they address ecological values holistically.

The frequent imperative to practice justice, righteousness, or nonviolence expresses religion's commitment to bringing sacred truths into social life. Under the pressure of environmental concerns, this commitment necessarily requires a comprehensive vision of collective, structural change that extends far beyond religion's usual subject matter. If we are to love our neighbor as ourselves, we had better think deeply about the ways our energy use damages his life by causing global warming, even if he lives eight thousand miles away. Yet significantly reducing the use of fossil fuels is clearly something we can do only through collective political action aimed at changing national energy policy. If we must not kill, we should not use pesticides that cause cancer; thus, supporting more organic agriculture on a massive scale becomes a serious moral matter. These and dozens of other examples indicate why ecojustice critically examines all aspects of our shared economic and political life. In the words of the Ecojustice Ministries, a Denver-based Protestant activist organization, "Faithful and ethical living is not confined to personal choices. In our globalized economy, it is absurd to suggest that personal choices alone can address the crises we face. Various forms of power—economic, political, military, intellectual and personal—must be taken into account in the ways that we understand the world and live within it."[92] In concrete terms, this means that when any serious theologian talks about the environment, he or she necessarily expresses support for certain concrete political policies, for instance, the need to monitor and restrict market forces, limit the prerogatives of corporations, make the government responsive to the interests of ecosystems and the socially powerless, reduce military expenditures, and direct technology toward sustainability. Here critical concepts that have been essential to secular political movements become the province of religion as well. Words such as freedom, democracy, rights, totalitarianism, capitalism, racism, sexism, globalization, and imperialism are freely used, and religious thinkers find themselves compelled to use ideas developed by theorists far from the world of faith. (This is perhaps less surprising than it looks. One should no more expect the Bible to enable us to understand global capitalism than to tell us how to build a computer!)

Many historians of religion, of course, would find this movement rather ironic. For a very long time, progressive political movements and established religions tended to be sworn enemies. Despite the occasional role of religion in social change—ministers seeking to abolish slavery, Quakers rejecting war—movements for democracy, workers' rights, women's equality, or economic justice could generally count on the local religious authorities to be their opponents rather than their allies, or to simply ignore the oppression in front of their noses altogether.

Yet, in the context of ecojustice, religious thinkers have had to turn to secular accounts of the dominant *social* structures to apply religion's fundamental *ethical* teachings.[93] Latin American Catholic feminist ecotheologian Ivone Gebara, for example, proposes a new model of the Trinity that recognizes people's connections to the rest of the universe (with the history of that universe defined by current science!) and sees the reality of the Trinity as a series of relationships understood politically as well as personally. These relationships, in which Gebara seeks to find the meaning of God as Father, Son, and Holy Spirit, include nature's continuous movement of creation and destruction and the diversity of cultures and races. If we find the Trinity in nature, Gebara tells us, we are a good deal less likely to casually or thoughtlessly ravage it; if we find the Trinity among other people, including those different from ourselves, we "could more easily overcome the different strains of racism . . . xenophobia, exclusion, violence, and sexism" that plague us.[94] For an ecojustice perspective, then, comprehending even the most basic of religious concepts, such as the Trinity, requires a political understanding of our moral situation.

Of the many social issues ecotheologians focus on, three hold particular importance: economic, racial, and gender justice. These issues, interestingly, represent a leading secular progressive movement of the past two hundred years. Each of these movements directly connects to environmentalism, and the moral commitment to ecojustice requires and recognizes the necessity to integrate them.

For example, one of the most ambitious descriptions of what an ecological society might look like, *For the Common Good: Redirecting the Economy toward Community, the Environment and a Sustainable Future*, is, significantly, the joint product of a pioneer Protestant ecotheologian (John Cobb) and a professor of economics and former senior economist for the World Bank (Herman Daly).[95] Daly and Cobb propose a rich combination of policy and value changes. They challenge existing economies of scale and current trade policies, suggest new ways to cultivate local communities and redesign educational priorities. And they address the cosmic meaning of human existence and the ethical standards that should guide it. Similarly, when theologian Dorothee Soelle speaks to what she takes to be the prospects of religion in the twenty-first century, she diagnoses the political ills of globalization—the pervasive influence of multinational corporations and economic institutions creating poverty and environmental ruin—along with the more familiar problems of Christian complacency or arrogance.[96] Above all, ecotheologians (and, as we shall see in later chapters, institutionalized religions and religious environmental activists) oppose the prerogatives of the market. Time after time the unbridled pursuit of profit and private control of the industry and natural resources are questioned, challenged, or blamed for human and ecological suffering. In what is surely one of the great ironies of religious history, theological voices from all the world's traditions are echoing some of Marx's most critical comments on a capitalist economy and the society built upon it. In particular, they question capitalism's endless economic growth, its reduction of human relationships and the earth to commodities, and its relentless drive to create a world of compulsive consumers.[97]

Ecojustice writings show that if religions, to their shame, have often endorsed the social status quo and the privileges of the wealthy, their teachings nevertheless also remain a repository of critical resistance to both. Islamic ecotheologians, for example, have been critical of the creation of an "elite that overconsumes and overproduces, and hence contributes to the ecological crisis by depleting the environment." Such behavior results in injustice for the entire world, and also violates a basic Islamic virtue of *hay'a* or "dignified reserve." It is the absence of hay'a, Nawal Ammar writes, that leads to "the disparity between the poor and the rich, a production system that is entirely dependent on the monopolies and big corporations, which in turn leads to a misdistribution of resources and overconsumption, authoritarian leaders, wars, disrespect for human diversity, and a way of life that depletes natural and human resources."[98]

Another dimension of ecojustice focuses on "environmental racism," that is, the fact that minorities and the poor in the United States, just like indigenous peoples worldwide, are exposed to a great deal more pollution than are the racially and economically dominant groups. Lacking social power, their lives are held as less valuable. Hence the environmental crisis is written on—and in—their bodies.[99] During the past twenty years a comprehensive concern with environmental racism developed with the constant input of black religious social activists.[100] Virtually every religious account of the place of nature in religious life now includes a focus on this topic. Larry Rasmussen puts the matter succinctly: "All communities, it turns out, are not created equal. Some get dumped on more than others."[101] African American Christian theologian Karen Baker-Fletcher talks of how "sociopolitical and economic systems allow" us to "place toxins in the neighborhoods of the poor and the colored."[102] Native American activist Thomas White Wolf Fassett, a national officer of the United Methodist Church, describes native peoples' resistance to having their lands become "national sacrifice areas," so polluted that they can never be cleaned up, and of the similarities between colonizing people and colonizing land.[103]

Ecojustice's concern with racism is joined by critical attention to an "ecofeminism" that focuses on connections between the oppression of women and the devaluation and destruction of nature. Ecofeminism takes as central the fact that for much of Western religion, philosophy, and science women were "nature" incarnate and thus lacked the value and importance of men. The initial justification for this dual subordination was rooted in the claim that women and nature both lacked men's holiness or closeness to God. As secular society and scientific discourse emerged in the seventeenth century, it was men's (self-proclaimed) rationality that was used to justify masculine social privileges. Interestingly, whatever else they disagreed on, both religious and secular institutions agreed that men deserved power over women. Deconstructing that power, ecofeminists argue, requires a changed understanding and valuation of women, nature, and men alike. This involves, for a start, a celebration of human beings' bodily existence, a denial that we are human predominantly because of our soul or mind, and recognition of the vast spiritual intelligence of both women and the natural world. Ecofeminism, in both its religious and secular forms, thus participates in ecotheology's need to develop a new self-identity.[104]

In many concrete social contexts, of course, class, gender, and race may be closely intertwined. For example, awareness of the combination of the cultural devaluation of women with their economic subordination has powerful religious and political implications.[105] In India, to take one instance,

Vandana Shiva has analyzed the distinct effects of deforestation policies on women, whose love of their surrounding ecosystems reflects the role those systems play in providing food, fuel, forage, and medicines.[106] Ecofeminism also describes how patriarchy shapes the effects of economic development. When export agriculture promoting a single agricultural commodity replaces subsistence labor, women in the local community see their standard of living sharply decline and the local landscape diminish.

In another example, one advocating an active role for Christianity in South African environmentalism, Denise Ackermann and Tahra Joyner describe how "the abuse of the environment and the imbalance of the distribution of male-dominated political power over centuries are intimately connected." In white-controlled South Africa, "conservation" meant protecting wilderness areas for hunting by expelling natives who lived in them, and population policy meant sterilizing black women and encouraging whites to have more children. Simultaneously, "capital-intensive agriculture . . . resulted in mass eviction of farm dwellers from their land and homes."[107] Their analysis, in other words, extends far beyond traditional theology and into the details of South Africa's racial, gender, and class relationships. Similarly, when Catholic theologian Gabrielle Dietrich offers a feminist perspective on ecology and social justice in the context of the fisherfolk of South India, she must examine traditional religious restrictions on "unclean" women that limited their access to public spaces. She is also aware of the destructive impact of capitalist development on traditional communities and how

> the cycle of indebtedness imposed by World Bank loans, branding social expenditure as wasteful, drives land prices up, enhances individual indebtedness and bondage, impoverishes people by inflation, dismantles the distribution system, and works toward fragmenting society and destroying nature at the same time. The sea becomes polluted and depleted of fish, the traditional skills are destroyed, the land is sold at exorbitant prices, and people are deprived of shelter and livelihood. Environmental protection gets divorced from the people's survival rights.[108]

I believe that ecotheology's social critique makes it the contemporary heir to the fusion of religion, social action, and moral teaching found in the work of Gandhi, Martin Luther King, and Latin American liberation theologians. In this capacity, it combines frameworks too often used in isolation or opposition. It does not make sense to ask if the widespread siting of toxic incinerators in African American communities is an environmental, a racial, or a class issue. Clearly, it is all three. War hurts us because it traumatizes people and the environment both, absorbs resources that could be spent for human welfare (education, health care, services for the elderly), and leaves behind polluted landscapes and decimated ecosystems. The more we see humans as a part of nature, the more it is clear that what we do to nature we do to each other—and vice versa. There is no way to be unjust, selfish, or cruel to one sector of reality and treat the rest morally. If we do not see the whole, we won't really be seeing much of anything else. To paraphrase Jesus: What you do to the least of these natural beings, you do to yourselves also.

∽

Ecotheologians are quite aware that the sources of human injustice and environmental destruction are in our hearts and minds as well as in social relationships. Unjust social institutions include a personality-shaping culture that needs to be criticized and resisted privately as well as collectively, in terms of personal values as well as laws, property, and policy.

This is particularly important because one powerful element of the environmental crisis in the first world—and among social elites everywhere else—is a driving psychic need for ever more consumption: more powerful cars, larger homes, ever faster computers, and a cell phone that can take pictures, download e-mail, play video games, and massage your aching neck muscles. This need is no longer confined to the West, as one of the "benefits" of the new global economy is the spread of these values throughout the world. In Thailand, Buddhist activist Sulak Sivaraksa laments, "The department stores have become our shrines, and they are constantly filled with people. For the young people, these stores have replaced the Buddhist temples."[109]

In this context, religions provide a rich resource, for, as Bill McKibben trenchantly observed, "Only our religious institutions, among the mainstream organizations of Western, Asian, and indigenous societies, can say with real conviction, and with any chance of an audience, that there is some point to life beyond accumulation."[110] It has been a long-standing religious claim that true human fulfillment cannot be found in wealth, addictive pleasure, or unrestrained consumption. The Talmud defines wealth as "being satisfied with what one has"; Christianity claims that wealth made spiritual development extremely difficult; and Buddhism centers on a rejection of any kind of attachment or unrestrained desire. Religious life is rooted in the idea that lasting happiness is found in the development of virtues such as acceptance, gratitude, love, appreciation, and tranquility, not gadgets that support a "lifestyle."

Besides their explicit teachings that a life of wealth and pleasure is ultimately unsatisfying, religions also contain instructions and practices about how to shift one's attention away from the addictive attractions of the market. Long-standing spiritual traditions offer resources that secular environmentalists—who share religions' rejection of consumerism but who often come off as pretentious moralizers—do not have. Some of these resources may be quite simple. For example, traditional Jews begin each day with a prayer thanking God for "returning my soul to my body," with an intention of gratitude rather than desire or complaint. Some would involve real changes in social life. Many ecotheologians have stressed the biblical idea of the Sabbath as a time when, as Abraham Joshua Heschel put it, "man's royal privilege to conquer nature is suspended"[111] and we accept the world for what it is rather than try to change it. And some require only a little common sense. Buddhist environmentalist Stephanie Kaza points out that in traditional Buddhist teachings, the sense organs "catch on fire" when brought into contact with flashy objects of desire.[112] One response to this fact is simply not to expose oneself to those things that are so calculatedly designed to provoke a needless craving. In other words, just stay out of the mall—especially if you frequently find yourself going there to buy a pair of socks and walking out with new shoes, two CDs, a scarf, and a large frappuccino.

❧

Ecotheology faces a global environmental crisis; thus, it is not surprising that its considerable achievements raise many difficult questions, a few of which I will now examine.

First, we have to admit that none of the many ways of describing the value of nature *in general* determines how we should resolve any *particular* conflict between humans and nonhumans. As living beings, we must consume other beings to live. In need of shelter, we displace and destroy, and with the development of culture and science we generate higher populations and greater power. At what point do we start limiting ourselves? When does the sacredness or moral worth we now see in nature lead us to sacrifice something of ourselves to protect it? It seems that when almost all ecotheologians talk about reverence for life or rejecting anthropocentrism, they generally mean that all species, all arrangements or collections of life, have value. Yet, when they apply these ideas of reverence to human beings, it seems that it is each individual, and not the species as a whole, that is the focus. Even if animal rights are defended and veganism proposed, our buildings, transportation, and production dislocate and devastate countless other beings. This is accepted as a matter of course, or, if it is lamented, there still remains a critical difference between our concern with people and our concern with nature. Running over a human child will always provoke more distress than running over ants. Short of the traditional and rather extreme Jain practice of starving to death to avoid consuming any other creature, more respect is shown to people than to animals and plants.[113] Whatever our theological *theory*, we privilege people in *practice*. Environmentalists tell us to privilege humans less; they don't tell us how we can—and certainly they themselves do not—live without privileging humans at all.

Yet, this way of living seems to lead us back to the idea of hierarchy: favoring humans because of our capacity for self-reflection, language, culture, or morality. Will this not return us to the kind of heedlessly brutal anthropocentrism that created the present mess in the first place?

The situation gets more complicated still when we consider conflicts within nature itself. For example, when ecosystem protectors clash with animal rights activists over killing imported feral pigs because the pigs devastate native Hawaiian species, with whom does ecotheology side? When illegal immigrants trying to reach the United States make a long trek through—and damage—ecologically sensitive wilderness areas on the U.S.-Mexico border, for whom do we grieve?[114] And if we feel everyone's pain, from the endangered species to the migrant workers, what do we do first? When we cannot side with both, who gets our support and protection?

Further, it is clear that subjective and not terribly rational feelings and perceptions often enter into day-to-day judgments about the value of different parts of nature. Our love for all of creation may turn out to be considerably more partial than we thought. We commit ourselves to saving the whales—but also to killing the ghetto rats. Like Lisa Sideris or Richard Fern,[115] we offer the general guideline of preserving the wild, but then seem to forget that nothing, after all, is more "wild" than an AIDS virus. Also, as James Nash points out, we have to factor into this discussion a distinction between the value a species may have because of its complexity and self-awareness and its value for an ecosystem as a whole. It's hard to imagine any terrible consequences to other life-forms (at least to nondomesticated life-forms) if humans disappeared. But if the nitrogen-fixing bacteria in the soil or the phytoplankton at the bottom of the ocean's food chain were to die off, the results would be irreversibly catastrophic.[116] From the standpoint of earth community, these simple creatures are much more valuable than we are.

We also need to ask about the human relationship to animals. With rare exceptions by particular faiths or for particular species, the religions of the world have generally taken animals to be legitimate objects for human use: in the past for food, work, and bodily products (fur, leather), more recently for unlimited medical and commercial purposes.[117] It is one thing to be concerned with biodiversity and lament the elimination of jaguars or orcas; it is another to challenge practices as central to modern society as factory-farmed meat or using 100 million animals a year in laboratories. On the one hand, it would seem that "treating nature as kin" would preclude some actions. On the other hand, serious vegetarianism is so far from the norm that advocating it would put religious environmentalism even farther from the mainstream of current social life than it already is. And the idea that we have no right to sacrifice animals to find cures for human diseases would seem to most people heartlessly cruel.

Despite the level of perplexity here, we should not forget that conundrums such as these haunt every moral system. We claim that our moral and legal systems value each person, and then engage in economic, industrial, and military policies that kill, maim, and afflict millions of those "very valuable" people. Conflicting rights—between private property and the public good, free speech and safety, the "right to life" and the "right to choose"—are the very stuff of introductory ethics courses, culture wars, and Supreme Court cases. Difficulties and contradictions do not invalidate ecotheology any more than they do the idea of human rights, though they do mean that environmental ethics may be a lot harder than it looks. At the very least, general principles—about human rights and about the value of and our kinship with nature both—can help establish the expectation that hurting or using other beings is a moral matter that requires reflection, honest self-assessment, and at times public justification.[118] This position has been accepted to some extent for people, but we are a long way from acceptance in terms of the rest of the earth. The new ecotheology is part of the effort to get us there.

Some ethicists will argue that these contradictions should propel us away from concentrating on the rights, or theological status, or ultimate value of nature and toward the question of ecological virtue. It will be more helpful, they argue, to think about human virtues such as temperance, humility, compassion, and self-control. The virtuous will be able to distinguish between need and want, between legitimate human ends and addictive compulsion. Clearly, no truly virtuous person could endorse either the crazy excesses of our global economy or the morally shattering disparity between decadent wealth and crushing poverty. Thus, Jeanne Kay argues that the Torah's key contribution to environmentalism is not the value it places on nature, but the ways its emphasis on love of God, following commandments, refraining from covetousness, and protecting the poor indirectly promotes an ethic of ecological responsibility.[119] Similarly, Louke Van Wensveen provides a whole table of "ecological virtues," showing that often, what will count as good reasons for a moral value will depend on what our sense of a good life is, and therefore that good environmental rules may be an outgrowth of a virtuous community.[120]

Then there is the question of what nature can teach us about how to live morally. If nature includes predation and symbiosis, cooperation and deadly competition, what (if anything) can ecotheology offer by way of an ethic that is particularly appropriate to an ecological age? When ecotheologians write eloquently about the moral lessons of our 14 billion–year universe story and the intricacies of interdependence, what lessons are we actually supposed to derive? One answer is that outside of certain clear truisms—yes, people are part of nature, and yes, if you mess around with your own ecosystem awful things can happen—substantive moral theory will still be left to the human realm. If we are to fashion an environmental ethic, it will have to grow out of what we think about other people and nature considered as in some sense like persons, not out of the behavior of nature in its own right. That is because an environmental ethic, like any ethic whatsoever, is necessarily about guiding our choices. And the rest of nature does not function in terms of choices in the sense of considering alternatives in the light of reasons—

only humans do. The redwood and the beaver may be our kin, but in terms of the actual practice of moral deliberation, the kinship is rather distant. This fact does not make us better, higher, or worthier. It makes us different.

Finally, ecotheology must continually wrestle with the fact that the environmental crisis, taken in its mind-numbing entirety, brings religion itself into question. If nature is evidence of God's power, grace, and love, if the earth is the body of God, what are we to make of strip-mined mountains or rivers choked with industrial waste? We can see nature as a sign of God, but what happens when the sign is torn to pieces or covered with toxic graffiti? Although certain Christian theologians find that the vulnerability of nature makes it resemble the vulnerability of the crucified Christ, it should be remembered that for traditional Christianity the crucified God was only one part of the Trinity, that God the Father was not nailed to the Cross, and that in any case, Jesus rose from the dead. If God can be found on earth, however, the environmental crisis makes God fragile, vulnerable, and potentially killable—with little guarantee of resurrection. If we still wish to retain the comfort of a transcendent and infinitely powerful Deity, we must also retain the idea that in some sense, God is outside of time and space, and not a creature of earth.

For those religions that do not center on the idea of God, or for those people who consider themselves "spiritual but not religious," problems arise concerning the role of nature as a source of solace and awe. In Taoism, for example, the idea of Nature as the model of balance, self-regulation, and virtue becomes questionable when natural relationships or forces have been tampered with—and made unstable or dangerous—by humans. Nondenominational spirituality often makes reference to the soothing, calming, and invigorating powers of nature. These powers become questionable when the sunlight is dangerous because of holes in the ozone layer or huge "dead zones" appear in the Gulf of Mexico because of runoff from industrial farming.

These brief considerations show that, despite all the work that has been done, we are still at the beginning of having adequate answers to many critically important ecotheological questions. John Cobb (who has been doing this work longer than most) observed in 1997, "Adopting nature as the context for doing theology does not settle issues so much as it raises them."[121] This should not surprise us. Thirty years is not a very long time for human beings to come to grips with an immense and historically unprecedented challenge. We have been wrestling with the idea of democracy, itself a profound change in social life, for three centuries, and many questions about its proper form and scope are still up for grabs, in religious institutions as well as society as a whole. If we consider the current storm of debate over gay marriage, we will see that the (roughly) 150-year-old question of gender equality is similarly marked by seemingly irreconcilable differences. Because it concerns an essential shift in our most basic understandings of who we are and how we should live, it should neither surprise nor disappoint us that ecotheology is rife with debates and unsolved questions.

❧

Yet, even as we assess the contributions of ecotheology, we must ask what difference any of this makes. For what a society's leading institutions *teach* about nature may tell us little or nothing about what it is actually *doing* in that regard. If we have read the Bible and know that most people in the United States are Christians, we might expect (mistakenly, in fact) this to be a country where the poor are cared for and wealth is shunned. A similar disconnect can be found in India, where many Hindus are violent, or in Thailand, where many Buddhists think wealth is wonderful. If Nietzsche's sardonic claim that "the last Christian died on the Cross" is something of an overstatement, it is also true that the prophetic and radical moral teachings of religion are too often loudly proclaimed, taught to children—and ignored. The ecotheological challenge to modern society is significant only if people will really put their religious principles into social practice.

This point becomes especially relevant when religious writers, as is often their tendency, stress the importance of ideas—especially mistaken ones!—in explaining the environmental crisis. Many non-Islamic theologians could easily adapt to their own faiths what Abdul Aziz Said and Nathan C. Funk say about Islam: "Failure to protect the natural environment does not represent a shortcoming in *essential Islamic precepts.* . . . Disregard for nature follows both from preoccupation with *imported models of state, economy, and society* and from an incongruity between long-established assumptions about the potential impact of human activities upon nature and the unprecedented *power of modern technology.*"[122] This statement leaves us all wondering why Islam—or Christianity, Buddhism, Judaism, or Confucianism—was unable to resist either these "imported models" or this new "power." If tradition has all the answers we need, why was it so easily sidelined by modernity? If correct ideas didn't work then, what makes us think they will have an impact now? Maybe, because the real causes of social life lie elsewhere, it makes little difference what people think. Perhaps we should instead focus on our systems of ownership and political power.

Although these are all serious considerations, they do not render theology irrelevant. If there has never been a simple correlation between what theologians (or churches) teach and what people do, ecotheology, like any visionary account of a better world, provides a resource that can takes its place among the many sources of how we think and act. It will compete with, and only occasionally win out against, social conventions, economics, personal gain, a virtual blizzard of media images, and pure human weakness. Yet there have been surprising instances when religious voices—against slavery or war, for instance—have made a real difference. If things work well, religious environmentalists will join abolitionists and pacifists as examples of motivated religious believers taking principled and highly significant public stands.

Ultimately, of course, the point is not to understand how valuable nature is, but to change the way we act toward it. Indeed, as we shall see, virtually every theme discussed in this chapter—from recognition of the reality of the environmental crisis to shifts in the religious understanding of nature, from a new sense of ecological personhood to hard-hitting criticisms of some of our society's most cherished institutions—has been echoed by leaders of the world's largest organized religions and is being lived out in political action designed by religious environmentalists to awaken their fellow citizens and shake the foundations of the social order.

Before we turn to the remarkable public presence of religious environmentalism, however, we need to ask whether it is ever a good thing for people of faith to bring that faith to our common political life.

CHAPTER 2

RELIGIOUS ENVIRONMENTALISM AND SECULAR SOCIETY

How is it possible for citizens of faith to be wholehearted members of a democratic society?

—John Rawls, *Political Liberalism*

Union in affection is not inconsistent with disagreement of opinion.

—William Penn

This chapter is aimed primarily at those devout secularists who believe religion should stay out of politics. As well, religious people who are convinced that religion can make the world better may want to see some detailed arguments in support of their position, especially by someone with decidedly progressive politics. They may be tired of the presumption that fundamentalism owns all of religion or that our only choice is between repressive religion and spiritless secularism. If the arguments here are persuasive, they will help people on both sides of the debate see that their options are not limited to those two depressing alternatives and that more fruitful relations between religion and politics are possible. Those who are confident that religion can play a positive role in modern democracy and don't feel they need any more reasons for that belief might go directly to chapter 3!

The opposition between modern democracy and traditional religion began three centuries ago. Seeking an end to centuries of bloody religious conflict, Enlightenment thinkers proclaimed that religion should be free—but private. Common concerns would be regulated by a political democracy in which each person's views counted equally; public policy would be bound by a doctrine of rights that protected each person's autonomy to find personal fulfillment in any way he or she chose, as long as that fulfillment left others with equal freedom to find theirs. Because modern society was religiously diverse, and because science possessed the rationality religion lacked, faith was to be excluded from the public realm. What we all needed to know we could learn from science. What we all needed to have would be produced by a modern industrial society. For the rest, nonrational personal beliefs and choices would be left up to each of us as private citizens. In particular, the government would neither support any particular religion nor allow religious beliefs to determine its policies.

This rather extreme version of the proper role of religion in modern society coexisted (not necessarily consistently!) with a widespread view that religion was for the most part a good thing, that most countries could take for granted a certain amount of religious homogeneity, and that religious institutions and education were, if not essential, at least highly useful in promoting social stability and personal morality. If the government was not to offer extensive direct support to one religion over another, it could take for granted that by and large people accepted the use of religion as an innocuous support for our collective good intentions. We would get the day off on major religious holidays, invoke God's blessing on the legislature, the army, and the local baseball team, and tell ourselves that we were "one nation, under God."

With some notable exceptions (such as the 1925 Scopes trial, in which a high school science teacher was found guilty of teaching evolution), this compromise seemed workable for many years. But in the past decades it has become increasingly strained. Many religious communities have felt attacked, excluded, and marginalized, both by public policies (abortion rights, exclusion of prayer from schools, French schools that forbid wearing traditional Islamic garb) and by an increasingly consumerist, sexualized, and hedonistic public culture. In response, numerous religious groups, often labeled "fundamentalists," have acted politically—and sometimes violently—to elect candidates, shape policy, and challenge the wider culture. In Iran, India, Algeria, and elsewhere, strong religious feelings, mixed in complicated ways with nationalism, patriarchy, and hatred of the West, have dominated governments or appeared as the rallying cry for militant mass movements.

On the secular side, many feel increasingly endangered by the specter of religious involvement in politics. Whereas faith communities typically believe that religion can only improve public life, secularists—and in particular, progressive secularists—see threats to democracy in general and to the gains of recent political movements (feminism, gay liberation, etc.) in particular. The extreme violence of al Qaeda and India's Hindu nationalists is taken as a warning of what the Christian Right in America could become. The progressive response to the idea of political involvement in politics is therefore sometimes negative in the extreme. Hold whatever religious views you wish, these observers often say, but keep them out of our political life, our economy, and our shared culture. This is a secular democracy.

Simultaneously, to make matters even more confusing, America in particular and parts of the developed world in general have witnessed the recent emergence of widespread nondenominational forms of spirituality. Borrowing from Eastern religions, love of nature, mystical elements of Western religions, indigenous traditions, and humanistic psychology, this spirituality is aligned neither with a militant fundamentalism nor with militant secularism.

These considerations are relevant here because religious environmentalism, like any other kind, necessarily attempts to influence such public matters as law, industrial policy, economic institutions, and agriculture. (Although the popular bumper sticker "If you're against abortions, don't have one" misses the point that pro-life forces think abortion is a kind of murder, it at least makes a modicum of sense. "If you're against global warming, stay cool" would make no sense at all. Environmental problems can *only* be solved collectively.) If religions should stay out of politics, then the idea of a specifically religious environmentalism is mistaken from the outset.

Further, religious environmentalism's natural allies in this endeavor are progressive political movements, precisely those that are often the most suspicious of religion's entry into public life. Because religious participation in politics is necessarily oppressive and undemocratic, the argument goes, environmentalists motivated by religious values should keep their motives to themselves, or at least to their churches and mosques. There is, after all, nothing environmentalists need from religion, though people of faith are certainly welcome if they leave their religious identities at home.

Not surprisingly, I reject this position, and believe that religious groups have (at least) as much right to enter the public realm as do trade unions, the National Organization of Women, or the Chamber of Commerce. Moreover, I am confident that secular culture, including politics and science, can learn a great deal from religious traditions and temperament. For all their limitations, religions still have a great deal to offer. There is, in fact, much in common between the secular goals of freedom, democracy, and human rights and religious aspirations toward justice and compassion. Yet, precisely because of the widespread tensions that do exist, this is a confidence that must be argued for, which is what I shall do here. Out of the many serious and wide-ranging concerns that surround the religious role in secular politics, I will try to resolve five central problems.

❧

Problem 1. *Religion, in essence, is undemocratic and oppressive.*

John Rawls, perhaps the most influential political philosopher of the past thirty years, asked, "How is it possible for those affirming a religious doctrine that is based on religious authority, for example, the Church or the Bible, also to hold a reasonable political conception that supports a just democratic regime? . . . How is it possible for citizens of faith to be wholehearted members of a democratic society?"[1] The premise of this question, a premise widely shared among liberal intellectuals and political activists, is that religion is at odds with democracy. Believing that they have "ultimate" support for what they do, people of faith assume that they are entitled to disregard what other people think. They are simply not open to reason or to compromise. In the popular magazine *The Nation* Ellen Willis wrote:

> As many devout believers will admit, there is *an inherent tension between religion and democracy.* The authority of the biblical religions—which are the main subject of this debate—is embedded in sacred texts, religious laws and ecclesiastical hierarchies that claim to transmit absolute truth and serve the will of a Supreme Being. Democracy, in contrast, depends on the Enlightenment values of freedom and equality, which are essential to genuine self-government. In a democracy, truths are provisional and subject to debate—which doesn't mean arbitrary, only arguable. A society grounded in democratic principles can neither restrict people's choices because they don't conform to religious truths nor give them privileged treatment because they do.[2]

The issue of the rationality of religious belief—whether religious values are somehow inherently less reasonable than secular ones—is the focus of the next section. Here my concern is with what Willis and Rawls think is the necessarily undemocratic nature of religion, how it opposes what Willis calls the "Enlightenment values of freedom and equality."

Can religion accept democracy? At least two widespread religious ideas, which seem to conflict with either majority rule or the freedom of the individual, make this a reasonable question. First, religions often claim that legitimate power is derived from God and from those who know what God wants. Our primary obligation is to obey not the will of the group, but that of our Creator and His representatives. Second, because religion gives us Clear Moral Standards rooted in Absolute Truths, individual behavior, for example, in sexual matters, should be bound by religious teachings.

It cannot be denied that a good deal of religious tradition and contemporary forms of fundamentalism make fear of faith reasonable. From the Bible's listing of punishments for those who violate the Sabbath to the Iranian religious police who beat women for disobeying dress codes, there has been and continues to be an element of religiosity that demands social and moral authority and that seeks to impose its own views, at times by any means possible, as widely as it can.

On the other hand, this is not by any means the *whole* story of religion, and that many critics present it as such reveals an unfortunate mixture of prejudice and ignorance. When secular adversaries talk about the disastrous consequences of religion entering public life, they do not mention Martin Luther King Jr., abolitionist ministers in the nineteenth century, avowedly religious antiwar activists, or the literally hundreds of religious organizations, publications, and Web sites that work for human rights. In these cases, religious people are *extending* democracy, not undermining it. Neither do critics of religion tend to make blanket generalizations about how awful secular political figures are when such people are found to be dishonest, self-serving, or repressive. When Richard Nixon resigned over Watergate, they were sure, the problem was that he broke the law and attempted to subvert democracy, not that he was secular. Yet the same may be said for violent and repressive religious figures: their problem is their violence and repressiveness, not their faith. If we applied the same kind of sloppy generalizations to secular political thinkers that secular critics do to religion, we might lump Strom Thurmond with Robert Kennedy, Barry Goldwater with Ralph Nader, and perhaps Stalin with FDR. In their blanket suspicion of *religious* "intolerance" and "repressiveness," secular critics tend to forget the many *secular* ideologies and political movements that have been no less undemocratic. The Chinese Communist Party, Nazism, Chile under Pinochet, and Iraq under Saddam Hussein are among the more flagrant examples. The point is that neither secularism nor religion is the problem. What threatens democracy is the basic idea that a minority has the right to impose its views by force on the rest of society, rather than go through the difficult and chancy process of convincing them with arguments. This view can be found in the religious and the secular alike.

The simple fact is that there is no uniform moral or political character to religious groups, any more than there is to nonreligious political movements. There are those who accept democracy and those who do not; those who choose force when persuasion fails and those who keep trying to get their point across respectfully. When the general secretary of the National Council of Churches, representing 130,000 congregations with 50 million members, says he is committed to "replacing fear, fundamentalism, and Fox News with making peace, ending poverty, and protecting planet earth," or when religious leaders in South Africa, Burma, and Poland play key roles in the struggle for human rights, we can see that in the real world, religion can sometimes be democracy's vibrant ally.[3]

Clearly, this was not always so. It is only through a long historical development that religion (not unlike the rest of society) has learned how to be democratic. Indeed, a new form of faith has evolved which is fully compatible with "democratic pluralism," societies in which people hold an irreducible multiplicity of worldviews and in which the power of government flows from the will of the people.

A number of historical developments sparked this change. In Europe, the Reformation created a welter of violently competing forms of Christianity, and it was in response to this seemingly endless violence that both the liberal political ideal of separating church and state and the liberal religious ideal of toleration of different theologies was born. Also, natural science's clear progress, compared to the intractable debates about matters of faith, made it doubtful that religious beliefs were rational. If consensus was impossible, perhaps all faiths were equally rational—or irrational. The social necessity of toleration and a new view of religious beliefs were also supported by the extensive contact among different faiths prompted by colonialism and globalization. As Catholics and Protestants encountered Hindus, Buddhists, and Taoists, many came to see that religious life could not be centered on finding the "right" set of views and dismissing everyone else as mistaken. Something else had to be more important.

Out of this interesting and complicated history two aspects of this new form of faith are key. First, there was a shift in what was taken to be the central aspect of a religion, a shift, we might say, from metaphysical theology to ethics. For instance, the influential seventeenth-century Protestant theologian Hugo Grotius argued that the essence of Christianity was the goal of a harmonious society, and that *theological* differences between different types of Christians—that is, different conceptions of God, the Trinity, the afterlife, or the role of the church—were trivial compared to what they shared *ethically*. Grotius's goal was "to give Christianity a new centre of gravity, replacing dogma and creed with a morality oriented to social peace . . . to fit the needs of deeply divided societies."[4] William Penn, the early and notable Quaker, put it simply: "As a variety of flowers may grow on the same bank, so may Protestants and Papists live in England. Union in affection is not inconsistent with disagreement of opinion."[5] In other words, kindness and mutual respect are more important than strict agreement on what we think about Heaven or the resurrection. It should be noted that although this attitude originated as a way to cool hostilities among Christians, it can at least in principle be extended to any religion—and even to any nonreligion—whatsoever. Taking the goal of social peace and mutual respect as central, many in the contemporary religious scene reach out to members of different faiths and to like-minded secular organizations, joining hands to support each other in areas of social justice, simple human concern, and the celebration of life.

Along with a stress on morality over theology, there is the progressive development of what might be called a "subjective" attitude toward faith. In this attitude, as evidenced, for instance, in the work of nineteenth-century Danish Protestant philosopher Søren Kierkegaard, beliefs *about* God are much less important than the degree to which a person commits himself or herself to a passionate relationship *with* God. It is not what we literally believe, but how much energy we put into that belief. Sincerity, authenticity, and integrity replace theological correctness. Or, as Kierkegaard put it, a passionate pagan is more "Christian" than a self-satisfied Lutheran.[6] When theology takes this turn, the goal is no longer to meet demands promulgated by an unquestioned authority, but for individuals to find their own way to God, and to know that they have done so through their own inner knowledge. This stress on personal passion continues the Reformation's rejection of the institutional authority of the Catholic Church, which it challenged by claiming that people could relate to God without the help of an institutional intermediary.[7] This viewpoint sets the stage for people to move from "dwelling" in a set religion to "seeking" spiritual growth.[8] In this process, there is little room to worry if someone else has it "right," for the emphasis is on finding one's own authentic path, not judging the correctness of others.

Many more historical details could be offered here: John Locke's *Letter on Toleration*, which argued that religious belief, by its very nature, could not be compelled; late nineteenth-century Reform Judaism, which replaced emphasis on the theological/metaphysical system of the Talmud in favor of the ethical teachings of the prophets; or the historic Vatican II conference of 1963–1964, which committed the Catholic Church to an open dialogue with and an acceptance of the rights, if not the truth, of other religious communities. In the contemporary world, these attitudes virtually define a widely shared attitude toward faith. Buddhist Thich Nhat Hanh claims it is *religiously* wrong ever to try to impose one's views on another. Gandhi read from the scriptures of several religions before his mass meetings, and Martin Luther King found no conflict between the highest ideals of democracy and religious truth. Catholic priests Daniel Berrigan and Thomas Merton repeatedly voiced their appreciation for the wisdom and goodness of practitioners of other faiths. Glenn Tinder has forcefully argued that Christianity is by its very nature a "dialogical" religion, and that Christians must be willing to talk to and learn from a variety of interpretations of religion, as well as no religion at all, if they are to be faithful to essential features of their own religion.[9] This list could be extended virtually indefinitely, which is why respectful dialogue among different religions and between religious and secular ethicists is everyday stuff.

This respect comes not only from changes in theology, but from an awareness of the mixed, and at times shameful, history of religion itself. As Evangelical Protestant Jim Wallis writes, "History and experience tell us that religious vision can turn into sectarian divisiveness, justifying some of our worst human behavior." Stressing that Christians have often *not* done so, Wallis quotes theologian Walter Brueggemann, who asserts that in the realm of politics, the contemporary Christian voice must speak "in a way that touches the shared human requirements of love, mercy, justice, peace, and freedom."[10] Even for those believers who still cling to the absolute truth of their faith, there may be a sense that the actual content of what they hold impels them toward compassion and respect for those who believe differently. As George Corey puts it, "What we have to recognize is that because God is the kind of God He is, our integrity as believers in Him *compels us to behave in such a way that tolerance, and not intolerance*, is our instinctive reaction; and that honest engagement with each other as valued by God becomes the context in which our differences are faced—and faced strenuously."[11] Paul Weithman argues that the critical reflection necessary for Christians to have a committed relationship with God is possible only in a society in which human rights are taken seriously.[12] In short, there exists in Christianity, and in comparable versions of other religions, what might be called "liberal" religion, whose attitudes toward faith, morality, and social life make it a fitting member of democratic societies.

Of course, some will say that all this is a perversion of the "real" faith, or that liberal religion is so accepting of difference, so supportive of every "politically correct" fad or interest group, that no real principles are left. It is simply a mish-mash that owes far more to liberal social attitudes and psychotherapy than to God and scripture.

This is a central area of disagreement in contemporary religion, occasioning passionate disputes between Orthodox and Reform Jews, fundamentalist evangelical Christians and liberal Protestants, Hindu nationalists and Hindu universalists. Those who criticize the liberal side often say that innovators have no right to change the old, tested, revealed truths. The liberals reply that what is now called "fundamentalism" was in its time just as much an innovation. Therefore, those who downplay metaphysics and stress ethics, view descriptions of God as metaphors rather than plain "facts," and commit themselves to religious ecology have the same right to innovate. Another way to put this point is to say, with certain modern Christian theologians, that there is always a difference between the essence of Christianity and the form it takes in a particular culture. "Christ" is an ideal, sought for but never completely realized. "Christianity" is the particular way that seeking is institutionalized at any given time. Christians must always refrain from the arrogant assumption that the particular form they have found is the final, perfect version.[13] A comparable perspective can be applied to any religion whatsoever.

This still leaves open whether or not liberal religion is a *good* or *holy* version of the faith. In response to this question, all the innovating liberal can do is describe how she understands the tradition, tell a story of how she got to where she is, and explain as fully as possible what religion in particular and society as a whole would be like if her views were accepted. In the absence of some cosmic revelation that we all recognize, or of some ethical code that can be proved valid to everyone, this is all that can be done for any religion—or any secular viewpoint, for that matter.[14]

This point is particularly important because, contrary to frequent charges against it, liberal religion need be no more unprincipled or sloppy than fundamentalism. Accepting an innovation such as gay marriage, for instance, does not mean that one accepts anything. It means choosing one interpretation of love and marriage over another and seeing scriptural commands to "love thy neighbor" as having more force than strictures against homosexuality. Far from "accepting anything," homophobia is now seen as a sin, or at least as a failure of imagination and spiritual development. Having female ministers, priests, and rabbis is part of a commitment to gender equality, which means a rejection of taken-for-granted male power. A commitment to environmentalism requires (at least) serious questioning of everything from individual consumerism to having CEOs of polluting industries as congregational officers.

In terms of the particular question of democracy, countless public statements by religious leaders criticize totalitarianism of any kind and use a language of human rights to endorse a legal system in which freedom of religion, speech, the press, and so forth are practiced. The strongest adherents of liberal religion's role in public life—from the civil rights movement of fifty years ago to contemporary religious environmentalists—accept the basic principles of the separation of church and state, that is, the simple idea that distinctly political processes such as voting and judicial appointment are the source of legitimate political power and that having achieved some kind of religious authority (such as being ordained) should no more propel one to political power than getting tenure as a professor or graduating from medical school.

As in the instances already mentioned—ending slavery, promoting racial equality, resisting dictatorships, supporting the rights of the poor—there have been many times when a liberal religious voice has been a source of *more and better* democracy, entering modern social life as a powerful and positive force. This simple but profoundly important fact, often obscured by the headlines about fatwas, fundamentalist attacks on feminism or gay rights, and religious leaders eager to support this or that war, should not be forgotten. If these positive contributions represent only a fraction of the religious community, the same may be said of the secular community as well, only a small part of which has engaged in activist support for social justice or human rights.

❧

Problem 2. *Religious beliefs are irrational or at best nonrational, and thus have no place in the organization of society.*

Secular society was shaped by the historical experience of the contrast between interminable religious disputes resolvable only by force or schism and orderly scientific progress. The very absence of shared ways to resolve conflicts within the religious community suggested that this entire dimension of human life lacked a rational basis. In response, many saw science as the source of objective truth and sought to exile religion to the realm of private life. Because, secularists claim, religious believers argue from premises (the existence of God, the truth of a particular scripture) that many others do not share and that have no rational justification in any case, expressions of their faith have no place in public life. It is neither fair nor respectful for a person to argue in support of governmental policies and potentially coercive laws on the basis of a faith that many fellow citizens do not share. One should only offer reasons that can be justified on the basis of shared premises. A citizen, argues philosopher Robert Audi, is obliged "not to advocate or support any law or public policy that restricts human conduct, unless [he or she] has, and is willing to offer, adequate secular reasons for this advocacy or support."[15]

In other words, when a religious person argues for his political viewpoint, he must do so as if he is not religious, for his argument will make no sense— and thus seem irrationally coercive—to someone who is not religious. And, because religion is *inherently* irrational—not the kind of thing for which reasons can be offered unless people have preexisting faith in its premises— there is no way the believer could *ever* convince the unbeliever that his (re- ligious) reasons do make sense. In a pluralistic society filled with people of different faiths and no faith at all, it is never appropriate to argue about public matters by appealing to "what Jesus would do," "what the Qur'an teaches," or "how we have been instructed by the Guru." If this lesson is applied to religious environmentalism, the implication is that it would make no sense to argue against a strip mine or oil drilling in the Arctic National Wildlife Refuge because these ravage God's Creation or violate religious moral norms about not wasting. Only common, shared, secular arguments will do—preferably, in the environmental context, ones generated by science.

Although I believe this position is fundamentally misconceived, I also think it possesses a large grain of truth. In a diverse society, a simple appeal to religious authority makes little sense. "Pass Law X [make abortion illegal, close liquor stores on Sunday] because Religious Authority Y [the pope, the Bible, the Vedas] says so" is a pretty weak argument to those who don't believe in the authority of the pope, the Bible, or the Vedas. Such statements may rally one's own troops and make them a more potent political force, but they will have little effect on, and be inappropriate to the point of seeming bizarre to, people outside the fold.

Yet religious arguments about political matters are rarely so primitive or simple-minded. They may ultimately rest on a particularly religious basis (more on that in a moment), but they often involve intertwined elements of scientific fact, practical considerations, and ethical values that may well be shared by religious and nonreligious alike. When Pope John Paul II argued against abortion rights, for example, he did not say simply "God forbids this," but offered a comprehensive account of the value of life, respect for "the human person," and the dire effects of this policy on women in particular and society as a whole. He warned that killing a fetus would translate into greater disrespect for life everywhere else.[16] The religious ideal he appealed to—universal respect for all people—is easily translatable into secular terms, and if his concerns about the consequences of abortion were well founded, many of them could resonate with the most devout atheist no less than the most devout Catholic.[17] Therefore, although many (including myself) disagree with his assessment of the meaning of abortion rights and will appeal to the rights of women and the effects of patriarchy as counterarguments, the pope's position was something with which secular voices can engage. It may be mistaken, but it is hardly hopeless nonsense.

Comparable examples of religious positions on political matters—from issues of war and peace to capital punishment—easily come to mind. For environmentalism, we might think of how conceiving of the world as "creation" can have powerful benefits in terms of how we orient ourselves to nature, whether or not we have faith in a literal Creator. With or without God, it may well be that looking at nature as a miraculous gift deserving of reverence is a good thing. In one sense, it clearly is a gift: a wondrous totality we neither made for ourselves nor "deserve." Similarly, because murder is as offensive to secular ethicists as to religious ones, the carefully researched claim that pollution is a kind of long-distance, slow-motion murder should be quite interesting to just about anyone, *even* if the person making the argument about the effects of pesticides is against murder because it is forbidden by the Ten Commandments. When we look at the policy statements of organized religion in chapter 3 and the goals of religious activists in chapter 4, we will see articulated positions that can appear quite reasonable to just about anyone.

Moreover, because we do not know how people will respond to these arguments, it makes no sense to try to rule out religion at the start. Until we have the conversation, we don't know what other people will find convincing! When Thomas Berry offers his spiritual reading of scientific cosmology, or Holmes Rolston finds evolution to be cruciform, or Thich Nhat Hanh invites us to see our interconnections with all beings, who knows in which listener a responsive chord may be struck? There was something compelling about Martin Luther King's combination of religious and secular language—of his prophetic calls for justice and appeals to constitutional rights. When the strength of his personality and the bravery of the movement he led combined with the full range of his ideas, he impressed and changed, rather than alienated, many nonreligious people. Ultimately, as Mary Segers argues, people like King (and Jesse Jackson, Mario Cuomo, and dozens of other public figures) combine religious rhetoric with forceful appeals to the public good.[18] As a matter of both strategy *and* common courtesy, religious people address the larger political community as broadly as possible, appealing to as many shared values as can be found.[19] In the end, it makes little difference if it is the prophet Amos or the ACLU who calls for justice: we can all respond.[20]

Yet, it may be replied, when Christians talk about how abortion may make women depressed or about how strip mining hurts the environment, they are using *secular* arguments. That's fine! Let them base their arguments on mental health and the effects of pollution—and leave out the Ten Commandments. It is when they invoke God or a "Holy Book" to support their position that the trouble starts. Their foundations, their appeals to God or Religious Truth, are not rational, and therefore should be omitted in public discussion.

In short, there are "rational" and "nonrational" ways to argue about public policy. Secular approaches are the first, and specifically religious ones the second. Religious environmentalists' *religious* reasons should be of no more public relevance than anyone else's private motivations for their politics.[21]

This position, which would sideline religious environmentalists from public life, presumes that there is only one rational way to argue about public issues, some manner of thought that is simply "right" for a democratic society. One well-known version of this position is Rawls's idea that democracy is based only on the general idea that all citizens are free and equal. Without the shared foundation of freedom and equality, democracy is impossible; with it, democracy can work. What religion might add to this is unnecessary and cannot be justified to people outside of the religious group in question.

The problem with this position is that it is either too weak to settle serious policy issues or so strong that religion, in a broad sense, is brought back in to social life. In the cases of abortion rights, animal rights, and capital punishment, to take three pertinent examples, simply appealing to freedom and equality will not do. Are fetuses, animals, and murderers part of the "we" who are free and equal? How do we deal with conflicting freedoms between the "right to choose" and the "right to life"? How do freedom and equality determine choices between punishment and rehabilitation or human welfare and that of nonhumans? No simple appeal to freedom and equality will answer these questions, yet answers must be found. And to do so, we will necessarily refer to or presume some comprehensive perspective on issues of life, human identity, and morality. We will turn to substantial religious or philosophical views to support our sense of what a person is, what our obligations to mother and fetus are, the moral status of animals, and what criminal and victim deserve. Without comprehensive ideas about morality, identity, goodness, and happiness, we cannot address these issues. Yet, it is precisely these comprehensive ideas that are addressed by religion, as well as by a wide variety of secular philosophical views. To say that the latter are rational and the former not is, quite simply, the sheerest prejudice.[22]

For a more detailed example in the context of environmentalism, consider the question of whether or not to develop a particular piece of wetland, home to an endangered species of butterfly, by building a large mall in an area with high unemployment. Does the promise of more jobs trump the loss of the wetland's ecological function (water purification, flood control, home to animals and plants)? Is it somehow more rational to say that more jobs are an absolute good but that protecting a particular ecosystem is mere sentiment? Is it irrational to say that endangered species, even if they have no obvious use for us, have a value of their own (as a creation of God, as a fellow being in the web of life)—but that it is simple common sense ("rational") to treat everything on earth as up for grabs? Is endless economic growth (higher incomes, more shopping) a "rational" goal, whereas that of tending and keeping the earth or having compassion on all beings is irrational?

The truth is that all these alternatives rest on comprehensive[23] views about matters such as the meaning of existence, the purpose of human life, and the proper standards of moral conduct, views that must come into play if we are to have any public policies whatsoever. Yet, though we can offer reasons in support of our comprehensive views, there is no definitively rational way to choose among conflicting versions of them. The notion that the world is a gift to be cherished is no more—or less—rational than the idea that it can be used any way we want. The idea that we exist to learn how to love all of life is as rational—or not—as the idea that we are essentially self-interested individuals and that he who dies with the most toys wins. The goal of preserving as many species as we can because they are our kin and companions is no less justifiable than the notion that we should care only about the ones we think are useful or pretty.

There is no inherently "rational" view of a flower, a river, or a mountain, or of deciding for more or less consumption, luxury, technological development, or world trade. In this sense, religion is neither more nor less rational than secularism. Each of these views, and countless variants besides, is equally compatible with "the facts." Offering a vision with as many details as possible is the best way to argue for our respective comprehensive views, not abstract appeals to some supposedly universal standard of reason. We can describe the environmental crisis and say how these different views contribute to or could help solve it. We can say what a world would be like in which the views we support held sway. In particular, I believe that an appeal to reverence for life as God's creation, a sense of awe and mystery that permeate nature, and cultivating a sense of kinship with other species is a profound contribution to society, one that makes it *more* rational—in the sense of more humanly fulfilling and less needlessly destructive. It is a distinct gift that religious environmentalists can offer to secular environmentalism and earth community as a whole. And just like those who hold the comprehensive views that direct the World Bank, Exxon, or Britain's Labour Party, I can offer serious reasons in defense of this view.

In so doing, I will be engaging in the best of what democracy can be. This is so because democracy is not simply about the exercise of personal choice in a society organized to further that choice through legal protections for personal rights. Freedom does not exclude, but rather presupposes certain shared views that are broader than individual rights. Because we do things together—educate our children, make war or peace, save or destroy the environment, build roads or bike paths—we will necessarily appeal to broad values that will guide us in these shared activities. The historical basis of American democracy as understood by its leading philosophers, jurists, and legislatures in the eighteenth and nineteenth centuries always incorporated the vision of a shared morality and the hope of collective virtue.[24]

Democracy, then, goes beyond individual rights and the separation of church and state to include a distinct way to discuss differences among our comprehensive views. It arose as a form of common association when appeals to the absolute authority of religious texts and inherited political power were no longer convincing. In the face of religious and social pluralism, in the absence of accepted authority, how was a political community to hold itself together? The key, argues Jeffrey Stout, is that a democratic community constitutes itself by a fundamental respect for the views of other people, and to the process of talking with them when views conflict.[25] Instead of imposing our will, we offer reasons for what we do—and hold others accountable by demanding reasons from them. In a broad range of social matters—foreign policy, education, economic policy, for example—it will be the results of such conversations (codified as voting) that determine the broad outlines of social policy.

To make the system work, we must cultivate certain distinct skills: form judgments and express them, listen to other people, and recognize the good of the community. We must be able to distinguish among several claims that a speaker is making so that we can separate the 10 percent we accept from the 90 percent we think mistaken. Speech in America, and throughout other democracies as well, clearly suffers from a paucity of these skills nowadays. If this is partly the fault of religion, it is partly the fault of many secularists as well. One need only listen to many conservative or liberal talk-show hosts to see what I mean. The problem, as with violence, is thus not with religion per se, but with those religious voices who do not understand or accept democracy, and with many secular voices who share the same failing. People of faith can be narrow-minded or open to learning; so can secular libertarians, Marxists, and Republicans. Evangelical Christians can be absolutely sure they have nothing to learn; so can feminists.

Finally, and perhaps most surprisingly, it has been pointed out that religion can actually help people participate in public life. Mary Segers, for instance, describes how the social context of religion provides a kind of training for democracy. It encourages people to take their social involvements seriously, to feel a moral responsibility to the community, and to express that responsibility through networking, organizing meetings, and delivering their message to the government.[26] Similarly, Allen Hertzke claims that religious lobbies support democracy by encouraging participation from people who are otherwise left out.[27]

If religions can sometimes act as if only their own flock matters, they also are a repository of values that stress a universality of moral concern. There is the Buddhist injunction to free all beings from suffering and the biblical demand that we care for the "widow, the stranger, and the orphan." Surely the idea that we are all made in the image of God bears no small affinity to that of "one person, one vote." In a society dominated by entrenched governmental bureaucracies, corporate strategies for growth, partisan political parties, and self-interested interest groups, the introduction of a little religious perspective on public policy might go a long way. And the direction it would travel would be toward the good of the public as a whole, not just that of Buddhists or Christians.

But, some will say, why do we need religion at all? Even if it has witnessed something of a resurgence in recent years, religion really is nothing but a projection of human needs, powers, and fears onto an imaginary realm. To be fully human, we must give up this fantasy of the supernatural.[28]

Ultimately, there may be no way to bring religious believers and militant atheists together. The former cannot conceive of a universe without a higher power, the latter can't believe the universe has one!

One response to this dilemma is to talk—or argue—about things other than the existence of God. We can discuss the value of Christian ethics without accepting that Jesus was the Messiah or Islamic strictures on the accumulation of wealth without believing that "there is no God but Allah." Religions are rich, complicated, and multifaceted cultural creations, only parts of which, and not necessarily the most practically important parts, have to do with God.

Also, we might see that in a sense, the difference between believers and unbelievers is not like that between those who do and those who do not believe in Santa Claus. It is, rather, more like the difference between those who find a painting beautiful and those to whom it is just a big blob of paint. Differences of artistic response are differences in taste, in temperament, and in the kind of attention one brings to a work of art. The same may be true for the realm of the spiritual. There is a sense in which theists and atheists do not always differ in "the facts" they are acknowledging, but in how those facts hold together, in what they mean. For religious people, the world—the same world the nonreligious confront—just means God. For the nonreligious, it simply does not.[29]

ᴥ

Problem 3. *Religious values are, at best, peripheral to environmentalism, which should be shaped by science, not faith.*

The relationship between religious environmentalism and science is both fascinating and complex. On the one hand, the new ecotheology is filled with references to cosmological accounts of the history of the universe, details of ecological interdependence, the latest research about global warming, and reports of cancer clusters near nuclear power plants. Never in religious history has a religious movement been so intimately connected with and dependent on science. Also, no environmentalist of any kind can envisage solutions to the environmental crisis without the participation of ecologically minded technology. We cannot simply abandon our current forms of energy production, transportation, medicine, or communication. Rather, we will have to transform them to more environmentally and humanly benign forms. Such sustainable technologies may be inspired by the moral demands of the new ecotheology, but they will be designed by engineers, architects, organic farmers, and city planners.

At the same time, religious environmentalists are extremely critical of a number of views that, if not actually part of science, typically accompany the view that science is the only authentic form of knowledge; or that nature is "really" what natural science says about it. Seeing nature solely as an object of study, to be manipulated in laboratory experiments and summed up in mathematical laws, religious environmentalists have argued, is an element of the environmental crisis itself. If all our knowledge is only oriented to control, historian Carolyn Merchant wrote, we end up with "the death of nature."[30] In place of a unique, organically connected totality, we will have bits and pieces, each one of which is reducible to its smallest parts, none of which really matters. We move from organisms to cells, from cells to molecules, from molecules to subatomic particles—and the irreplaceable character of living animals, interrelated ecosystems, and a planetary ecological balance is lost.

This reductionist view of the natural world has, ironically, been challenged by a number of scientific theories in the late twentieth century, but it had unquestioned supremacy for a very long time, and still exists in some forms today. The result is a perspective that is blind to the essential complexities of ecosystems and the way life unfolds through webs of mutual interaction. If things can be known only by reducing them to their most basic elements, then life as it has evolved and exists now cannot be known at all. And if it cannot be known, it cannot be loved or protected, only controlled, used, bought, and sold.

It is not only these general, quasi-philosophical ideas about science of which religious environmentalists are critical; it is also the actual practice of science in contemporary society. For science, despite its pretensions to being a product of pure rationality, is in fact deeply shaped by the particular societies in which it functions.[31] The choice of problems to be solved, areas of research, and acceptable forms of technology developed all greatly depend on who pays for the science and technology in question. If science is to be the ultimate authority on ecological questions, we still need to ask: Whose science?

To explain this point, consider the painful example of breast cancer. This virtual epidemic is understood and researched in ways that are particularly fitting for certain groups but not necessarily those who suffer from it. Most often, it is treated as a personal tragedy, a lifestyle problem (smoking, bad diet), or a genetic problem: as a disease needing a cure. This view predominates *despite* a great deal of research suggesting the powerful environmental role in cancer in general and breast cancer in particular.[32] Why, then, is there so much more emphasis on cure than cause? On medicine for those with cancer rather than stopping the environmental causes before any medicine is needed? One reason is that thinking of breast cancer as millions of individual "cases" rather than as a public health issue is beneficial for a powerful cancer establishment of foundations, treatment hospitals, and research centers. As physician Janet Sherman points out, "There is a massing, in a few hands, of the control of production, distribution and use of pharmaceutical drugs and appliances; control of the sale and use of medical and laboratory tests; the consolidation and control of hospitals, nursing homes, and home care providers. We are no longer people who become sick. We have become markets. Is it any wonder that prevention receives so little attention? Cancer is a big and successful business!"[33]

The orientation of breast cancer research toward cures rather than causes is a particular instance of a general truth: in modern society, scientific research is virtually always integrated into corporate and governmental institutions. These shape the form of the research and thus foreclose certain kinds of solutions to critical problems. One commentator argues, "To a large degree, universities have been taken over by money managers and academic entrepreneurs who are looking for financially lucrative research. . . . Research that reveals degradation of our natural resources, . . . exposes charlatan claims of companies, or . . . investigates the environmental causes of disease usually offer[s] no financial benefits to the university."[34] Similarly, when we consider that the directors of major cancer institutions are often managers of polluting industries, we should not be surprised that roughly 98 percent of cancer research is oriented to cure rather than prevention. For a time, one of the medical directors of prestigious Sloan-Kettering, perhaps the most respected cancer treatment and research center in the country, was Leo Wade. Wade had been the medical director for Standard Oil of New Jersey, a member of the Manufacturing Chemists Association, the American Petroleum Institute (a lobbying group for oil companies), and the National Association of Manufacturers. Is it any wonder that Wade ridiculed efforts to control chemicals in the environment as "both futile and suspect"? In the same vein, many of the carcinogens ignored by the American Cancer Society are "by-products of profitable industries in which its directors have financial interests."[35] When Occidental Petroleum CEO Armand Hammer chaired the National Cancer Advisory Panel, a group with direct access to the president, his appeal for $1 billion in funds contained precisely zero percent for study of the carcinogenic effects of the oil industry.[36]

This common problem, which is reproduced throughout society in everything from energy policy (big power plants and more oil drilling instead of renewable energy and conservation) to transportation (private cars over buses and subways), shows why science should not be the sole voice of environmentalism. To reveal the dimensions of the problem and conceive of solutions, of course, science *is* absolutely essential, but science *itself* must be critically examined for its own limitations and downright biases. Given the possible distortions of science and the way scientists have contributed to environmental problems, the centerpiece of environmentalism should be public forums in which issues of safety, efficiency, progress, health, nature, and humanity can be discussed and debated. This would promote a democratic public culture in which human needs, respect for nature, and public safety are considered and evaluated.[37]

Scientists are essential to this process, of course, but they are not its sole authority. Because everyone has a physical body that is affected by pollution, and virtually everyone has some stake in the natural world, all of us need to be part of the deliberative process. In countless cases—from the effects of CFCs on the ozone layer to consequences of overuse of antibiotics—"scientific" knowledge and modern technology proved dead wrong, irresponsible, or downright destructive. Further, we have seen many instances when laypeople warned that technologically sophisticated processes would be disastrous both for their surrounding nature and themselves. They protested against the "expertise" of the scientific experts, were ignored—and in the end were proven right. Large-scale dam development in Thailand, designed, no doubt, by highly trained engineers, failed completely and had to be replaced by traditional water management methods. Large-scale fishing in Newfoundland—enormous and enormously sophisticated trawlers that strip-mined the sea day and night, 365 days a year—wiped out a fishing industry that had been sustainable for generations.[38] In both cases, the local people had said quite clearly that things were going wrong.

Of course, because local, scientifically unsophisticated people are often right about ecological balance in their own community does not prove that being "native," any more than being scientifically trained, is a guarantee of being right. As philosopher Meera Nanda shows, in the case of modern India, "traditional knowledge" often includes religiously legitimated superstitions that support local forms of injustice.[39] Natives may know not to overfish; they may also "know" that women will pollute the sea if they do the fishing, or that inoculations against disease are harmful. Some environmentalists, particularly ones who wish to side with peasants or native peoples against multinational corporations and corporate science, have at times overstated the value of "local knowledges," claiming that their beliefs, no matter how wrong to us, have absolute validity in their own context. Because of the tendency of local knowledge to sometimes support local forms of injustice, this is a profound mistake. Just as modern science can be an apparatus of corporate or military power, so "what the natives know" can support the local priests or the local men.

This long excursion into science may seem to have taken us far afield. It has been necessary, I think because science, like democracy, is often used as the concept that opposes, and should be used to curb or restrict, religion. Yet, just as we cannot exclude religion from the democratic conversation at the outset, so we cannot replace that conversation with scientific expertise.[40]

In both cases, the messy, difficult, contentious process of collective decision making, in which all can be given a respectful hearing, is essential.

∾

Problem 4. *Involvement in politics is bad for religion.*

There are some contemporary theologians who believe that the attempt to shape public policy is a distraction for religion. Neither politically conservative fundamentalists nor liberal religious activists, they believe that the duty of the faithful is to construct their own internally purified community, and to thereby "testify" to the value of their faith. The task of religion, they tell us, is religion, not politics: to focus on ultimate goals and absolute moral imperatives, not to seek positions in government, engage in horse-trading to satisfy group interests, or jump on the bandwagon of social reform.[41]

Perhaps the most forceful exponent of this view is Stanley Hauerwas, whose position is all the more interesting because he rejects both the theological liberalism of the left and the often conservative political orientation of the right. He believes that Christianity is the only true religion, but that because its focus is on love, it cannot express that truth in an oppressive way. He also believes that Christian morality forbids participation in war, and, in a forceful essay written in response to September 11, 2001, rejects a military response. When asked what, as a Christian, he would do about 9/11, his answer was precise: as a Christian, it is not his job to construct a foreign policy, but to demonstrate through his life in community that Christian values are the message of God.[42]

Hauerwas's position, which can be extended without much difficulty to any other religion, is important: if Christians do not shape a foreign policy, they do not need to shape an environmental one either. If creating the Kingdom on earth (or achieving Buddhist Nirvana, following the Jewish Mitzvot, etc.) requires that one give exclusive attention to religious rather than social and political matters, then religious environmentalism is a distraction from religion. Rather than rejecting religious environmentalism because it will harm political life, it should be rejected because it will harm spiritual life.

Though I have (not surprisingly) sharp disagreements with this position, I also believe it contains an important message. If religions enter the public sphere simply to achieve political power and cheerfully utilize dishonest, instrumental, or purely utilitarian tactics to get it, something of vital importance will be lost. Religious values must guide not only the goal, but the means as well. Politically oriented Christian fundamentalism that supports its agenda with vitriol for its opponents has forgotten basic Christian scripture. Loving your neighbor—not to mention loving your enemies—is, after all, supposed to be at least as essential to Christianity as prayer in schools,

curbing pornography in the media, or making abortion illegal. On the progressive side of the aisle, it will not do to pursue global ecological compassion
in a mean-spirited way, even though the stakes are very, very high. Exactly
how these values will be reflected in environmental activism may be difficult
to work out in practice, but at least the overriding principles are clear.

The danger that political activism will strip religion of its principles can
be averted. That is why Martin Luther King and Gandhi are so universally
respected—not simply for their personal courage and devotion or the success
of their movements, but because their participation in the hard-nosed realm
of politics was guided by values derived from religious traditions: nonviolence, the willingness to take pain onto oneself to change the moral and legal
climate, and an attitude of respect for one's opponents. The meaning of what
they were doing was clearly explained to the general public; their own relations with their comrades were generally honest and respectful; and they did
not seek power or wealth for themselves.

Further, it is not only *possible* for religious values to be brought into political life, it is also religiously *necessary*. Moral teachings are essential to every
religion, and in the modern world, we simply cannot fulfill those moral teachings without political involvement. If we are to be moral, we must also be
political. As Reinhold Niebuhr put it seventy years ago:

> The tendencies of an industrial era ... tend to aggravate the injustices from
> which men have perennially suffered; and they tend to unite the whole of hu-
> manity in a system of economic interdependence. They make us more con-
> scious of the relations of human communities to each other.... [As a result,]
> we can no longer buy the highest satisfactions of the individual life at the
> expense of social injustice. *We cannot build our individual ladders to heaven
> and leave the total human enterprise unredeemed of its excesses and corrup-
> tions.*[43]

Consider, as a simple example, one of the essential Ten Commandments,
a cornerstone of Jewish and Christian ethics alike: "Thou shalt not kill" (or,
depending on the translation, "murder"; Exod. 20:13). The simple fact is that
given the environmental consequences of modern life, following this com-
mandment is not so easy. Technology confers an ethical complexity on the
most mundane of routine daily activities. It is like a magical connecting rod,
creating moral bonds where none existed before. Simply using my car to go
the supermarket can increase global warming, threatening the lives of entire
nations subject to increased flooding or violent weather. Yet simply not driving leaves the entire system intact. Traditional religions or more contemporary forms of individualistic spirituality tend to concentrate on situations
where people have pretty much total control over the moral character of
their actions. We are told, as individuals, not to steal, lie, or kill. Now, however, a host of everyday actions—from paying taxes to using air condition-

ers—have consequences that are not chosen by us personally and cannot be changed by anything we do by ourselves. Hannah Arendt coined the chilling phrase "the banality of evil" to refer to the "ordinary" person who fulfills bureaucratic tasks that contribute to genocide.[44] In less dramatic ways, all of us who pursue "normal" lives in advanced industrial society contribute to various kinds of ecological ruin.

It is obvious that the large social structures that connect *our* electricity use—and the acid rain caused by the emissions from our power plants—to the death of someone *else's* forests are only occasionally, or to a limited extent, a matter of anyone's conscious ill will. We certainly bear no malice to the forests, or to those who depend on them for firewood, fodder, and herbs. The Mega-Mega Power Company doesn't want to hurt the forests: they simply want to make a profit and are burning oil or coal to do so, and perhaps making a few judicious campaign contributions to lessen government regulations on emissions. In the context of the environmental crisis, then, instead of immediate forms of violence, calculated attempts to hurt or rob, we find that Thomas Merton's words of four decades ago still ring true: "Violence today is white collar violence, systematically organized bureaucratic and technological destruction . . . abstract, corporate, businesslike, cool, free of guilt-feelings and therefore a thousand times more deadly than the eruption of violence out of individual hate."[45] In the case of acid rain, we find a national energy policy, campaign contributions made in the hope of getting a break on environmental regulations, personal dependence on too much power use, psychological addiction to power-draining gadgets, and the threat of economic slumps if we don't have constant, high-energy economic "growth."

Just like the powers of physical machines, the large bureaucratic machines we call governments also extend the moral reach of our actions. As global systems of production and consumption enmesh us in global moral relations, so do the connections forged by taxation and national allegiance. This is especially true for a nation such as the United States, which is both a democracy and a world power. As a democracy, it contains the political space for citizens to register dissent from policies they consider immoral; as a world power, its actions can seriously affect people's lives throughout the world. When our government supports a World Bank loan that will uproot indigenous tribes and flood rain forest containing endangered species, some of the moral responsibility belongs to those who pay taxes.[46]

As a result of this *technological* and *political* complexity, seemingly endless *moral* questions arise. Should we pay taxes to a militaristic government? Should we abandon our cars and use public transportation to lessen our contribution to global warming, knowing that such a move would put a deep strain on our ability to fulfill *other* moral responsibilities? Do we have to alter our lives dramatically to consider ourselves decent people? How can we help create a more just society and world?

If we are to "love our neighbor as ourselves," Catholic monk Charles Cummings tells us, we must realize that "in the current era of ecological awareness, we are beginning to see that celebrating Eucharist implies a commitment not only to our neighbor but also to all God's creation. . . . As our neighbor is an image of God, so also is the material world."[47] The bleak truth is that unless we totally withdraw from society, we will be participating in morally questionable collective forms of life, forms that can be made more moral *only* by political change. Latin American theologian Gustav Gutierrez sums up the situation: "The neighbor is not only a person viewed individually. The term refers also to a person considered in the fabric of social relationships, to a person situated in economic, social, culture, and racial coordinates."[48] Clearly, the point extends to any other religion that teaches justice and compassion: in short, to every religion whatsoever.[49]

❧

Problem 5. *Religion has become increasingly irrelevant to modern life,*
so a religious environmentalism is not needed and will make
no real contribution.

From the mid-nineteenth century to the present, many sociologists and historians accepted some form of what is often called the "secularization thesis."[50] They believed that a combination of factors—pluralistic societies, the social power of science, the daily experience of technology and bureaucracy—would reduce the political power and personal importance of religion. Religion would become increasingly private and progressively less active in the public world, as the state, scientific expertise, and personal choice replaced its functions of controlling society, answering questions about the natural world, and shaping morality.

As plausible as this thesis seemed, history has shown that the jury is still out on the fate of religion in modern times. This is partly so because not every society has responded the same way to modernity. Northern Europe seems in some way to confirm the secularization thesis, but the United States does not, and countries such as Russia, Japan, and Italy are a confused mixture of religion and secularism that is hard to categorize. The thesis is also challenged by the fact that religion did not, in fact, have to choose between remaining exactly the same as it was in (say) 1700 or disappearing. Rather, as indicated in my description of liberal religion, it could also *change*. It could, for example, adapt to pluralism, democracy, and science and yet remain a vital force in the life of people who practice it. Although the religions that made these changes have become *different* from any form of religion we've seen before, that does not mean they are not *religious*.

Perhaps the most important reason we have not seen a simple and direct secularization is that for a significant segment of the American (and world) population, the exclusively secular perspective that would sideline religion from social life is itself questionable. A purely secular society seems to leave people with no real reason to do anything but shop, amuse themselves, and seek power and wealth. It can lead to an exploitive and impersonal sexuality, a cheapening of human relationships, a life in which people learn the price of everything and the value of nothing.[51] Wonder, awe, reverence, self-awareness, or even the simple peace of a quiet Sabbath become harder and harder to come by. Most important, there is nothing to sustain us as communities, and the lack of community devastates all of our human relationships, leaving us with fractured marriages, pointlessly rebellious teenagers, and businesses that will purvey physically and culturally poisonous material without ever thinking that they have a responsibility to anything but the next quarterly report. Too many politicians and professionals have a similar lack of concern for anything but self-advancement.

Further, science and technology, touted in the nineteenth century as unmixed sources of progress and happiness, have revealed a dark side. We have experienced the threat of nuclear war and the wastes from nuclear power plants, the human-created hole in the ozone layer and the ghastly spectacle of genetic engineering that puts ears on mouse backs and causes flies to grow eyes on their legs and wings. We have seen a pesticide transmuted into a gas that kills people (Zyklon B, the gas used in Nazi concentration camps, was first used to eradicate insects from old buildings). Later, we discovered that pesticides kill people even when they are aimed at bugs. Many things don't work as well as we thought—and as we've been told—they would. One need only think of the high technology and the real-life consequences of traffic gridlock, urban sprawl, or the way the overuse of antibiotics has led to new and virulent strains of bacteria. As a result of such experiences, emerging areas of the scientific transformation of everyday life, such as the claim that genetically modified foods are safe and healthy, are met with deep skepticism.

That skepticism has its roots partly in straightforward health concerns, but also partly in a quasi-spiritual—or at least value-oriented—attitude that "nature" deserves a certain respect for both its own good and ours. It is also connected to the idea that when any human enterprise—science, technology, politics, or a high school football team—aims solely at goals such as power and wealth, disastrous consequences follow.

In the absence of science as a guiding authority for social life, people have rediscovered or sought to create other kinds of knowledge: the kind that comes from awareness of one's own needs and social situation[52] and practices such as meditation, mind-body medicine, and visualizations. For many, the alternative to spiritless secularism is the life of the spirit and the values of great spiritual teachers, both within and outside of established religions. The distinction between technical expertise and wisdom, obscured by an Enlightenment mentality in which everything that is not science is written off as literature,[53] becomes operative once again. In all these developments, space is made for both traditional religion and the new forms of spirituality—and thus for a potentially socially influential religious environmentalism.

How many people can chart a *religious* course in modern society, avoiding both violent fundamentalism and spiritless secularism? Is it enough to make a difference? This is perhaps an impossible question to answer. Paul Ray and Sherry Anderson designate as many as 50 million Americans as "cultural creatives," people who possess a significant new sensibility about personal and social life.[54] This sensibility includes concern for environmental destruction and global problems, suspicion of unrestrained technological development and economic growth, spiritual involvement that is ecumenical rather than fundamentalist, support for women's equality and community needs, and a rejection of the notion that happiness can be founded in individualistic consumerism. Clearly, there are comparable groups, of exactly how many we cannot be sure, throughout the world.

Religion sees the self as more than the consumer, the taxpayer, and the pursuer of wealth and pleasure; the religious spirit teaches a reverence for life, as opposed to the hands-off, keep-your-distance perspective defined by individual rights. Further, this contemporary religiosity offers a view of human beings in which our goal is inner knowledge and moral rectitude. The culture of religious life emphasizes virtues such as gratitude, compassion, and self-awareness, virtues that (it is believed) have the long-term advantage of promoting a long-term sense of fulfillment for the practitioner *and* a more harmonious and just society. In the context of environmentalism, reverence means that certain things are not for sale and not exchangeable for other "consumer preferences."

Religious environmentalism is one part of a global movement that seeks to integrate the most creative, humane, and hopeful parts of both secular society and religious tradition. We cannot know now whether there are enough such people to stem the tide. Comparatively few African Americans marched with King, or Indians with Gandhi, or women with the feminists of the late 1960s. And considering how few secular environmentalists there are, at least relative to the task before us, it is heartening to see a significant resource emerging from an unexpected place. In any event, it is often not the sheer numbers of a social movement that determine its success, but the force of its commitment and the truth of its claims. A breathtakingly new force on the social and cultural scene, we will just have to see what kind of long-term effect religious environmentalism can have.

Now let us look at what it says it wants to do and some of the things it has done.

CHAPTER 3

SUSTAINABLE RELIGION

> We affirm that the world, as God's handiwork, has its own inherent integrity; that land, waters, air, forests, mountains, and all creatures, including humanity, are "good" in God's sight. The integrity of creation has a social aspect, which we recognize as peace with justice, and an ecological aspect, which we recognize in the self-renewing, sustainable character of natural ecosystems.
>
> —Taken from ten affirmations adopted by the World Council of Churches Convocation in Seoul, March 1990 (These linked ecological concerns with social justice and asserted "that the land belongs to God. Human use of land and waters should release the earth to replenish regularly its life-giving power, protecting its integrity and providing spaces for its creatures.")

Under the pressure of the environmental crisis, theologians have proven that religion can think ecologically. But theologians—anyone telling us what our traditions really mean or how we as religious people should act—can occupy a variety of positions within a faith. They may be central or marginalized, representative or idiosyncratic. Indeed, history reveals many religious thinkers who made remarkably modern-sounding statements about the awe-inspiring and even holy qualities of nature, yet who were largely ignored by the wider religious community.

So our next step is to examine religions as *institutions*: to look at public commitments by individual leaders and key groups. What these are saying to their followers and the wider world will tell us, at least in theory, to what degree the critical messages of religious environmentalism are supported in the world religious community.

Of course, we may wonder if such statements have much importance. After all, religions have been preaching many values—peace instead of war, justice for the poor, the unimportance of wealth, love of neighbor—for millennia, and it is (to say the least) not altogether clear that they have been having any effect on the broader society. A casual glance at the contemporary world scene does not reveal a place where religion's ethical teachings, with the possible exception of rather repressive ideas about gender, are taken very seriously.

On the other hand, because we don't know what society would be like without them, it is quite hard to know what effect religious moral teachings do have. Certain kinds of distinct and highly valuable activities—Catholic hospitals, India's Sikh community providing millions of free meals a day, nearly a thousand professional Mennonite peacemakers seeking to resolve conflicts throughout the world—are motivated by religious ideas and supported by religious institutions. Further, even if few of its self-described followers are as faithful as they should be, religion's moral teachings at least tell us that people can act for reasons other than the desire for money, power, and pleasure, and that such reasons can be spoken of by widely respected and authoritative leaders and groups.

It might also be argued that in most of the world, religions do not have the legal or political power to confront anything as sweeping as the environmental crisis. Although this is true, in a sense it makes my point rather than contradicts it. The state coerces, the world of business controls your wallet, but religion commands through love, devotion, community, and tradition. For good or ill its mandates represent a marriage of what its serious practitioners care deeply about and what they believe, most deeply, to be right.[1] This fusion provides leverage for social change, a leverage that can potentially transcend economic "rationality," narrow self-interest, and the struggle for political rule.

If religions too often do little but reinforce the status quo, at other times their values vigorously counter the dominant ideas of society, its reigning "common sense." Religions can teach a perspective on how to live that one is not likely to learn in the army, the factory, law school, or on the football field. This is important, because if a great deal of social history shows that money, power, and pleasure are what people usually want, it also contains many instances when people act out of moral beliefs. Parents devote themselves to their children, soldiers die for their country or their comrades, people work to ameliorate society in the name of universal ideas. These actions cannot be reduced to narrowly construed self- or group interests. They express the human capacity for love and care, as well as our ability to take a critical look at existing social life and seek a better one—to make a new world on the basis of what we think good, sensible, or holy. The ideas that motivate such actions may come from personal experience, historical change, intuitions, or God—but they must be articulated before they can be lived.

Environmentally destructive policies sometimes seem inescapable. Socially powerful economic institutions put profit before long-term sustainability. Ordinary people are materially dependent on the imperatives of business, and in any case, large numbers of us in the richer nations (and increasing numbers in the poor ones) are psychologically hooked on consumption. These deep connections mean that any serious environmental challenge to current policies could be met by businesses refusing to invest, thus causing an economic downturn and widespread financial hardship. With corporate spokespeople and a corporate-dominated media shaping the debate as "jobs versus nature" or "trees versus people," political support for environmentally sane policies would melt away. On the personal side, a proposal for "less growth, more green" in social life would threaten our own emotional dependence on consumerism. We hope for a continually better life for ourselves and our children, defining "better" as "richer, bigger, faster, more."

It is possible that religious environmentalism could help unravel this complicated knot. Its challenges to society's most powerful institutions and our own psychic limitations are rooted in long-standing values that command wide respect. For a tremendous number of people throughout the world, religion is a repository of hope and trust.[2] If that hope and trust are accompanied at times by bored complacency or a near contempt based in familiarity, at least it is there. Religion is, quite simply, the single strongest alternative to government, corporations, and consumerism.

In this chapter, I examine a series of powerful statements by religious leaders and institutions, giving the reader an indication of their scope and seriousness. Toward the end of the chapter I raise some critical questions about how these environmental commitments relate to political life, both in society at large and within religious institutions themselves. I must emphasize that I am presenting a small fraction of what is out there. Encouraging, sympathetic, and often extremely bold declarations have come from the vast majority of the world's religions. If you are a member of one of the world's faiths, it is almost certain that some of your leaders have shown that they know there is a problem and that something quite fundamental has to change in the way we live. Would that such a widespread response were forthcoming from the world's industrialists, political leaders, labor unions, consumers, or philosophers.

∾

To set the stage for more detailed accounts, we can begin by sampling a few dramatic statements by leaders and institutions.

The headline of a 1997 *Los Angeles Times* article read: " 'Harming the Environment Is Sinful!' Declaration by Bartholomew I, Orthodox Christian leader, Is Believed to Be a First by a Major Religious Figure." In his speech to a symposium on religion, science, and the environment, this leader of 300 million Orthodox Christians from North and South America, Europe, and Asia was unflinchingly direct. "To commit a crime against the natural world is a sin . . . to cause species to become extinct and to destroy the biological diversity of God's creation . . . to degrade the integrity of the Earth by causing changes in its climate, stripping the Earth of its natural forests, or destroying its wetlands . . . to contaminate the Earth's waters, its land, its air, and its life with poisonous substances—these are sins."[3]

This dramatic statement was not the first evidence of environmental concern to come from an Orthodox leader. In 1989 Bartholomew's predecessor, the ecumenical patriarch of Constantinople, Dimitrios I, issued a patriarchal message calling for thanksgiving and supplications for all creation to be offered on each September 1, the first day of the Orthodox ecclesiastical year. In 1991 an Eastern Orthodox conference committed itself to theological study and practical action: from congregational recycling and energy conservation to support for environmentally friendly tax policies and investing in green businesses. Bartholomew himself sponsored a broad symposium on pollution in the Black Sea, which borders several countries in which Orthodox membership is sizable.

But what Bartholomew did in the clearest terms possible in the Santa Barbara speech was link destructive environmental practices with the most basic and powerful of religious categories. Pollution was not simply a policy problem, an oversight, or a technical glitch that could be fixed by more technology. It was a sin.

Further, in a move that directly related to law and public policy, Bartholomew advocated criminalizing antienvironmental action: "If human beings treated one another's personal property the way they treat their environment, we would view that behavior as anti-social. We would impose the judicial measures necessary to restore wrongly appropriated personal possessions. It is therefore appropriate for us to seek ethical, legal recourse where possible, in matters of ecological crimes."[4]

More decentralized, and typically characterized by social conservatism, America's Evangelical Christian churches are perhaps one of the last places from which one would expect powerful environmental statements to emerge. Yet, in an authoritative and sweeping document, "On the Care of Creation: Evangelical Declaration on the Environment," hundreds of ministers, lay leaders, and heads of evangelical educational institutions stated in no uncertain terms that environmentalism had become central to their Christian mission. They also were not averse to the language of sin, committing themselves to "repent of the way we have polluted, distorted, or destroyed so much of the Creator's work." Acknowledging the full scope of the crisis, they spoke of "(1) land degradation; (2) deforestation; (3) species extinction; (4) water degradation; (5) global toxification; (6) the alteration of atmosphere; (7) human and cultural degradation." Rooting themselves directly in biblical precepts of the goodness of creation and human responsibility to represent God on earth, they specifically rejected "attitudes which devalue creation, and which twist or ignore biblical revelation to support our misuse of it." They called for social change so that economies may be "godly, just, and sustainable" and so that public policies would "embody the principles of biblical stewardship of creation."[5]

In the spring of 2005, national evangelical leaders, representing umbrella groups with some 30 million members, committed themselves to changing U.S. policy on global warming and called meetings attended by members of the Senate and representatives of the Bush administration. "Because clean air, pure water, and adequate resources are crucial to public health and civic order," read part of their twelve-page statement, "government has an obligation to protect its citizens from the effects of environmental degradation."[6]

Like Evangelical Christianity, Judaism, too, is decentralized. Certain rabbis may have more standing or followers than others, but there is no religionwide structure of authority. Yet certain key institutions are granted an informal respect and possess public visibility and clout. The Jewish Theological Seminary is the premier educational institution of American Conservative Judaism, a branch of Judaism claiming a million members and purporting to marry modernity and tradition by combining the Talmudic rigidity of the Orthodox and the more liberal attitudes of Reform. For nearly twenty years, the chancellor of the seminary has been history professor Rabbi Ismar Schorsch. Schorsch achieved national recognition on environmental issues through his participation in a Middlebury College symposium, televised nationally by Bill Moyers, titled "Spirit and Nature: Religion, Ethics and Environmental Crisis," during which he shared the podium with the Dalai Lama. Working closely with Vice President Al Gore, Rabbi Schorsch helped create the National Religious Partnership for the Environment, an interfaith coalition with a wide range of educational programs for faith groups and society as a whole. A leading spokesman among Conservative Jewry the world over, he is not hesitant to take Jewish tradition to task and advocate a fundamental transformation. It is a mistake, he argues, to use Judaism's rejection of paganism to propel Judaism into an "adversarial relationship with the natural world." When that is done, "the modern Jew is saddled with a reading of his tradition that is one-dimensional. Judaism has been made to dull our sensitivity to the awe inspiring power of nature. Preoccupied with the ghost of paganism, it appears indifferent and unresponsive to the supreme challenge of our age: man's degradation of the environment. Our planet is under siege and we as Jews are transfixed in silence."[7]

∾

The Catholic Church is the largest centralized religion on the planet. With more than a billion members, financial resources in the hundreds of billions of dollars, and a vast array of universities, schools, charities, hospitals, and media, it is the single most important nongovernmental institution on earth. For these reasons, its development of ecological awareness deserves detailed study.

Even with a distinctly hierarchical structure—ecclesiastical and financial power spreading downward from the Vatican in Rome to large-scale archdioceses headed by archbishops, smaller concentrations led by bishops, and then local parishes—the church is by no means theologically or politically homogeneous. In what is virtually an entire world of cultural values and political perspectives, liberation theologians in Latin America blend Marxism with Christian ethics, feminist nuns demand an end to gender inequality in the church, and burgeoning ranks of Catholics in Africa and Asia tend to be socially conservative and vociferously anticommunist. In the context of this variety, a commitment to Catholicism does not necessarily imply acceptance of all of the statements of its leadership, any more than a commitment to being an American implies respect for the current president or not cheating on one's taxes.

Still, church authorities—and, as we shall see here, the pope in particular—possess enormous influence. They do so directly by the power of their office and indirectly through the charismatic effect that their office has on Catholics worldwide. One only need consider the enormous crowds, often in the hundreds of thousands or even millions, who turned out to hear John Paul II address the faithful on his world tours. A pope's statements may not command instant obedience by every Catholic, but they do generate enormous interest, are widely cited and reproduced, and get taught in schools and seminaries. They may even legitimate the expression of preexisting views that require an initial support by the Highest Authority before they can be widely accepted. Some will follow what a pope says simply because he says it; others will emphatically disagree. In either case, the pope's views tend to become a central part of the fabric of Catholic faith for their time.

So when the pope turns green it is Big News.

Let us consider in detail the development of a serious commitment to ecology by John Paul II in particular and in other parts of the church as well, a commitment all the more significant because it required some fundamental shifts in Catholic doctrine.[8]

John Paul II became pope in 1978. He inherited a church that, in the Vatican II conferences of the early 1960s, had sought to bring itself into modernity. This goal required that the church face key social problems, including political conflict centered on issues of wealth and poverty, communism's persecution of the church in Eastern Europe, relations with a religiously pluralistic world community, and the continually nagging question of birth control. The many positive accomplishments of Vatican II incorporated resolutions to work with people of goodwill around the globe, acknowledgment of the desperate plight of the poor and oppressed, and a new sense of how contemporary historical conditions affect long-standing theological doctrines.

Ecological problems were decidedly not on the church's agenda during this period. Since the late nineteenth century, the church had had other political matters in mind. In *Rerum Novarum* (*The Condition of Labor*, 1891), Pope Leo XIII had focused on "the social question" with a decidedly pro-development perspective.[9] His central interest had been issues of justice, labor, and property. In defending capitalism against European socialists, he offered extensive justifications for private property, especially the idea that human labor, the source of private property, develops unused wilderness and thus improves common life. Yet Leo also supported a decent form of life for workers, suggesting that the prerogatives of private property were limited by the moral good of the community. This position offers a later opening for environmentalism, for it leaves unsettled the question of how we should respond when "development of wilderness," and by implication all other forms of human labor, no longer improves, but vastly diminishes, our collective life.[10] At the very least, asserting that the economy was subject to moral constraints is in harmony with the environmentalist critique of industry's damaging effects. Theologically, Leo's use of Thomas Aquinas, who defined nature as an essential source of knowledge about God and argued that God loved all existing beings, raised interest in a potential source of more positive attitudes toward the natural world.

But these remained possibilities only. It was not until the early 1970s that even brief mentions of ecological damage appeared in important church statements. For the most part, the church saw nature as resources for human labor or a creation that signaled God's grandeur and generosity. It had not yet become "the environment"—an imperiled kin.

In the following decades, all this changed, beginning with the church's response to the rise of secular environmentalism, the first Earth Day celebrations of 1970, and the United Nations–sponsored Stockholm meeting (1972) on sustainability (which was addressed in sympathetic terms by John Paul's predecessor). It slowly became clear to the church that throughout the world, ecological issues were central to human existence.

A powerful rhetoric of ecological concern marked John Paul's papacy from the outset. In 1979 he proclaimed Francis of Assisi the patron saint of those who would seek to protect the environment. In his encyclical (the most authoritative of papal statements) *Redemptor hominis*, he challenged the validity of unquestioned faith in science and technology, pointing out that even with our "previously unknown immense progress" the world still "groans in travail" from phenomena such as "the threat of pollution of the natural environment in areas of rapid industrialization . . . or the prospective of self-destruction through the use of atomic, hydrogen, neutron and similar weapons." John Paul's focus was not just on the consequences of particular technologies gone wrong. His questioning went further, warning that there is something fundamentally wrong with humanity's treatment of nature:

> Exploitation of the earth not only for industrial but also for military purposes and the uncontrolled development of technology outside the framework of a long-range authentically humanistic plan often bring with them a threat to man's natural environment, alienate him in his relations with nature and remove him from nature. Man often seems to see no other meaning in his natural

environment than what serves for immediate use and consumption. Yet it was the Creator's will that man should communicate with nature as an intelligent and noble "master" and "guardian," and not as a heedless "exploiter" and "destroyer."[11]

John Paul's overall ecological vision is rooted, commentator Charles Murphy tells us, in his reading of Genesis. After creating the earth, God sees it as "very good"; because God values creation, we are obligated to treat it respectfully and carefully. Human dominion over the earth entails serious responsibility for it.[12]

Despite this appeal to scripture, we need to recognize that the book of Genesis has been part of Christianity for two thousand years; it was only in the late twentieth century that its teachings were applied to the environmental crisis. Thus, no matter how much John Paul might claim that his position was inspired by tradition, it was a tradition almost never used this way in the past. An "ecological tradition" was really an innovation, for the meaning of a foundational text had to shift. Yet, because what was being appealed to was actually *in* Christianity's most basic text, this was an innovation that strengthened, rather than threatened, the integrity of the faith.

Philosophically, the pope's environmentalism was in part an extension of his personal stress on the moral centrality of the "human person." During his philosophical training, this stress had focused solely on humanity's special capacity for moral freedom and subjective experience. These unique qualities, he believed, were the foundation for universal moral norms of respect, care, and nonviolence. As his ecological awareness developed, he began in a limited way to include nature in this framework, and thus to expand his moral horizon beyond a purely anthropocentric limit. Human relations with nature, he wrote in 1987, are bound by ethical constraints and thus not simply matters of technique, convenience, amusement, or human satisfaction: "When it comes to the natural world, we are subject not only to biological laws but also to moral ones, which cannot be violated with impunity."[13]

It is remarkable that John Paul II, in more than two decades of statements that followed his ecological awakening, talked about nature as having its own value, meaning, and even subjectivity. If we reflect on the exact language he used, we see that we cannot, after all, "communicate" with something that has no point or purpose of its own. Nor can we be "alienated" from something that is not essentially connected to ourselves. This dramatically new element only increased over time. In a 1987 statement from a discussion of how to bring nonindustrialized countries into the realm of modern industrialized economies, he wrote, "Thus one would hope that all those who, to some degree or other, are responsible for ensuring a 'more human life' for their fellow human beings, whether or not they are inspired by a religious faith, will become fully aware of the urgent need to change the spiritual attitudes which define each individual's relationship with self, with neighbor, with even the remotest human communities, *and with nature itself*, and all of this in view of higher values such as the common good."[14]

As evidenced by his decisive World Peace Day statement of 1990, John Paul's assessment of the importance of ecological issues continued to develop. In that statement he spoke of how "world peace is threatened not only by the arms race, regional conflicts and continued injustices among peoples and nations, but also by a *lack of due respect* for nature, by the plundering of natural resources and by a progressive decline in the quality of life." Like war, like abortion, like unrelieved poverty, then, ecological destruction is a moral issue, one evidencing a "lack of *respect for life.*" The consequences of this lack of respect include global warming, toxic industrial products, unbalanced ecosystems, and deforestation.[15]

In statements such as these, we see that the pope's firmly established rejection of much of modernity as a "culture of death" was expanded to include ecological damage. By a culture of death, one commentator tells us, he meant "hopelessness . . . social death, the death of culture, the death of the family, the death of moral commitment, the death of faith, the death of the possibility in the belief in higher values."[16] This general idea was used as the basis of strong condemnations of war, unnecessary poverty, abortion, cheapened sexuality, interpersonal violence of all kinds—and our treatment of nature. Ironically, in his sweeping denunciation of much of modern culture, John Paul II resembled many of the most radical secular critics of modernity. Icons of the left from Herbert Marcuse to cultural feminism also condemn militarism, mindless media, commercialized sexuality, and horrible disparities between the rich and the poor. Like John Paul, they see an administered society at war with life, heading toward a time when all we have left are the "social engineers and the inmates of closed institutions."[17] This kind of social critique is also essential to many (although clearly not all) environmentalists, who see the mistreatment of nature and people as evidence of a profound alienation from life. The similarities of all these broad social criticisms create a surprising common ground where other differences—most notably John Paul's rejection of some of the essential demands of feminism and gay liberation[18]—would seem to preclude any sympathy whatsoever.

By including respect for the earth with other central moral concerns the pope made it clear that caring for creation is an essential part of the faith. It is not something added on, a temporary and contingent application of the "really important" principles. Even if humans have a "greater and higher fraternity" with each other than they do with nature, Catholics are reminded that "respect for life and for the dignity of the human person extends also to the rest of creation, which is called to join man in praising God." To this end, John Paul recommended ecological education, international coordination, actions by individual states, and a critical examination of concentrated wealth and immoderate lifestyles.[19]

In 2000, John Paul II made a definitive statement of our kinship with nature, a statement that embodies a profound change for Catholicism: "This discovery of a transcendent presence in creation, must lead us also to redis-cover our *fraternity with the earth*, to which we have been linked since cre-ation (cf. Gen 2:7). This very goal was foreshadowed by the Old Testament in the Hebrew Jubilee, when the earth rested and man gathered what the land spontaneously offered (cf. Lv 25:11–12). If nature is not violated and humiliated, it returns to being the *sister of humanity*."[20]

It is worth noting that a sense of kinship with nature was at times present in premodern Catholic teachings, notably those that viewed the material world as a sign of God's greatness and power. Individual theologians had celebrated the presence of God in nature; others, such as Aquinas, had talked about how God's goodness was bound up in the integrity of the entire created world, not simply based in human individuals or even humanity as a whole.[21] Yet the dominant strands of Catholic tradition had been at best ambivalent about nature.[22] A profound distance between the worth of humanity and that of nature was generally taken for granted, with the latter placed well below humans in a detailed cosmic hierarchy. If nature was a gift from God, it was also something to which we should not be attached. As our fundamental purpose on earth was to merit an eternity in heaven, the earth was really just a temporary testing ground.

Further, Catholic reverence for nature had greatly diminished since the Middle Ages. With the rise of modern science and the disenchantment of nature, the church grew less interested in the material world as a source of understanding of God.[23] The problem of nature, if it existed at all, concerned its role in the proof of God's existence, not in its own value. Or it was the problem of how to get enough nature and spread it around fairly—issues of wealth, poverty, and class conflict.

Perhaps more important, for a good deal of its existence the church had been at war with any tradition that celebrated the sacredness of the earth. In this it reflected its Jewish roots, for any close reading of the Hebrew scriptures reveals the consistent struggle between the followers of the "sky God" Yahweh and those surrounding groups who had fertility rituals and sacred groves.[24] As Christianity spread first through Europe and later throughout the world, it consistently faced indigenous traditions with com-parable beliefs. Such beliefs were dismissed as idolatry and paganism and often violently persecuted. Therefore, although nature could retain its sym-bolic function as evidence of an unseen God, any sense of it as a presence with its own reality and importance was largely expunged from the Catholic sense of the sacred, especially at the level of major statements by its lead-ership.

Given its history, then, the Catholic Church might be considered one of the last places for environmentalists to look for allies. But this is no longer the case. Under the enormous pressure of the environmental crisis, the church as a whole is coming to realize that ecology is a central moral issue, and that this issue cannot be resolved without an essentially new perspective on the meaning of nature. As we shall see, the pope's statements, powerful in their own right, have helped spark and legitimate a wide range of public commitments and activities.

Of course, Catholic environmental statements and actions cannot be attributed solely to the pope's statements. Every Catholic lives in a world in which the environmental crisis is registered on the media and can be felt in daily life—in everything from summertime unhealthy air warnings to the sight (and smell) of polluted rivers. In all probability, it was the combination of their own daily experience and the pope's increased focus that helped motivate the Filipino bishops' poignant and heartfelt 1988 plea "What Is Happening to Our Beautiful Land?," a remarkable document in which virtually every theme of ecotheology is registered and grounded in concrete national experience:

> All the living systems on land and in the seas around us are being ruthlessly exploited. The damage to date is extensive and, sad to say, it is often irreversible. ... Within a few short years, brown eroded hills have replaced luxuriant forests in many parts of the country. We see dried up riverbeds where, not so long ago, streams flowed throughout the year. Farmers tell us that, because of erosion and chemical poisoning, the yield from the croplands has fallen substantially. Fishermen and experts on marine life have a similar message. Their fish catches are shrinking in the wake of the extensive destruction of coral reefs and mangrove forests.

To respond to this crisis, the bishops see themselves in solidarity with

> tribal people all over the Philippines, who have seen the destruction of their world at close range, [and] have cried out in anguish. Also men and women who attempt to live harmoniously with nature and those who study ecology have tried to alert people to the magnitude of the destruction taking place in our time. The latter are in a good position to tell us what is happening since they study the web of dynamic relationships which support and sustain all life within the earthly household.[25]

Alongside the depth of the suffering in this statement it is crucial to notice how the bishops moved beyond Western religion's typical pattern of spiritual arrogance. Instead of dismissing them as primitive, the bishops recognize and respect the "anguish" of "tribal people." Instead of proclaiming the virtues of religion over science, they seek to work with those "who study ecology."

The bishops also questioned the usually assumed values of "progress" and "development," contrasting the original biological diversity of the Philippines with what the country has become under modern agriculture, fishing, and industry. "It took millions of years of care and love to mold and reshape this land with all its beauty, richness and splendor, where intricate pathways bind all the creatures together in a mutually supportive community. . . . How much of this richness and beauty is left a few thousand years after human beings arrived at these shores?" Speaking of road building in rural areas, they write, "There is no denying in some areas our roads have improved and that electricity is more readily available. But can we say that there is real progress? Who has benefited most and who has borne the real costs? The poor are as disadvantaged as ever and the natural world has been grievously wounded."[26]

Here even a serious Catholic stewardship model—the idea that the remedy for the environmental crisis is essentially to use the earth for human good more wisely and responsibly—is transcended. As in the pope's later statements, but in a bolder and more pained form, nature itself has a kind of presence, integrity, and value. It is not merely a resource, even a resource given by the Creator. For we cannot "wound" a resource; nor can we be part of a "mutually supportive community" with one.

To heal these wounds and save the human-nature community, the bishops say, we must oppose "human greed and the relentless drive of our plunder economy." Efforts to do so will be aided by knowledge of tribal Filipinos and the inspiration of environmental activists from the (Hindu!) Chipko of India to the Greenbelt of Kenya. The ultimate goal of this work is to "protect endangered ecosystems . . . and to establish just human communities in our land. . . . Commitment to work for justice and to preserve the integrity of creation are two inseparable dimensions of our Christian vocation." The seamless connection between environmental concern and social justice found in ecotheology, as well as a sense of global solidarity that transcends the bounds of Christianity, is here repeated by the leaders of a national church of nearly 80 million people.

U.S. environmentalism reaches back to the nineteenth century. In the past two decades the national face of the American church, the United States Council of Catholic Bishops, has become part of that tradition. As late as 1986, however, this was not the case. In that year the USCCB issued "Economic Justice for All," a major statement on wealth and poverty, class relations, and consumerism. Strikingly, the thoroughly anthropocentric document paid virtually no attention to environmental issues—and this more than a decade after the sweeping national environmental legislation of the 1970s (the Clean Air and Water Acts, creation of the Environmental Protection Agency, Endangered Species Act, etc.). It did not recognize environmental justice issues or that ecological concerns were part of a just economy. Even though a few earlier high-level American Catholic documents had examined ecological issues—notably a 1975 Appalachian bishops statement about destructive effects of local mining and a 1980 Nebraska bishops statement concerning land stewardship and agriculture—these declarations were treated as essentially regional matters, limited in applicability, and still somewhat distant from the main work of the church.[27]

Yet in 1991, only five years after "Economic Justice for All," having been inspired by John Paul II, the rise of secular environmentalism, and a pained recognition that this was a global problem confronting humanity and nature alike, America's bishops put forth the powerful document "Renewing the Earth." Building on many of the pope's ideas, this statement is also significant for its assertion of the holiness of the universe and its recognition of the significant role of the secular environmental movement.

> The whole universe is God's dwelling. . . . Throughout history, people have continued to meet the Creator on mountaintops, in vast deserts, and alongside waterfalls and gently flowing springs. In storms and earthquakes, they found expressions of divine power. But as heirs and victims of the industrial revolution, students of science and the beneficiaries of technology, urban-dwellers and jet-commuters, twentieth-century Americans have also grown estranged from the natural scale and rhythms of life on earth.
>
> For many people, the environmental movement has reawakened appreciation of the truth that, through the created gifts of nature, men and women encounter their Creator. The Christian vision of a *sacramental universe*—a world that discloses the Creator's presence by visible and tangible signs—can contribute to making the earth a home for the human family once again.[28]

In the Catholic tradition, we should remember, a sacrament is a religiously organized experience that reveals God's presence. To say that we live in a "sacramental universe" is to assert the ability of nature to show us God.[29]

It is of great importance that the bishops' assertion of the sacramental quality of the universe goes hand in hand with a direct and unqualified recognition of the role of the environmental movement. Like ideas of democratic government and workers' rights, environmentalism is something the church has had to learn about, at least initially, from outside sources. A statement such as this indicates not only a willingness to learn, but also an ability to acknowledge that it has done so. This development is a significant example of the openness to both other traditions and secular political movements that I described in chapter 2. This openness, I believe, does not signal the collapse of religion, but its growth. The statements cited here retain a powerful sense of the holy, a commitment to seeing the universe as created by God and the necessity for humans to live according to God's will. In opening to the insights of a secular political movement, Catholicism has not diminished, but grown.[30]

By the 1990s, then, both the pope and important organizations of bishops were on record as environmentalists. Yet the important general statements we have been discussing—and dozens more that could be cited—are not the end of the matter. The church's commitment to environmentalism has been ongoing and serious, with numerous action campaigns, from resisting urban industrial pollution in Kenya to a special task force on children's health and the environment in the United States. Of this extensive and impressive list, two particular examples deserve attention here.[31]

However important large-scale position papers by the pope or bishops' councils may be, they can also leave ordinary Catholics somewhat in the lurch. The local parish priest, after all, does not have a PhD in philosophy as John Paul II did, nor does he have a bishop's staff of assistants, helpers, and housekeepers to support him in going to national meetings and releasing impassioned environmental statements. Outside of the importance that attends institutionally based statements by an organization of the size and status of the church, how are the world's Catholics to make this issue their own?

Recognizing this dilemma, the USCCB did not rest with "Renewing the Earth," but committed time and money in preparing resources for local use.[32] By 2004 it had created three of these resources kits, mailing one of each to all of America's nineteen thousand Catholic parishes. The kits have such names as "God's Creation and Our Responsibility" and "Renewing the Face of the Earth" and include precisely the kinds of material that enable theology to become the subject matter of the daily life of a local parish: source material for sermons, precise and accessible summaries of the church's teachings, suggestions for prayer and worship, opportunities for environmental action, and examples of such action taken by other parishes. The kits strongly emphasize that these issues are part of a concern with "environmental justice"—that the "environment" includes people as well as trees, and that, as the pope had stated clearly, justice for humans and justice for nature are intertwined.

These kits enable a neighborhood priest, who has to deal with myriad local concerns and personalities, to jump-start a focus on environmental issues. In them we can see a transmission belt that runs from the highest level of Catholicism to the small church on the corner. Along with other activities of the USCCB's Environmental Justice Task Force, they contribute to what its director claimed in 2004 as his greatest victory: "We have in the last ten years helped to connect religion and concern for creation, for nature. We've helped people realize that caring for the environment is part of your religious faith as a believer . . . a way to say 'Yes,' to say 'Thank you,' to God."[33]

How to apply a green Catholicism on the parish level is one problem; understanding how it might be applied—in living detail—to an entire region is another. As valuable as are local activities suggested in the parish kits, such as making a church energy-efficient or supporting local recycling efforts, many environmental concerns cannot be understood or responded to by a parish, a city, or even a state. Protecting a coastline, preserving a vast wilderness area, dealing with an entire region's air-quality problems—such issues require a level of understanding and action that fits somewhere between the global theology of John Paul II and the concerns of your nearest vestry. And they also put to the test the generalities on which programmatic statements often rest. It is one thing, after all, to talk about the web of life and healing the wounds of nature. It is another to confront possible conflicts between preserving forests and keeping jobs in the logging industry, power from dams and having rivers for salmon to spawn in, the need for organic agriculture and the cost of fruit at the local supermarket.

The Columbia River is over a thousand miles long and encompasses a 259,000-square-mile watershed in Washington, Idaho, Oregon, Montana, and British Columbia. In January 2001, the Catholic bishops of the region, after a three-year process of reflection, research, consultation with environmental professionals, and community meetings, presented "The Columbia River Watershed: Caring for the Creation and the Common Good," a glossy 12,000-word brochure with scenic pictures, extensive quotations from the Bible, John Paul's 1990 address, and "Renewing the Earth," and a detailed account of the threats and practical responses to the ecological and human turmoil of the region. The bishops offered an "ecological vision" in which the "common goal" of industry and environmentalists would be the "well-being of the entire community of life"; agriculture would be as organic as possible; mining would not endanger water, fish, air, or land; environmental damage from logging operations would be paid for by logging companies, not pawned off on the public; and alternative energy sources would be developed. And all this within a framework in which, as in the Filipino bishops' statement, both the inherent value of the land and the ecological wisdom of native peoples are acknowledged.

The Columbia bishops' tone is serious but nonconfrontational. Yet its repeated claim that respect for the living community of the earth—and not just for people—is a distinctly religious value stands in dramatic contrast to the dominant economic and political culture of the United States (as well as to most of Christianity until recently). Even without a direct criticism of clear-cutting or pollution from extractive industries, their call for corporations to be bound by the "common good" would, if taken seriously, make for significant improvement. In the context of fierce public debates that are often dominated by economic concerns of logging companies and loggers, or the "interests" of agribusiness or sportsmen, the church articulated a perspective in which nature as well as people, the common good along with individual rights, are honored. If the secular environmentalists of the Columbia River region had been putting forth a similar vision, probably none could do so with as much fanfare, attention, or possible effect. Certainly none could do so with the built-in audience that could be commanded by the leaders of the region's nearly 2 million Catholics.

∾

World Buddhism has much less centralized authority than Catholicism. At times, certain teachers may rise to prominence, and within certain traditions (e.g., Tibetan Buddhists) there may exist a localized hierarchy, but there are no worldwide, institutionally based guarantees of influence or prestige. At the same time, where Buddhism is the national religion, as in Mongolia, the recognized Buddhist leadership approaches the position of cultural authorities, and devout Buddhists who hold political power may take religious teaching seriously in shaping national policy. Further, the recent rise of Buddhism in the West generally and the United States in particular can be tilted in an environmental direction when Buddhist spokespersons who have achieved near celebrity status commit themselves to the necessary connections between Buddhism and ecology.

Statements about these connections are worth noting both in their own right and because, despite all the differences in underlying theology, institutional organization, and cultural history, they reveal some instructive similarities to Catholicism.

The Dalai Lama has for more than thirty years been the leader in exile of the Tibetan nation, as well as the world's most famous Buddhist monk. Although he has not written a separate book on ecology, his concern for the matter is often present in his writings, and part of his public program for Tibet is to make the country an ecological refuge.[34]

As a traditional Buddhist who has spent much energy representing his religion on the world stage and trying to forge connections of sympathetic concern for a nation without a country, the Dalai Lama typically puts his position in the most general and widely acceptable terms. He describes himself as speaking as a human rather than as a Buddhist. In that sense, a good deal of what he says about the environment is simple common sense: we are destroying resources essential to our happiness and that of our descendents. We do this not out of evil, for these errors, like all human faults, stem from ignorance. Still, "if we develop good and considerate qualities within our own minds, our activities will naturally cease to threaten the continued survival of life on Earth." This change will show respect both for people and "for the natural right to life of all of Earth's living things."[35]

For the Dalai Lama ecological wisdom comes not from recognizing the holiness of nature or from seeing the world as God's gift. It emerges, rather, from spiritual virtues such as mindfulness and selflessness. In his stress on the universally human causes of the crisis, he seeks a universally human solution. Not "This is what Buddhism teaches about nature" or "Here are the rules from scripture," but "Our current form of life will keep us from being happy." In this sense, his concern is a familiar application of the Buddhist principle that ignorance and attachment always breed suffering, while compassion and detachment make for a peaceful heart.

After the Dalai Lama, Vietnamese Zen Master Thich Nhat Hanh is probably the world's most well-known Buddhist. An initiator of "engaged Buddhism," which applies Buddhist precepts to social problems and encourages the involvement of Buddhists in movements for peace and social justice, Nhat Hanh left his native Vietnam in the 1970s. Since then he has become internationally famous for his work with refugees and his simple, accessible, yet profound presentation of Buddhism. His traditional roots are shown by his repeated emphasis on the essential Buddhist concepts of mindfulness and interdependence. Through the practice of meditation and the persistent application of meditative focus to all aspects of life, he teaches, we can enhance our simple enjoyment of life and decrease our enslavement to anger, greed, or fear. Ecologically, careful attention paid to everyday life and the earth as a whole reveals a profound interdependence. Quite simply, everything is connected to everything else.

So far, of course, this is standard Buddhism, essential to the religion for twenty-five centuries. But just as John Paul II used the ancient text of Genesis as a support for a new Catholic environmentalism, so Thich Nhat Hanh applies mindfulness and interdependence to the ecological crisis, at times with novel and important results. For example, if we seek to understand who we are as living beings, he tells us, we find that we "inter-be," we exist with a host of other beings, from the energy-producing sunlight to the microbes that help digest our food. Indeed, because humans are made from all the elements of the environment—water, iron, calcium, and carbon, for example—the very distinction between human and nonhuman becomes unimportant.[36] Acting as if there were a rigid separation between humans and other life forms, and even animate and inanimate existence, is mistaken. How can we consider ourselves superior to beings on which we are so dependent? We need plants for food and trees to clean the air; without water or air we'd be dead in days or minutes. Because humans need nonhumans, because the living depend on the inanimate, the best way to care for humanity is to care for the entire world. "We *are* trees, and air, bushes, and clouds. If trees cannot survive, humankind is not going to survive either."[37] The traditional "Bodhisattva vow" of Mahayana Buddhism—"I vow to save all beings"—thus takes on new meaning, for under the threat of environmental destruction, all beings need saving in a dramatically new way.

As a Buddhist, Nhat Hahn looks at the issue, he tells us, "from the viewpoint of mental health."[38] We have become the cogs in the wheel of a vast machine that reproduces itself through habitual and unthinking acceptance. The only way out is through the development of a persistent and unblinking awareness of how we are actually living, of our own moment-by-moment response to daily life. Are we rushing around in frenetic activity, too busy to pay attention to the consequences of our acts? Are we receiving the love and nurturance we need, or trying to fill an emotional and spiritual void with consumption? Are we polluting our minds with media junk—a pollution that is the psychic analogue to what we are doing to forests and rivers? Are we living with enormous wealth while the rest of the world starves? Do we think that we can achieve real peacefulness while others are at war? These states of mind, he tells us over and over, rest on mistaken ideas about selfhood and happiness. To overcome them we must be aware of how they are shaping our lives. This awareness can be furthered by traditional Buddhist meditation, by dwelling on all the beings that make our lives possible, by slowing down and breathing when the phone rings instead of rushing to answer it, and by cultivating compassion even for the CEO of the local polluting company. The goal of mindfulness, he stresses, is most definitely not to adjust the individual to a damaged and damaging social order, but to create an inner peace that will be expressed in action that counters the destruction. Yet the environmentalist won't last long, and won't be very successful, is he or she is motivated by anger or desperation. We must care for the activist as well as the environment.

The goal of meditation and Buddhist virtue, then, goes far beyond personal peacefulness. If the Catholic tradition, and indeed Western religion generally, stresses nature-as-Creation, obligations to God, prophetic calls for justice, and love of neighbor, the Buddhist vision of the Dalai Lama and Thich Nhat Hahn centers on the simple assertion that our conquest of nature is making us profoundly unhappy. Nuclear waste, toxic pollution, vastly unequal standards of living, the poor starving and the rich needing Prozac—all these form a totality and cannot be dealt with in isolation.

Thich Nhat Hanh frequently describes the unpleasant facts of the environmental crisis, referring to everything from the number of trees cut down to make the Sunday *New York Times* (75,000) to how long we must wait for nuclear wastes to stop being poisonous (250,000 years). He has no doubt that "the harmony and equilibrium in the individual, society, and nature are being destroyed. Individuals are sick, society is sick, nature is sick."[39] This inclusive assessment should remind us of John Paul's criticism of the "culture of death," for in both cases, religious leaders make no bones about a sharp and sweeping negative judgment of modernity. Both are unafraid, that is, to see the environmental crisis as a sign and a part of social crisis, rather than as a series of disconnected technical problems solvable through a series of disconnected technical responses. And in this judgment, both can make common cause with environmentalists who offer a similarly comprehensive critique.

As with some of the claims of the Catholic hierarchy, these statements, provided by widely acknowledged representatives of world Buddhism, point to changed social reality and a changed faith. As John Paul II and the bishops have shown that environmentalism is integral to a Christian life, so the Dalai Lama and Thich Nhat Hanh have claimed that Buddhism is incomplete without awareness of and response to this particular social problem and the larger mess of which it is a part.

In this effort they are joined with Buddhists from around the world. In developing countries such as Sri Lanka and Thailand, dramatic environmental damage—with disastrous consequences for forests, rivers, coastlines, and people alike—has been written off as the reasonable costs of frantic economic "growth." Buddhist leaders in these countries have been outspoken in their condemnation of a model of economic development in which nature and the poor are casually sacrificed. In May 2004, Buddhist monks and nuns from Cambodia, Laos, Thailand, and Myanmar met in Phnom Penh to share experiences, make contacts with secular environmental NGOs, and plan for future actions to protect forests, wildlife, coastlines, and people.[40] The Southeast Asian Monks Federation for the Environment was established, which will further existing environmental work and expand connections with concerned agencies, such as the World Wildlife Federation. (Interestingly, the meeting was partly funded by the World Bank, which, through a "Forests and Faith Initiative," has supported religiously based action for conservation in nearly a dozen countries.)[41]

Perhaps the most interesting case of Buddhist environmentalism is developing in Mongolia. Newly emerged in 1989 after seventy years of communist control, Mongolia is recovering a Buddhist tradition that was fiercely suppressed by, among other things, the murder of tens of thousands of monks. Although Mongolia has been eager to attract foreign investment for economic growth, it has also introduced strict controls over development in relation to environmental issues: extending restricted status to a significant percentage of its forested land, making special provisions to defend biodiversity, and trying to preserve the unique and seriously overfished taimen, a freshwater river fish that can grow to seven feet long.[42] Critically, these decisions are often explained by Mongolia's *religious* orientation. Its current prime minister, Nambaryn Enkhbayar, has offered a detailed explanation of the relationship between Buddhism and environmentalism, particularly in the context of Mongolia's traditional nomadic population:

> Buddhism considers the creation of a good balance or, let us put it in a broader sense—of a healthy environment where everyone and everything can enjoy freedom to realize or improve its potential—is the condition for the qualitative development.... In other words Buddhist philosophy proceeds from understanding that real, qualitative development is based not on theory of contradiction of two or multiple polarities (or interests) but rather on the notion of interdependence of everyone and everything.[43]

Enkhbayar's commitment to a distinctly Buddhist perspective on development and environmental policy led him to become in 2003 the first international president of the Alliance of Religions and Conservation, a UK-based organization linking religion and the environment throughout the world. His commitment is shared by Mongolia's Buddhist leaders. On Buddha's birthday in 2001, they announced the reinstitution of centuries-old logging and hunting bans on Buddhist sacred sites and sacred nature reserves. These sites include over 10 percent of Mongolia's forests, home to many rare and threatened species of plants and animals. The monks supported the bans by appealing to Buddhism's wide-ranging reverence for life and to recently recovered ancient Buddhist and shamanic texts that hold surprisingly modern insights into erosion control and resource management.[44] Indeed, sometimes the recovery of Buddhism and the protection of nature go hand in hand, as in the wide-ranging Uur project, which seeks to conserve taimen as a viable species, create a regional Buddhist outreach program on the importance of the river and the fisheries, restore the local Dayan Derkh monastery, and develop working relationships between Buddhists and conservationists.[45]

The Mongolian population has responded favorably to these conservation efforts. This is a particularly important fact given the difficulty of maintaining a sound ecological policy in the face of severe poverty. When people lack basic necessities, it is often hard not to choose the quicker, easier (at least in the short-term), more polluting solution to their problems. The presence of religious support has increased the legitimacy of a slower, more careful, more sustainable development. When appeals to the aesthetic, economic, or even health value of nature fails, religious environmentalism may yet strike a deep responsive chord.

∾

In the modern world, love and justice are manifest in our behavior as producers and consumers, citizens or government officials. That is why contemporary religion's serious ethical commitments require involvement in politics—in our collective efforts to shape the way we live as communities, nations, and an interconnected world. And that is why when religious leaders—such as Bartholomew, the Evangelical Environmental Network, Ismar Schorsch, John Paul II and the bishops, Thich Nhat Hanh, the Dalai Lama, and Nambaryn Enkhbayar—commit themselves to a serious environmental stance, they face a potentially explosive question. Besides criticism of particular policies (pesticide use, fossil fuels) and our collective moral failings (selfishness, greed), what proposals do they offer concerning the basic structure of society? Religious environmentalists support human rights and reject consumerism and vast disparities between rich and poor. But what about basic *economic* institutions? In particular, as so many of the environmentally destructive practices are undertaken by corporations, is it possible for a profit-driven, free market society to function without dangerously harming the environment? If religion can become green, can capitalism as well—or does it have to be replaced by something else?

Among secular environmentalists there are a variety of answers to this question: from the conservative notion that technological developments and the free market will solve all environmental problems, but can do so only after capitalist-led industrialization; to the far leftist belief that only some form of socialism can be sustainable. Within the religious community, few major statements confront the issue directly, though virtually all of them speak of the necessity of corporations—no less than government, workers, and consumers—acting to promote a common good that includes nature as well as people. But these general admonitions do not tell us how much of such action can be generated by moral persuasion and how much by government constraint. And if there is to be government constraint, should it stop at the level of regulation, or proceed to outright collective ownership of the major economic institutions?

In answering this question, religious environmentalism faces a series of conundrums that confront all stripes of political theorists and political movements. On the one hand, capitalism has typically been the most effective form of economic development and thus can be seen as the most reliable source of a social life of material security. Given the scope of poverty throughout the world, this is no small matter. At least in some places, moreover, the relative freedom of the economy from political power under capitalism allows for the development of democracy and basic human rights. In some times and places, capitalism, economic growth, and political freedom have gone hand in hand.

Yet advanced industrial capitalism, especially in its current global phase, has proven itself extremely ecologically destructive. Virtually everywhere large-scale market-oriented economic activity has taken place, the environment has been enormously degraded. Further, the economic benefits of this activity, many argue, are hardly unmixed. The comparative abundance it has produced in Western Europe, the United States, and Japan has been matched by devastated local economies, increased gaps between rich and poor, and hundreds of millions of people subjected to steadily worsening economic conditions in many parts of Latin America, Asia, and Africa.[46] Capitalism produces dazzling technology and wealth for some, while the rest languish in social dislocation and brutal deprivation. The predominant thrust of world-dominating multinational corporations tends toward untold costs to nature and people alike. Only governmental power, applied at the urging of popular movements, can keep corporations from clear-cutting forests, polluting rivers, heating up the atmosphere, or overfishing the ocean and from reversing environmental gains by lobbying legislatures, controlling scientific research, supporting antienvironmentalist publicity campaigns, and influencing public education.[47]

To bring the argument full circle, we can ask what the alternative is to the present system. State-controlled economies have tended to be inefficient and conducive to political dictatorships. Socialism has too often meant that a political elite replaces an economic elite, and a monopoly on all forms of power shuts down intellectual creativity and political dissent. Further, self-described communist governments, such as the Soviet Union, typically pursued industrialization, military power, and popular support at the expense of long-term environmental sanity, easily matching the capitalist world for environmental damage.[48]

Within the broad contours of the social experiences just sketched, to make matters even more confusing, there are many complicating cases. Socialist Cuba has pursued sustainable, community-oriented, organic agriculture. Capitalist (albeit social democratic) Germany and Denmark exercise strict controls over pollutants and food additives.[49] Republican president Richard Nixon supported the first major environmental legislation in the United States, whereas China has a dismal environmental record even though its current economic development remains under the control of a centralized government (though, to be fair, environmental awareness has recently been factored into China's latest long-term economic plans). There are cases of major corporations such as British Petroleum and Toyota on their own initiative taking serious steps to make their production and their products "greener" and "cooler,"[50] and there are cases where organized labor or the population as a whole—that is, the broader community that would run things in an economically democratic or socialist form of government—chose jobs, income, or other short-term gains over the long-term health of people and the environment. On the one hand, the practice of "industrial ecology" has led firms to ecologically precise, close to zero-emissions factories that blend into their surroundings and consume a minimum of energy. On the other, the implementation of NAFTA has led to the liberation of capitalism in the form of hundreds of small, highly polluting factories causing untold ecological and human damage just south of our border with Mexico.[51]

This complicated and confusing terrain of politics and economics leads some in the religious community to argue that outside of legal guarantees of human rights, the structure of our social system is comparatively unimportant. At bottom, they say, the real question is a spiritual one. Whether the economy is controlled by private corporations or by the minister of planning and ecology, it is the underlying goals and attitudes that will determine the outcome. Only if the mass of the population turns from the pursuit of wealth, technotoys, and greed can the environmental crisis be surmounted.

There is some real truth in this position. Any major social change—moving from dictatorship to democracy, extending human rights to women—requires that fundamental attitudes and values shift. We cannot expect the dominant laws and institutions to change if people remain the same. But surely this does not mean that laws and institutions do not matter, as if they themselves are not enormously effective in changing people's attitudes and values! Clearly, personal change and social change go hand in hand.

Further, any serious environmentalism must at some point confront the question of what particular social policies it recommends. And it must hazard a guess about whether those policies are likely to be implemented in the current system or require another one. For even though no system can guarantee ecological sanity if people are not ecologically sane, some systems may be more conducive to sanity than others.

For the most part, major religious statements on environmental issues seem to presume that political reform, economic moderation, and ethical exhortation can bring capitalism to its senses. Capitalism's in-built tendency toward uncontrolled growth, foisting environmental consequences onto the population at large, and promoting consumerism can be restricted and sustainability, conservation, and environmental concern can be enforced. Given that there is no significant global socialist movement at this point in time, and that governmental environmental action has frequently coexisted with some form of free market economy, this reformist position may be the only realistic one. In any event, because most religious believers are not socialists, it would make little sense to call for the immediate eradication of private ownership of the means of production—even more so given the frequent leftist antipathy toward, and in many cases outright persecution of, religion.

Yet these strategic concerns leave unanswered the question of whether ecological sustainability is like the eight-hour workday or social security, a reform that capitalism (at least in certain parts of the world) can live with. On the most immediate level, those who say it is not compatible can point to rain forest tribes whose lands were taken to grow Big Macs, local fishermen whose traditional catch was wiped out by huge mechanized trawlers, or victims of a lead smelter in East Dallas. Capitalism, they would argue, requires endless growth and gives so much power to those who control corporations that even well-intentioned governments are always several steps behind in the effort to make capitalism environmentally responsible. Modern production has global effects, involves countless workers from every corner of the earth. It makes no sense to leave it to the control of a small cadre of self-interested and often conscienceless owners.[52]

Because capitalism is such a global system now, evaluating its effects requires a global standpoint. Reforms and regulations in one place often lead businesses to migrate to more hospitable locations. If constraints are imposed *here*, factories will move *there* as corporations take advantage of cheap labor and compliant national governments to engage in highly polluting production.[53] Thus, it may do no good to defend capitalism by pointing to successful environmental reforms in the United States, as those reforms are linked to ecological decline in other countries.

A similarly broad view of environmental reforms is required for any particular country as well. The antienvironmental behavior of the Bush administration, for example, shows that whatever compatibility with environmentalism capitalism achieves in one period can be undone in the next.[54] Laws can be repealed, policies reversed, scientific reports can be rewritten or suppressed, new policies labeled misleadingly, and protected land lose its special status.[55]

Even in the rosiest scenario of environmental reform, there is the nagging fear that capitalism will never be able to advocate less growth. Even if pollution diminishes, the unending multiplication of buildings, roads, and commodities is likely to leave little room for anything else on this earth. Capitalism without growth, growth pursued as the Holy Grail of economic life, would not be capitalism. Yet that is the change, at least for the developed world, that may be necessary. We need to create and value a steady-state economic life, finding hope for the future in something other than endless amounts of *more*.

Finally, given the current rate of global warming, desertification, devastation of rain forests, reduction of the world's fish, and strange new chemicals in our bloodstreams, do we have the luxury of waiting for reforms to do their work? Even if capitalism can be reformed, by the time that happens, will there be anything left to save?

On the other side of this crucial argument, capitalism's defenders point to its boundless capacity for social and technological innovation, as well as the way it has incorporated seemingly impossible reforms—from union rights to environmental regulations themselves—in the past. Because only a capitalist economy is compatible with individual freedoms, they argue, only under capitalism will environmentalism be the free choice of the population, not something imposed by bureaucrats. Besides, typically government control does little but make things worse: hampering innovation, raising costs, failing to deal with key issues. Orienting tax and regulatory policy in the right direction and getting out of the way of entrepreneurs who will make money by being clean and green is all that is needed. If technology created these problems, technology can solve them. But the creative spirits who can fashion such technology will only be choked off by government interference or collective ownership.[56]

We can get a sense of how serious institutional statements of the religious community respond to these debates by looking at positions on the extreme ends of the political spectrum. By "extreme," let me be clear, I do not necessarily mean "wrong." Given the scope of the problems, it may be that only extreme measures will succeed. And though I personally tend to the left side of just about any spectrum one could think of, the overall situation is so complex and confusing I believe it is important to listen to anyone who thinks he or she can make it better. Because of the scarcity of our numbers relative to the size of the task, I also believe that every environmentalist needs every other environmentalist. Whatever our sense of the ultimate solutions, there are often plenty of short-term goals on which we can work together. And if capitalism can truly be ecologically reformed, so much the better. If it cannot, authentic (and not just pseudo-) environmentalists will, sooner or later, get the point.

To begin on the politically conservative, right-wingish side of the spectrum, consider the Cornwall Declaration of the Interfaith Council on Environmental Stewardship, a group seeking to serve "humanity and ecology through faith and reason."[57] The statement combines sincere environmental concern with repeated warnings against the overreactions and misconceptions that riddle the rest of the environmental community, including religious environmentalists.

Signed by a group of fifty Jews, Protestant, and Catholic clergy, professors, and leaders of lay organizations (e.g., Focus on the Family, the Faith and Reason Institute), the statement celebrates "political and economic liberty and advances in science and technology." It asserts that a clean environment is a costly good; consequently, growing affluence, technological innovation, and the application of human and material capital are integral to environmental improvement. The tendency among some to oppose economic progress in the name of environmental stewardship is often sadly self-defeating.

Whatever mistakes have occurred or problems arisen, the statement reassures us, do not require serious questioning of modernity, free market economics, or technology, but rather improvements in all of these. The statement is also critical of what it takes to be unfounded concerns with population growth, global warming, and species loss, taking these issues to be speculative, having limited consequences, and lacking substantial evidence. People may fuss about them, but they either aren't really happening or they can be handled without too much trouble. There are, however, many problems that do deserve serious attention. These are predominantly in developing nations: "inadequate sanitation, widespread use of primitive biomass fuels like wood and dung, and primitive agricultural, industrial, and commercial practices; distorted resource consumption patterns driven by perverse economic incentives; and improper disposal of nuclear and other hazardous wastes in nations lacking adequate regulatory and legal safeguards." To respond to such problems, we need a "serious commitment to fostering the intellectual, moral, and religious habits and practices needed for free economies and genuine care for the environment."

It is fascinating how much the Cornwall Declaration shares—and how much it does not—with the kinds of statements we have looked at so far in this book. On the one hand, there is repeated appeal to nature as God's creation and to humanity's special place within creation as careful stewards. But there is none of Pope John Paul's criticism of misdirected technology, of Bartholomew's language of sin, or of Buddhist teachers' negative judgments of consumerism. There is no sense that the environmental crisis calls for profound social change. There is, rather, faith that ecological balance can be achieved only by private property, individual initiative, and freedom from government interference.

For the most part, the signers of the Declaration find serious environmental problems only in poor countries that have yet to receive the blessings of capitalist development and democracy. Problems in third world countries that are caused by the first world—pesticides illegal here that are distributed there, the effects of global warming that are already causing island nations to evacuate their population—are simply not seen. Nor are problems, such as those connected with environmental racism, that unfairly affect certain groups *within* the developed world. There is no mention of how the blessings of capitalism translate into monstrously high cancer rates (caused by uranium extraction) on Native American reservations, or of how coastal Alaskan villages are being submerged by rising sea levels and melting glaciers (caused by global warming). There is no sense that corporate power over media, government, and science can distort even mild-mannered environmental regulations in developed and underdeveloped countries alike. And perhaps most important, the signers do not even consider what would happen to world ecology if even a fraction of the developing world began to approach the level of resource use or greenhouse gas emissions of the United States or Western Europe—an eventuality most ecologists contemplate with enormous dread.

An immediate contrast in tone, orientation, and size of the group in question can be found in the World Council of Churches. This international coalition includes more than 340 churches, denominations, and church fellowships in more than a hundred countries and territories throughout the world and represents some 400 million Christians.[58] Critical questions about market capitalism permeate WCC documents, most notably in relation to the growing powers of the dominant institutions of globalization. These questions often focus on detailed levels of policy or law, but they also cast doubt on the system as a whole. For example, in 2003, in preparation for a meeting with the World Bank, WCC general secretary Konrad Raiser questioned "the allegedly irrefutable logic of the prevailing economic paradigm."[59] Simultaneously, representatives of seventy member churches signed a document stating that "nothing less than a fundamental shift in political-economic paradigms is necessary." In recent years, the WCC's support of ecojustice has typically gone hand in hand with criticism of globalization. This critique sees the widespread growth of poverty, the privatization of natural resources, the encouragement of national debts, and vastly unequal distribution of wealth and consumption of resources as connected to worldwide environmental problems.

To take but one example, we can examine the WCC's participation in the 2000 United Nations Framework Convention on Climate Change, an international meeting centered on how regulations and policies can lessen global warming. The WCC roundly criticized "powerful economic and political interests in some of the richer countries [which] are mounting campaigns to try and persuade the public that the science is faulty and that ratifying the Kyoto Protocol and implementing this commitment will lead to economic disaster."[60] Appealing to the same theological views about creation and stewardship as the Interfaith Council, the WCC takes a diametrically opposed view of the reality and causes of global warming. The statement singles out British Petroleum, Shell, and Exxon-Mobil as examples of "transnational corporations" that bear responsibility for emissions.

The WCC statement on climate change policies included a highly detailed description of the effects of global warming and completely rejected having wealthy nations pay off their vastly excessive emissions at the expense of the undeveloped world.[61] In quite a radical moral initiative, the WCC also called for "contraction and convergence": allowing each country an equal amount of emissions per capita. This measure would allow developing countries some increase, but require that developed nations reduce their emissions dramatically. The earth, said the WCC, is a "Global Commons" and should be governed by norms of justice, not the prerogatives of private property:

> In the use of the global atmospheric commons *all human beings have equal rights*. In practice, some of us have taken an unfair share of this commons. Any system of global atmospheric management must acknowledge this fundamental right. *Any system of global atmospheric management which appears to establish an individual or corporate property right in the atmosphere must be recognized as fundamentally wrong.* Property rights allow for the possibility of exclusion. Exclusion from access to the atmosphere equals death. The human community agrees that human lives may not be mortgaged and human rights may not be sold or exchanged. We need to recognize that the global atmospheric commons may not be traded.[62]

Although the WCC's position is much closer to my own than that of the Interfaith Council, I know that many questions can be raised about it as well. For one thing, the WCC does not say how to accomplish the transition to a fundamentally new "political-economic paradigm," especially as the beneficiaries of the current paradigm control the current social order. Given that the Western nations are democracies, how would they make palatable to voters an appeal to significantly lessen energy consumption, or even stop its increase? How well, after all, would "No Economic Growth" do as a campaign slogan? Further, adopting anything like the WCC's principles on global warming would require unprecedented acts of international human solidarity. How would such solidarity emerge? Can we really imagine asking people in Texas or Montana to trade in their SUVs for Honda hybrids so that people in Ghana or Guatemala can have better lives? Also, if a free market will not solve our economic needs, what evidence does the WCC have that some other system will do better? Finally, because churches have not tended to directly support progressive or green political parties, what organization would make the wonderful religious proclamations come to life? Are such sweeping environmental demands little more than ecological repeats of other warm and fuzzy religious maxims, as often repeated and as rarely followed as "Love thy neighbor" and "Blessed are the peacemakers"?

Even if these pointed questions are not answered, the WCC's position is a clear call for popular movements and a powerful regulatory mechanism to restrict, if not to eliminate, corporate economic and social power. Seeking the good of the world community rather than that of any restricted group, religious environmentalists often find themselves compelled to such an extremely progressive, one might even say radical, political viewpoint. Although exceptions such as the Interfaith Council exist, for the most part, environmentalism drives religious groups to the political left. This is a remarkable development. To anyone familiar with earlier relations between religion and leftist politics, it is no small irony that the WCC's criticisms of globalization are far more sweeping and severe than those of the AFL-CIO.

In the end, perhaps, the crucial differences between the WCC and the Interfaith Council turn on their respective interpretations of the history of capitalism and their confidence that another system is possible. Because their ecological readings of scripture are not that far apart, their sharp political and economic disagreements show that environmental policies can never be shaped by theology alone. Our various attitudes toward science, governmental policy, and the economy—or, we might say, our overall political viewpoint—will also come into play. Thus, religious ethics compels believers not only to engage in political life, but also to adopt political ideologies to direct that engagement. These political ideologies are no more contained or determined by religious tradition than are the designs of the local minister's cell phone. There is nothing in Genesis, no matter how ecologically interpreted, that will tell us whether free market capitalism can be reformed, whether extending private property or limiting it will be better for nature and human health, or whether the World Bank can be taught to seriously include ecological concerns in its loans or should be scrapped entirely.

This point is significant because religious voices sometimes describe themselves as above or outside politics, simply applying Universal Truths rather than being partisans. This claim is naïve in the extreme. *Any* serious environmental position has serious political implications, for any serious environmentalism requires that we make basic changes in the way we do things. These changes will, at least in the short run, tend to favor some groups over others: organic farmers over pesticide manufacturers, workers who produce solar panels over workers who assemble SUVs, local tribes over corporations that want the oil that lies under the tribes' villages. Thus, religious environmentalism cannot avoid being political, for it must take positions on questions of who will and who will not benefit from a particular policy, law, or regulation.

If religious environmentalists wish to claim any special status because they are religious, it must be not by being above or outside of politics, but by pursuing politics in a distinctly religious way. Taking the lead of spiritual social activists from Martin Luther King Jr. and Gandhi to Burma's Ang San Suu Kyi and our own Daniel Berrigan, this means, I believe, to do so honestly, compassionately, and courageously. It means to maintain a profound personal respect for one's bitterest opponent, to be open to criticism and rethinking, and to be as detached as possible from the pursuit of personal power or success within the movement. It does *not* mean trying to maintain an impossible political neutrality.[63]

❧

Ecotheology and institutional commitment are important. In a world where the imperatives of growth, consumption, military power, pleasure, or immediate survival predominate, simply naming long-term, comprehensive and inclusive goals and values is a step toward an alternative to the current level of harm. If statements by the pope or the Dalai Lama are not likely to make a secular anthropocentric turn in his gas-guzzler and vote for the local Green Party, they can and do help committed Catholics or Buddhists reexamine the meaning of their faith. Further, for middle-of-the-road types who have mixed feelings about whether all this stuff is really that important, they serve as additional reasons to take environmental issues seriously. These statements are, at the very least, another link in the chain of a worldwide environmental movement.

Yet, if things are messy in the public world, they can be equally vexing within religious institutions themselves, for political questions involve not just how religious leaders say the wider world should be run, but the conduct of religions as well. This is a problem because, I believe, most religions still have to confront the full seriousness and complexity of the moral demands of environmentalism. On the one hand, the strength of many statements indicates that this has become a serious, central matter. How we treat nature is a moral question and thus an essential part of our religious identity, no more a matter of personal choice than stealing or adultery. When Bartholomew calls pollution a sin, or the Filipino bishops tell us that the pursuit of justice and the integrity of creation are inseparable parts of a Christian vocation, their faithful followers have been told that environmentalism is now part of their faith.

At the same time, and here lies the heart of the problem, both the leaders and the followers of world religion—just like everyone else—face a disquieting reality. When Bartholomew calls polluting the world a sin at a conference in California, surely he knows that his airplane trip to the conference, just like every other jet flight, damaged the ozone layer. Each religious environmentalist in the developed world, and probably many in other places as well, plugs into the same power grid, drives a car, eats food produced by unecological agribusiness, and in all likelihood doesn't recycle every little bit of paper used in writing the rough drafts of his or her impassioned statements on ecology and faith. From the pope to the rabbis to the world-famous Buddhist teachers (and the author of this book), we are all involved, all somewhat guilty.[64]

When religions adopt environmentalism, then, they face a daunting moral complexity. On the one hand, it would be an attractive prospect to think of corporate polluters (or your neighbor who drives a Humvee) being no more welcome in religious settings than pornographers or child abusers. One has a hard time imagining the producer of *Deep Throat* on the board of directors of the local temple or church. Yet any comparable rejection of those most responsible for the environmental crisis does not occur. If bishops talk of refusing communion to politicians who support abortion rights, surely they could do no less to those who would gut the Environmental Protection Agency, or to the corporate executives whose huge financial contributions pressure the government to do so. Yet, neither the money nor the participation of CEOs of clear-cutting logging companies or pesticide manufacturers are turned away by religious institutions. The idea, as far as I can tell, has not even crossed anyone's mind.

Still, this may be a good thing. In the end, thundering, self-righteous denunciations of polluters, despite the difference between them and ordinary citizens, will probably not work. After all, the self-righteous denouncers, we know, are also part of the problem. The priest who watches the Playboy Channel must treat Hugh Hefner with compassion, and the ministers who drive to work rather than riding a bike must admit to their own failings even as they argue against low-mileage cars, tax breaks for the auto industry, and too little government support for public transportation.

Like other moral problems, this one can be a profound opportunity for growth. Surely for those who are not saints (which would seem to be just about all of us), the essential (but too often unrealized) task of moral life has always been to combine principled morality with compassion for human weakness, a compassion partly rooted in awareness of our own failings. The trick, of course, is to balance the two: an excess of compassion and self-awareness can cripple our ability to name sin, immorality, and unethical conduct for what they are; too much righteousness can make us arrogant, supercilious, and addicted to the pleasures of moral superiority. Dealing with the complexity of the environmental crisis poses this dilemma in perhaps its starkest form. It will be enormously interesting to see how religions learn to deal with it.

CHAPTER 4

RELIGIOUS ENVIRONMENTALISM
IN ACTION

We come here as multi-racial and multi-cultural witnesses to shed light on long-term health consequences associated with toxic waste. . . . We are here to name the sin of environmental racism and to renew our call for real and lasting environmental justice in order that the burden of toxic waste will be shared by all—and not just some.

—The Rev. Henry Simmons, board chair, Justice and
Witness Ministries of the United Church of Christ, protesting
a plan to incinerate nerve gas in East St. Louis, April 20, 2002

By depleting energy sources, causing global warming, fouling the air with pollution, and poisoning the land with radioactive waste, a policy of increased reliance on fossil fuels and nuclear power jeopardizes health and well-being for life on Earth.

—"Let There Be Light," an open letter to President George W. Bush,
signed by thirty-nine heads of denominations and senior leaders of
major American faith groups, May 18, 2001

When unethical harvesting of trees is infringing on the health of the land, on sacred mountains, then we have to protect it.

—Earl Tulley, Diné (Navajo) Committee Against
Ruining the Environment, quoted in *Ernie Atencio*, "After a Heavy
Harvest and a Death, Navajo Forestry Realigns with Culture,"
Western Roundup, October 31, 1994

WASHINGTON, DC, MAY 3, 2001

After two days of meetings and lobbying, prayer services and press releases, fifty-year-old Episcopalian priest Margaret Bullitt-Jonas, accompanied by twenty-two other ministers, priests, rabbis, and lay people, many in their clerical robes, moved toward the gates of the Department of Energy. Nearly 150 supporters looked on as the slender, dark-haired Bullitt-Jonas knelt in prayer. Capital police demanded that she and her fellows leave, and when they refused, they were arrested.

This action, which drew participants from as far away as Alaska and California, was focused on the energy policy of the Bush administration, and in particular on its stated goal of drilling for oil in the Arctic National Wildlife Refuge. The protest had been organized by Religious Witness for the Earth, a network of religiously oriented environmentalists from diverse faith traditions "dedicated to public witness in defense of God's creation." Signed by Protestants, Catholics, Jews, Buddhists, and Muslims, the call to demonstrate had declared that ANWR should be protected as a sacred place for its native inhabitants, a haven for wildlife, and a "cathedral for the human spirit to glory in God's handiwork." "As a born-again Christian, President Bush must understand that creation is sacred," said Rev. Fred Small, cochair of RWE. "His drill-and-burn energy policy endangers not only the wonders of nature but human existence itself. Despoiling the earth is sacrilege, and exhausting its resources is theft from our own children."

For seventeen of the twenty-two RWE members arrested, it was their first time behind bars, something that ordinarily would be considered shameful. Yet, Bullitt-Jonas tells us, she was inspired to participate because during Easter Holy Week, while pondering the sufferings of Jesus, she felt that she needed to witness against today's "greedy mindset that the earth is ours to devour."[1] "I felt," she writes, "as defiant as a maple seedling that pushes up through asphalt. It is God I love, and God's green earth. . . . We may have nothing else, but we do have this, the power to say, 'This is where I stand. This is what I love. Here is something for which I'm willing to put my body on the line.' "[2]

HEADWATERS FOREST, HUMBOLDT COUNTY, CALIFORNIA, JANUARY 26, 1997

It was Tu B'Shvat, the Jewish "New Year of the Trees," and 250 celebrants had enjoyed a traditional ritual meal honoring the place of trees in human life and the bounty of God in providing them.[3] Then about ninety people walked over a boundary line into a six-thousand-acre section of old-growth redwoods owned by the Maxaam Corporation, a section that Maxaam planned to cut. In defiance of Maxaam's orders, the celebrants-turned-demonstrators planted redwood seedlings in a denuded stream bank.

Over the preceding eighteen months, three local rabbis had pursued Maxaam CEO Charles Hurwitz, a leading member of the Houston Jewish community. They had asked him to "turn completely," in Hebrew to make *tshuvah*, and cease cutting the ancient trees. His willingness to despoil the area, they argued, violated Jewish ethics. They wrote to him that they were praying that God would "soften your heart and give you clear guidance so that your future actions might reflect the wisdom and generosity of Jewish tradition."[4] They had taken out ads in national papers arguing that the old-growth redwoods of Headwaters provide critical habitat for several endangered species and pointing out that whereas only 150 years ago the redwood forests of Oregon and California covered 2 million acres, now less than 4 percent remain.

Perhaps because many of the protestors wore traditional Jewish prayer shawls, perhaps because they had been careful to inform Maxaam and the police beforehand of their plans, the authorities allowed the civil disobedience to proceed without arrest. "At a place where demonstrators before have been met with billy clubs, nightsticks, and arrests, we are now walking freely," said a local environmental activist who had been struggling to protect the areas for years. "It reminds me of the parting of the Red Sea."[5]

∾

Religious environmentalism is a worldwide movement of political, social, ecological, and cultural action. As expressions of a particular religion, in ecumenical alliances with other traditions, through loose networks of spiritually committed activists, and in coalitions with secular environmental organizations, hundreds of groups have resisted global warming, destructive economic "development," dangerous toxic waste dumps, reckless resource extraction, mindless consumerism, and simple waste. In a wonderful pattern of interfaith cooperation, believers have shown that they are capable of actively working with people whose theologies are quite different from their own. Contrary to the widespread secular liberal belief that religion is inherently antidemocratic, religious environmentalists have shown both a broad openness and a deep civic concern.

The two actions described above are themselves part of ongoing movements and campaigns. Religious Witness for the Earth continues its work to this day, its accomplishments including a 2002 Interfaith Service of Prayer and Witness for Climate Action, held inside the Massachusetts State House and in the capitols of every other New England state. The goal was to call on the New England governors to actually implement their agreed-upon climate change action plan. Later, in well-publicized actions in Northampton and Lynn, Massachusetts, activists challenged fuel-hogging SUVs and confronted representatives of automobile companies. In 2003, a public Witness for Creation at the UN drew three hundred participants from surrounding areas.

RWE's leaders have consistently claimed the mantle—and the tactics—of committed religious social activism. "I wanted to explore," said Fred Small, "how to apply the lessons of Gandhi and Martin Luther King, Jr. to a challenge of comparable moral urgency."[6] In their commitment to direct action, says cofounder and United Church of Christ minister Dr. Andrea Ayvazian, they have "upped the ante" for religious leaders, demanding political action along with a greener theology.[7]

The "Redwood Rabbis" actions in Northern California are part of environmentalist efforts by the larger American Jewish community. In these efforts, two organizations have been central. The Shalom Center, headed by veteran social activist and Jewish Renewal rabbi Arthur Waskow, helped design the Tu B'Shvat seder and has long been engaged in bringing a Jewish presence to key environmental issues. The Center's activities have ranged from promoting "Olive Trees for Peace" in an effort to forge peaceful ties among Jews and Palestinians, to its current campaign against the uncontrolled power of "Big Oil," which, they charge, "incites war, endangers the earth, intensifies the asthma epidemic, corrupts U.S. politics, and shatters indigenous peoples in Africa, Latin America, and Asia."[8]

The Coalition on the Environment and Jewish Life (COEJL) began in the spring of 1992 when, partly at the invitation of Al Gore and Carl Sagan, the leadership of the major organizations in American Jewish life, eminent rabbis, denominational presidents, and Jewish U.S. senators gathered in Washington, DC, to create a specifically Jewish response to the environmental crisis. The following year, COEJL was established as a joint project of the Jewish Council for Public Affairs, the Religious Action Center of Reform Judaism, the Jewish Theological Seminary, and several other organizations. The Coalition is now a national organization of Jewish environmental concern, education, and activism, with chapters in twenty-five states and Canada, national offices in New York City, San Francisco, and Washington, and a yearly budget of nearly $1 million. It draws institutional support from twenty-nine national Jewish organizations, including some of the largest and most powerful. On the national scene, it has prodded Detroit to produce cleaner and more fuel-efficient cars and offered free congregational energy guides to make synagogues greener. Action by its forty regional affiliates range from the Boston group's integral role in publicizing environmental justice issues, to Philadelphia's help in organizing a demonstration against the disastrous environmental policies of the Bush administration, and Vancouver's advocating of eight environmental actions for the eight nights of Chanukah ("turn down the thermostat," "skip a car trip," "recycle your paper," etc.).[9]

Recently, COEJL has been instrumental in facilitating information exchange and joint projects between environmentalists in the United States and Israel. Its most important contribution, says its representative in Washington, is "the fact that the American Jewish community has become increasingly focused on energy policies, global warming, conservation, and on the environment in Israel. People don't wonder who COEJL is and what the environment has to do with being Jewish any more."[10]

Much of what follows in this chapter focuses on the United States, but a good deal does not, for, contrary to stereotypes of environmentalists as effete, politically correct, white liberals from rich countries, religious environmentalism is truly a *global* phenomenon, involving members of virtually every religious group, race, and culture on the planet.

To get an idea of this global character, consider some of the work of the internationally oriented and UK-based Alliance for Religions and Conservation, which emerged in 1996 after the World Wildlife Fund convened a meeting of five major world faiths to discuss their relation to ecology. Since then, the member faiths of the Alliance have grown to nine, and the organization— often in partnership with local governments, environmental groups, development programs, and even the World Bank—has initiated and supported projects throughout the world. In 2000 the ARC hosted a celebratory meeting, "Sacred Gifts to a Living Planet," in Nepal to honor actions to care for the environment undertaken by religions throughout the world. A brief description of a few of the thirty-six gifts ARC has recognized will indicate how widespread religious environmentalism is.

In 2000, Madagascar fishermen were convinced to stop dynamiting the ocean for fish, a practice with disastrous long-term results to fish populations and undersea coral ecology, when local Islamic authorities ruled that the practice violated the Qur'an's injunctions against wasting God's creation. The fishermen had been blithely ignoring both government pamphlets and strict laws forbidding the use of dynamite. As ARC leader Martin Palmer put it, "By throwing sticks of dynamite into the sea, they could haul in almost guaranteed catches and it took so little time."[11] It was only when their sheiks— who had been brought together by joint efforts of the ARC, the London-based Islamic Foundation for Ecology and Environmental Science, the World Wildlife Fund, and CARE International—applied the Qur'an to dynamite fishing and declared the practice decidedly un-Islamic that things began to change. Since then, dynamite fishing has been dramatically lessened and plans for sustainable fishing have emerged. (A remarkably similar story unfolded among Hindu fishermen and an endangered shark species off the coast of India.)[12]

Appeals to Islamic teaching are also central to Saudi Arabia's commitment to protect its biodiversity, a project directed by its National Commission for Wildlife Conservation and Development. "The reserve's creation and management embodies specific Islamic rulings relating to the sustainable management of natural resources especially through the concept of 'hima,' a traditional method of protecting range land and water resources."[13] Explaining its goals, the commission directly links theology and ecology:

> Islamic teachings maintain that nothing has been created without value and purpose; all creatures are signs of the Creator and glorify Him in unique ways, and all have been given roles by which they contribute to the common good. Hence man in his role as steward on the earth is obliged to conserve them in

all their forms.... The Commission acts as the custodian over the integrity of the biodiversity of the Kingdom.... Although man has the right to use these resources, he is not permitted to abuse them. He is required to pass them on to future generations in an unimpaired condition.[14]

Half a world away from the Saudi desert, researchers at the Beijing School of Traditional Chinese Medicine are trying to protect endangered species by looking for alternative ingredients for traditional medicines. Treatments for a variety of illnesses call for components such as tiger penis, bear gall, and rhinoceros horn. Despite international bans on the hunting of many of these animals, the high price they fetch encourages widespread poaching. Arguing that use of endangered species violates Buddhist and Taoist principles of balance in nature, and thus is bad for both the environment and the soul, these world-renowned Taoist physicians are changing long-used prescriptions. The wide-ranging authority of the Beijing School will lessen the use of endangered species by traditional practitioners and perhaps save a few from extinction.

From fishermen eking out a living on the African coast and poachers drawing a bead on endangered rhinos in Africa we go to India, where the Sikh community has committed itself to a three-hundred-year project of energy conservation. Through their network of 28,000 temples, Sikhs provide free meals for tens of millions of people a day. By adopting solar power and fuel-efficient technology, they hope to reduce energy consumption by at least 15 percent. Some of the largest temples have also initiated a series of projects to raise ecological awareness, reduce pollution, and improve damaged ecosystems. Actions include tree planting, promoting solar energy, encouraging recycling, and improving water management.[15]

Forests in Sweden, Japan, and Lebanon protected by Lutherans, Shintoists, and Maronite Christians, Jewish synagogues in England and Buddhist pagodas in Cambodia proclaiming a new green gospel, a rubbish dump converted to a park by Muslims in Cairo and U.S. Methodists confronting Staples about selling paper whose production causes toxic dioxins in the water and air— the list continues. These examples show that religious environmentalism, though not necessarily stemming the tide of environmental destruction, has become a worldwide force for a cleaner, healthier planet and for more moral relations among human beings and between human beings and other species.

In the rest of the chapter, I explore some examples of this exciting movement in greater detail. We will first see how activists in southern Africa and in small Catholic communities in the United States care for the land on which they live, responding to immediate contexts of life and livelihood. I contrast their intensely local actions with the campaigns of international networks aimed at the critical but more remote issue of global climate change. We will also get a sense of how significant political differences can exist within the environmentalism of one particular faith, comparing an emphasis on individual environmental action by a Taiwanese Buddhist organization with the truly revolutionary economic and social perspective of Sri Lanka's Sar Movement. Next I briefly describe the decisive role of the United Ch Christ in the emergence of environmental justice as a critical concept for religious and secular environmentalism alike, a concept that has literally transformed much of the world environmental community. As a special case of environmental justice concerns, I then examine indigenous environmental activism, whose unique character is rooted in the distinctly ecological character of indigenous spiritual traditions and the intense cultural connections between indigenous peoples and their land. Finally, we will see some examples of the important ways religious environmentalists have made common cause with secular ones.

Activist religious environmentalism goes beyond theology and public declarations. It is directly aimed at changing the world: by making new laws, stopping harmful practices, creating better ways to produce and consume, healing the earth, and nurturing human beings in their relations with the rest of life. *Politically* it seeks to generate a collective force of voters, demonstrators, long-term activists, tree planters, and energy conservers. *Ecologically* it treats the earth with care and respect, hoping to replace our current system with organic agriculture, habitat restoration, the conservation of biodiversity, alternative technology, and renewable energy. *Morally* it pursues justice in the distribution of negative ecological effects.

ZIMBABWE

Chivi District, April 8, 1993

Having taken communion at a tree-planting Eucharist conducted by a member church of the African Association of Earthkeeping Churches (AAEC), the Rev. Solomon Zvanaka addresses the seedling he is about to plant: "You, tree, I plant you. Provide us with clean air to breathe and all the other benefits which Mwari [God] has commanded. We in turn will take care of you, because in Jesus Christ you are one with us. He has created all things to be united in him. I shall not chop down another tree. Through you, tree, I do penance for all the trees I have felled."[16]

Shrine of Mwari, Matopo Hills, Masvingo Province, January 17, 1992

After years of brutal drought that left nearly half a million people receiving food handouts, the spirit mediums of the Association of Zimbabwean Traditional Ecologists (AZTREC) have come to hear instructions from Mwari issue from a mysterious cult cave. An ancient female voice tells them, "The

world is spoilt. I shall give you only sparse rains. . . . Persevere with the planting of trees! I shall keep my hand over you."[17]

These two scenes highlight the remarkable coalition of Independent African Christian churches and traditional African religions in a groundbreaking coalition to repair the ravaged landscape in southern Zimbabwe's Masvingo province. The coalition, formally known by the slightly intimidating
title of the Zimbabwean Institute of Religious Research and Ecological Conservation (and more easily as ZIRRCON), has played an important role in
reversing ecological decline and galvanizing African peasants to act in their
own defense. ZIRRCON was the initiative of Marthinus L. Daneel, a
Rhodesian-born professor of theology who developed contacts with both
Christians and traditionalists while researching the role of religion in Zimbabwe's independence struggle in the 1980s. With some prompting by Daneel, communities facing denuded countryside, eroded hillsides, and deteriorating riverbanks committed themselves to a "war of the trees" in 1988.
Mobilized by a common threat, this cooperative effort between unlikely allies
grew to a province-wide organization with forty salaried employees, the majority of chiefs and mediums in the area, 150 churches with nearly 2 million
members, eighty women's clubs, and thirty youth clubs. It has planted over
8 million trees in thousands of woodlots, raised awareness about and applied
religious sanctions against damaging wildlife and water practices, placed ecological issues in a framework of social action and political liberation, and
roused peasants from resigned passivity.[18]

The accomplishments of ZIRRCON embody many of the distinct characteristics of religious environmentalism. Perhaps most dramatic, this is a
strikingly *ecumenical* effort, one all the more remarkable because it involves
strikingly different religions. Far more than a matter of Methodists working
with Catholics or Christians with Jews, ZIRRCON is an alliance between
Christianity and spirit- and ancestor-centered religions that have wildly different religious beliefs. It is the kind of alliance that for centuries would have
been unthinkable, for Christians would simply have rejected the traditionalists as ignorant. Yet, in the context of their environmental vocation, most of
the members of the Earthkeeping Christian churches have maintained an
attitude of respectful comradeship with the non-Christians. As Daneel said
in an early assessment of the partnership, "The mediums should wage war
against deforestation in terms of their own beliefs and the churches should
do so on Christian Principles. Each movement should have its own religious
identity but they should recognize the value of each other's contribution."[19]
Bishop Machokoto, after being elected AAEC president, warned his fellow
Christians, "We must be fully prepared to recognize the authority of our
krallheads and chiefs. For if we show contempt for them, where will we plant
our trees? . . . Let our bishops in their eagerness to fight the war of the trees
not antagonize the keepers of the land. . . . Let us fully support our tribal
elders in this struggle of afforestation."[20] Comparable moves were made on

the traditional side. For example, it was Daneel's role in the founding of ZIRRCON that enabled him to be the first white man to attend the ceremony of the cult oracle described above. Similarly, though conflicts among different Christian denominations did not disappear, they tended to pale into insignificance in the context of meetings, conferences, shared rituals, and ecological efforts.

This was not the first time either the traditional or the Christian churches had responded to a critical social issue. Their political sensibilities and capacity for decisive action had been proven in the struggle for independence. In that struggle, both groups had made important contributions, including supporting military actions, providing resources for fighters, and lending their social prestige to the struggle. Just as Fred Small appeals to the history of social activism of Gandhi and King, and (as we will see below) some of the "Green sisters" in the United States see themselves as having been formed by the civil rights, antiwar, and feminist movements of the 1970s, so ZIRRCON could view its war of the trees as a continuation of activist religion from the past. Its religious environmentalism is, and has to be, political.

We have seen that religious environmentalism is both rooted in tradition and a creative transformation called forth to meet the demands of the environmental crisis. This creative tension was present in ZIRRCON as well. For a start, traditional religion had always involved beliefs and practices to help conserve land, water, and wildlife. As one observer says of some remaining forests of the Zambezi basin, not too far from ZIRRCON's Masvingo province, despite the economic pressure to use the land for cotton, a few key areas—because they were religiously protected—have been preserved: "If they weren't sacred, the forests would have been long gone."[21] Yet, as valuable as traditional values and practices were, they depended on a steady-state subsistence economy. Increases in population, profit-oriented deforestation, overuse of water for commercial farms, soil erosion, and a decade-long drought created something profoundly new. In response, traditional religious leaders have changed Africa's "age-old religio-ecological values into a modern programme of environmental reform."[22] Mwari morphed from a rain god into a god of ecology, and it turned out that the spirit ancestors would no longer be satisfied with the observance of age-old ecological taboos against taking certain game or felling sacred trees. They now demanded that people heal the land, reforest the earth, and protect the water. Believers could not simply perform religious rituals to convince God to bring rain; actual ecological work (i.e., tree planting) had to be done to help make it happen.

Although the African Independent Churches already had a strong sense of social engagement, they, too, had to change. The face of Jesus had to be seen in the trees and the water, and the power of God had to be understood as an Earthkeeping power that Christians were compelled to manifest in their own lives. Every Christian was urged to recognize his or her responsibility for the health of the land. In a sermon in 1991, Daneel reminded his listeners,

"Whenever you celebrate Holy Communion, be mindful that in devastating the earth we ourselves are party to destroying the body of Christ. We are all guilty in this respect."[23] And indeed, it is an essential part of the compelling ritualistic innovation of the tree-planting Eucharist that *all* participants, from the most humble peasants to the most senior bishops, confess their ecological sins of cutting trees without planting, overgrazing the land, or injuring the riverbanks—and *then* proceed to plant a tree.

Concern with the land is a life-and-death matter for these residents of Masvingo. But their environmentalism goes far beyond purely instrumental or conservationist values. They know that caring for the earth is good for people—but that is not the only reason they do it. In the quote that began this section, it is striking that Rev. Zvanaka did not simply ask God to bless the seedling in the hope that his parishioners would have healthier soil and more rain. Rather, he talked directly *to* the seedling, including it as part of a community sanctified by Christ. Environmentalism for these churches is a matter of love for creation as well as enhancing their own material well-being. As God's love was manifest in the creation of the earth, so those who believe in God are to imitate God by showing their love for what God created.

We find in the case of ZIRRCON that once again religion has a particularly important role to play in environmentalism because of its distinct capacity to motivate. When the spirit mediums of AZTREC told their followers that they were obeying the demands of their ancestors, unprecedented ecological activity followed. When the African Independent Churches took on the task of environmental stewardship, people acted, something that usually did not happen in response to the appeals of governmental experts or secular environmental organizations.

The fusion of tradition and innovation, human and ecological concern, ecumenism and political action that we find in ZIRRCON is not limited to one province of Zimbabwe, but is echoed in many other parts of the region. South African churches, many of which played a crucial role in the struggle against apartheid, for example, are engaged in a variety of ecological activities.[24] In the 1990s, the Faith and Earthkeeping Project functioned in almost every South African province, stimulating interest in environmental care in religious circles and working with religious groups to develop community-based environmental conservation projects, including tree planting, water protection, urban greening, and recycling. In the town of Philadelphia, a Dutch Reformed congregation led a successful struggle against building a toxic waste facility. In the poor, rural district of Umzimvubu, Anglican bishop Geoff Davies, after a decade of working to bring ecological concern into the heart of the church, formed the Umzimvubu Sustainable Agriculture and Environmental Education Programme, which supports local communities wishing to start sustainable gardens and offers advice on earth care, land reclamation, and recycling. Davies, popularly known as the "Green Bishop," also drew wide notice for his outspoken criticism of a government plan to build a large toll highway though Umzimvubu, arguing that it would be an ecological and human disaster, flagrantly disregard international conferences on biodiversity held in South Africa, and violate South Africa's own laws.[25]

More recently, an umbrella organization, the Network of Earthkeeping Christian Communities in South Africa, has organized conferences, sent representatives to national and international meetings, and chronicled detailed struggles in local towns and villages. The stated commitment of the Network is ecojustice: in an inclusive vision, love of God's creation takes its place alongside resistance to unjust corporate power, foreign investment, distorted forms of economic development, the oppression of women, and genetically modified crops.[26] Here environmentalism is a key element in determining how economic development affects people's day-to-day existence. In the words of a retired priest and development worker from Umzimvubu, "Sustainable agriculture can liberate us from the chains of dependence and starvation."[27]

Traditional African religions have always been keyed to the health of the land. Any serious Christian who cares about the life and death of his or her neighbors must sooner or later recognize that responding to environmental damage is part of that care. Therefore, it is not surprising that from Masvingo to Umzimvubu—and in countless other places—religious leaders, congregations, and organizations are an essential part of environmental activism in Africa. Whether they can do enough, soon enough, in the face of that continent's enormous poverty, illness, and widespread governmental and ethnic violence, remains to be seen.

FAYETTEVILLE, ARKANSAS, JULY 15–18, 2004

The sixth annual and tenth anniversary meeting of Sisters of Earth, a loose network of nuns, combined "panels and presentations about sustainability, institutional and congregational greening, eco-spirituality, earth literacy, bioregionalism, and social justice with ritual, celebration, and song."[28] An altar was constructed with material from the different bioregions of the nearly ninety participants, who joined in a newly created ceremony honoring endangered species, focusing specifically on select animals and plants from the United States and Iraq. The directors of the Denver-based grassroots organization EarthLinks shared how they combined devotion to the earth with care for people, seeking to empower the socially powerless by connecting them to earth community.[29] Other speakers criticized genetic engineering and described their resistance to mining companies that literally cut the tops off mountains and leave behind millions of tons of refuse in nearby communities.

Like ZIRRCON, the Sisters of Earth focus their attention on the human connection to the earth, seeking to repair a deeply injured relationship. Yet, as inhabitants of the world's richest country, their immediate context takes a very different shape. Whereas many in Africa find that ecological damage threatens them on the basic level of food and water, most in North America face sterile urban or suburban settings, an ever increasing sprawl in which everything looks increasingly alike. Unless we live in California or Florida, the vast majority of our food comes from hundreds or thousands of miles away, most of it nearly tasteless, laced with additives, or genetically engineered. We are much more likely to confront obesity than starvation, and farming is something conducted by multibillion-dollar agribusinesses using poor migrant workers made sick by pesticide exposure. Our closest connection to the land is at best a small garden and lawn on which we lavish chemical fertilizers and carcinogenic pesticides. Ravaged landscapes are pawned off on the poor and people of color, especially on Native Americans, whose lands bear huge burdens from mining, toxic incineration, and coal-fired power plants. And all this is embedded in a cultural frame in which humans have pretty much unchallenged rights to use, consume, and abuse the rest of the earth at will.

Against this ecological and social background the Sisters of Earth, an informal network of some three hundred Catholic nuns, took shape in the early 1990s. Many of the women were inspired by the ecotheological teachings of Thomas Berry, particularly his stress on human kinship with the rest of life and the way he situated human beings within the cosmic history of the universe and the path of evolution. Some were long-term veterans of progressive politics, having been active in the antiwar, women's, and human rights movements from the 1970s on. Some were recently awakened, partly by the statements of Pope John Paul II and bishops from Appalachia to the Philippines and partly by recognition of the seriousness of the environmental crisis and the immorality of American individualism, consumerism, and anthropocentrism. These diverse origins have led them to a common goal: to, as one observer writes, "reinhabit the earth," to live and teach a form of life in which humans treat the rest of the earth with respect and care, integrating themselves into their own places sustainably and gently.[30]

Sisters of Earth try to infuse these values in their personal lives, the way their communities function, and in contributions to surrounding towns. Their activities include organic gardening, land conservation, reducing consumption, using alternative building materials, solar heating, and hybrid vehicles, and building wildlife sanctuaries. As Carol Coston, cofounder of Santuario Sisterfarm in Texas, says, they want to "find a way to live lightly on the earth."[31] Chris Loughlin, director of the Crystal Spring Earth Literacy Center in Massachusetts, estimates that more than five hundred people help support their community farm and enjoy its organic produce; New Jersey's Genesis Farm serves six times that number and has educated nearly seven hundred people in its extended "earth literacy" courses. EarthLinks of Denver created a "BioBox" program that teaches elementary school students about their bioregion and links children from different regions. They also involve homeless people in gardening projects to help raise both their income and their pride, while connecting them to the healing benefits of gardening.[32] Santuario takes as its focus the preservation and promotion of diversity, in social as well as ecological forms. Quoting Indian ecologist and globalization critic Vandana Shiva, they maintain, "An intolerance of diversity is the biggest threat to peace in our times; conversely, the cultivation of diversity is the most significant contribution to peace—peace with nature and between diverse peoples." To this end, they seek to "bring awareness of the dangerous loss of biodiversity and the exploitation of economically impoverished peoples by multinational corporations that have been usurping the seed lines developed over centuries by small farmers and indigenous peoples around the world."[33] The political implications of this project are reflected in its name, the Rosa y Martín Seed Project, which echoes the names of two Peruvian Dominican priests who sided with native peoples against colonialism.

While the sisters applaud the work of groups like the Sierra Club and the Audubon Society, they seek a format for their work in which the spiritual dimension of a kind of universal respect and care is essential. As Mary Romano of EarthLinks puts it, any real change in our environmental practices "must come from a place of love." Echoing Thomas Berry, Chris Loughlin says she hopes Crystal Springs activities—community-supported agriculture, hosting retreats on ecocosmology—will help people develop a new sense of self and create caring relationships with the web of life. To take one small example of this attitude of ecological respect: parts of Genesis Farm are simply off-limits to people. While the farm is committed to growing organic food for human consumption, they also want to leave part of the earth to itself.[34]

The Sisters of Earth also seek to be a force for this changed consciousness in their local communities. Mary Romano, who practices an eclectic spirituality, says that EarthLinks' greatest accomplishment is the way it helps "people establish a personal relation with the natural world, which then enables people to make positive changes in personal life." Miriam MacGillis, who oversees Genesis Farm's 140 acres and nearly quarter-million-dollar annual budget, takes deep joy in the way the farm serves as an "amazing developer of community. Individuals, families, children—they grow up with a cultural life tied to the farm."[35]

Along with their stress on moral change and community organizing, many of these women have a clear sense of the larger social and political implications of what they are doing. They may not couch their concerns in leftist rhetoric, but they have no doubt that society, no less than their organic gardens, requires decentralization, diversity, and interdependence.[36] As politically committed environmentalists, they engage in "disrupting shareholder meetings of corporate polluters, contesting the construction of garbage incinerators, and combating suburban sprawls."[37] Although most activity is lo-

cal, some have been active with national or international agencies. Jane Blew-
ett of Earth Community Center in Maryland monitors UN debates on
sustainable development, having spent years working for an internationally
oriented Catholic social justice organization. She regularly conducts workshops on "Justice for People, Justice for Earth: Two Sides of the Same Coin."
Other sisters are engaged with Worldwatch, the Environmental Defense
Fund, and Greenpeace.[38] Gail Worcelo of Vermont's Green Mountain Monastery, which she cofounded with Thomas Berry, puts it simply: her goal is
the health of the total earth community, and thus she resists processes and
products that unbalance that health or privilege one part over another. Dominican sister Carol Coston offers a direct criticism of global capitalism: "Its
tendency to look only for the bottom line makes it impervious to its effects
on local economies. Instead of growing for their families, people are made
to grow for export." Further, "when agribusinesses develop genetically modified seeds, they threaten the livelihood of small farmers throughout the
world, as well as pose a danger to seed stock biodiversity."[39]

Finally, Sisters of Earth manifest a profound ecumenical respect for other
religious paths. Many are open about what they have learned from Buddhist
meditation or earth-honoring indigenous peoples. Non-Catholics work at
their centers; yoga and meditation are taught at their conferences. "We welcome all people of goodwill," says Miriam MacGillis. Like the different groups
in ZIRRCON, the Sisters of Earth have both maintained and transformed
their religious allegiance. They remain Catholic, but Catholicism for them
now unfolds in the context of a 14-billion-year-old universe. They believe in
the Trinity, but now see Father, Son, and Holy Spirit as permeating all of life,
including human beings who have different names—or no names at all—for
God.

If this small group of activist women is not likely to lead a revolution,
they are keeping alive the hope that human relations with the earth can be
repaired. Each of the centers is a small oasis amid the temples of hypercon-
sumption and the cavalier abuse of the land. Each center offers a place where
we can honor something of which many have only the faintest memory.
Ultimately, what they teach and the way they live is part of the promise that
we can change—here and now—some of what we are doing. However many
lives they touch, this is a profound contribution to global environmental
action.

☙

For the most part, African Earthkeepers and the Sisters of Earth are responding to their immediate surroundings: planting trees and protecting local wildlife and water, growing food with love and intelligence rather than chemicals,
and trying to live a bit lighter on the earth. On the other end of the spectrum
of environmental concern are global problems, the causes and effects of

which may be separated by thousands of miles. These problems, too, are being addressed by a variety of religious environmentalists.

The most momentous of such problems is global warming. By all serious scientific accounts, this process is already well under way. The many aspects of this calamity—warmer temperatures to be sure, but also droughts, extreme weather events, and increases in insect activity and disease—are affecting people from hurricane-ravaged New Orleans to flood-ravaged Bangladesh. As with most social problems, those in the third world suffer disproportionately, enduring suffering all the more unjust because it is first world industrialization (with the United States alone responsible for 25 percent of greenhouse gas emissions) that is the source of third world misery.[40] Near the Arctic Circle, the Inuit are facing deformed fish, depleted caribou herds, dying forest, starving seals, and emaciated polar bears and losing entire coastal villages as the ice melts and the water level rises.[41] Island nations in the South Pacific are simply disappearing, as thousands of natives have to leave their islands because the waves come ever higher. In previously agriculturally self-sufficient southern African Lesotho, a long-term drought driven by higher temperatures has created the looming threat of famine.[42] And so it goes.

Of the many religious groups that have spoken out about global warming, the World Council of Churches, representing faith groups encompassing some 400 million members, has been particularly clear and decisive. The Council, whose strong and actually quite radical public statements on environmentalism we have encountered already, has (along with a number of associated and subsidiary groups) manifested a significant public presence in this area. The Council's position on global warming, as on environmental issues in general, evolved from the 1970s on.[43] Because it forms the context for its global warming work and exemplifies the hallmark pattern of religious environmentalism's evolution, that evolution is worth recounting.

In the early 1970s, the widely publicized Club of Rome report "Limits to Growth," probably the first instance an internationally respected group asserted that the earth could not support unending industrial development, helped spark environmental concern in the WCC. From then on, its major programs included reference to environmental issues, beginning with the significant but clearly anthropocentric goal of "just, participatory and sustainable societies," and moving by the 1980s to the more ecologically inclusive values of "justice, peace and the integrity of creation." As we have seen in everything from the ecological evolution of Pope John Paul II to the way Genesis Farm restricts part of its land from human contact, one hallmark of religious environmentalism is a deep commitment to acknowledging the value of all life. WCC's transition from "sustainable societies" to "the integrity of creation" signals that movement in the context of this international Christian alliance.[44]

Another crucial aspect of religious environmentalism is the development of an environmental justice perspective. From an initial sense of environ-

mentalism as concerned with how we treat nature, there arises recognition
of the connections between environmentalism and more familiar social justice issues. During the 1980s, intense discussions on the "relationship of socioeconomic justice and ecological sustainability" unfolded at WCC con-
gresses and group meetings.[45] And at its historic 1990 world gathering in
Seoul, the WCC was able to affirm ten principles linking the economy, justice,
ecological health, war, and racism. Seeking to sharpen its position in response
to the new world economy, the 1998 General Assembly in Zimbabwe adopted
a long-term program to critically assess globalization, paying special attention
to its intertwined economic, ecological, and social effects. By 2004, the Council's subgroup on environmental justice could sum up globalization's most
damaging practices: multinational corporations moving outlawed operations
to developing countries, the shipping of toxic wastes from industrialized
nations to the economic south, free trade agreements that restrict the capacity of national governments to adopt environmental legislation, destruction of southern rain forests to provide exotic timber for northern consumers,
and pressure on poor nations to engage in ecologically destructive agricultural practices to produce cash crops for export in order to service foreign
debt payments.[46]

The WCC's work on global warming embodies moral respect for nature
and political criticisms of globalization. Its observers have been present at
many of the major international conferences and meetings on climate change,
for example, sending representatives to monitor, advocate, and lead religious
services at UN climate change negotiating sessions. During the widely publicized 1992 Conference on Environment and Development meetings in Rio,
the Council stated in no uncertain terms that climate change was a moral
and theological matter, not simply a scientific or economic one. In these
international contexts, the Council's representatives constantly emphasize the
negative effects of climate change on human beings, assert that the world's
poor should not be expected to suffer for the industrialization and unsus-
tainable consumer needs of the rich, and offer a vision of a society that is
sustainable for humans and nature alike.[47]

The truly global nature of climate change provides a remarkable, perhaps
unparalleled, motivation for ecumenical work. If there were ever an issue that
clearly reveals the commonalities of human beings despite differences in religious belief, ideology, or culture, this is the one. Thankfully, many people
of faith have recognized this fact, and have forged interfaith coalitions as well
as alliances with secular environmentalists.

As one example, consider the Interfaith Global Climate Change Network,
itself a joint project of the Eco-Justice Working Group of the National Council of Churches, COEJL, and the National Religious Partnership on the Environment. Together, NCC and COEJL have organized eighteen statewide
interfaith climate change campaigns. These groups see themselves squarely
in the emerging tradition of religious care for the earth and concern for the

connections between humanity and nature. The North Carolina chapter, for example, is a coalition of "various spiritual traditions" committed to "turning human activities in a new direction for the well being of the planet" and for the sacred task of *preserving all eco-systems* that sustain life."[48] The effects of global warming, the coalition warns, will "fall disproportionately upon the most vulnerable of the planet's people: the poor, sick, elderly."[49] The thirty-six signers listed on the group's Web site include rabbis, Buddhist priests, Roman Catholic and Episcopal bishops, and ministers from the Lutheran, Unitarian Universalist, Quaker, Baptist, Methodist, and United Church of Christ denominations. The frequent use of the term "spiritual" in the group's call signals an acceptance of the variety of paths to God; acknowledgment of the sacredness of the earth announces an end to theological anthropocentrism; naming the special vulnerability of the poor opens the way for an account of irrational and unjust social institutions and for common work with secular liberal to leftist organizations. The challenge to existing political and economic arrangements is direct and serious.

The nearly twenty chapters of the coalition have organized meetings with business leaders, local governments, and congressional representatives. They have made visible public statements, educated local congregations, and offered practical ways for religious buildings to become more energy-efficient. Several kindred Interfaith Power and Light organizations offer detailed energy audits of congregational buildings and provide technical help in utilizing renewable energy sources.

Along with their own efforts, religious environmentalists have engaged in many coalitions with secular environmentalists, particularly on the issue of climate change. Perhaps the most interesting of these alliances involves widely publicized joint efforts with—of all groups—scientists! If we remember the centuries of conflict between religion and science—from the Catholic Church's punishment of Galileo to religious resistance to Darwin's theory of evolution—we will be struck by the cultural significance of cooperative efforts between the two. These efforts began in the early 1990s, when thirty-four internationally recognized scientists wrote an "Open Letter to the Religious Community," appealing for a combined effort in defense of the environment, an effort much in need, these *scientists* asserted, of a "religious dimension" and a "sense of the sacred."[50] Several hundred religious leaders from around the world responded, and there followed in June 1991 the "Summit on the Environment," a joint meeting of scientists and religious leaders. The summit issued a "Joint Appeal," initiating perhaps the most high-level cooperation between these long-standing cultural antagonists in history. The appeal acknowledged the scope of the environmental crisis and called for a variety of "diverse traditions and disciplines" to respond to it. Pride of place in the list of environmental concerns was global warming, with its expected consequences of increased drought, depleted agriculture, destruction of the "integrity of ecosystems," and creation of "millions of environmental refugees."

Along with noted scientists, signers included the leadership of the WCC, the Rabbinical Council of America, the American Baptist Church, the National Conference of Catholic Bishops, the Greek Orthodox Archdiocese, and the Episcopal and Lutheran Churches.

Thirteen years later, another joint science and religion statement, focused exclusively on global climate change, was sent to the U.S. Senate to urge passage of the Climate Stewardship Act, legislation committing the United States to restrict its greenhouse gas emissions. In the context of broad consensus among scientists worldwide, the letter asserts:

> The United States has both responsibility and opportunity. With 4% of the world's population, we have contributed 25% of the increased greenhouse gas concentration which causes global warming. Moreover, we uniquely possess technological resources, economic power, and political influence to facilitate solutions. However, policies that devalue scientific consensus, withdraw from diplomatic initiative, and seek only voluntary initiatives do not seem to us adequate responses to this crisis.[51]

Signers included the head of the American Association for the Advancement of Science, the founder of the Wood's Hole Oceanographic Institute, a Nobel prize–winning chemist, the president of the National Council of Churches, and the general secretary of the United Methodist Church.

These statements, it should be emphasized, are more than just new theology. By joining forces with scientific leaders, widely considered our society's arbiters of rationality and its best sources of sound public policy, religious leaders are announcing a decisive intention to influence social life in a way that *combines* a spiritual vision with empirical science. Faith here is not a substitute for or alternative to science, but a way of understanding and working with it. Faith expresses the indispensable factor of the human response to the world—both the natural world, which requires protection, and the human world, which, in its unrestrained industrialization, has gone astray and needs new direction. The fact that 4 percent of the world's population produces 25 percent of the greenhouse gases does not by itself tell us that something must change; only a commitment to basic human moral equality will do that. If we do not believe that we should love our neighbors as ourselves, or that all people are made in the image of God, or that the rich nations do not have a presumptive right to inflict ecological disasters on poor ones, then the bleak truths of global warming will mean little. When religious leaders speak out in this context—offering their vision, trying to affect public policy—they are in effect saying, "These facts have powerful ethical implications; here is how we should respond to them." Their voices move arcane issues of industrial policy and economics, energy sources and conservation, into the realm of ethical life, personal and collective responsibility, and even (gasp) sin, a movement with potentially quite powerful political implications.

For it is typically only when long-established ways of life, especially those that benefit the socially powerful, receive a *moral* challenge that they can be *politically* changed. Freeing the slaves, granting equal rights to women, and now making fundamental changes in our relation to nature are possible only if we change our moral assessment of slavery, male domination, and unrestrained production, consumption, and pollution.

The language of the religion-science statements was necessarily measured, somewhat cautious, and noninflammatory. More flamboyant and exuberant, as well as controversial and just plain fun, was the Evangelical Environmental Network's "What Would Jesus Drive?" campaign. Endorsed by hundreds of ministers and lay leaders of Evangelical Christianity, promoted by a tour through Bible Belt centers in Texas, Arkansas, Tennessee, and Virginia that ended at the country's largest Christian rock festival, "WWJD?" promoted "ways to love your neighbor as we strive together to reduce fuel consumption and pollution from the cars, trucks, and SUVs we drive." The campaign started in February 2002 with a Detroit press conference, meetings with auto industry executives, and support from non-Evangelical religious leaders. Over the ensuing months it received massive press coverage, with thousands of newspaper, radio, and TV stories in the United States and throughout the world. Its guiding document made the religious implications of gas guzzlers crystal clear:

> Obeying Jesus in our transportation choices is one of the great Christian obligations and opportunities of the twenty-first century. Pollution from vehicles has a major impact on human health and the rest of God's creation. It contributes significantly to the threat of global warming.... Making transportation choices that threaten millions of human beings violates Jesus' basic commandments: "Love your neighbor as yourself" (Mark 12:30–31); and "Do to others as you would have them do to you" (Luke 6:31).[52]

The campaign was significant for a number of reasons. For a start, Evangelical Christians are generally socially conservative, far from the usual collection of Volvo liberals, aging hippies, and young "crunchy" types identified as environmentalists. Also, the campaign was not limited to a mild-mannered and widely acceptable celebration of the beauties of nature or bland generalities about "stewardship" and "creation." This was (by God!) an effort of "biblically orthodox" folk, an in-your-face challenge to religious conservatives who believe that "religion in politics" means being against abortion rights, pornography, and gay marriage and for the nuclear family, tax breaks for religious groups, and prayer in schools. "WWJD?" redefined Christian morality to include pressuring government and business leaders to increase fuel efficiency and develop mass transit and, as un-American as it sounded, encouraged their fellow citizens to walk, bike, or take the bus instead of driving. It carried a deadly serious message in a slightly playful way and bore the unmistakable stamp of religion entering the public arena to demand a change in business—or at least driving—as usual.

❧

I have made much of the political significance of religious environmentalism, stressing how it leads to serious criticisms of the existing social order. Yet it would be a mistake to think that every religious environmentalist, or every activist campaign by a religious group, carries this stamp. Within the ranks of religious environmentalists there are mild-mannered reformers as well as wild-eyed radicals, advocates of small, personal, local change as well as those who would initiate an ecological revolution and remake the world.

To see how these variations can coexist within the same religious tradition, it will be instructive to compare two sizable, nationally important, and internationally influential social movements from the world Buddhist community. Both are well-supported, influential, grassroots organizations started by far-thinking and charismatic leaders. Both are sustained by the integrity of their guiding principles and the moral commitment of their members. Yet their respective places on the political spectrum between individual and institutional change could hardly be greater.

TAIWAN

A central player in the development of the new Southeast Asian economies, Taiwan is also massively polluted, facing dying rivers, contaminated soil, and dangerously poor air quality.[53] In the 1980s, an environmental movement emerged, and among its ranks were a number of Buddhist and Christian organizations. The largest and most influential of the former was the Buddhist Compassion Religious Tzu-Chi Foundation, which had been founded as a neighborhood philanthropic association in the mid-1960s by a Buddhist nun, Cheng Yen. Beginning with a group of thirty housewives who would put aside 13 cents a week for donations, Tzu-Chi has grown to a major force in Taiwan and a presence in several foreign countries. It has established hospitals and a medical/nursing school, distributed over $20 million in charity funds in Taiwan and abroad, and is currently engaged in a wide variety of educational, cultural, and health care projects. A truly international force, it has provided flood relief in Thailand and Mexico, free medical care in Indonesia and California, helped handicapped children in Malaysia, and organized a beach cleaning in Singapore (after which volunteers watched a video of Cheng Yen speaking on "Compassion for Mother Nature").[54]

Tzu-Chi's guiding principles are taken directly from the moral teachings of Mahayana Buddhism.[55] Members commit themselves "to support one another through love and wisdom, and to walk hand in hand on the Path of the Bodhisattvas," which means, quite simply, to seek to end the suffering of every living being in the universe. They seek "Purity in our minds, Peace in the society, and a disaster-free world," and they hope to achieve these by "Kindness, Compassion, Joy, and Giving through helping the poor and educating the rich." Oriented toward enlightenment rather than devotion to God, Buddhist environmentalism is based as much in personal virtues such as nonattachment and wisdom as in the imperative to care for nature. Yet the mental outlook these personal virtues promote—for example, detachment from compulsive cravings—provides the basis for a radical critique of any culture that seeks the endless multiplication of desires and requires correspondingly high levels of production and consumption.

With this general perspective as a foundation, Cheng Yen committed herself to applying Buddhist insights to the social world. Such an application, she taught, calls for deep personal change if it is to succeed. "Environmental protection must start from the mind ... if everybody can get rid of greed, anger, delusion, and pride, then all people can help each other and work together to open up a piece of clean land."[56] A clean environment is an essential element of physical health, itself a corollary of the mental purification taught by Buddhist meditation.

Cheng Yen's explicit calls for environmental protection began in 1990 and have since focused on recycling and avoiding the use of polluting products. Because of her track record of integrity and generosity, Tzu-Chi was able to mobilize wide support in response to her call. "Between July 1990 and November 1996, 6,000 to 7,000 people per month were involved with the [recycling] program.... About 275,000 tons of paper, aluminum cans and metal cans were collected per month," saving more than 30,000 trees. In a single day in 1992, 176 tons of waste paper was collected in six hours.[57] The communal center of Tzu-Chi is run by principles like those of the Sisters of Earth: paper is recycled, organic cleaners are used, car travel is minimized. Nuns have "collected waste paper from the trash, wood chips from wood shops, wooden molds from building sites, and wooden boxes. This trash, which would otherwise be dumped, is recycled by the Tzu Chi environmental protection volunteers."[58]

Cheng Yen's vision for Tzu-Chi focused on compassion and concern, support for those in need, and an associated joy of selflessness which is the hallmark of the serious Buddhist. Although Tzu-Chi has created some institutions (hospitals, schools), it does not focus on a political transformation of society. Its offers no pointed critique of globalization, does not protest World Bank development schemes, and leaves issues of democratic control of major social institutions to others. It helps to clean up parks, not to punish polluters, to promote the inner joy that comes from generosity rather than directly confronting the conditions that make generosity so desperately needed. For this it has been criticized by a Taiwanese Buddhist scholar for too much stress on inner transformation rather than social change, for allowing the government and the industries to pollute rather than confronting them.[59] Despite these limitations, its contributions are undeniable.

SRI LANKA

Like Tzu-Chi, the Sarvodaya Movement is also rooted in Mahayana Buddhist principles of compassion, generosity, and personal contentment. Yet it resides at the other end of the political spectrum, seeking nothing less than a full-scale, nonviolent social revolution that will fundamentally reshape modernization both in its country and throughout the developing world. The Sanskrit word *sarvodaya* was used by Gandhi to mean "the benefit of all." A. T. Ariyaratne, the Sri Lankan science teacher whose vision brought Sarvodaya into existence, uses it in a self-consciously Buddhist sense: "Everyone wakes up." In 1957, Ariyaratne sparked the movement by arranging for student volunteers from the college he taught at to work—building roads, improving sanitation, teaching basic literacy—in a few of the poorest and lowest caste of Sri Lanka's 24,000 villages. Out of this simple beginning there grew with remarkable speed a national organization coordinating volunteer efforts in thousands of villages, creating preschools, offering agricultural education, forming groups for women and teenagers, aiding countless development projects, and touching the lives of nearly 4 million people.[60]

Sarvodaya was always distinguished by the idealism of its workers, its focus on the poor, and its inclusion of women and members of minority Tamil and Muslim communities. Even more important, however, were the distinct goals that shaped its activities. For Ariyaratne personally and Sarvodaya as an organization wanted a transformation of Sri Lanka into a society governed by broadly interpreted Buddhist ideals, brought about by Gandhian methods of nonviolence, spiritual discipline, and inclusion. Central to this process, they taught, was a subjective awakening: to a sense of self-worth, compassion for and cooperation with others, and active engagement in community life. This awakening would create a society very different from the acquisitive, high-technology nation sought by the Sri Lankan government, and taken by the dominant institutions of global capitalism to be the hallmark of a successfully "modernized" country. In a truly radical political and spiritual stance, Ariyaratne flatly rejects this image of success, opting instead for a humanly and ecologically sustainable society in which there is neither Western-style affluence nor crushing third world poverty. "In production-centered society, Ariyaratne says clearly, "the total perspective of human personality and a sustainable relationship between man and nature is lost sight of."[61] As a commentator puts it, "Sarvodaya's main message is that human suffering cannot be alleviated merely by material means. . . . All its projects are meant to serve the specific needs of a local community that has been reawakened . . . to the ancient virtues of interdependent sharing and caring, joint suffering, and compassionate interaction."[62]

As Tzu-Chi began in charity work, Sarvodaya initially focused not on environmental issues but in support of a comprehensive, morally oriented reshaping of Sri Lankan modernization. It envisaged quasi-independent villages controlled by local citizens through an engaged democracy, in which all basic human needs would be met, many by subsistence labor rather than the marketplace. The result would be a kind of Buddhist socialism, for the goal of economic life would not be continual industrial expansion and ever growing consumer "needs," but balanced support for all facets of a moral and humane life. As abstract as this sounds in principle, Sarvodaya's success has always depended on being clearly grounded in the details of village life. It seeks the "liberation of the goodness that is in every person," but sees that process as unfolding in concrete and highly practical actions such as preventing soil erosion, teaching literacy, building schools and roads, purifying water, and conserving biodiversity. For Sarvodaya, the problems of economic development, in fact, parallel those of spiritual development. "The root problem of poverty," argued Ariyaratne, is "personal and collective powerlessness." Yet awakening is not an isolated process of spiritual practice, but something that arises out of "social, economic, and political interaction . . . interdependent with the awakening of one's local community."[63]

Environmentalism is a natural consequence of this program. Thus, it is not surprising that Sarvodaya constantly makes references to environmental protection and respect for nature. Its goals for national awakening include protection of the environment, biodiversity, the use of appropriate technology "without destruction of nature or culture," and avoiding dependence on "exploitative international economic relationships."[64] The maldevelopment pursued by the central government and international agencies such as the World Bank were not just against Buddhist principles, they damaged human beings. "We believe," wrote Ariyaratne, "that poverty, powerlessness, and related conditions are directly linked with affluence imbalances, and injustices in the exercise of political and economic power and other advantages enjoyed by the few over the many. What is necessary is not a palliative, but a strategy for a total, nonviolent revolutionary transformation." Waging peace in the face of a protracted and bloody, ethnically based civil war, Ariyaratne called for ecological sustainability along with economic and political justice as part of a comprehensive peace plan.[65]

During the 1960s and 1970s, much of Sarvodaya's expansion was supported by a consortium of European donor agencies, which were impressed by its large number of volunteers and effectiveness at creating village-wide organizations. It also received government cooperation and support to help build centers and staff its operations. Yet with this growth and dependency inevitably came conflict. Ariyaratne's stress on the integration of religious values with economics and his vision of decentralized political power and civically active peasantry were ill adapted to mainstream models of modernization. The donor consortium, for instance, aimed to separate economic development from other kinds of growth, valuing projects that generated income rather than community-supporting subsistence labor or improvements in women's social position. Seeking a society with neither wealth nor poverty, Sarvodaya rejected the exorbitant, technologically sophisticated projects favored by the international agencies and its own government. Buddhist virtues of modest consumption would not fit Sri Lanka for participation in a high-tech global economy; microcredit schemes would not lead to large industrial projects.

From Sarvodaya's point of view, such projects typically devastated the local ecology and did little for the people who were most closely affected by them. Ariyaratne lamented, "By the side of gargantuan dams are parched fields that poor farmers watch disconsolately and with mounting discontent. Under the electricity lines which carry power from the dam to the cities and factories live people who have no permanent structures to call homes and hence are not eligible for that electricity."[66] Guided by traditional Buddhist ideals of universal compassion, and applying those ideals through engagement with the critical social problems of his society and nation, Ariyaratne was able to chart a course past destructive models of what third world communities needed. In doing so he has committed himself, and with him a remarkably large and widespread organization, to a fundamental transformation of social life. Although not defined by its environmentalism, concern for ecology and biodiversity is integral to this transformation. Sarvodaya's religious cast gives it its distinctive character, and its enormous range of positive contributions indicates just how important religious environmentalism can be.

∾

EAST ST. LOUIS, ILLINOIS, APRIL 20, 2002

Facing a decision by the U.S. Army to have Onyx Environmental Services incinerate tons of neutralized nerve gas, residents of one of the nation's most environmentally contaminated neighborhoods protested. Among their supporters were members of the United Church of Christ's Justice and Witness Ministries, who led a public demonstration in opposition. Drawing on the UCC's history of involvement in environmental issues, Rev. Bernice Powell Jackson, then executive minister of the Ministries (and now president of the National Council of Churches!), asked some pointed questions:

> Did East St. Louis' high asthma rate among its children factor into Onyx's decision? Or was that fact even considered at all? Were all segments of the community—especially those most likely to be affected—involved in the decision making process? Can the burden of disposing potentially toxic wastes be

shared equally among all communities and not borne by the most vulnerable members of our society? Should East St. Louis continue to bear an unfair burden for our nation's waste?[67]

This last pointed question is a hallmark of the environmental justice movement, a movement spearheaded initially not by Greenpeace, the Sierra Club, or the World Wildlife Federation, but by the United Church of Christ. Environmental justice and the related idea of environmental racism center on the simple but crucial fact that environmental burdens are distributed unequally: people of color and the poor are much *more* likely to face polluted air and water in their communities and much *less* likely to have attention paid to their plight by either government institutions or environmental organizations. African American, Native American, and Latino communities have served as the dumping grounds for industrial waste, pollution from production and incineration, and the toxic by-products of mining. The integration of an environmental justice perspective has been a crucial part of the development of all aspects of religious environmentalism, from ecotheology and institutional commitment to political activism. It has decisively enlarged a conservationist ethic that had focused almost exclusively on the fate of nature and more traditional political agendas that had been limited to people. For secular environmental organizations that place environmental justice alongside nature preservation, it means a potentially much larger constituency. Simultaneously, socially marginalized groups of African Americans in East St. Louis, Latinos in New Mexico, or Native Americans in Wyoming can now feel that environmentalism concerns their lives as well as pandas and rain forests. In general, recognition of the class and racial nature of the environmental crisis was among the most important steps in helping environmentalism move into the mainstream of political life as a potentially unifying focus of political action, rather than remain the province of comparatively privileged groups.

From what is perhaps the first environmental struggle in which race played a key role, religion has been an essential part of the environmental justice movement. The struggle was sparked by North Carolina's 1982 decision to dispose of its toxic PCBs (a suspected cause of cancer and reproductive, immune, and endocrine problems) in Warren County, the area with the highest percentage of African Americans in the state. Residents accused the state government of picking their county because of its racial makeup. Warren County Concerned Citizens, a biracial group based in a local Baptist church with the active leadership of its minister, began a lengthy process of protest, resistance, and civil disobedience. More than five hundred residents and supporters were arrested, including activist members of the United Church of Christ and a U.S. congressman. The campaign received national attention and helped spark an increase in political militancy and political representation for Warren County's black community.[68]

Having taken a committed role in the Warren Country struggle, the UCC's

Commission for Racial Justice (formed in the early 1960s to work for "justice and reconciliation" in both the church and the broader society) began to study patterns of environmental contamination in U.S residential areas. Five years later it issued its landmark study, *Toxic Wastes in the United States*, which conclusively documented that race was the most important variable in determining the location of hazardous waste facilities, even taking precedence over socioeconomic status. What this meant for people of color was frightening: 60 percent of "black and Hispanic Americans and about half of Asian/Pacific Islanders and Native Americans lived in communities with uncontrolled toxic waste sites"; three of the five largest commercial hazardous waste landfills, accounting for almost half of capacity in the country, were in predominantly black or Hispanic communities; the more toxic facilities a community had, the more likely it was to have a high percentage of racial minorities.[69]

Along with its wealth of technical details, *Toxic Wastes* helped begin the critical process of thinking about the relation between race and pollution. It discussed how economically and socially marginalized racial minorities frequently lacked the social power, financial resources, and government connections possessed by white communities. To poor people, offers of jobs and tax revenues from toxic facilities could be attractive, and legal resources for resistance were often lacking. "Poverty, unemployment, and problems related to poor housing, education and health" meant that attention usually focused on immediate problems of survival, rather than on longer-term issues of environmental protection.[70] Such communities, in short, were vulnerable— and a consequence of that vulnerability was poisoned air, water, and earth.

Building on the national publicity of *Toxic Wastes*, the UCC convened a historic meeting, the first National People of Color Environmental Leadership Summit, in 1991. Called by the UCC's Benjamin Chavis, who had overseen the preparation of the 1987 report, the Summit gathered six hundred people from all over the United States, Canada, and the Pacific. Delegates heard Cherokee chief Wilma Mankiller describe resistance to Sequoyah Fuels' uranium conversion facility, Dolores Huerta of the United Farm Workers talk of the effects of pesticides on farm workers, and Pat Bryant from Louisiana's Gulf Coast Tenants Organization talk about a "billion pounds of poisons" dumped into the "cancer alley" between New Orleans and Baton Rouge.[71]

On the basis of their experience, the delegates affirmed seventeen "Principles of Environmental Justice." These are worth quoting at some length, because in a remarkably clear way they show the integration of the spiritual and the political, concern for nature and for human beings, challenges to corporations and governments that has been the most important hallmark of religious environmentalism:

1. Environmental justice affirms the sacredness of Mother Earth, ecological unity and the interdependence of all species, and the right to be free from ecological destruction. . . .

3. Environmental justice mandates the right to ethical, balanced and responsible uses of land and renewable resource in the interest of a sustainable planet for humans and other living things.

4. Environmental justice calls for universal protection from nuclear testing and the extraction, production and disposal of toxic-hazardous wastes and poisons. . . .

7. Environmental justice demands the right to participate as equal partners at every level of decision-making including needs assessment, planning, implementation, enforcement and devaluation. . . .

10. Environmental justice considers governmental acts of environmental injustice a violation of international law. . . .

14. Environmental justice opposes the destructive operations of multinational corporations.[72]

Both *Toxic Wastes* and the Summit—organized, overseen, and financially supported by the United Church of Christ—have had a remarkable impact. The Summit itself had outside observers from Greenpeace, the Sierra Club, the National Resources Defense Council, and the Environmental Defense Fund. These groups had been alerted by the earlier report and also by a letter directed to the ten major U.S. environmental groups and signed by hundreds of activists in 1990 who charged the groups with failing to recognize environmental racism, a lack of diversity in their organizations, and often making policy decisions without including those affected in the process.[73] In the next few years, virtually all of these groups made significant policy shifts. Feature articles on environmental racism and the environmental justice movement appeared in their publications. They began to acknowledge and support campaigns in places and with groups they had previously ignored, vigorously seeking participation from people of color.[74]

Having given the problem a name and begun the process of understanding it, the environmental justice work of the UCC prompted further research. For example, a study chaired by environmental scholar Robert Bullard (who earlier had connected toxic waste siting and race in Houston)[75] revealed that penalties for violating hazardous waste laws in areas having a high percentage of whites were 500 percent higher than those applied in areas with large minority populations. The fines averaged $335,566 for Euro-American districts, $55,318 in minority ones.[76] Countless other studies have been done since then, and "environmental justice" has become part of the standard lexicon of the environmental movement everywhere it is studied.

Whether or not the specific *terms* are used, the *concepts* of environmental racism and environmental justice have spread far beyond the borders of the United States. Global environmental activists can see environmental injustice in the way Shell Oil and the Nigerian government collude in the oil production that has devastated the Ogoni peninsula. They can ask by what right does Philadelphia dump 15,000 tons of its toxic ash on Kasai Island off the mainland capital of Canabry, Guinea. And why the United States is the only industrialized county that has refused to ratify the Basel Convention, which forbids rich countries from exporting toxic waste to poor ones.[77] Such questions continue the initial connections made in Warren County and *Toxic Wastes in the U.S.*

The change registered on the governmental level as well. In 1994, less than three years after the Summit, President Bill Clinton issued an executive order directing federal agencies to "make achieving environmental justice part of [their] mission by identifying and addressing disproportionately high and adverse human health or environmental effects of [their] programs, policies, and activities on minority populations and low-income population."[78] Although the George W. Bush administrations have worked to undo Clinton's order, and although there are questions about how much was accomplished even under Clinton, it is nevertheless true that the concept of environmental justice has entered the mainstream of even comparatively conservative governmental environmental policy.[79] It is no accident that in 1998 EPA head Carol Browner issued an unprecedented order overruling Louisiana's approval of a PVC plant in Convent, a largely African American region that already had several toxic facilities. Sixteen years after Warren County, a real victory in the global war for environmental justice was won. Religion—in the form of the United Church of Christ's efforts, insights, and energy—could take a significant amount of credit for that victory.

This victory did not stem from a new perspective of world-famous theologians or the somewhat impersonal rhetoric of an Earth Day celebration. It was achieved because of direct connections among people who knew each other. And the churches' role depended on their moral rootedness in the everyday lives of their communities. Countless comparable actions, less well-known but equally the result of the simple moral ties between local religion and the daily life of community throughout the world, could be added. In India, the Sankat Mochan Foundation, led by Hindu priest and civil engineer Veer Bhadra Mishra, has received international recognition for pioneering work in organizing to restore ecological health to the Ganges River.[80] In southern Brazil, local church activists joined in an antidam movement, first to help protect peasants' land and later in support of a more inclusive concern with the region's ecology.[81] As the most important institution of civil society, poised uneasily between the formal structures of government and the private life of families, religion is at times the most powerful resource in any struggle against entrenched injustice.

Indeed, several commentators have argued that for environmentalism to succeed, it must be rooted in community life, moving beyond centralized organizations, national laws or policies, and single-issue campaigns keyed to a particular wilderness area, pollutant, or endangered species. Labeled by some "civic environmentalism," this model relies on informal networks of people concerned with the enduring existence and sustainable development of a particular locale.[82] It involves creative planning for the future as much as stopping some practice that is damaging, and the health of the human community as much as the health of the land. It focuses precisely on what is close at hand, in the hope that *this particular place* can be restored and sustained. Civic environmentalism can be found in a neighborhood coalition in Oakland, California, locally based conservation in rural Colorado, urban agriculture in Boston's Dudley Square, and in Africa, when natives are integrated into the ecotourism of national parks instead of being expelled so that the "wilderness" will be purely "natural" (except for the white tourists).[83] Religious environmental activists, connected to their neighbors through myriad congregational activities, church suppers, and midnight masses, are particularly suited to be active participants in civic environmentalism. As this chapter indicates, they have done so throughout the world already.

DURANGO, COLORADO

Before she could walk, Lori Goodman was taught that all parts of the world are connected, and that as a matter of course, you are to show respect for all your elders, human and nonhuman alike. A religious environmentalist virtually all her life, the connection between spirituality and caring for the earth was not something she had to realize or develop. Our true worth, she learned, depends on the quality of our relationships to people, animals, and the land—and not on how much "we can hoard and keep." As she grew up, however, she came to see the technical details clearly: "If you damage one part, all the other parts get damaged as well. For example, toxic waste dumps will come back to your water."[84]

It is not surprising that Goodman is a Native American, a Navajo, for proper relations with the earth are central to most native religious traditions. As Gail Small, whose work for the Northern Cheyenne parallels Goodman's with the Navajo, puts it, "Environment, culture, religion, and life are very much interrelated in the tribal way of life. Indeed they are often one and the same. Water, for example, is the lifeblood of the people. . . . Indeed, there is a profound spiritual dimension to our natural environment and without it, the war [to protect their lands] would not be worth fighting."[85]

Goodman's activism has centered on Diné (a Navajo word meaning, roughly, "the people") Citizens Against Ruining our Environment (Diné CARE). For nearly twenty years, Diné CARE has sought to defend the Navajo and their lands against a variety of threats.[86] In 1988, it successfully organized in the town of Dilkon to prevent the siting of a toxic waste incinerator and dump, overcoming pressure from the tribal governments to acquiesce and fears of their own powerlessness. As cofounder of the Indigenous Environmental Network, CARE has helped scores of native environmental activists exchange information, resources, and support. In the early 1990s, they kept an asbestos dump from their sacred mountains and resisted a tribal timber industry that was literally clear-cutting the reservation's forests and destroying the character of some of their tradition's most important sacred sites.[87] In the course of the struggle, which pitted Diné CARE against a Navajo-operated sawmill, one of its leading activists died mysteriously. Since then, the assault on Navajo forests has declined significantly.

Perhaps most important, from 1998 to the present Diné CARE has worked to bring justice to victims of uranium mining by forcing modification of the Radiation Exposure Compensation Act. Uranium had been mined on Navajo land since the late nineteenth century, but during World War II and the cold war the intensity of mining increased dramatically. Yet the Navajo people were never told of the dangers of uranium mining, nor how to lessen its effects on miners, their families, and their communities. In Navajo communities near the "tailings" left from old mines, the cancer rate can be as much as seventeen times the national average, and contaminated abandoned mines fill with rainwater and get used by livestock. Leading a coalition of radiation victims from the ranks of uranium miners as well as the "downwinders" who had been exposed to radioactive fallout from weapons tests in Utah, Diné CARE helped make government compensation for these victims more accessible. It has also tried to completely prohibit any future uranium mining on Navajo lands.

The struggle for sustainable forests, like the management of other resources on indigenous lands, typically pits the long-term interests of native culture and community against timber or mining industries that have a commitment only to short-term profit. Because short-term profit can be sizable, there are often conflicts within tribes as well as between tribes and white-owned corporations, as certain members of the community—often those with political power—opt to avail themselves of a percentage of the money flowing in. In Diné CARE's case, for example, pushing to curtail timber sales and prevent waste dump siting set them at odds with tribal leaders. It was only their ability to generate publicity and rally large numbers of ordinary Indians that enabled them to succeed.

The situation faced by Lori Goodman and Diné CARE is replicated throughout North American native communities, and indeed much of the world. On one side are native groups whose culture and history tie them to a place, an ecology, a way of life. As Goodman says, "Our land is our sacred books. We know the places we walk on."[88] *Where* they are is as essential to them as the Bible or the Qur'an is to Jews, Christians, and Muslims. On the other side is a world of nation-states, global corporations, and culturally alien communities, all seeking to extract as much from the land as possible. Timber in Minnesota, rivers in northern Quebec, coal in Montana and Wyoming, rain forests in Brazil—these are often the last frontiers for low-cost mining, cutting, damming for "cheap" power, or cattle raising. Further, as the political power of previously colonized countries throughout Africa, Asia, and the

Middle East grew, the comparative powerlessness of native groups made them attractive sites for "development"—or for destructive use. Native peoples, like African Americans in urban settings from East St. Louis to Chester, Pennsylvania, are almost always marginalized groups, less liable to put up a fuss when they are ravaged by pollution. Suffering from poverty, lack of education, emotional depression, and cultural dislocation, they can be easy to divide.[89]

Finally, like Sri Lankan peasants whose rivers are dammed to make electricity for someone else, native peoples are for the most part suffering pollution while someone else benefits. Gail Small has worked for more than a decade to resist the effects of coal and gas production complexes that power Los Angeles and Seattle but not her own reservation. The Western Shoshone Defense Project, focused on tribal lands in Nevada and Southern California, has resisted nuclear testing and nuclear wastes, threats that are part of someone else's foreign policy and someone else's nuclear energy.[90]

Despite the David and Goliath feeling of many native struggles, some impressive victories have been achieved. Through aggressive court action, for example, Native Action got the Environmental Protection Agency to classify the Cheyenne region a Class-One airshed, which meant that nearby stripmining was subject to vastly stricter EPA air quality standards. They also "launched court proceedings that resulted in a nationwide moratorium on all federal coal leases.[91]

Pollution, of course, is bad for everyone: we all suffer from higher cancer rates, more birth defects, the exorbitant costs of global climate change, and the loneliness that comes as biodiversity diminishes. Yet environmental destruction of native lands is also a kind of cultural genocide. When these lands are contaminated, rivers dammed, and traditional game rendered toxic through mercury or PCBs, indigenous groups can simply die as a people. Given the role of culture in sustaining people's sense of identity and personal well-being, it is often a kind of quasi-physical genocide as well, as the loss of culture all too often leads to epidemics of depression, suicide, family instability, and drug and alcohol abuse.

For generations indigenous groups have been guided by perspectives that stress ecological balance, preservation, and reciprocity rather than the characteristically modern attitude of "improvement," "development," and taking as much as we can as fast as we can. As a number of writers have suggested, this is often not so much a matter of finding the sacred in nature, as if the Western concept of God were now identified with the earth. Rather, it is a sense of respect and care—a moral, psychological, and spiritual relationship that can be characterized as "social" as much as "holy."[92] A marvelously clear (and clearly racist) statement of the distinct environmental consequence of this worldview can be found in an 1874 newspaper editorial condemning Indians for resisting a gold rush into the Dakotas: "What shall be done with these Indian dogs in our manger? They will not dig the gold, nor let others dig it. . . . They are too lazy and too much like animals to cultivate the fertile soil, mine the coal, develop the salt mines, bore the petroleum wells or wash the gold."[93]

As one historian puts it, "Virtually all Americans at the time saw the 'Indian problem' as the perpetuation of Indian cultural patterns and land use incompatible with those of the larger society."[94] Yet, what is from the dominant white point of view a willful and unreasoned refusal to "develop" is from the native point of view an ongoing commitment to their *particular* place. Moving "somewhere else" after having ruined this piece of land is simply not an option—or at least, not an option that is compatible with the continued existence of the group as it understands itself. As the Central Land Council of Australian Aborigines makes clear, "For us, land isn't simply a resource to be exploited. It provides us with food and material for life, but it also provides our identity and it must be looked after both physically and spiritually. If we abuse our land, or allow someone else to abuse it, we too suffer."[95]

Thus, for most native traditions, "religious environmentalism" is redundant. Their traditions simply are environmentally oriented. Unlike the dominant themes of Western religions, which stress heavenly salvation and purely interpersonal morality, or the Hindu and Buddhist pursuit of liberation from the sufferings of embodied existence, native traditions believe that the well-being of people and nature are inextricably linked:

> Tribal members observed elaborate systems of proscription—taboos—governing the essential activities of hunting, planting and harvesting, and insuring that individuals would not disturb the web of agreements by which animals and plants consented to offer themselves up to meet human needs. Through traditions of myth, ritual, community identity and moral action, then, tribes were often not easily inclined to see themselves in positions to sell land or extinguish title to other human beings, but rather as dependent upon the greater-than-human power embodied in the land.[96]

This set of distinct attitudes and practices is one reason "Native American environmentalism" is not limited to defensive actions in response to pollution or clear-cutting. Rather, the intelligence of the native worldview is at times shown in their management of their own lands. To take but one example: the Menominee tribe has been in control of its forest resources since 1854, when the Wolf River Treaty created their reservation. In appearance, its 220,000-acre forest in northeast Wisconsin looks wild and untouched. Yet in truth, it has been highly managed—in a sustainable way—by the tribe. Over 2 *billion* board feet of lumber have been removed, yet the total mass of wood in the forest is greater than it was a century and a half ago. Towering white pines fill the forests, along with ruffed grouse, eagles, ospreys, woodcocks, bobcats, coyotes, otter, marten, fox, white-tailed deer, and bears. With many of its members still living close to the land, the forest provides meat and furs, maple syrup and ginseng. Continual monitoring assures the Menominee that their forest will continue for generations, serving human needs while maintaining its own ecosystemic integrity. As one elder said, "Everything we have comes from Mother Earth—from the air we breathe to the food we eat—and we need to honor her for that. In treating the forest well, we honor Mother Earth."[97]

Of course, one should not romanticize native traditions nor overgeneralize about them. There are, for instance, eyewitness accounts of Indians killing large numbers of buffalo and taking only a small piece of the carcass. Some evidence suggests that as many as fifteen large mammal species were wiped out by native hunting between 12,000 B.C.E. and 1000 C.E.[98] It may be that native environmentalism had to be learned, that the knowledge was not some magical, spontaneous genetic endowment.[99] As radical environmentalist Dave Foreman asks, "Is the land ethic of the Hopi a result of a new covenant with the land following the Anasazi ecological collapse seven hundred years ago? Would the hunt ethics of tribes in America (and elsewhere) have been a reaction to Pleistocene overkill?"[100]

Indeed, this may well be the case for indigenous peoples throughout the world: perhaps they learned to honor the earth after having some experiences of the consequences of *not* honoring it. The point, nonetheless, is that for the most part, they learned the lessons of their histories and over the course of generations developed a deeply religious sense of their interdependence with the earth, a sense that was expressed not only in myth and ritual but in limitations on hunting, fishing, and farming, in literal management of the ecosystem.[101] Given the difference between their technological powers and our own, we can only hope that contemporary societies will learn such lessons without making mistakes of comparable scope—where we have not done so already.

The insatiable demand of the dominant society for land and production, of course, does not make the prospects of native environmentalism particularly bright. Key victories have been won, but throughout the world the onslaught continues. Thankfully, the same sensibility that leads indigenous activists to the struggle sustains them in it. When I asked Lori Goodman what she does about despair over her losses, she seemed genuinely surprised. "We don't feel despair," she said. "No matter what happens. We know we are not going to beat them, but at best we can delay them, and perhaps end up with something sustainable. In the meantime our ceremonies, our prayers, our celebrations—they keep us going."[102]

✿

If there is hope for native peoples throughout the world, it will come because they have aligned themselves with nonnative environmentalists, in particular the environmental justice movement of the larger societies in which they live. Throughout the world, cooperation among different types of people is often the key to success in environmental struggles. As we have seen in the example of the religion-science cooperation on global warming, religious environmentalists are actively engaged in working alliances with and becoming members of secular environmental organizations and campaigns. Often, there is no clear division between the secular and the religious in the environmental community (even if, as many of the Sisters of Earth feel, some need an organizational home base with a strong spiritual dimension). In fact, although in some countries (e.g., Islamic ones) religious motives will be sufficient to mobilize political change, in those in which religion and government are separated it is in the broadest possible coalitions that religious environmentalism can make the largest possible impact. This fact has not been lost either on religious environmentalists or on secular ones, and their increasing cooperation, as we'll now see in two telling examples, is one of the most hopeful signs in the world environmental movement.

In January 2002, a remarkable ad appeared on TV stations in Georgia, Arizona, North Dakota, Indiana, Missouri, and Delaware. With a background of uplifting new age music and a series of breathtaking images of mountains, rivers, and tundra, the ad told viewers, in language familiar to virtually every secular environmental organization, that America's energy needs could be better met by conservation and renewable sources than by drilling in the Arctic National Wildlife Refuge. And there was more: in language that would have fit perfectly with the Religious Witness's civil disobedience at the Department of Energy, the ad also proclaimed that Americans have a deep obligation not to ruin the land that is in our trust, but to "keep our promise to care for creation."

The combination of secular and religious vocabulary was no accident, because the ad was a joint project of the Sierra Club and the National Council of Churches. Sierra's executive director Carl Pope, feeling a real need to reach out to communities of faith, had initiated contact with the NCC's secretary general, former Pennsylvania congressman Bob Edgar. After taking, Edgar says, "about thirty seconds to think about it" before agreeing, the NCC provided advice on how to phrase the issues and lent its name and influence. The Sierra Club put up the money and directed production. Interestingly, within the Sierra Club there was some serious discussion about whether to do the joint ad and, if so, how: the word "God" was taken out at the last minute, but the word "creation," though opposed by some, remained. Afterward, a large volume of positive responses came to both groups.[103] And the follow-up on both sides has been impressive. The Sierra Club now spends upwards of $100,000 a year in outreach to faith communities and to offer support to religious environmentalists. The NCC and its members partner with Sierra in several contexts, from climate change work in New Mexico to clean water campaigns in Arizona and environmental justice work in Louisiana.

The Sierra-NCC ad was one moment in a long campaign to protect ANWR and redirect America's energy policy. Focused on India, the extensive struggle to defeat the Narmada complex has had a distinctly international character. The religious element in this struggle has been one piece of the puzzle, and its role indicates something of the importance, as well as the difficulty and the complexity, of the real-world politics in which religious environmentalists are involved.

In the late 1980s, the Indian government proposed its largest ever public works project: a series of 30 large, 135 medium, and 3,000 small dams to harness the waters of the Narmada and its tributaries, ostensibly for flood control, irrigation, and electric power. Alarmed over the possible human and ecological effects of the project, long-time Gandhian nonviolent social activist Baba Amte, whose extensive political and humanitarian work included successfully resisting large dam projects in Maharastra in the early 1980s, organized a meeting of dozens of India's leading environmentalists. They estimated that the projects would flood more than 200,000 acres of pristine forest and fertile farmland, threaten the existence of endangered species, and displace as many as 300,000 local villagers, most of them tribal people or untouchables. Out of that meeting was born Narmada Bachao Andolan (Save the Narmada), an ongoing organization that has opposed the dam complex by a wide variety of means, from legal challenges and public protests to international pressure and civil disobedience.[104]

Opposition to the Narmada dams was based in a fascinating mix of religion, science, and simple human decency. Like the Ganges, the Narmada has a sacred character for the tribal peoples who live near it. For them, the dams are a kind of desecration. Further, the benefits of this sacrilege, according to critics, were vastly overrated and would in any case be selectively distributed to the corporations paid for building the dams and the comparatively small percentage of city dwellers who would receive the electricity. Interestingly, opposition to large dams in India was justified as much by science as by religion, for large dam projects, so beloved by development agencies and central governments in the third world, have for the most part proved to be environmental and human disasters. They have destroyed ecosystems, created tens of millions of "refugees from development," and produced comparatively little in the way of benefits. Riverbanks are eroded for tens or even hundreds of miles downstream; fertile sediment stays behind the dam, worsening fishing and farming; and submerged villages release toxic chemicals into the water. Even in terms of irrigation, small-scale dams tend to work much more efficiently.

When the negative environmental and human effects and the astronomical costs of construction are factored in, the electricity produced is neither cheap

)r clean. Ironically, the World Bank, long a strong supporter of large dams (including the Narmada project), in 2002 undertook its own study of their effectiveness and concluded that by and large they had had unjustified ecological and human effects.[105] (Strangely, this has not stopped them, along with numerous other private and public development organizations, from funding the Narmada project.) In his challenge to the Narmada dams, Baba Amte put this matter clearly nearly fifteen years before the World Bank got the point: "I will not let my beloved state of Gujarat fulfill a death wish by adopting an antediluvian technology. The science of large dams now seems to belong to the age of superstition; the coming century belongs to the technology of mini and micro dams and watershed development ensembles."[106]

Narmada Bachao Andolan has been struggling for seventeen years, trying to halt the dams, limit their height, or at least get recompense for the refugees they create. And they have not done so alone. *The movement against the Narmada dams has been truly global in scope.* International environmental NGOs, such as Oxfam, the Environmental Defense Fund, and the International Rivers Network, publicized the case, offered support, and publicly protested at World Bank meetings. Indian environmentalists and civic activists have joined with tribals in demonstrations and protests, challenging state and national governments.[107]

Like other international struggles—against the James Bay hydroelectric plant in northern Quebec, or nuclear power, or global warming—the Narmada campaign incorporates secular analysis and religious reverence, a sophisticated critique of failed technology and a near instinctive sense that some rivers should be left intact. The worldwide scope of these campaigns indicates, against all dire warnings to the contrary, that there is no inherent incompatibility between science, technology, the political defense of human rights, environmentalism—and religion. Religious environmentalists—activists defending God's creation or Mother Earth, the entire globe or their own villages—have become an essential part of an international movement for a sustainable future.

CHAPTER 5

ENVIRONMENTALISM AS SPIRITUALITY

> Upon entering those groves a spirit of awe and reverence came over me.... In the stillness of these mighty woods, man is made aware of the divine.
>
> —Richard St. Barbe Baker, pioneering international advocate of
> ecological tree planting for conservation, on first seeing redwoods,
> from Karen Gridley, *Man of the Trees: Selected Writings
> of Richard St. Barbe Baker*

> There is broad acceptance among Greenpeace staff that the work is quintessentially spiritual, though definitions of what is meant by the term vary.
>
> —Christopher Childs, public spokesman for Greenpeace USA, in
> *The Spirit's Terrain: Creativity, Activism, and Transformation*

The passion and commitment that Religious Witness for the Earth brought to its nonviolent civil disobedience in protest of the Bush administration's plans to drill in the Arctic National Wildlife Refuge, as well as the spiritual overtones of the National Council of Churches and Sierra Club ad—these were not lost on some less than friendly observers. In May 2002, *Detroit News* columnist Thomas Bray criticized environmentalists for waging an irrational "jihad" with "grim religious determination" in defending the ANWR, a defense he saw as based in a "faith" in wilderness and a distrust of the beneficial tendencies of democratic capitalism. In a similar vein, two timber companies sued the National Forest Service for being influenced by the "religious" motives of environmentalists (including the well-known Julia Butterfly Hill, who spent two years living in a redwood to protect it from being cut) in the defense of old-growth forests. The director of one of the groups attacked in the suit was disturbed to learn that he was thought to be involved in Gaia worship: "I realized that they were trying to make us look like witches or something—I'm a practicing Methodist, for goodness sake."[1]

While these critics of environmentalism typically refuse to question the religious quality of their own faith—in dams and power plants, unending "development" and a rising gross national product—they are clearly right about one thing: a good deal of environmentalism does have a "religious," or at least a "spiritual" dimension. Compared to other progressive political movements of the past two centuries—for democracy, in support of rights for workers, women, or racial minorities, against colonialism, or for more economic justice—environmentalism bears remarkable and crucially important affinities with religion. These affinities make the emerging alliance between secular environmental organizations and institutional religion particularly appropriate, and they mean that at times it is quite difficult to talk about the relationship between religion and environmentalism because the two so shade together that it becomes hard to tell them apart. In the contemporary environmental movement, even those groups totally unconnected to religiously identified organizations are often inspired by a political ideology, or at least a moral sensibility, with powerful religious overtones. This sensibility has been present in much of environmentalism since its origins in the mid-nineteenth century and has evolved into a comprehensive worldview that in many respects is often undeniably spiritual in nature.

I will make the case for these rather broad claims by showing how many of the essential elements of *religion* have been present—even at times dominant—in *environmentalism*. As an individual response to life on earth, a social movement, and a heartfelt hope for the future, environmentalism comprises experiences, beliefs, and actions that make it the near kin, if not the sibling, of much of religious life. If my claims here are correct, then we should not be surprised when environmentalists and people of faith work together.

∾

An enormously varied global movement, environmentalism's goals range from the preservation of wilderness to the cleaning up of toxic waste dumps, from creating clean, cool, and green technology to protecting biodiversity. At one end of the environmental spectrum we find direct actions aimed at stopping some particular instance of "development" or some concrete industrial practice. When the women of India's Chipka movement physically encircle the trees of their beloved forest (which provides herbs, fodder for animals, and firewood) to save them from being chopped down, when Greenpeace plugs the outflow pipe of a chemical factory, when thousands protest "free trade" agreements that would cripple communities' rights to limit ecological degradation, environmental politics means putting your body on the line to protect both other species and human beings. At the other end of the spectrum we find attempts to influence world culture through teaching, writing, films, Internet sites, and art. In between these two poles are a host of governmental and nongovernmental institutions and activities: government regulation of pesticides, lobbying to protect wetlands, resisting environmental racism, researching the duplicity of the chemical industry, organizing neighbors to clean up a local river.

When does this wide spectrum of green politics have a religious or spiritual aspect? Well, despite my rather sweeping claims, this will not always be present. If we seek to preserve a forest so that we can hunt big game in it (one of the original motivations for wildlife preservation efforts),[2] or if our sole concern with pesticides is their effect on human health, then our approach to environmental issues has little to do with a comprehensive vision of the value of all of life. When pioneer of urban and occupational health Alice Hamilton reported on workplace and residential pollution in the early twentieth century, or National Forest Service's first director (1898–1910) Gifford Pinchot called for rational management of national forests to benefit a constantly growing economy, environmentalism was no more religious than attempts to sterilize a wound or make comfortable furniture.[3] In such cases, nature is simply a background to human goals and needs, and the earth itself material for us to use as we will.

But there is more, much more, to environmentalism. In the experiences that give rise to it, the beliefs that motivate it, and the actions to which it gives rise, it is frequently, perhaps even predominantly, religious or spiritual.

∾

But what is religion? Facing difficulties that plague practically every attempt to define "obscenity," Supreme Court Justice Potter Stewart acidly stated, "I shall not today attempt further to define the kinds of material I understand to be embraced. . . . I know it when I see it." We might well say the same of religion. This is probably the case because long before we try to define the word abstractly, we have concrete experiences that give it meaning. We are taught to pray or hear about the prayers of others, take our place in churches or synagogues, see crosses hanging from people's necks, listen to actresses thank God for their Academy Award, hear politicians invoke the Lord's blessing on their country (and political party), and find that most weddings or funerals have a priest, minister, or rabbi running things. If a few instances confuse us—Scientology, astrology, devout atheists, peyote rituals—for the most part we nevertheless know religion "when we see it." Similarly, despite a certain vagueness and ambiguity, we make free use of the word "spiritual." And even though people will refer to themselves as "spiritual but not religious," it seems that the two have a great deal in common. Spirituality, we might say, is really a kind of religiosity, one that is less oriented to a fixed creed or defined denomination, more committed to the long path toward spiritual truth than permanently dwelling in a settled religious community.[4]

Spirituality is more likely to celebrate purely personal experiences and less likely to tell everyone else exactly what God is like. Yet, as there is nothing we think of as spiritual that cannot be found, even if only at the margins, in the world's religious traditions, I hesitate to make a sharp distinction between the two.

To make the case that environmentalism includes deeply religious or spiritual elements, however, I have to say at least a bit about what I take the terms to mean, and to do this I will break down "religion" and "spirituality" into what I believe are their essential elements. If my account is accurate, readers will find that my list of these elements corresponds to their own understanding.

To begin with a disclaimer, we should be clear that although much of religion focuses on the belief in revelation from a Supreme Being, much of it—for instance, Buddhism and Taoism—does not. Also, although religions typically center on formal creeds and ongoing institutions ("the church"!), there are wide exceptions to this rule as well. Islam's Sufis, Catholic medieval mystics, and renowned Zen Buddhist teachers have existed within a broadly religious framework without emphasizing such things.

Therefore, I will cast a wide net and focus on some common and significant aspects of religious life that allow us to demarcate it from other spheres of life: to distinguish religion from the practical, the accumulation of wealth, power, or social status, the development of scientific knowledge or technical power, and even (though this is a tricky one) from achieving social justice. For convenience and clarity I consider these elements under three main headings: characteristically religious or spiritual *experiences, beliefs,* and *actions.* In each case, we will see that the essential aspects of religious life have analogues in the realm of environmental concern.

⌘

Pursued by his enemies, afraid for his life and his throne, King David experienced a moment of grace which he recorded in a poetic prayer that has given people comfort for centuries: "The Lord is my shepherd, I shall not want," says the Twenty-third Psalm, indicating a trust in God marked by gratitude and serenity. When a follower of the Buddha finally entered into meditation fully, he told a friend that he was able to let go of any sense of "I am this, this is mine, this is my self."[5] When the orchestra and chorus burst into the *Et Resurrexit* section of the Bach B Minor Mass—an explosive and ascending melody that propels the believer into an awareness of the miracle of Christ's entry into Divine Life—devout Christians may experience a sense of overwhelming joy: a joy, we might note, that is always available, because for the Christian, Christ's resurrection is a permanently recurring miracle that gives meaning and hope to human existence. When we celebrate the Sabbath, Judaism, Christianity, and Islam tell us, we should feel delight, thankfulness, and rest. It is a time to appreciate what has been given to us, to see it as the gift of a generous God, and to take a break from thinking about how we can get more.

These are a few of the distinctive experiences fostered by religious life. Their most important shared feature is the way they take us beyond the conventional ego, beyond a frame of mind in which we calculate our interests, compete with those around us, struggle for success, seek to control the world to get what we want from it, or unendingly complain about every damn thing we don't have. In the experience of God or Ultimate Reality or Spirit, we are less depressed, bored, anxious, and selfish and more grateful, joyous, and serene. We taste exuberance or tranquility, reverence or awe, a deep confidence in the universe or a sense of how much of the universe will always be an enthralling mystery. Finally, because we feel we have achieved communion with an immensely powerful source of meaning, a force or intelligence much vaster than ourselves with whom we can, in some sense, communicate, we no longer feel so *alone*.

For thousands of years religious writings have described these experiences as the product of encounters with God, or with states of mind stemming from meditation, prayer, and contemplation. Yet they are also to be found at the heart of environmentalism. It is precisely because for many of us the encounter with the rest of life on earth—indeed at times with the universe as a whole—provokes profound feelings of awe and reverence, mystery and serenity, that we commit ourselves to its protection.

The connection between nature and powerful, religious-like emotions is a familiar theme in the classic nineteenth- and early twentieth-century nature writers, writers who also were active in or guiding lights of the emerging social movement of environmentalism. Over and over, Thoreau and John Muir, John Burroughs, and Sigurd Olson describe the transformative quality of wilderness. Thoreau celebrated a "wildness" that is "the preservation of the world" and tells us, "When I would recreate myself, I seek the darkest woods, the thickest and most interminable and, to the citizen, most dismal, swamp. I enter a swamp as a sacred place, a *sanctum sanctorum*. There is the strength, the marrow, of Nature." A keen observer of his surroundings, knowledgeable in natural history, Thoreau also regarded nature in a decidedly spiritual light: "The highest that we can attain to is not Knowledge, but Sympathy with Intelligence. . . . Nature is a personality so vast and universal that we have never seen one of her features."[6] John Muir's celebration of (and lobbying for) California's Sierra Mountains in the late nineteenth century eventually helped give rise to Yosemite National Park. Of his first encounter with them he wrote, "No description of Heaven that I have ever heard or read of seems half so fine."[7] Sigurd Olson, whose life in the rugged lake country of northern Minnesota produced widely read books and articles, suggested in 1938 that what we learn from wilderness "are spiritual values . . . a familiar base for exploration of the soul and the universe itself. . . . With escape comes perspective. Far from the towns and all they denote, engrossed in their return to the old habits of wilderness living, men begin to wonder if the speed and pressure they have left are not a little senseless."[8] John Burroughs, a contemporary of Muir's whose writings on birds made him equally famous in his day, reassured his readers, "Nature we have always with us, an inexhaustible store-house of that which moves the heart, appeals to the mind and fires the imagination—health to the body, a stimulus to the intellect, and joy to the soul."[9] During a long ramble in the countryside he described a kind of mystical perfection that could be found through a commonplace encounter with the sky: "The office of the sunshine is slow, subtle, occult, unsuspected; but when the clouds do their work, the benefaction is so palpable and copious, so direct and wholesale, that all creatures take note of it, and for the most part rejoice in it. It is a completion, a consummation, a paying of a debt with a royal hand; the measure is heaped and overflowing!"[10]

These few examples signal a widespread fact: it is quite common, says historian Michael P. Nelson, for people to argue for the preservation of wilderness as "a site for spiritual, mystical, or religious encounters: places to experience mystery, moral regeneration, spiritual revival, meaning, oneness, unity, wonder, awe, inspiration, or a sense of harmony with the rest of creation—all essential religious experiences."[11]

These experiences are not merely the passing pleasures of ecological aesthetes, but are often integrated into lives of environmental activism. Engaged in a fight to prevent the Yosemite's magnificent valley Hetch Hetchy from being dammed, Muir raged, "Dam Hetch Hetchy! As well dam for water-tanks the people's cathedrals and churches, for no holier temple has ever been consecrated by the heart of man."[12] As a twenty-four-year-old the Jewish forester Robert Marshall, early advocate for wilderness conservation and a founder of the influential Wilderness Society, spent Yom Kippur 1925 walking in the Idaho mountains and for three hours meditated in silence while sitting on a rock. The experience, he claimed, was for him more religiously effective than traditional observance: "In Temple . . . it has in the past been impossible to banish [trivial] thoughts from my mind, and, at best, fasting, hard seats and dull sermons are not conducive to deep thought. Therefore, I feel that my celebration of Yom Kippur, though unorthodox, was very profitable."[13] Richard St. Barbe Baker, who pursued a lifelong vocation in support of tree planting to repair landscapes, improve agriculture, purify water, and orient humanity to cooperation with rather than unthinking control over nature, often wrote of how forests led him to awe and reverence.

It is important to note that such attitudes toward wilderness are not, as some might suppose, relics of earlier times when people were "more religious" than they are now. During three recent seminars on the "value of wilderness" hosted by the National Forest Service, accounts of the economics of lumber and consumer preferences for outdoor recreation were persistently joined by acknowledgment of the "intrinsic value" of wilderness, and of how it sustains and elevates humanity's spiritual life.[14]

Of the many religious experiences to which wilderness gives rise, one deserves special mention: a sense of the dissolution of the ego, of the boundaries that sharply divide one's own self from others. Sigmund Freud termed this experience "oceanic," and it has been a hallmark of religious mysticism in virtually every tradition one can think of. A good deal of spiritual practice, from long periods of meditation to extended fasting to intense prayer, has as its goal a lessening of our sense of separation, of rigid demarcation, between "me" and the rest of creation. Such experiences are also common in relation to nature. At certain crucial moments, ecofeminist Charlene Spretnak wrote in 1990, we manage to attend fully to what is around us, and "at that moment the distinction between inner and outer mind dissolves, and we meet our larger self."[15] A century and a half earlier, Ralph Waldo Emerson described how going into the woods provides a "perfect exhilaration," enabling a man to "cast off his years" and be forever a child. "Standing on the bare ground,— my head bathed by the blithe air, and uplifted into infinite space,—all mean egotism vanishes. I become a transparent eye-ball; I am nothing; I see all; the current of the universal Being circulates through me: I am part or parcel of God."[16] As traditional religions revere those times when we are overwhelmed by the presence of God, or feel our ego dissolved in meditation, so people have for centuries acknowledged the power of nature to take them out of their normally constricted sense of self.

This expanded sense of self prompts an extended sense of fellowship as well, one in which we feel for all of nature (including people, we hope!) the kinds of moral sentiments held dear by traditional religions: to love our neighbors as ourselves (Christianity and Judaism), to "spend of your substance, out of love for Him, for your kin, for orphans for the needy, for the wayfarer" (Islam, Qur'an *2:177*), or to respond to anyone's pain as if it were our own (Buddhism). To use Jewish philosopher Martin Buber's terminology, each animal and plant, even each mountain and river, becomes a "thou" rather than an "it."[17] In Baker's words, "A Tree is a real thing, it has a personality. It is a living entity. Is it too much to believe that it responds to the love that is given to it? . . . We shall tread softly when we enter the sanctuary of the woods, seeing we are in company with tree beings who respond to our love and care."[18]

This sense of kinship extends to the whole as well as to the particular elements that make up the whole. American nature writer and inspirer of the radical deep ecology group Earth First! Edward Abbey suggested that love of wildness is "an expression of loyalty to the earth, the earth which bore us and sustains us, the only home we shall ever know, the only paradise we ever need."[19]

It must be stressed that the language of love, awe, and reverence, of nature's capacity to heal and comfort, are not, as some might suppose, simply the province of poetic and private individuals, of a Thoreau in a cabin by Walden Pond or an isolated nature writer whose affection for nature is solely literary. Rather, for many in the environmentalist community, these kinds of experiences of nature are essential to *why they became active environmentalists*, and to why they continue the struggle throughout their lives. Muir helped created America's national parks and founded the Sierra Club, Marshall the national forest system. Baker spent his entire adult life trying to regenerate lost forests, helping protect redwoods in California, creating a tree-planting society among native Kenyans, and improving tree cover for fields in India and Australia. Spretnak has been a political activist in the American green movement for decades.

To take a less well-known but critically important example from recent American history, consider Howard Zahniser, who spent seven years drafting more than sixty versions of what became the 1964 Wilderness Act, an act that set aside more than 9 million acres of the United States as places human beings could visit but not impact and in which the marks of human activity would be absent. The Wilderness Act was an enormously detailed, highly technical legal accomplishment, not the stuff of religious enthusiasm or spiritual musing. Getting it passed required extensive lobbying, negotiating, consulting, and coalition building by Zahniser and his allies. Yet, in "The Need for Wilderness," after giving the more tangible recreational, scientific, and ecological values of wilderness their due, Zahniser went on to emphasize that "the most profound of all wilderness values in our modern world" is its ability to help us "know a profound humility, to recognize one's littleness, to sense dependence and interdependence, indebtedness and responsibility."[20]

Another conservation professional, chief economist and social science coordinator for the National Forest Service's Inter Mountain region David Iverson, speaks of "a spiritual element to the land: you can feel it every time you're out there." Influenced by a childhood filled with experiences of nature, by Aldo Leopold and Edward Abbey, Iverson heads the remarkable organization Forest Service Employees for Environmental Ethics, a group of professional foresters who oppose our government's tendency to treat the woods simply as raw material. Their goal is not only to manage the land efficiently, but to pass it "with *reverence* from generation to generation."[21] Of all the words that could have been used in this simple statement of intent, it is striking that an essentially religious word was chosen. In a review of *Nature and the Human Spirit*, a large collection of essays by foresters and environmentalists, Iverson points out that such a volume could not have been possible in the past, and that its endorsement by high-level administrators indicates that the long-standing taboo against speaking of the forests' spiritual meanings may be weakening.[22]

In general, says experienced forester Robert Perschel, many of his fellow paid staffers of the 250,000-member Wilderness Society find a spiritual sensibility underlying their work. If the culture of professionalism forbade a great deal of discussion of that dimension, it still could be tapped. During the Society's annual week-long staff meeting, Perschel initiated an hour-long discussion by asking participants to bring in "sacred objects," something to indicate why they were doing the work they did. "Amazing things came out," he says. "One man talked about taking walks with his dying mother through pine forests where she had played as a child. A woman who had worked for the merchant marine described seeing a pod of whales suddenly shooting out of a massive wave during a typhoon, and her staring into the eyes of one of them who was magically suspended in front of her." Perschel, former head of the Northern Forest Alliance and current environmental director of the Garrison Institute, believes that in the environmental movement, "You can always make a connection to someone about some special moment. Maybe it came in the Grand Canyon, maybe in the backyard, but there is always that common thread: that there is more to us than just the self, there is the larger community—from the family and the town and the nation, to all of nature, the whole universe."[23] The environmental crisis demands, says Perschel, far more than "rational management": "We have no hope unless we infuse the debate over the environment with the deep emotional and spiritual connections that it warrants and that will be required for a great social transformation."[24]

These sentiments are echoed by one of the giants of the modern conservation movement, Brock Evans, whose work with the Sierra Club, Audubon Society, and Endangered Species Coalition has put him on the front lines of environmentalism for forty years. Evans, who calls himself a confirmed Episcopalian, finds easy compatibility between his Christianity and his environmentalism: as the bumper stickers on his car read, "Extinction is not stewardship" and "Love Creator, Love Creation." Evans's work (and, he says, that of very many of the people he has worked with over the years) is rooted in experiences that are "akin to religious feelings." It is about realizing, he says, "how the species, the land, the fish, the mountains . . . how *everything* interacts." This realization began, for him, in a powerful personal encounter: "The first time I ever stood on a mountain peak I could see a vast area of forests and mountain and lakes, I heard the sound of running water in the distance . . . a powerful, feeling rose up, like some profound chord struck deep within me."[25]

Many of the sentiments quoted so far reflect a widely held sensibility that "nature" means "wilderness" and that therefore environmentalism should be keyed to wilderness protection, to preserving areas of the earth untouched by humanity. From Thoreau to Abbey this perspective was crucially important during the first century of American environmentalism. Yet the underlying premises—and even the basic decency—of this perspective have been seriously criticized in recent years. Historian William Cronon complained that the ideal of a place completely without humans in which we can fully be ourselves reflects the romantic fantasies of privileged men who never had to work the land for a living, a flight from history which "offers us the illusion that we can escape the cares and troubles of the world in which our past has ensnared us."[26] Equally important, the creation of national parks as a preserved wilderness in which only tourists were allowed frequently required forced restrictions on Native Americans or poor whites who for generations had used the areas for hunting and fishing.[27] Comparable complaints have been raised about the export of the American wilderness ideal to third world countries, where the "preservation of nature" often requires the expulsion of natives.[28]

As pertinent as they are, these criticisms no more invalidate the religious factors of environmentalism than criticisms of a traditional religion automatically entail *its* complete rejection. For one thing, Cronon's point that the concept of nature is a human construction and that the meaning of wilderness (at one time a fearful and threatening waste, at another a refuge from industrialization) varies over time, show, if anything, yet another affinity between religion traditionally conceived and environmentalism. What, after all, is more humanly shaped, more subject to historical change, than our understanding of God? As human beings, we always experience religious realities through a human lens, whether in the way we interpret scripture or in our response to inspired prophets. Historical developments in politics, economics, or technology, contact with other cultures, the entry of previously marginalized voices into religious life—all these lead to transformations in theology, ritual, and religious experience.

The same pattern holds for what we take to be the meaning and value of the natural world. Our sense of nature, no less than our sense of God, has a history. In neither case does this mean that religious attitudes toward the one or the other are inauthentic or misconceived.[29] Indeed, it is not difficult to trace two profound changes in the experience of nature in the past two centuries. The first occurred in the mid-nineteenth century, when it became clear that nature could be deeply affected by human beings. Although its awesome power was still manifest in powerful storms or the grandeur of mountains, the enormous changes in the American landscape, combined with the explosive growth of cities, represented a pretty clear writing on the wall to those who saw that their wilderness "temples" would soon be overrun. It is out of this sensibility, as well as a growing sense of the disconnect between technological development and human well-being, that the nineteenth-century preservationist tradition emerged. This tradition continues to the present, and has included environmental activists and thinkers like Marshall, Zahniser, and Abbey and environmental groups such as the Wilderness Society, Earth First!, and the Nature Conservancy.

Yet, even while a concern for untouched areas and wild places remains a focus for many, the past forty years of environmentalism has come to see its object of reverence not as a nature untouched by humans, but as an ecological network, a web of life, in which humans, other animals, plants, and landscapes are all fully enmeshed. When Martin Luther King Jr. was speaking of how all humans were joined in an "inescapable network of mutuality,"[30] a comparable vision animated Rachel Carson, whose fame as a natural history writer and opponent of reckless and destructive pesticide use make her a centerpiece of modern environmentalism. Carson's warning about the effects of chemicals such as DDT in some ways resembled decades earlier studies of industrial wastes or consumer products (the muckraking *100,000,000 Guinea Pigs*, a critique of health effects of chemicals in common consumer products, was a 1933 national best-seller),[31] but her own sense of what she was doing was radically different. For Carson's focus was neither human health alone, nor nature in and of itself. It was, rather, the two joined, as in King's phrase, in "inescapable mutuality." For Carson, and for countless environmentalists since, we have moved from wilderness to ecology, from "nature as precious refuge" to "nature as all of life," from protecting some wild places "over there" to realizing that, as Barry Commoner remarked in his "Seven Laws of Nature," "everything is related to everything else" and consequently there simply is no "over there."[32] As the Catholic Church discovered through the course of the nineteenth century that democracy was a social value worthy of support, or many contemporary Protestants have fundamentally altered their sense of the place of women in religious life, so a good deal of spiritually oriented environmentalism has learned not to divide humanity and nature.

Crucially, this view recognizes wildness as a feature of life that can be discovered anywhere: the birch tree in my backyard or the ants scurrying across the sidewalk as much as the rain forest.[33] Therefore, "sacred nature" is not served by fencing off a few special bits while the rest are poisoned. In any case, whatever is being done to the rest of the world will eventually affect "nature preserves" as well. This unavoidable and creative tension—between environmentalism as the protection of separate areas and environmentalism as the celebration of life wherever it appears—is mirrored in religion. For there is a similar split between religion thought of as an alternative to and even an escape from the crass and corrupt social world and religion as a spirit that animates every aspect of our everyday lives. Like those religious teachings that stress finding God not only in church but in washing dishes or earning a living, ecological environmentalism sees as its goal preserving the sacred character of nature by a thoroughgoing transformation of the entire fabric of human society—for only such a transformation will reflect the sacred character of all of life.

It is probably true that the two perspectives, though often represented as alternatives, are both necessary. In traditional religion, we may get the most powerful experiences of the sacred when we are somewhat sheltered from the cares of life, and in environmentalism of nature when we are in the wilderness. Yet to keep such experiences from being little more than passing moments of emotional uplift, we need to realize that their real function is not momentary exaltation, but to inspire us to bring holiness or love of nature to every aspect of our lives.

∾

If religion, as many think, begins in overpowering experiences of ecstasy, awe, deep peacefulness, or cosmic gratitude, it clearly does not end there. Such *experiences*, perhaps regrettably but certainly necessarily, give rise to characteristically religious *beliefs* about what the sacred is and how it should be understood. If such beliefs have too often caused conflict, they nevertheless remain an ineluctable part of religious life. Humans cannot engage in any activity—politics or science, commerce or movies—without telling themselves and each other what they believe about what they are doing. Religion is no different.

The enormous variety of claims by the world's religions may make any attempt to offer a neat definition of "religious belief" nearly impossible, yet I think we will at least head in the right direction if we realize that one function of specifically religious beliefs is to offer some kind of objective support for the powerful emotional encounters just described. In the context of the human relationship to nature, religious teachings are a way of saying that our awe and reverence, delight and trust are rooted in reality, that the intensity of our gratitude is matched by the value of that for which—or to Whom—we feel grateful, and that the deepest principles of the universe in some sense make this a place in which we can fully be at home. Whether those principles are identified with a transcendent God or with the idea that we can achieve full Enlightenment, they offer us assurances that our most vibrant religious experiences arise not because of some accident of our personal psychology, but because of the True Nature of things.

To explore the key spiritually oriented beliefs of the environmental movement we can begin with David Iverson. For him—and, he believes, for many of his fellow Forest Service employees as well—the spiritual quality of the woods is not just a matter of a passing *experience*, but gives rise to a powerful *belief* in the "inherent value of the forest as part of an ecosystem."[34] The earth, its ecosystems, the species that dwell upon it—these are all deserving of respect and care. The inclusiveness of this vision should remind us of those religious teachings that encourage us to reach beyond our normal circles of care: the Torah's revolutionary stress on the importance of moral concern with the powerless ("the widow, the stranger, and the orphan," "the blind and the lame"); Mahayana Buddhism's resolute commitment to save *all* beings. Similarly, the spiritual elements of environmentalism commit us to recognizing intrinsic value beyond the boundaries of our species.

This moral commitment derives in part from another central idea of environmentalism: that rigid distinctions between humanity and the rest of nature are mistaken. Starhawk, a widely recognized leader in the recovery of earth-based religion as well as a political activist, tells us that "the earth is alive, part of a living cosmos . . . spirit, sacred, Goddess, God . . . is not found outside the world somewhere—it's in the world: it *is* the world, and it is us."[35] Recognition of this immanence of the divine, she says, naturally leads to a sense of community with the rest of the earth. Aldo Leopold, whose ecologically oriented writings on game management and forestry helped define the "land ethic," argued that humans should behave like "plain citizens" rather than "conquerors" of the earth. "We abuse land because we regard it as a commodity which belongs to us. When we see it as a community to which we belong, we may begin to use it with love and respect."[36] Geologist Liberty Bailey, whose early twentieth-century writings on ecology had a significant impact on Leopold, instructed his students to live "not as superior to nature but as a superior intelligence working in nature as a conscious and therefore as a responsible part in a plan of evolution, which is continuing creation."[37]

Recognizing the value of nature and asserting our kinship with it alters our sense of what we humans are as much as it does our beliefs about it. We cease to identify solely with our particularly human capacities: with language and history, social position and ethnic group. Just as traditional religions often demand that we see things from the point of view of the sacred rather than that of "common sense" (which would tell us, certainly, that the meek will not inherit the earth, that happiness lies in fulfilling desires rather than overcoming them, and that prophetic calls for justice are hopelessly naïve), so environmental spirituality asks us to recognize a different self from that with which we have generally been taught to identify. "We need wilderness," cautioned Edward Abbey, "because we are wild animals ourselves."[38] "We are a part of the wildness of the universe. That is our nature," wrote Howard Zahniser.[39]

Because of our membership in this wildly extended family, encounters with our kin can have remarkable effects. Barry Lopez, whose wide-ranging fiction and nonfiction works are all oriented to the appreciation of nature and those human communities who have retained their long-term connections with it, suggests that affinities with nature can lead to transformative or healing psychological benefits. Our minds and spirits are shaped by connections to the land as well as to our families and communities. As we can learn deeply from stories about people, so we can be touched by tales of wolves or caribou, storms or sea voyages. At times these stories, not unlike the effects of spiritual discipline, can help heal a broken spirit: "Inherent in story is the power to reorder a state of psychological confusion through contact with the pervasive truth of those relationships we call 'the land.' "[40] From biologist and environmentalist E. O. Wilson's claim that humans are genetically predisposed to attend to and appreciate nature ("biophilia") to Bill McKibben's suggestion that nature has lessons that we won't find on TV, the idea that moral value and spiritual insight can be found in the natural world pervades the environmental community.[41] In historian Thomas Dunlap's

:: "Environmentalism spoke to the human need for a place and purpose in the universe and looked for a way of living with nature inspiring enough to guide people over a lifetime and change society's goals as well."[42]

◆

Environmentalism can function as a religion because it begins with religious emotions and connects them to an articulated set of beliefs about our place in the universe. As most religious traditions have their myths of origins and sense of human destiny, as they tell us who we are and what we should try to become, so environmentalism conceived of as a comprehensive view of human life does the same. John Burroughs wrote, "In intercourse with Nature you are dealing with things at first hand, and you get a rule, a standard, that serve you through life. You are dealing with primal sanities, primal honesties, primal attraction; you are touching at least the hem of the garment with which the infinite is clothed."[43] For environmentalists, this means that humans' superior capacity for knowledge gives us a special responsibility. As E. O. Wilson cautioned (in terms that should remind us of ecotheology), "Humanity is exalted not because we are so far above other living creatures but because knowing them well elevates the very concept of life."[44]

Thus, the emotional experience of our kinship with the rest of nature, as well as our actual physical connection to and dependence on it, has deeply important moral implications. As the relations of marriage, parenthood, or work confer on us blessings and demands, responsibilities that we cannot shirk and unique satisfactions we can get nowhere else, so our membership in earth community creates moral relations to a vast array of other beings. If we want to know who we are and what we must do, much environmentalism tells us, we must acknowledge these relationships and take them to heart. I am not sure a more precise expression of a "religious" sensibility could be imagined.

Because everything we do here (global warming, acid rain, PCBs in the food chain, etc.) will cross the artificial boundaries protecting a preserved area, environmentalism must reshape the entire society. It cannot confine "nature" to special parks or reserves while accepting business as usual in the rest of social life. It must offer a total perspective on how we produce and consume, grow our food and heat our homes; it must affect healing, education, transportation, and technological innovation (for a start!). Any true religion makes serious demands of people—to live according to God's will, to renounce attachment—and environmentalism asks us for a similarly encompassing commitment: to learn to cooperate with nature, to see it as a partner rather than simply dominate it. This theme of cooperation rather than control is repeated constantly in the contemporary environmental literature. It is perhaps its defining belief and most cherished moral value. As Thomas

Dunlap observes, it was Rachel Carson's stress on this point that engendered her critics' most extreme wrath:

> Environmentalism asked society and all humans to acknowledge that we were part of nature. Rachel Carson establishes that theme at the beginning of the environmental movement with her demand that we be humble before the forces of what shaped us and her condemnation of "the control of nature" as a "phrase conceived in arrogance, born of the Neanderthal age of biology and philosophy, when it was supposed that nature exists for the convenience of man"—words her critics saw as an attack on the foundation of Western civilization.[45]

Yet, many would argue, the very idea of cooperation with rather than domination over nature, though (perhaps) appealing in the abstract, is impossible in practice. Don't humans need to eat, build houses, and watch TV? Don't deep ecologists and ecofeminists use antibiotics to treat their kids' ear infections? And don't we all use computers and drive our cars?[46] Isn't all this talk of cooperating with nature simply an armchair philosophy that evaporates once we leave our armchairs and start to deal with real life?

These questions are not easily answered. It is interesting, however, that comparable ones can be asked of any religion. Can people really love their neighbors as themselves or (harder still) love their enemies? Isn't it unrealistic to expect people to completely submit to God or overcome all their desires? And even if we want to, how are we to live by religious values when serious moral conflicts arise: when one neighbor is at war with another, or when our "desires" are really about wanting health and a decent life for our families? Isn't it true that when they leave their mosques and churches and temples (or get up from their armchairs), religious people act like everyone else? In the end, aren't all grand religious values completely utopian?

All these uncertainties are valuable for placing a check on the widespread tendency of the faithful to grandiosity and hypocrisy, but they do not tell the whole story. In fact, many people do bring unrealistic and utopian religious values to play in their lives, at least some of the time, even if they cannot do so always. The kindness, generosity, selflessness, and compassion we find in the world clearly do not require a religious foundation—but they do often have one. In exactly the same way, the difficulty of living as a "plain citizen" of the biotic community, of being partners with nature rather than its master,[47] need not dissuade us from attempting it. In both cases, the impossibility of *completely* fulfilling the moral demands in question does not mean we should not try to fulfill them *as best we can*. The Talmud is clear on this point, succinctly teaching that although no one is expected to "finish the task" (of healing the world from suffering, injustice, and imperfection), no one is allowed to refrain from beginning it either.[48]

The fact that there are numerous complex and confusing environmental issues should not obscure the fact that there are many issues that are neither. Many difficult choices have to be made, but some should be pretty easy. For example, it is not hard to see that one functions more as a plain citizen of or a partner with nature when one farms organically than when one drenches the land in chemical pesticides and fertilizers (thus slowly destroying its capacity to sustain any life whatsoever); or when one minimizes human impact through energy sources that do not change the earth's climate or create toxic wastes; or when one no longer gets minerals out of the earth by cutting the tops off mountains and dumping poisonous by-products into the nearby watershed. There are countless cases—from gas-guzzling cars to the little "ready" lights on appliances (which use more energy per year than that consumed by some entire nations)—where the conflict is not between the legitimate needs of us (humans) and them (the rest of the earth), but between reasonable environmental stewardship and greed, sloth, and moral sloppiness.

Further, those who criticize the values of environmentalism as unrealistic fail to realize that it is precisely the task of spiritually oriented environmentalism—just like other authentic spiritual perspectives—to challenge what "really" exists now and try to replace it with something better. These are not confirmations of common sense, of "what we all know to be the case," but forms of resistance.[49] Like great religious teachers, environmentalists give us a new way to think about how we ought to live, offering an alternative to values based only in fame, money, power, or the good of one's own family and nation. Baker claimed that the worth of a forest was not measured solely by the price of its lumber. Rachel Carson told us that introducing a child to the natural world can create a "sense of wonder" that will serve as an antidote to the "boredom and disenchantments of later years, the sterile preoccupation with things that are artificial, the alienation from the sources of our strength."[50] These are values that, just like the Christian emphasis on peacemaking and humility or the Taoist on a truly balanced life, serve as an alternative to conventional estimations of worth. As David Brower didn't want to be caught dead "in any heaven without canyon wrens,"[51] so environmentalists cannot accept moral codes that discount the health of those wrens, and of the canyons they inhabit, the rivers that run through the canyons, and the oceans, land, and sky that surround them.

Yet, despite *similarities* between the beliefs of traditional religion and spiritual environmentalism, it might be objected, the crucial *differences* that exist are far more significant. The most important of these has to do with the idea of God. When Brower, called by some the single most effective environmental leader in American history, says, "For me, God and nature are synonymous," he is, after all, collapsing Divinity into the earthly, the natural, and the finite.[52] Indeed, it is precisely this assertion of the divinity of the earth, with its overtones of idolatry or paganism, that often alienates some members of the religious community from environmentalism.[53] Though it is true, we might say, that many environmentalists think of nature in the same *way* people of faith think of God, the differences in the *objects* of belief are so significant that they create an impassable divide between the two. Religion just does require a sense of a transcendent Deity, and therefore collapsing divinity into nature is at odds with what religion is. If this claim does not hold for all religions, it would seem to be true for Western religion, African religion, and a good deal of Asian religion as well.

This point is well taken, and I do not wish to suggest that every spiritual perspective is the same as every other one, or that there is no difference between finding the divine *in* nature and believing in a God Who transcends space and time. Yet we need not be so quick in agreeing that the distinction between nature spirituality and religion, even Western monotheistic religion, is absolute.[54] Even within Western religions certain minority currents have stressed the ways holiness can be found in, rather than outside of, the earth.

We might consider one example from Judaism, a religion that has always stressed the nonmateriality and transcendence of its Divinity. The Baal Shem Tov, the late eighteenth-century founder of a particularly mystical and ecstatic form of Judaism known as Hasidism, wrote, "The world is full of wonders and miracles, but we take our hands and cover our eyes and see nothing."[55] It is interesting to ask what exactly could be meant by this. Clearly, the statement does not refer to the well-known miracles of the Bible—the parting of the Red Sea, the sun standing still in the sky before the walls of Jericho—for the world is not *filled* with such rare occurrences. They are miracles precisely *because* they are so rare and extraordinary. Rather, the "miracles and wonders" of which the Baal Shem Tov speaks can only be those things, including those elements of the natural world, that we experience every day: the sparrows that flit from bush to tree in the yard, the progression of the seasons, a crescent moon glimpsed at twilight. These are miraculous because of their beauty and constancy, because of the comfort and joy they bring us, and because we know that they are gifts we have neither created nor earned. And the same sense of the natural world as illuminated by grace (even if we've seen this stuff countless times), as calling forth wonder, gratitude, and a profound sense of surprise right along with our sense of familiarity, is exactly what environmentalists are talking about. Thus, if there are real differences between many traditional religions (though clearly not all of them) and environmentalism, there are also real affinities.

Another of those affinities, and perhaps the most painful one, is the striking similarity between modern forms of the Problem of Evil and a deepening sense of nature's vulnerability. Of course, painful questions about how an all-powerful God can coexist with seemingly unjustified human suffering have been a fixture of religious life at least since Job. Yet the well-nigh limitless mass slaughters of the twentieth century have given this dilemma a new meaning and a new urgency. Auschwitz and Cambodia, mass starvation in a world of computer networks and jet planes, the unendingly repressive governments and the casually callous rich—all these have made the promises of

God's redemptive power seem rather empty. At the very least, faith in God has been tested as perhaps never before, for the very foundation of religious life seems strangely—and sadly—absent just when He or She is needed most. The faithful may still believe in God's infinite power and that "in the end of days" everything will be made clear, but for many, the reality of human experience had made the daily life of devotion strained and seeing God as all-powerful increasingly difficult. As a fellow prisoner in a Nazi concentration camp said to Elie Wiesel, "If God knows what is going on it is terrible; and if He doesn't it is also terrible."[56]

The distressing contours of the environmental crisis make this true for much of environmentalism as well. The temples that Muir and Baker found in the forests have been cut down for hot tubs, overrun with ski resorts and cell phone towers, or are dying from acid rain. Countless species of insects, plants, and birds, each a unique product of evolutionary labors across millions of years, are lost each week. The once comforting sunlight must be blocked so that it doesn't give us skin cancer, and the tropical storms, feeding off energy provided by our fossil fuel addiction, get more frightening every year. The beauties of nature remain, and of course the universe as a whole is far beyond our reach, but the earth—our unique and treasured home—has been deeply wounded. The consolation and inspiration we get from nature is now mixed with our compassion, even our pity, for it. If spiritual life requires trust in the power and grandeur of that which it adores, then spiritual environmentalism and traditional religion (at least of the theistic kind) are in the same, at times foundering, boat.

~

Along with experience and belief, religion is also about action: the performance of particularly religious actions such as prayers and rituals, the structuring of daily life according to distinctly religious codes of conduct, and the creation of a moral community. Here, too, environmentalism has a clearly religious dimension.

As Orthodox Jews must carefully ensure that several hours elapse between eating meat and dairy products, a care entirely lost on everyone who does not observe the traditional Jewish dietary regulations, so environmentalists often develop an awareness of and a set of restrictions concerning what they eat, drive, and wear, the settings of their air conditioners and furnaces, what they put on their lawns (if they even grow grass at all!), and how they recycle their used paper. Thus, in personal life, environmentalism offers a series of choices about daily behavior that encompass the smallest details with an exacting discipline.

These actions, it should be noted, though "practical," are not solely about consequences. Of course, each energy-efficient lightbulb will save so many pounds of carbon dioxide from contributing to global warming, and each time I use my bike instead of the car I lessen the local smog a tiny bit. But most environmentalists know that the real ballgame is institutional, legal, and deeply economic—not personal. Global warming will be changed by new laws governing our energy policy, not individuals buying better lightbulbs; air pollution is significantly lessened by major environmental regulations, not Roger on his bike.

Yet the point is that the religious quality of everyday environmental actions is not measured solely by its immediate effects. It stems, rather, from a characteristically spiritual sense that everything we do has moral meaning. Regardless of how much any given act helps to conserve resources or heal the earth, it must be done anyway, for "this is the kind of person I wish to be" and "it just is the right thing to do." Even if the world is going to hell in a handbasket, even if we cannot change anyone else, we will at least have the satisfaction of knowing we are doing the right thing.

This sensibility is often a particular mark of the religious spirit, for such a spirit tends to see itself in a cosmic context in which everything we do has meaning—because God sees it, because it improves our karma, because our purpose on earth is to live godly lives whether our cause triumphs or not. This religious sensibility is manifest in environmental contexts by the deep feeling that what we do matters, even if we cannot get the right law passed, shut down the polluting factory, or save the whales. Because of the reverence and awe and comfort we *feel* from nature, because we *believe* that it is both our closest kin and the very ground of our being, we will *act* in a way that honors and cares for it. We will not waste or pollute, kill needlessly or cause pain—no matter how many of these things are being done by others.[57]

Living with care and love for earth community requires inner as well as outer action. If we are to take only what we really need, then we must spend some energy asking ourselves how much, how many, and how often we actually do need to take, eat, or use. Asking such questions, as well as engaging in the behavior they may prompt, further reveals the religious quality of environmentalism. For any serious religious dedication includes a lifelong attempt to mold the self in accord with the deepest truths of the universe. Religious action may be aimed at a larger goal—repair of the world, sustaining the community of believers—but it also shapes personal conduct. Similarly, environmentalists stress that personal as well as collective well-being depends on harmony with "laws of nature." From vegetarianism (or, better, veganism) to hybrid cars (or, better, bicycles), the ardent environmentalist has parameters of behavior that require self-discipline and self-knowledge as well as public duties.

Environmentalism can also include that hallmark of religious life: ritual. If the decentralized nature of the environmental movement necessarily entails the absence of any widely shared rituals, that doesn't mean such behavior is absent, only that such rituals that do exist will be individualized, idiosyncratic, and a little harder to pin down. Rituals can be found, serving the purposes that rituals always do: focusing attention, expressing emotion, and arousing energies in ways that simply verbal responses to our religious life cannot.

To take but one example: camped in the western Brooks Range of Alaska, overlooking a rolling tundra on which he saw caribou and wolves, red fox and grizzlies, Barry Lopez made a habit of taking evening walks to study the ground-nesting tundra birds. "I took to bowing on these evening walks. I would bow slightly with my hands in my pockets, toward the birds and the evidence of life in their nests—because of their fecundity, unexpected in this remote region, and because of the serene Arctic light that came down on them, like breathing."[58]

What is this bow but a ritualized way of showing respect? Of acknowledging a sacred value by expressing in one deeply personal gesture a response to the magic and mystery of the natural world? Like most rituals, Lopez's bow is, paradoxically, a kind of communication, in some ways more primitive and embodied than any purely verbal exchange. It is an answer to a call already heard, a reality already felt: an offering to the Holy (whatever that happens to mean for us) in which we do *our* part—God (or Spirit, or Nature) having *already* done His. In the more familiar world of institutionalized religion, similarly, we do not know exactly what it means to God that we bow to the altar when we enter a church, how that slight flex of the knees registers on the Divine Mind. Yet our concern at that moment is not with God, but with ourselves: with constructing a life in which a relation to the Divine is essential, and in which, having received so many blessings from God, we cannot help but offer something in return. We will bow as we enter the church because we wish to register in our body a sense of the reality of God. To remind *ourselves* (presumably God already knows) in Whose Presence we are and therefore how we should comport ourselves. And when Lopez bows to the tundra, the birds, and the sky, he is doing the same. The intense reality of the long Arctic twilight and the astonishing plethora of life he finds within it make him want to be the kind of person who expresses his delight, gratitude, and respect. And so . . . he bows.

∾

Environmentalists do not confine themselves to private gestures, no matter how meaningful. They are environmentalists not just because of what they feel, believe, or do in their personal lives, but also because of what they manifest in the realm of public action. It is here that the political goal of large-scale social transformation and the spiritual habits of self-discipline and self-transformation come together.

One telling example is a form of political action that tends to be a distinct characteristic of religious activism, its most familiar example the Quaker-inspired practice of "witnessing" in response to a collective moral failing. In the context of environmental politics, witnessing may take the form of civil disobedience at a nuclear test sight, interfering with the slaughter of marine mammals, or plugging the outflow from a polluting factory. Through the example of the moral engagement of an individual or a small group, these actions aim to raise public awareness of and resistance to dangerous and damaging activities. Yet they are typically *not* part of a carefully long-term strategy, one that, if carefully followed, might be expected to lead to "victory." These are not steps from a calculated plan so much as cries of the heart. Often, in fact, such actions arise just when the situation seems hopeless— when the whaling ships, the military, or the polluters have the power, money, and public sentiment overwhelmingly on their side. If we are not to sink into a depressed and cynical passivity, a religious rather than a purely secular understanding of political action is needed. For at this point, a religious consciousness tells us that in some deep sense there are forces (or a Force) in the universe on which we can call and to whom we owe allegiance, and that it is important that we bear witness to that allegiance, no matter what the final results.

Not unlike the discipline that leads us to be environmentally responsible in our private lives, our concern at such a time cannot be with a reasoned assessment of our chances of success, but with making as powerful a moral statement as possible. Such an attitude can be found throughout environmental activism: "Greenpeace's well-publicized actions in the face of pollution or mammal killing,"[59] the ragtag army of tree-sitters in California redwood forests, or antinuclear demonstrators in Germany. These activists publicly express their moral concern, at times at risk of arrest or personal harm. They hope that other people will respond, but don't have much hope that they will. Again, it is only because of a deep sense of connection to fundamental structures of meaning and value in the universe that they can undertake action in this way. If this is not a hallmark of a socially engaged spirituality, what is?

In many instances of environmental activism, all the elements discussed so far come into play, and it can be surprisingly difficult to distinguish environmentalism from religion at all. Feelings of reverence and kinship for nature, beliefs about its inherent value and our essential connections to it, and the need to shape our own actions on its behalf come together to form a distinct combination, nearly a fusion, of religion and politics. Consider as one example of this phenomenon the Shundahai Network, a Utah-based coalition that seeks to end nuclear testing, prevent the storage of nuclear waste in Nevada's Yucca Mountain, and replace nuclear energy with clean, sustainable power. Although it places particular emphasis on its links to Native American groups—working, for instance, with the Western Shoshone against continued nuclear tests and Utah's Skull Valley Goshute to stop a high-level nuclear waste dump on their reservation—the Shundahai Network is nevertheless a racially mixed organization. And although it takes inspiration from the writings of Western Shoshone spiritual leader Corbin Harney, it does not bear the stamp of a particular native tradition. In support of its long-term goals it has organized and participated in "nonviolent direct actions, demonstrations, workshops, and conferences."[60] Its members—Native Americans, peace and justice activists, environmentalists—come from a variety of religious traditions and from none. Yet, says current executive director Pete Litster, a spiritual presence permeates everything the group does: "Every event, every meeting—starts with prayer. Our peace encampments at the test site begin with a sunrise ceremony and sweat lodges. We recognize the earth as mother and our relations with every living thing as essential to who we are. Contamination is not just bad for people, it's a sin. For us, the spiritual and the political just can't be separated."[61]

∾

Any political movement can have religious motivations—one need only think, for example, of the religious aspect of the civil rights movement—yet I believe that there is a particular kind of universality to environmental politics that leads it to converge with spirituality.[62] Having overcome its earlier tendency to make a sharp separation between nature-as-wilderness and humanity, a good deal of environmentalism has come to embrace a perspective in which *all* of life matters. Although environmental organizations often make common cause with other "liberal" groups over issues such as women's rights, poverty, or racial discrimination, the former are apt to have a more inclusive vision of their ultimate goals. Movements that focus on what some particular group of people want or need, on their rights and their history of oppression, often tend to ignore or downplay the wants, needs, rights, or oppression of others. If identifying with some particular group does not, as some have said,[63] *necessarily* lead to a consciousness and a politics based in opposition, struggle, and even violence, it certainly has in fact led in that direction. Historically, too much of progressive politics has been interest group politics, and too often the difficulties, if not downright failures, of movements stem from the limited, partial interests that were pursued. The history of the labor movement shows repeated tendencies to favor one group of workers over others: craft workers over less skilled industrial workers, white workers over blacks, men over women. Feminism has had its own troubles with racial and class issues, as well as with the splits between straight women and lesbians. Anticolonialist movements have foundered on issues of human rights for their own people, and nationalist movements have felt free to oppress indigenous groups.[64]

As criticisms of its dominant organizations by people of color attests, environmentalism has had difficulties in this regard as well, at times devaluing humanity as a whole or ignoring crucial political distinctions such as gender.[65] Yet, unlike other movements, it is led by its essential ideas toward universal inclusiveness, toward a commitment to the flourishing of all of life.

To a great extent, environmentalists are necessarily concerned with the destiny of our species and the value of the earth—or at least all living beings—as a totality. It is true that this may bode ill for certain occupational categories—pesticide manufacturers, for instance, or dam builders or SUV salesmen. Yet this vision at least holds the promise that, because the goal is the liberation of everything that lives, no group of humans will be neglected. Given environmentalism's stress on holistic thinking, on the value of all parts of the ecosystems, there is less likelihood that whole groups of people will be devalued. More than political movements for gender and racial equality or workers' rights, environmentalism therefore often has to be both political *and* (in a very broad sense) spiritual. Its concerns are as close and familiar as the emissions from our cars, as global as the World Trade Organization's refusal to allow countries to restrict the importation of carcinogenic pesticides, and as cosmic as our deepest questionings about humanity's proper place in the universe.

Ecotheology's journey toward environmental justice has been taken by secular environmentalism as well. Religiously *and* politically, this means the full integration of the human with the natural, as well as a comprehensive concern with, literally, everyone. In its growing maturity, environmentalism has become more liberatory in its intent, more keyed to a rootedness in community, more sensitive to the interplay between nature preservation and the preservation of indigenous cultures. It has realized that it cannot just aim to ban one chemical or save one species of whale. Rather, it must point to a fundamentally new form of society, one based in a radical kind of democracy and a universal human concern. *And* one that values plants and animals, particular ecosystems, and the entire web of life.[66] If the scope of what has to change is daunting, only such a change can speak to the scope of the crisis we face. Like any good religion, then, environmentalism requires a total commitment, a total transformation, a radical—and I use the term advisedly—conversion.

In short, environmentalism is *not* interest group politics applied to old-growth forests and toxic waste dumps. It is, at its best, a vision in which all forms of life have their place and receive respect and care. If not every environmentalist sees it this way, and if there remains a strong cultural tendency within the movement to downplay this aspect, indications of the truth of what I am saying are not hard to find. Thus Petra Kelley, long-time leader of the German Green Party, a group represented in the national government of a major European nation, wrote, "We must learn to ... recognize the interconnectedness of all living creatures, and to respect the value of each thread in the vast web of life. This is a spiritual perspective, and it is the foundation of all Green politics."[67] The Forests Stewards Guild, an informal network of foresters and other resource management professionals, seeks to promote policies that are both "economically *and* ecologically" responsible. The chair of its board recently cautioned members to remember that human (at least short-term human) and fully ecological perspectives may be at odds, and not to use our limited human perspectives "to justify creating forests of diminished ecological value."[68] In other words, foresters must think for trees as well as for people.

Such spiritually inclusive values may be more explicit in environmental organizations focusing on wildlife protection or wilderness conservation, but they can be found in other places as well. One example is the Southwest Organizing Project (SWOP), a New Mexico-based multiracial membership and multiethnic organization whose focus is on racial, gender, and economic justice. The Project is committed to an environmentalism centered on the places where people live, work, and play, and it focuses on elementary issues of pollution in the air, water, and land. At the same time, it embraces the full statement of environmental justice created at the 1991 People of Color Leadership Summit. This statement includes a commitment "to reestablish our spiritual interdependence to the sacredness of our Mother Earth."[69]

The use of this statement is not accidental, says a SWOP staffer, because the belief that environmental issues include concerns for nature as well as for people can be found throughout the organization. "Most people here," I was told, "are very spiritually connected."[70] Similarly, Greenpeace International, resisting toxic chemicals and nuclear power, trying to save the oceans and old-growth forests and slow down global warming, seeks above all to protect "the ability of the Earth to nurture life in all its diversity."[71] Clark Stevens, media spokesman for Greenpeace USA, is clear about this: "Of course the basis of what we do is love and respect for the earth. We are connected to all of life."[72] The National Resources Defense Council, well-known for its aggressive legal action for environmental causes, echoes this sentiment, seeking to "protect the planet's wildlife and wild places and to ensure a safe and healthy environment for all living things."[73] Friends of the Earth International, with more than a million members in affiliated groups in sixty-eight countries, requires that members combine democratic, nonsexist process with commitment to the major environmental issues of their homelands.[74] Its overall goals include protecting the earth against further deterioration, repairing damage inflicted on the environment by human activities and negligence, and preserving the earth's ecological, cultural, and ethnic diversity. They do this because "human life depends on it, and because there is a widespread sense that the earth is kin to us."[75] The hallmark of all these organizations is the inclusiveness of their vision, the scope of the social transformations they would create, the all-encompassing healing they seek.

At its best, the religious spirit has a similarly inclusive goal. We are all, says the Bible, made in the image of God. We all, says Buddhism, suffer and deserve release from our pain. Each community, says the Qur'an, has its own purpose and value. Any violence against one of us, teach the Jains, can only hurt us all. Looked at in this light, the universal mission of truly compassionate religion and truly global environmental politics naturally converge, at least in the attempt to forge the widest possible social and ecological ethic. Both believe that there are things that deserve reverence, that self-examination and spiritual practice make the most important kind of sense, and that there is more to human well-being than money, power, and pleasure.

This convergence need not embarrass environmentalists. The fusion of religion and politics at the heart of much of the world's environmentalism is a prophetic alternative to modernity's currently reigning faith, the one that stresses the "holiness" of economic growth, ever more complicated gadgets, and hyperstimulating media spectacle. The values of this faith are not a *religious* (nonrational, faith-based) alternative to a *secular* (rational, oriented to evidence) system. Rather, they are a no less rational alternative to the current values. (In fact, if we examine comparative long-term effects, they are a good deal *more* rational.)

That these current values are themselves taken "religiously" is indicated by the fact that they are so rarely questioned, that their adherents find it next to impossible to believe that anyone could doubt them, and that they have been pursued with a blind devotion often heedless to the damage they cause. There is, I believe, certainly no more "rational justification" for "development at any price" than for the claim that nature has inherent value or that the earth is holy. Referring to the conflict between native peoples and economic development over the proposed building of massive, ecosystem-destroying and native people-uprooting hydroelectric dams in James Bay, Ontario, David Kinsley puts the point well:

> If hunting animals is a sacred occupation among the Mistassini Cree, building dams to harness power for electricity is equally sacred for many members of modern industrial society.... The conflict between the Cree and [Quebec political leader] Bourassa, then, is not so much a conflict between a religious view and a secular view as it is a conflict between two contrasting visions of the nature of human beings and human destiny, that is, two conflicting myths about the place of human beings in the natural order, two contrasting ecological visions.[76]

No society can function without some comprehensive framework of values. Every time we apply (or fail to apply) the Endangered Species Act, or choose between energy efficiency and more oil drilling (no matter where, or with what effects), we are expressing a sense of what is important to us, how we ought to live, and what we regard with reverence. The spiritual dimension of environmentalism offers us a fresh choice of how we should answer those questions. Deeply embedded in the environmental movement from its inception to the present, it makes environmental politics particularly fertile ground for an alliance with explicitly religious voices.

CHAPTER 6

OPENING THE HEART
The Ritual Life of Religious Environmentalism

One: God speaks through rocks and trees and water,

People: And the words "peace be with you" are heard.

One: God speaks through budding flowers and twinkling stars,

People: And surely "peace be with you" is heard.

One: God speaks, and is still speaking, when every living creature on earth breathes:

People: "Peace be with you. Peace be with you."

(Pause)

One: But some do not hear the words.

People: Some do not hear God speaking through the land or the sea or the air.

One: They doubt.

People: God speaks, but they do not hear.

(Pause)

One: God speaks, but do we listen?

People: Must we touch the scars on the soil or put our hands through the ozone layer to believe?

> —Earth Day Service Prayer, United Church of Christ, in Kelly Jo Clark,
> " 'God Speaks, Earth Speaks,' A Contemplative Prayer Based on
> John 20:19–31," in *Integrity of Creation Sunday, Second Sunday of
> Easter, April 18, 2004, or Earth Day, April 22, 2004*, Justice and
> Witness Ministries, UCC, 2003, Ecojustice Ministries

Often, the heart of religious life resides not in abstract theology or moral action, but in ritual. Ritual's repetitive nature provides a comforting constancy in a relentlessly changing world; the symbolic material of candles and wine, special foods and familiar melodies touches our emotional center in a way that little else does. When they have become authentic for us, religious rituals soothe our spirits or raise them to ecstasy, giving us a brief taste of the indwelling Spirit of God, Goddess, or Life.

Religious environmentalism has given rise to prayers, rituals, and forms of meditation that embody celebration, concern, and contrition. These include Christian prayer services for Earth Day, new Buddhist meditations, fresh significance given to old holidays, and the creation of innovative and original forms of observance.

This chapter describes a sampling of the many religious practices that are designed to help us honor the earth and feel the depth of our connection to it. These practices express a twofold character now indelibly stamped on the nonhuman world. On the one hand, as *nature* it has an integrity, beauty, and majesty that lead us to see it as a gift from God or a Sacred Presence in its own right. On the other hand, as the *environment* it is threatened and polluted by human action. We feel awe and love as we stand before nature, fear and grief as we regard the environment.

The new rituals of religious environmentalism are designed to help us meet the spiritual, moral, and political challenges of nature's new meaning. They provide a shared psychic space in which we can experience the full range of feelings we have about the natural world, and they encourage us to change our personal and collective lives in response. Reflecting the universal quality of the dangers from environmental deterioration and our collective responsibility for it, religious environmentalism's rituals often manifest a deeply ecumenical quality and often honor the wisdom of indigenous traditions. For individuals, they can help sustain the work of ecological activism; in public settings, they can make political statements more accessible and less threatening to bystanders.

∾

Like the idea of religion itself, the concept of ritual is perhaps best explained by pointing to the many examples of it in our experience: prayers repeated so often that they seem to be known by the lips as much as the mind ("Our Father, who art in Heaven"); lighting candles to begin the Jewish Sabbath or kneeling for daily prayers in a mosque; the focused breathing of Buddhist meditation or the particular hand gestures (*mudras*) of yoga; the careful construction of a Native American sweat lodge; or the delicately sipped wine of communion. The world of ritual is coextensive with virtually all of human civilization, from the cave drawings and goddess statues of the earliest recorded cultures to this year's Christmas Eve midnight mass in Manhattan.

The universal presence of ritual is no accident, because rituals are not simply patterns of action that we repeat mindlessly from one generation to the next. Rather, we maintain them because they play a wide variety of distinctive functions. We do them—and they do for us.

For a start, rituals play a powerful role in emotional life: they can help us *express* deep feelings, from the sadness that comes out during a funeral to the heartfelt joy of blessing God for Creation. They can also *arouse* emotions, in the way a stirring hymn lifts us from depression to gladness, or the sacrament of confession prompts us to feel sincere regret for our misdeeds. And they can *soothe* us, as meditation helps us detach from anger, or the familiarity of Sabbath prayers and Sabbath rest makes it easier to put aside anxiety or alienation.

Beyond these intensely personal experiences, rituals are felt to bring us closer to the wider world of divine energies. A particular sequence of words and gestures, the use of ordinary objects invested with extraordinary efficacy, our own suddenly focused intentions—these are directed to attract God's attention, balance our role in the universe, and improve us morally. The words may in themselves be perfectly ordinary ("Take, eat") and the materials pedestrian (a glass of grape juice, a cracker), yet they are organized to expand our consciousness of the sacred and connect us to it.

In addition, rituals enable us to acknowledge particularly important aspects of human existence: the changing of the seasons, the anniversary of a father's death, the transition of a child to adulthood, the consecration of a marriage. In our collective ritualized acknowledgment of the importance of these life cycle events we commit ourselves to being the kind of people who respond morally to them. As we ask God to gather up the soul of the newly deceased, or express gratitude for the birth of a child, or bless the bride and groom, we are saying that we will do what we can to honor the dead, help care for the child, or support the marriage.

Because we are using rituals to order our own psyches and connect them, through our religious community, to the sacred, rituals can heighten attention and moral seriousness. In the meditative practices of Buddhism, adherents are instructed to examine the underlying structure of their desires and compulsions, with the goal of realizing that these are inherently unsatisfying and have been causing unhappiness rather than real satisfaction. Thus, the ritual of Buddhist meditation, in which a spiritual intention is both embodied in and buttressed by ceremony (the special posture and gestures, the familiar cushion, the meditation hall, the incense), can enable the practitioner to change her mind about what is really important in her life. A ritualized prayer for God's help, if we pray from our hearts, can prompt us to ask "What is it I *really* need? Which of my desires are authentic and have real integrity?" We might ask God for healing, but not for an upward surge in the Dow Jones average; for compassion, patience, and hope—but not for revenge.

Because religious people tend to engage in and receive the benefits from ritual collectively as well as individually, as congregations of whatever faith or tradition, rituals serve the further function of creating community. Having chanted the sutras or shed tears for the dead, celebrated the birth of Jesus or declared our willingness to submit to Allah *together*, we forge ties based in a particularly rich intimacy. These ties link us through a common view of our place in the cosmos, shared emotional joys and pains, and moral commitments. We know that at times the collective energy of the group far outweighs what we could generate alone, and that whatever benefits we've received from ritual life are heightened because others practice along with us.

It might be objected, of course, that a great deal of the time rituals are simply empty gestures: well-known prayers are recited by rote while one thinks about playing golf or tomorrow's appointments; one drowses off on the meditation mat. And certainly religious rituals, like any other human activity, can be done with little passion or attention. In and of themselves rituals do not guarantee serious introspection or authentic community. When it comes to deepening our relation to God or Spiritual Truth, there are (unfortunately) few guarantees.

Yet surely these observations apply to all human endeavors. Marriage does not guarantee fidelity, voting cannot ensure real democracy, and sophisticated technical training can leave a scientist without a serious commitment to expanding knowledge. All these must be done with energy, honesty, and commitment if they are to succeed. Similarly, if (and only if) we devote ourselves to them, religious rituals can provide powerful techniques for self-transformation. They can at times move us to a place in waking life that resembles the resonance of dreams, or serve as a bridge between our existence as physical beings and as carriers of cultural meaning.

For religious environmentalism, rituals can link theology and political action, motivating us to take part in ecological activism. They also serve to sustain us *in* our political and religious lives—for we are not simply ethical agents or faithful believers, but human beings who must be supported morally and emotionally as well as physically. We need the comfort, reassurance, and celebration that rituals offer almost as much as we need food, shelter, and companionship. Finally, as rituals have traditionally served to create communities of believers, so ecological rituals provide collective opportunities to celebrate our kinship with life, atone for our failings, and deepen our commitment to care for the earth.

In the prayers of the Shundahai Network, the Tu B'Shvat seder of the Redwood Rabbis, and the tree-planting Eucharist of Zimbabwe's ZIRRCON, we have already encountered examples of ritual. Now let us look in greater detail at this rich and continually evolving source of sustenance, action, and community.

❧

Nature-centered rituals are as old as religion itself and can be found in all traditions, including those that have focused on a transcendent God rather than the presence of Spirit in earth community. Hindu and Native American, Jew and Christian have all honored the natural world as a sign of God, celebrated the cycle of the seasons, and praised God for Creation. Mayans would pray for the right to clear a field; the Hindu Artharva Veda XIX asks for blessing and peace on the land, earth, and water; and medieval Catholic mystic Hildegard of Bingen exalted "the fiery life of divine essence . . . in the waters . . . the sun, moon, and stars."[1] Yet, as powerful as these examples are, we must be clear that we have crossed a great historical divide, and that nothing from the past can mean exactly what it did before.

Consider, for example, the simple prayer of Rabbi Nachman, a leading figure in the creation of Hasidic Judaism in the late eighteenth century:

> Master of the universe
> Grant me the ability to be alone;
> May it be my custom to go outdoors each day
> Among the trees and grass—among all growing things . . .
> May I express there everything in my heart
> And may all the foliage of the field—
> All grasses, trees, and plants—
> Awake at my coming,
> To send the power of their life into the words of my prayer
> So that my prayer and speech are made whole.
> Through the life and spirit of all growing things
> Which are made as one by their transcendent Source.[2]

The basic idea of this prayer, that the natural world has a spiritual energy that can augment that of humans, has a strikingly ecological tone. Its words promote, probably more effectively than the tomes of theologians, a respect and care for "all grasses, trees, and plants" that would be welcome in any environmentalist setting.

Yet, it is noteworthy that I came across Nachman's prayer in a book published by Shomrei Adamah, the first self-consciously Jewish environmental organization in the United States, an early and important force in contemporary Jewish environmentalism. The creation of a book subtitled *Classic Quotes on Human Beings and the Environment* already implies that there is some rising need for us to think specifically about this particular connection, for such books simply were not created in the past. What has changed, in effect, is that although Nachman would have had little problem finding "trees and grasses" with which to "be alone," for most twenty-first-century Americans it is not so easy. We would probably encounter other people. We would almost certainly hear a human-made machine before very long.[3] There is a special poignancy to our need of the natural world, and a special—and historically unprecedented—fear that a great deal of the force Nachman hoped to find in nature is on its way out. We may still pray using Nachman's words, but in some ways our hearts are heavier than his, our need greater, and the distance between us and the help we seek much farther. In today's world, Nachman's prayer means something very different than it did for its author. Any one of us might, like Nachman, feel the support *of* trees as we pray, but Nachman did not have to pray *for* the trees, nor acknowledge that he was part of a collective form of life that was—by acid rain or urban sprawl—destroying them. The delight with which we contemplate nature is now tinged by fear, sadness, regret—and perhaps a touch of guilt as well.

These considerations mark much of religious life. When a contemporary Jew recites the Nishmat prayer as part of the traditional daily morning service, a prayer that begins "The soul of every living being praises you, O God," a new and pained awareness can arise. As species by species many of the earth's living beings are being extinguished, mixed in with their praise of God may well be the last gasp of life. When a Christian celebrates Easter as the rebirth not only of Jesus but of all life as well, she may wonder how many types of fish or monkey failed to make it through the winter. How can nature be a source of inspiration for Taoists and Native Americans when it has been so ravaged?

These dilemmas compel religious traditions to change, and of course, there is nothing new about religions doing new things. Religion is always in a near constant state of renewal, and most of what we think of as our tradition was at one point someone else's innovation. This includes the meaning of rituals as well as their content. We can retain the language and gestures but integrate that form into a different set of personal and collective struggles. What Arthur Waskow says of some of the more ecologically relevant aspects of Judaism is equally true of all the world's faiths:

> At Tu B'Shvat [a holiday celebrating trees] we can plant the trees that together make up the Tree of Life. At Pesach [Passover] we can eliminate the swollen chameytz [leavened bread and other foods that Jews throw out in preparation for this holiday] that makes our lives swell up, and live instead a week of simple living.... And we can face not only the dark side of Pesach, the chameytz and the plagues, but also we can as the tradition teaches read together the Song of Songs, that lovely evocation of a spring in which humanity at last learns how to live in loving, playful peace with all of earth as well as with each other.[4]

❧

While the meanings of Nachman's prayer or the Nishmat are changing, religious environmentalists are creating new prayers, and new ritual forms in which to insert those prayers, to reflect our current quandaries.

Perhaps the most accessible and familiar version of this creative endeavor is the addition of ecologically oriented prayers to traditional religious services. The Ecojustice Task Force of the National Council of Churches, not content with proclamations, lobbying, letter writing, and demonstrations, has for several years created special services for Earth Day, mailing a copy to *each one* of the NCC's 170,000 member congregations. For April 21, 2002, the packet of worship resources included the following:

> On this Earth Sabbath, we open our minds to learn about ecological threats to the health of present and future generations and to the whole community of life.
>
> We reach out our hands to bring healing and change, for the sake of the children of the earth—past, present, and future.
>
> The prophets Isaiah and Hosea said: The land lies polluted under its inhabitants. The beasts of the field, the birds of the air, even the fish of the sea are dying.
>
> God of mercy, we confess that we are damaging the earth, the home that you have given us. We buy and use products that pollute our air, land, and water, harming wildlife and endangering human health.
>
> Forgive us, O God, and inspire us to change.
>
> Chief Seattle said: Whatever we do to the web of life we do to ourselves.
>
> God of justice, we confess that we have not done enough to protect the web of life. We have failed to insist that our government set standards based on precaution. We allow companies to release dangerous toxins that destroy fragile ecosystems and harm human beings, especially those among us who are most vulnerable.
>
> We are connected with those who have gone before us: the martyrs and heroes, all the ancestors who invested themselves for the sake of future generations, and we are connected with those who will come after us.
>
> Our ancestors and descendents support us—we are their champions.
>
> We are related to the earth and all its creatures in a web that cannot be broken without injury to all.
>
> The earth and our fellow creatures support us—we are their advocates. We are connected to Jesus Christ, who reveals God to us, sends us the Spirit, and sends us out in his name.[5]

Many of the critical elements of religious environmentalist ritual—celebration of Creation, contrition for sin, commitment to change—are voiced here. Among the most striking is the clear enunciation of the intimate connections between humans and nature. "We are related to the earth . . . we are connected to Jesus Christ," this service reminds American Christians, and though nothing in it suggests (contrary to David Brower) that "Nature is God," the placement of our relationship to nature in between our ties to other people and to Divinity suggests the moral seriousness, even sacredness, of that relationship. Coupled with the forthright admission of ecological sin, this is a prayer that simply could not have been written before the late twentieth century, no matter how often one repeated psalms that celebrated God's presence in the natural world.

It is also noteworthy that this Christian prayer service includes, without apology or caveats, a quote from a Native American. This choice should bring to mind the long period in which American Christians committed themselves to eliminating the spiritual and ethnic identities of native peoples, during which it was illegal to teach Indian children their heritage. After such a history, the inclusion of Chief Seattle says more than "Native peoples have some ecological wisdom." It affirms, rather, that the words of an indigenous religious leader have enough holiness to be a vehicle for Christian worship.

This affirmation is perhaps the fitting completion of the process that began with ecotheology and continued through statements by major religious groups and cooperative political activism. To a religious person there are few things more personal, more spiritually intimate, than prayer. To welcome the words of a different tradition—one despised for so long—is in itself to make a dramatic statement not just about what Christians think about *Native Americans*, but what they think about *Christianity*. As the new ecological theology preaches kinship with the earth, so the environmental crisis creates a new kind of *human*—and thus potentially religious—kinship. Because we are all physically part of one creation, economically and socially part of one increasingly global system of production and consumption, so we can now envisage everyone as spiritually related as well. The depths of our shared grief, the intensity of our common fear, and the integrity of our mutual commitment to change—these emotional, moral, and political realities create the possibility of a truly ecumenical practice. As the members of ZIRRCON noted, this does not mean that all theological differences disappear. Protestants (even liberal ones!) will not become Native Americans nor will Native Americans become Protestants. It means, rather, that *now*, under the fierce demands of the environmental crisis, *what it means to be a Protestant Christian includes the possibility of celebrating the words and insights of someone from a different faith*. As all significant historical changes—from the rise and fall of empires to the emergence of modern technology and liberated women—are registered in religious life, so the environmental crisis, when taken seriously, leads to a powerful ecumenism of ritual.

∾

Because the environmental crisis is unique in human history, the prayers to which it gives rise may well be unlike anything we have ever had to pray before. People have always had moral failings, but they have never had to confess to devastating creation, or felt the need to pray for the health of the earth as an endangered whole. Likewise, the environmental crisis is prompting prayerful wishes that would not have even made sense in earlier times. The following instance comes from the pastor of a Christian congregation in Nigeria's Niger Delta, where oil development has devastated the local air, water, and land and where the national government and multinational oil companies have joined forces to violently repress local resistance to that devastation.[6] The prayer concentrates in a few sentences the human costs of our dependence on fossil fuels, and how at times the only solace religion can bring to those bearing those costs is an opportunity to ask, as simply and clearly as possible, for some help: "We pray to God on this holy morn that no petroleum oil will be discovered in our communities. Indeed, Lord, let the oil underneath our houses and farms drift away from us. Lord, spare us the pains and the misfortunes and diseases that petroleum oil brings to our people and to our farms and rivers. Lord, protect us from further harm in the hands of those who want our properties, Amen."[7]

Ecological prayers can also take the form of recognizing that human beings simply have not learned what they need to learn, and that things will perhaps have to get worse before they get better. In an intensely personal meditation, environmentalist, farmer, and devoted Christian Wendell Berry laments that God's grace of a created and bountiful earth has not taught us to live carefully, gratefully, or wisely—and that we will have to learn these virtues through a much more painful lesson. Knowing full well what will happen if his prayer is answered, he nevertheless calls out to God: "We have failed thy grace, Lord, I flinch and pray, send thy necessity."[8]

∾

As customary in their own way as Sunday morning services are for Christians, Buddhist *gathas* are short, often poetic, verbal formulas that draw attention to truths of deep import and provide focus for moment-to-moment awareness both in and out of meditation. Traditional gathas have focused on the inevitability of death, the inherent frustration of attachment to desires, and the "emptiness" of any idea of a fixed personal identity. Not unlike prayers in Western religions, they may also serve to express intentions to act in a certain way or a hope that other beings may be free from pain.

Now some leading Buddhist teachers offer them as ways to deepen our awareness of our inescapable connections to nature and of the consequences of an often destructive modern form of life. These new gathas combine a seemingly simplistic attention to mundane details with pointed and at times profound lessons whose simplicity belies their importance. They share an underlying assumption that awareness—or lack of awareness—is a key element in what is going on. While greed, fear, and attachment all have their role, they are much more likely to dominate our consciousness and behavior if we turn a blind eye to the way we are living. These ritual formulas, if taken seriously, can help us pay attention.

> *When recycling:*
> Garbage becomes rose.
> Rose becomes compost—

Everything is in transformation
Even permanence is impermanent.

When planting trees:
I entrust myself to Buddha;
Buddha entrust himself to me.
I entrust myself to Earth;
Earth entrusts herself to me.[9]

In these short pieces, Vietnamese Buddhist teacher Thich Nhat Hanh connects the "ecological actions" of separating the recycled cans or planting trees to basic Buddhist teachings about the universality of change and the sheltering comfort of Buddha's personal example. The point is not, of course, that these gathas tell a Buddhist something he didn't know before. All Buddhists know that everything is in transformation, but this gatha helps them find that most ancient of Buddhist lessons in the most pedestrian of ecologically friendly activities. All Buddhists take refuge in Buddha as the source of the Dharma, but here they are reminded that the refuge they seek is also offered by the earth! Just as traditional Buddhist doctrine rejected belief in fixed and separate identities, which might divide people from each other, or the sacred from the mundane, so there is no difference between caring for the earth and caring for our own spiritual development. The truths of the big blue plastic recycling bin, overflowing with empty cat food cans and last week's newspapers, are in their own way the very truths taught by the Buddha.

In an even more explicitly ecological mode, American Zen teacher and cofounder of the Buddhist Peace Fellowship Robert Aitkin offers us some "verses for environmental practice":

When I stroll around in the city
I vow with all beings
To notice how lichen and grasses
Never give up in despair

Preparing the garden for seeds
I vow with all beings
to nurture the soil to be fertile
each spring for the next thousand years

With tropical forests in danger
I vow with all beings
To raise hell with the people responsible
And slash my consumption of trees.[10]

A familiar phrase from Buddhist prayer, "I vow with all beings," is here joined with ecological care and environmental activism. Buddhist students who might have been committing themselves to freeing all beings from pain or eradicating all desires are now invited to envisage and support more complex and earthly goals: political action, mindful consumption, and protecting the long-term fertility of their garden's soil. These are goals worth praying for, implies Aitkin, as deserving of a Buddhist's attention as any of Buddhism's more traditional concerns.

Finally, Buddhist environmental activists are bringing newly created gathas into the context of political action. For example, in April 1994 fifty Buddhists gathered to celebrate Buddha's birthday at the Nevada nuclear test site. On a newly constructed altar they placed offerings and then recited sutras and engaged in walking meditation. In a well-publicized civil disobedience, some walked over the boundary and were arrested. One of their leaders offered the following prayer: "All merit and virtue that may have arisen through our efforts here, we now respectfully turn over and dedicate to the healing of this beautiful sacred land and to all beings who have been injured or harmed by the weapons' testing on this place, so that the children of this world may live in peace free from these profane weapons."[11] A prayer for healing of the earth, or for peace for children, is hardly new. What is striking, however, is *where* this Buddhist prayer is being offered: at the site of nuclear tests, a source of cancer-causing fallout, as destructive a force of the human and natural worlds as can be imagined.

Does it make any difference that these protestors *prayed* as well as protested? That it was a *religious* service as well as a political act? Or that the religious, the moral, and the political were here so intertwined? I cannot help but think it does. For the participants, the religious framework is at the least an invitation to engage in this action as genuinely and authentically as possible. It helps them overcome the near universal human tendency to anger, arrogance, unnecessary hostility to "enemies" or the pursuit of power within the group, tendencies all too common in activist political circles.[12] Of course, there is no more guarantee that religious people will enter political life in a respectful and compassionate way than that secular people will. Sadly, religious mannerisms can themselves be an invitation to oppressive self-righteousness. Yet if one is truly committed to loving one's neighbor or seeking happiness for all living beings, then the use of ritual can help focus and develop that commitment. We all have values that we would like to embody, but because of stress, emotional immaturity, or lack of moral discipline, we fail. If we believe that our religion commits us to these things, then invoking religious values when we engage in public acts may help those qualities emerge. This is perhaps especially relevant in the context of environmental concern and action, where the stakes are so high and the losses we have already endured so great.

One reason rituals transform behavior is the sense of timelessness they can generate. When they are deeply felt, religious services transport us out of the normal time of alarm clock settings and doctor's appointments, of getting there on time and three weeks later. Rather, we are encouraged to feel that events can happen both at one time and at all times: that the liberation from Egyptian slavery takes place each Passover, that the crucifixion and the resurrection of Jesus happen each Easter, or that meditation suspends both memories of the past and dread of the future. Religious practices also encourage us to sense that human identity—who we really are—is not nearly so fixed as we generally suppose. Jesus can be found in the face of the poor; Buddha Nature is present in the simplest person and the commonest object. Like their capacity to arouse powerful emotions or focus attention, rituals can thus also break the boundaries of conventional social ego—and in doing so, make a positive contribution to contexts of political struggle that have been witness to countless disappointingly destructive manifestations of that ego.

The power of ritual can transform those who witness the act as well, for it invites a comparable seriousness on their part. There is, or at least their can be, a significant difference between the often antagonistic, confrontational, and even quasi-violent (at least in speech and manner) tone of a typical public political action and the measured solemnity and inclusiveness of a religious ritual. A ritual calls on the onlooker to join or at least respond to a shared set of meanings, whereas a purely secular demonstration often creates a context of friends and enemies, drawing a line in public space that says "You are either with us or against us."

To take one example of this power of religious ritual to engage public understanding and support, consider the case of Thailand, where "forest monks" have taken action to resist a devastating pattern of deforestation. This pattern was part of a comprehensive project of economic modernization, which included integrating Thailand's economy into the global market and depleting its natural resources at an alarming rate. So committed was the government to inculcating the mental habits of modern production and consumption that it went so far as to forbid the teaching of the traditional Buddhist value of "*santhuhi*—austerity or contentment with what one has."[13] Although the major governing body of Thailand's extensive system of Buddhist monasteries went along with this ruling (raising serious doubts about the authenticity of its religious commitment!), a small number resisted. In response to the destruction of forests in northern Thailand, the abbot of a monastery extended the ancient ceremony of ordaining monks to the ordination of trees, including the symbolic act of wrapping them in the traditional saffron robes of a monk: "If a tree is wrapped in saffron robes, no one would dare cut it down. So I thought that perhaps this idea could be used to discourage logging, and I began performing ceremonies on trees in the forest near the temple. I called the ritual an 'ordination' to give it more weight. The term 'tree ordination' sounds weird to Thai people since an ordination is a ritual applied only to men. This weirdness has helped spread the news."[14]

❧

Along with traditional prayers and ceremonies getting new meanings, the environmental crisis has also given rise to fundamentally new forms for ritual.

A striking example of this is the Council of All Beings, an experiential process designed by Buddhist and deep ecologist Joanna Macy and Australian rain forest activist John Seed. These councils, says Seed, were created "to end the sense of alienation from the living Earth that most of us feel, and to connect us with new sources of joy, commitment and inspiration that follow from union with Gaia."[15] The extensive ritual, which can be done in hours or extend for a few days, was created in 1985 and has been performed in the United States, Russia, Europe, and Australia. It unfolds in three stages: mourning, remembering, and "speaking for other life-forms."[16] Reflecting Macy's profound contribution to ecological spirituality, this structure rests on the premise that human beings have deep emotional ties to the earth, and therefore experience powerful feelings of loss and fear in the face of the environmental crisis. As traditional Jews mourn for the destruction of the Temple in Jerusalem, or Christians reflect on the sufferings of Jesus, so the Council begins with shared acknowledgment of loss. The remembering section brings to mind the panorama of cosmic history, starting with the Big Bang and moving through the long ages of evolution. It prompts participants to an awareness of their place in a shared cosmic drama rather than leaving them to the purely personal or social histories on which people usually focus.

The center of the ritual, the Council itself, requires participants to project themselves into the identity of another life-form and to speak for that form to the other members of the group. Like children, poets, or shamans, speakers engage their capacity for empathic connection beyond the ordinary realm of the human ego. If the voices that emerge are necessarily anthropomorphic, they are not totally so, for although humans are different from other life-forms they are also the same: also examples of life, products of evolution, and citizens of a common earth.

In the context of the Council, participants hear both warnings and counsel:

> I am lichen. I turn rock into soil. I worked as the glaciers retreat....I thought nothing could stop me ... until now. Now I am being poisoned by acid rain.
>
> Your pesticides are in me now. The eggshells are so fragile they break under my weight, break before my young are ready to hatch.
>
> It is a dark time. As a deep-diving trout I offer you my fearlessness of the dark.
>
> As rainforest, I offer you my powers to create harmony, enabling many life-forms to live together.[17]

This Council of All Beings ritual is the ceremonial analogue of several crucial themes. The most important of these, one that has been stressed by theologians, major denominations, and religious environmental action, involves the deep ties of kinship and care between humans and the rest of nature. A living sense of these ties has been lost to much of modern society, and a central goal of religious environmentalism is to reawaken it. Thus, although the Council itself presumes no particular religious commitment, it expresses the experiences and hope of virtually all who have tried to respond to the environmental crisis, whether in a Jewish, Christian, or Muslim celebration of the earth's creatures as God's creation; a Buddhist "Jewel Net of Indra," in which each part of the universe reflects every other part; a Taoist stress on imitating nature's balance; or a Hindu emphasis on nonviolent, compassionate action. Whatever stories traditional religions tell about God, humanity, the Divine, or Enlightenment, they must now—more than ever—include a sense of the fate of the earth. However we think of ourselves as humanly religious—as believers in Jesus or Allah, seekers of an end to suffering or of unity with God—the rest of the earth now forms part of our congregations.

Yet, it is not enough simply to assert all this in straightforward language. A kind of emotional technology must be devised to enable us to feel it, to have an *experience* of kinship and remembering, to allow us to internalize the personal meaning of our ecological beliefs. As the Jewish observance of Passover begins with the words "Tonight, each Jew should feel as if he or she had just gone out of Egypt,"[18] so the Council of All Beings seeks to generate the felt quality of identification with the rest of earth community.

The ecumenical nature of the Council of All Beings is echoed in a number of similar rituals that have been developed throughout the environmental community. Genesis Farm's Miriam MacGillis has developed the "Cosmic Walk," in which participants follow a long rope in a spiral marked with significant moments in our universe's history. As in the Council of All Beings, the Cosmic Walk connects the physical body, emotional openness, and a focused awareness of the reality of our place in cosmic time. A few selections from a much more extensive list provide a glimpse into what someone taking the Cosmic Walk would encounter:

> Today we take a glimpse at the beauty of the Story, something of its deep mystery. It is the story of the universe, the story of Earth, the story of the human, the story of you and me.
>
> From the great mystery, all of us came to be. From the void, from the dark, came the light and the spark. Some 15 billion years ago, a great ball of fire expanded outwards into the creation of the Universe—space and time, shadows and light. The universe expands and cools rapidly. After a million years, things cool sufficiently for hydrogen and helium to bring with them new forms of matter....
>
> 4.5 billion years ago, our Solar System forms from the remains of the supernova explosion. The sun and a great disk of matter emerge—all the planets and other members of our solar system family. Here begins the story of what will become one blue-and-white pearl of a planet....
>
> 1 billion years ago, Organisms begin to eat one another in the predator-prey dance that promotes the vast diversity of life as predators pick off the least healthy members among their prey species....

150 million years ago, Birds emerge as direct descendants of certain dinosaurs whose foreleg bones evolve into wing bones, jawbones into beaks and scales into feathers. Birds!

114 million years ago, Flowers evolve gorgeous and overt sexual organs, making themselves irresistible to insects by way of colors, perfumes, and delightful nectars. The Earth adorns herself magnificently and invites the sky creatures into a new dance. Flowers!

4 million years ago, Hominids leave the forest, stand up, and walk on two legs. They move over the surface of the Earth eventually spreading themselves over all six continents. . . .

100 thousand years ago, Modern Humans emerge. Language, shamanic and goddess religions, and art become integral with human life.[19]

At this point, I can almost hear someone muttering that all these rituals are little more than quasi–new age fluff, far from the seriousness of authentic faith. Following a rope or talking for lichen, indeed! How can they even be spoken of in the same breath as taking Holy Communion, celebrating Passover, or honoring Krishna?

Although I sympathize with this concern, I believe that what really distinguishes Communion or a seder from the Council of All Beings is simply the familiarity of Communion and a seder to us, their long-standing embeddedness in our culture, and not their content or structure. If the new ecological rituals seem a little hokey, so do all rituals when removed from the communities that practice them and the religious intentions that give them meaning. Is not a Passover seder, after all, in many ways just like the Cosmic Walk: a ritualized retelling of an ancient story to help us understand where we came from and who we are? And the little tricks that facilitate that telling—a special mixture of apples, wine, and nuts that resemble the mortar used by the Jews as they worked for Pharaoh, having the questions that start the seder asked by the youngest child—what are they but methods of focusing attention on that history, little different in and of themselves than walking along a rope arranged in a spiral? Are not the reenactments of the Stations of the Cross but a way of helping Christians sense their connectedness with the sufferings of Jesus, a connectedness that must be consciously cultivated despite frequent protestations of faith, as for the most part ordinary people do not accept their sufferings as Jesus did? And isn't that exactly what the Council of All Beings is doing: cultivating our sense of commonality, despite all the differences, with lichen, trout, and wolves?

We should remember that a good deal of the force of any ritual resides in the intentions of those who engage in it, rather than the objects used, the gestures performed, or the particular string of words recited. Or, to put it another way, the power of these objects, gestures, and words cannot be separated from the intensity of our purpose. Of course, it is essential that the contents of the ritual in question fit something deep in the structure of our experience and hope. It helps if the words of the prayer are poetic rather than dull, that the meditation posture facilitates calm and even breathing, and that Christmas occurs when the nights are long and Easter in the spring. But without intention, none of this would mean very much. And what is tradition but intention historically repeated? The new rituals of ecological religion lack such historical repetition, not because of their own inherent lack of value, but because the environmental crisis is itself so new.

∾

Rituals can become habitual and unthinking, yet they can also be powerful sources of awareness. Framing a period of observation or experience with a ritualistic sense of seriousness and importance can help us look at things we take for granted in a fresh way, and because we discover this newness ourselves, the ritualized observation is far more powerful than a discursive statement or plain description could ever be. Elias Amidon, for example, adapts traditional Buddhist meditation practices to help his students develop "Mall Mindfulness."[20] Gathered in the splendid palaces of consumption, confronting the endlessly repeated message that one really, really needs to buy something, the students are instructed simply to be aware of it all: to witness the place without buying, eating, or even talking. What comes to mind, Amidon tells us, is a deepened sense of the psychic mechanisms by which individuals are bound to the process of unnecessary consumption, as well as the "trail of disruption" throughout the world that the production of all this stuff has cost.

In an exercise that is in some way the converse of mall mindfulness, I require students in my Philosophy and the Environment course to keep a "plant journal."[21] Each student must pick some particular plant—a blade of grass, a tree—and sit with that plant three or four times a week, recording his or her experiences. I tell them to study the plant, talk to it, listen to it, touch it, and smell it. If the plant were to become extinct, they should be able to tell the world what has been lost. Any (legible!) record of this experience is acceptable—including writing over and over that they think the assignment is a waste of time and that their professor is an idiot.

After years of this assignment, I have seen, time and again, a kind of magic unfold for the students who perform it. I remember one fellow in particular: tall and muscular, a football player–fraternity member–beer drinker type who usually dozed or fidgeted during the extended visualizations I led in class and clearly wasn't buying much of my deep ecology–radical environmentalist–tree-hugger message. I was reasonably sure the course meant next to nothing to him. At the end of our seven-week term, I read his journal and found something surprising. For the first two weeks, he did nothing but record his disdain for the plant, the plant journal, and his dopey professor. Then he began to notice the details of the small tree he had chosen. By the fifth week he had named the tree "George" and looked forward to visiting it. His final entry read: *All the other trees have their leaves and George doesn't. I'm really worried about him.*

Someone might suggest that there is nothing specifically "religious" about any of these new rituals. They do not mention God, don't take place in a church or mosque, and follow no traditional rule. They are really just psychological exercises. As with the criticism of the Council of All Beings as new age fluff, there is some truth here. Mall meditations and tree journals certainly reflect a more generalized moral focus and eclectic spirituality than they do any particular theology. Again, however, the lines between these ecological ritual practices and traditional religion are not as clear as one might suppose. Mall awareness exercises and tree journals ask us to think morally and spiritually about the meaning of human existence, to deeply question how we are living, and to widen our horizon of love and care. These are the very stuff of serious religion, whether in the call of the prophets or the psychological insights of the Buddha. We might remember in this regard Protestant theologian Paul Tillich's definition of faith as "man's ultimate concern," by which he meant that the substance of God was to be known not through set theological principles but by the human capacity to rise to a place of utmost devotion.[22] Further, the very lack of any *specific* traditional religious orientation to these new ecological rituals means that they are easily adopted by any *particular* religion. When hundreds of Christian congregations in Great Britain commit themselves to "greening" their own buildings, they often engage in a celebration of the particular plant life in their church yards. When Sikh communities commit themselves (for the next three centuries!) to lessen their ecological impact, they develop awareness of their own consumerist issues.

There is an easy movement toward broad ecumenical acceptance in all forms of religious environmentalism, whether one is rooted in a traditional religion or a newfangled "spirituality." This is no accident, but reflects the actual reality with which we are confronted. Whatever the differences in our beliefs, we all have a physical body, live on the same earth, and confront the same polluted air and diminishing biodiversity. As there is striking commonality in the way all religions celebrate birth and mourn death, so there is an underlying commonality in what we all have to do in regard to the environment. That is why the same new rituals can be easily adapted to different traditions and why each tradition's new rituals can easily speak to those who worship in dissimilar ways.

Time alone will tell which, if any, of these newly devised rituals will become repositories of the kind of intention and repetition that have attached to "traditional" religion. Given the newness of religious environmentalism, and the scope of the crisis that prompts it, we will be creating new rituals for a long time. Prayers will be written, tried out, and discarded. Engaging ceremonies like the Council of All Beings or the Cosmic Walk will be found intensely meaningful for some and leave others cold. The focused attention of mall mindfulness or plant journals will prove effective or be forgotten. This uncertainty means only that we are at the beginning of a long, difficult, but also exciting task: to fashion spiritual lives that meet the challenges of human life in this strange, new world.

Essential parts of human culture, religions have faced numerous challenges throughout their history. One need only read the Bible, carefully, to see how many generations it took to create a tradition that spoke to the moral demands of family, community, and public life. For the past five centuries religions have been challenged by the modern state, nationalism, human rights, the nuclear threat, and a globalized economy. Making sense of these world historic changes in religious terms has always included creating new rituals. Religious environmentalism, for all its accomplishments, is really just beginning its version of this enormous task.

❧

It is a distinct characteristic of human beings that we live in a world not just of physical objects and natural laws but of beliefs and values, of a shared sense of what things are worth and why we are here. The physical world naturally possesses its own objectivity and reality; the human world of values and meanings exists only because we believe in it. Ultimately, claimed anthropologist Roy Rappaport, the task of ritual is to provide a foundation for this human world, to make it "real" through repeated, serious patterns of action.[23] Through tradition and repetition, focused attention and symbols, rituals confer a kind of shared reality on a way of thinking and being. In the context of environmentalism, this means that we will not see our lives as unfolding in a God-created universe unless we celebrate the creation that surrounds us on earth; we will not take the value of mindfulness seriously unless we seriously meditate; and the Sabbath will become a special day not simply because we are told it is by a holy book, but because we *make* it special with its own songs and prayers, meeting in congregations and refraining from work.

The meanings supported by the rituals of religious environmentalism are as varied as the traditions, communities, and personalities involved. They will range from a sense of the new universe story to the awareness of recycling, from taking a focused look at the mall to asking God's forgiveness for our greed and moral failings. Ultimately, however, I believe that two related and profound values permeate all of these rituals: the reality of our *kinship* with the rest of earth community and the importance of finding a way to *balance* our needs, desires, and lives with theirs.

David Abram has suggested that the traditional task of a shaman in indigenous cultures was to find some sustainable, moral, and enduring way for the human community to live in its surroundings, surroundings for which indigenous communities felt love and respect even as they hunted, ate, and used them.[24] Often living at the edge of the village, near the "wild" areas, able to go into trances and communicate with the spirits of eagles or leopards, skilled in the uses of plants for physical and psychic healing, the shaman was a kind of intermediary between the human community and the rest of the world. Her rituals were oriented to sustaining balance and integration with nature. And, she taught, if this balance were lost, the human community would suffer along with everyone else.

Many would say that we have come a long way since then. Our knowledge of how the world works and our technological power have "progressed" immeasurably. Relations with nature can be set by science, politics, and commerce. We will enshrine the laboratory, vote on the fate of the wetland, and find "balance" on our credit card statements and the national debt.

It is my belief, and that of virtually all the religious environmentalists discussed in this book, that this will not do. All the facets of the environmental crisis—from the communities already washed out by rising sea levels caused by global warming to the decimation of the world's fisheries—tell us that we need a new sense of meaning. It has become increasingly clear that if we do not find mutuality with the earth, we will endure lives of continually diminishing value. This will not necessarily mean some dramatic, once-and-for-all apocalyptic *event* in which everything is lost. Rather, we may simply endure a steady deterioration of the air, the water, the land, and our own bodies.[25]

In a culture that often lurches between denial and hysteria, where a series of current crises make it hard to see the long-term decline, how can we focus on these problems, take in their seriousness, and respond? How can we remember that our need to balance ourselves and the rest of the creatures is as real as our need for human love and a healthy culture? It is the task of rituals to help us as we face the truth and try to change: to hone our awareness, reaffirm our intentions, and goad us to action. If we enter into rituals with an open heart, they will also help us express our regret, mourn the dead, and receive some comfort for our losses.

CHAPTER 7

FIVE FACES OF RELIGIOUS ENVIRONMENTALISM

> I knew then that I was no longer acting on behalf of myself or my human ideas, but on behalf of the Earth . . . on behalf of my larger self, that I was literally part of the rainforest defending herself.
>
> —John Seed, *Thinking Like a Mountain*

Grand ecotheological manifestos, bold statements of church leaders, and public actions of ongoing organizations are created only because particular people have chosen to live a certain way. Why do they do so? What kind of people are they? What is the human face of religious environmentalism?

I sought some answers to these questions by asking five religious environmentalists to talk personally about the roles their religious identity and their concern for the earth play in their lives. I wanted to see what led them to the work they do, what makes the work particularly difficult, what they were proudest of, and how they kept themselves going when things, as they often do, seem bleak. I tried to get a varied group, not so much in terms of tradition, but in terms of age and gender, personal background and type of work done, spiritual style and political orientation.

Despite many differences, certain basic and important similarities emerged. These include a wide-ranging commitment to care for the human and non-human alike, a faith in the possibility of deep change, and a refusal to despair—no matter what happens. Although at times these articulate and engaged people feel impatience or grief, their underlying motivation is love: of the earth, other people, and the Sacred. Fiercely engaged in efforts to save wilderness, curb global warming, challenge powerful social institutions, or protect land that is essential to their people's survival, their efforts have played a powerful role in the growth and development of religious environmentalism. Indeed, you will recognize their names or work from earlier chapters of this book. Here we can listen as they tell, in their own words, a little of the personal side of their journey.[1]

❧

Service by creation to people must be reciprocated with service back to creation. Stewardship does not allow taking without giving back. Instead it returns creation's service with returned human service that is given in appreciation, gratitude, and care.

—Calvin DeWitt, from "Biblical Foundations for Christian Stewardship," in *Encyclopedia of Religion and Nature*

A large man with a booming, often laughing voice, a broad open face, and piercing eyes, Cal DeWitt is an Evangelical Christian, a University of Wisconsin biology professor, and a leading figure among American Christian environmentalists. Yet DeWitt is not one of the liberal Protestants or progressive Catholics who make up most of this group. His roots and his community are among Evangelicals, a group that is typically opposed to liberalism, serious environmentalism, and associated social movements such as feminism.

Cal DeWitt has managed to remain within the Evangelical community while speaking out and organizing for environmental commitments. His scientific expertise gives him a unique knowledge base from which to speak about ecological problems and sustainable solutions. His line-by-line familiarity with, and love for, the Bible has an instantaneous religious authenticity. His traditional faith and up-to-the-minute environmentalism, combined with an almost brash optimism and an unhesitating willingness to have a good time, make him a unique figure on the environmental scene.

I first encountered him at a conference on religion and environmental issues at Harvard Divinity School. After an erudite and highly effective lecture on the relationship between classic biblical texts and our environmental obligations, he took questions. "Professor DeWitt," asked an earnest young African American woman, "all this stuff about caring for the earth sounds great, but how can you really communicate these ideas to people who live in the inner city? There isn't any nature there for them to love." Cal leapt to his feet with a gleam in his eye. Obviously he'd heard this sort of thing before. "Not at all," he chuckled. "In fact, I love to take a bunch of city kids on a real nature walk, right where they live. You can find dozens of species of insects in any vacant lot, a whole little forest of organisms just growing up in the cracks in the sidewalk. There are city birds, squirrels, mice. Once you get the kids down on their knees and give them a little looking glass, or have them listen to the sounds early in the morning in spring, they're hooked."

DeWitt's biography contains a whole series of recognitions and accomplishments. As designer and director of the Au Sable Institute in Michigan, he has built a system of religious environmental stewardship education in partnership with sixty Christian colleges and universities across North America, with campuses in northern Michigan and western Washington and at sites in southern Florida, eastern Africa, and southern India. Decades of community conservation efforts have included saving three hundred acres of riverine forest in the Detroit metropolitan area and establishing the Calvin College Ecosystem Reserve in Michigan and the thousand-acre Waubesa Wetlands Scientific and Agricultural Reserve in Wisconsin. He has been consulted by members of the administration, State Department, and Congress and was a principal in preventing the weakening of the Endangered Species Act when in 1995 he appeared in Washington, DC, on *Fox Morning News*, Secretary of the Interior Bruce Babbitt's office, and a major press conference with a cougar from the Columbus, Ohio, Zoo proclaiming, "The Endangered Species Act is *our* Noah's Ark. Congress and special interests are trying to sink it!" Among his nearly one hundred published papers are a pioneering scientific work on the physiological and behavioral ecology of the desert iguana and pathbreaking essays on Christianity and ecology.[2] He has also been one of the guiding lights of the Evangelical Environmental Network, which we encountered in chapter 3.

What led you to join religion and environmentalism?

From my earliest youth, religion and science just seemed all part of a piece. I always thought that the Bible, theology, and science were interwoven. This was part of what we called "two books theology." Nature and the Bible—God is the author of both. And they should both be studied together.

And your passion for the earth, how did that come about?

I had a little painted turtle when I was three. It fascinated me. While fishing with other kids, I was distracted by turtles. I tried to find every type of turtle in Michigan, caught them in the wilds, went looking for them in the lakes and marshes. One thing led to another, and before long I had my own little backyard zoo: reptiles, amphibians, parakeets, even a cockatiel. Thirty-nine parakeets at the peak of my work with birds! I would spend hours and hours just observing them all, fascinated, watching lizards eating ants and everything else. This was long before I knew anything about "environmental problems."

So when did that awareness set in?

I was doing dissertation research on the desert iguana, especially about how they regulate their body temperature. So I spent the summer of 1961 in Palm Desert, in California. Toward the end of my work, the first house of a new development was started next to my study site, and ads promised people that there was water nearby. But there wasn't. They'd just brought in a truck with water. A few miles to the west they leveled the dunes to build, and then the new house foundations cracked as wind whipped out the sand beneath. I realized then that people could consistently deny the lessons of nature, and even tell lies about their developments. Then in my early teaching at University of Michigan–Dearborn, I taught courses that brought me to know things more globally. I came to understand that what I saw in the desert was happening nearly everywhere. I studied the Rouge River, saw aluminum boat hulls etched by acid in the water, an inch of fat on the surface of the river from a local rendering company. Once-productive and -beautiful rivers were being used as industrial drains. I was horrified.

Did your training as a scientist lessen your religious faith?

Not at all! In church we sang songs that celebrated creation, in the Psalms we celebrated the earth and all the wonderful creatures, and at the end of every worship service we sang, "Praise God all creatures here below." All this stuff was in my head, my heart. I still hear those words every day. So I realized instantly that pollution and destruction of the earth were a violation of scripture. It was easy to see that polluting God's community was wrong. Also, I grew up with stories of people helping other people, of people fixing things when they were broken. This, I thought, was really broken and I would try to help fix it.

Yet most Evangelical Christians have different priorities.

Yes, the "Moral Majority" just never seemed to realize that "creation" is a gift from God, or that, as the Bible says, it is in Jesus Christ that "all things are reconciled"—not just people, but *all* things! Some Christians saw what I was saying right away, but others seemed just to think about the next life and take little care for what's happening in this one. For me, the Creator is not just outside this world, He is also at work within it. Believing that God is on the sidelines in creation would deceive us and put the whole world, including the Christian community, at risk. Such an interpretation of Christianity is very mistaken and clearly overlooks the message of Revelation 11:18 that those who destroy the earth will themselves be destroyed.

With all you've done, what are you proudest of?

I feel really good about the accomplishments of the Au Sable Institute Forum, an annual meeting of scientists, theologians and practical people who worked to develop a well-founded stewardship ethic. I proceeded on this with the belief that solid biblical research, in the context of a deep scientific understanding of the world, would lead towards responsibility to the earth. In conducting these forums we had to move from just thinking about a theology of creation to seeing how biblically based ethics could be developed and applied to environmental problems . . . and we did! We'd pick a theme, bring in a wide range of scholars, and all sorts of things emerged from our interactions that we had not yet thought deeply about. For example, and this is important in Evangelical circles, we discovered that God's Kingdom and the "New Jerusalem" would come on earth, not somewhere in the heavens. On the very practical side, we had a farmer whose family lives near the Institute who farmed beautifully and productively using a combination of the Bible and *Mother Earth News* for his farming instruction. He grew wheat, for example, not because it would produce much grain in the northern Michigan climate, but because his cows liked it for bedding and the stubble he left three inches high captured blowing dust and contributed to the building up of the soil.

What led me to all of this is a pretty simple idea: the cultures which had used the Bible as their rule of faith and practice for over two thousand years must have found some very substantial ecological wisdom in it. I knew it was there—we just had to find it. So I stepped forward in faith. God—and all the people who interacted at the Au Sable Forums—answered. We contributed very much to a theology of creation that develops an understanding of Christian environmental stewardship.

> *How do you see religious environmentalists connecting*
> *to secular environmentalists?*

You know, it's quite remarkable that people seem to have forgotten that a lot of American environmentalism came out of a deeply religious conviction. John Muir, after all, founded the Sierra Club to protect the "great book" of the Sierras, from which he read the "glacial scriptures" while moving along on hands and knees. Just like in Psalm 104, Muir tells us, "God makes the winds—and the snowflowers—his messengers." And these snowflowers join together to form snow that soon is pressed into ice that does God's appointed work—releasing Yosemite from its rocky "sepulcher." And then there is Republican president Teddy Roosevelt, a product of seven generations of the Dutch Reformed Church in New York, stemming back to the time it had been New Netherlands. One wonders about the "two books theology" Roosevelt might have contemplated with John Muir during their visit together in Yosemite. And how thinking this way helped bring the numerous national parks and reservations that Roosevelt created into existence, preserves that would save these scriptures of Creation.

What has happened is that their religious conviction to save pages from the book of natural revelation has been largely secularized. It's almost funny: the secular environmentalists forget their religious roots while working to preserve Creation, and many Christians profess God as Creator while allowing the testimony of Creation to be diminished.

Cal, despite all you've done, the environment is not in great shape.
What keeps you going when things seem bleak?

What can I tell you? I'm always hopeful, always have several projects going on at the same time, trying to anticipate future problems and deal with them before they get out of control. When bad things happen I try to feel challenged, not overwhelmed. God is in control, not me. But I am here, as the rest of us are, to do God's work in the world. I remember that I work for the Lord, listen to some Bach, and think how I can make something beautiful from what's left now.

Besides, if you live your life to be faithful to God, you know even if you're not "successful," you'll be faithful. Every step taken in faith is a note or stanza in a psalm to God. Real joy bursts forth when we maintain our lives as living psalms.

ℭ

Should we be introducing prayers for the earth into every service in all our synagogues and churches, all our mosques and temples? Should our congregations be teaching eco-truth to our teens and adults, as an integrated part of religious studies?

—Arthur Waskow, at Shalom Center

With his commanding gaze, long gray hair, and bushy beard, Rabbi Arthur Waskow looks like he might have stepped right out of the Old Testament. Yet his colorful clothes, often including a rainbow-designed *kipah* (traditional Jewish head covering) and *talit* (prayer shawl), make you wonder if he stopped in the 1960s counterculture on his way from Mt. Sinai. Indeed, Waskow, who has combined an intensely spiritual Judaism with an intense political activism for three decades, did emerge from the movements of the 1960s, movements that took as their aim the ending of racism, sexism, economic injustice, militarism, and, yes, environmental destruction.

Waskow's long history of spiritual innovation has led him to be recognized as one of the leaders of Jewish Renewal, a form of contemporary Judaism that fuses politically progressive social values with passionate and joyful practice. Since 1983 he has directed the Shalom Center, a network of Jews who draw on Jewish tradition and spirituality to "seek peace, pursue justice, heal the earth, and build community."[3] Widely known for his writings on contemporary Jewish spirituality, his specifically environmental writings include editing the groundbreaking two-volume *Torah of the Earth: Exploring 4,000*

Years of Ecology in Jewish Thought and *Trees, Earth, and Torah: A Tu B'Shvat Anthology* and writing *Down-to-Earth Judaism: Food, Money, Sex, and the Rest of Life*, in which ecological themes are seamlessly connected to the everyday practice of a Jewish life.[4] He frequently appears on NPR and has published op-ed pieces in major newspapers. In 1996, Waskow was named by the United Nations a "Wisdom Keeper" among forty other religious and intellectual leaders.

A charter member of the civil rights movement who worked on voter registration in the 1960s and helped found the progressive think tank the Institute for Policy Studies, Waskow has a PhD in history, was ordained as a rabbi in 1995, and has made his presence felt in virtually every significant political issue of the past thirty-five years, from antiwar struggles in the United States to healing the wounds in Israel/Palestine, from critiquing budget priorities of the U.S. Congress to working for interfaith cooperation on peace, justice, and ecology.

Continually searching for effective ways to communicate his fusion of religious and political values, Waskow is currently leading the Shalom Center in a new project entitled Beyond Oil. This campaign aims to make global oil companies accountable to democratic oversight and to seek alternative energy sources that do not stimulate climate disaster, war, disease, political corruption, and the ruin of indigenous communities.

Arthur, you were among the first to connect religion and environmentalism. How did that happen?

You know, it comes out of all the other values we were wrestling with in the 1960s. In my first Jewish book, *The Bush Is Burning* [1969], I wrote about the connection between powerful corporations pushing workers around, stopping unions, exploiting consumers—and also exploiting and damaging the earth. Oppressing the earth—and oppressing people. It's the same pattern, the same absence of any sense of responsibility. And during this time my sense of Judaism's commitment to issues of injustice was also growing. The pharaohs of Egypt, it seemed to me, were replicated in unjust social power right before my eyes.

Certainly Judaism and the Jewish experience have lots of ecological dimensions. The Torah tells us not to destroy the trees of our enemy; contemporary Zionists planted trees to renew the environment of Israel. When I wrote *Seasons of Our Joy*, it started as a book on holidays and tradition and new forms of celebration. Then I saw how rooted the Jewish cycle of holidays is in the sun, the moon, the seasons. Our Purim holiday is about spring as well as a victory over anti-Semitism; our summer observance of Tishah B'av relates to the passage of the sun as well as historical experiences of loss. I realized that being Jewish is not just about people. We are rooted in the earth as well as in our human tradition.

One of the first places I put this together was in a project with other folks like [former U.S. congresswoman and peace activist] Bella Abzug and [Jewish Renewal leader] Shlomo Carlebach. We raised money to plant trees in Vietnam, after the U.S. government's policy of destroying their forests with bombs and chemicals. We had a weeklong celebration of Tu B'Shvat there.

In the 1980s it was pretty easy to see the threat of nuclear war as making for the ultimate ecological catastrophe. I saw this through Torah: like Noah, we had to try to save the earth. The Shalom Center was founded on the nuclear issue. But we saw it as more than just peace for people. Nuclear war would mean a Holocaust for all of life—so gradually the element of ecological concern that had been an aspect of our work became the central lens to view all other issues. Two rabbi friends of mine wrote a new Tu B'Shvat seder that I published in my journal *Menorah* in the early 1980s.[5] It prays for the protection and celebrates the existence of all the trees, of all life—not just those in Israel. Before you knew it there were Jewish ecology groups, Jewish environmental activists, a national network working on everything from global warming to the relationship between pollution and cancer. The whole thing took off, and we at the Shalom Center kept pushing for a stronger line, a more radical line.

As a Jew myself, I know that environmentalism wasn't big in the Jewish community until recently. What kinds of responses did you get to your work?

Well, first thing, they thought I was kind of a pagan! Then, as a general awareness of environmental stuff grew, they wanted to know, sincerely: "Is the earth a Jewish issue?" The more liberal Jews—reconstructionist, reform, feminist—had no problem. But it's been a tough sell in the more traditional and conservative communities. Yet now a lot of people see that Judaism is, and should be, deeply concerned. Keep in mind that for almost two thousand years the Jews didn't really have any land to care for. We were always strangers. So Rabbinic Judaism, of the Talmud, of our years after we left the Holy Land, wasn't interested in much more than not wasting resources or giving rules for when you could or could not have a business like a tannery in an urban area. So we had to go all the way back to biblical Judaism to find a real sense of responsibility for the land. We had to read it again.

Have you faced any unexpected obstacles to your work?

I think the Jewish community has to decide how far it will go, how seriously it will take the issues here. At the Shalom Center we are now organizing a specifically Jewish campaign against the oil industry, these mammoth corporations who have played such a big role in global warming, destroying indigenous communities, and motivating the Iraq war, whose pollution causes inner-city asthma. They are the pharaohs of today's world. Just like the pharaoh, their unconcern for others is leading to an ecological catastrophe. As pharaoh ignored his advisors, President Bush got reports from the EPA and even the Pentagon on the effects of global warming. He just dismissed them. It may sound dramatic, but I really believe it: the oil industry and their bought politician friends are like drug lords. We need to kick the oil habit if we are to live a decent life.

Now this is all pretty radical stuff—frankly, I don't know how much of the Jewish community will come along.

So much of your writing and activism brings religion and politics together. Is there anything in particular you feel you've learned from more secular environmental politics?

Yes. I think we learned about how serious work here needs up-to-the-minute science, comprehensive policy, and religious values. The three together. There's no need, and in fact it hurts us, to split the politics and the science from the Torah.

What do you consider your greatest accomplishments in this area?

Bringing Judaism into the world, into the wild, into real political struggles. I took part in a campaign to save some of the last redwoods in northern California, and we had a beautiful Tu B'Shvat seder—and did some civil disobedience by planting redwood seedlings on the land the logging company wanted to clear-cut.

Another one—this was great!—was to celebrate my sixty-fifth birthday. My wife said, "C'mon, Arthur, do some wild religious-political act!" It was the seventh day of Sukkot, our week-long harvest festival, when we are instructed to "dwell in booths" in the land. The seventh day is a special celebration called Hoshanah Rabbah. We joined forces with some another Jewish groups and a lot of local conservationists for the Hudson River. We went to the banks of the river, praying the Hoshanah ["God, please save us"] prayers, and while the traditional prayers for the special day focused on famine and drought, we also talked about General Electric dumping PCBs in the river for years. The tradition also says celebrate the seven days of creation with seven prayers and seven dances and to beat willow branches on the earth near the rivers to remind God we need rain. So that's what we did. We had three hundred Jews from up and down the Hudson, twelve nuns, and an elder of the Iroquois tribe, who carried the Torah in one of the dances. Pete Seeger sang "Haveinau Shalom Aleichem [We bring you greetings of peace]" with us.

Arthur, what sustains you during difficult times?

Shabbat! We are taught that the Sabbath is a little taste of what the world will be like after the messiah comes. Every Sabbath is a memory of the future, of that time when we finally get it together—when we make peace with the planet, act like a part of it and not an enemy. So for one day a week the world is perfect and beautiful. Sometimes I will lead services and I try to make the davenning [prayers] part of the healing of the earth. We stand in a circle, see each face as the face of God. We bring the faces of trees, of grasses, of animals into our minds, because all of these differences are evidence of God's gifts to us. We focus on the name of God that in the Western alphabet comes out as "YHWH," with no vowels, and we learn to hear that name as breathing: "YYYYHHHHWWWWHHHH." So we hear each breath, of every life-form, as the name of God. As it says in the prayer book, "The breath [or soul] of all life praises your name." What we breathe in is what the trees breathe out. So we see their faces as also the face of God—the green faces of God.

⁓

Eventually, the environmental movement will prevail. The question is, how many will suffer and how much devastation will be irreversible, before it does?

—Rev. Fred Small

Ramrod straight, lean, and handsome, with the kind of innocent, youthful WASP face that makes you wonder if he just came from a tennis match at the club, Unitarian Universalist minister Fred Small is the guiding light of Religious Witness for the Earth, an interfaith group best known for its direct action demonstrations and civil disobedience, mainly focused on energy issues, in New England and Washington, DC.

Younger in age and a much more recent convert to religious environmentalism than Waskow or DeWitt, Fred Small had at least two earlier identities before he became a minister. As a folksinger and composer (hailed by Pete Seeger as "one of America's best songwriters"), Fred wrote and performed powerful, affecting, and inviting songs that celebrated the goodness and courage of all kinds of people. These songs, which engage topics from life in a wheelchair to Hiroshima, have been performed around the world and recorded on seven albums. Their images of a new kind of relationship between men and women led Fred to be honored by the National Organization of Men Against Sexism for his work on gender justice.

Before he was a singer, however, Fred was a lawyer—and an environmentalist, earning a law degree and a master's degree in natural resources policy at the University of Michigan and working for several years as staff attorney at the Conservation Law Foundation. In 1996, Fred entered Harvard Divinity School in preparation for Unitarian Universalist parish ministry. He is now pastor of First Church Unitarian in Littleton, Massachusetts.

Your first job was with an environmental group. Why?

I grew up in the suburbs of New Jersey, where "being outdoors" meant playing tennis. Yet I managed to find some woods to wander around in. They really beckoned to me. When I read about Native Americans I sensed there was something in their attitude towards nature that the culture around me lacked, though I had no idea how to say what was missing. When I was eighteen I did an Outward Bound solo camping trip in the Boundary Waters area. I didn't have any grand religious vision—I was too busy keeping the spiders out of my sleeping bag and not starving! But I felt deeply connected to the woods and the waters. Somewhere around that time I happened upon two articles on population growth and earth's resources in my grandmother's *Readers' Digest*. The articles said, very simply, that the earth is a closed system and we couldn't sustain population growth forever. The lightbulb went off in my head.

What sparked your commitment to connecting religion and environmentalism?

Well [laughing], first I had to become religious! During the years I was an environmental lawyer, and then my folksinger years, I was pretty much an agnostic, even an atheist. I was just nonreligious, alienated from the Episcopal Church of my childhood. I was your basic secular humanist; nothing in spiritual life spoke to me. Then, in the 1980s, I had some pretty rough years following the end of a relationship. I sought out something to ease the pain. That led me to [Vietnamese Zen Buddhist teacher] Thich Nhat Hanh, and to a serious meditation practice. From there it was a pretty easy move to Unitarian Universalism, where I can walk a spiritual path without having it dictated.

So by the time I became a minister I was still a strong environmentalist and I'd become religious, but I hadn't put them together yet.

So? How did that happen?

The spark for Religious Witness for the Earth came from two pretty unlikely bedfellows: George W. Bush and Gandhi. I had hope for the environmental movement during the campaign in 2000, that Gore had some real environmental values. But when Bush was elected, I was just despondent. The movement had made great strides in the 1970s and 1980s, but since then everything slowed down. With Bush as president it looked like we were head-ing in the wrong direction. The movement was going to be spending all our time defending stuff we'd won years ago.

So I began to see that whatever we'd been doing hadn't been enough. We had to imagine a new way of doing environmentalism, a new way to shift people's ideas and change policies.

At this time I was reading a lot about Gandhi and studying the [essential Hindu text] *Bhagavad Gita*. You see, the greatest problem for me is that I'm so attached to "results," to "winning," to "getting it right." With that attitude, choosing the right action becomes, well, terrifying. I think, "If I'm right, smart, courageous, then I can make everything turn out okay. But if I don't do it right, then things will be ruined. And it's all up to me!"

The responsibility just felt overwhelming. The *Gita* says: act the best you can, and leave the results up to God. Just focus on the task before you. That's all you can do. So this simple idea just liberated me to act, even if I was going to fail. It took a huge weight off my shoulders.

And then I looked at what Gandhi did politically, and even more to Martin Luther King. The idea was simple: spiritual social activism, the power of their combination in India, in the civil rights movement here. And I wondered: could it be possible to tap into the same devotion, courage, and sacrificial zeal, but now on behalf of the environment? Just like civil rights, you know, the environment is a moral issue. When we abuse the environment we steal from future generations, not to mention the victims, near and far, in the present. It's also a crime against nature. Now, I know not everyone feels that way about nature, but I certainly do. But that's not really a problem, because it's pretty clear that if we just took care of what we were doing to hurt people, that would be a big change in itself.

What do you think is your distinct contribution here?

What I wanted to do was take prayer out of the sanctuary and into the streets. Religious groups—well, we are really good at issuing resolutions, quoting scripture, and calling on other people to act. This is not enough! Look at the way the religious leadership mobilized against the war in Iraq. They could, they should, show the same level of commitment about envi-ronmentalism. We have to be articulate, but we have to take action as well. Education, recycling, using a little solar power in a church—they're all great, but we need more. Like Gandhi and King, we have to confront society to be more just.

It's one thing to feel bad about pollution and buy organic
vegetables, it's another to engage in civil disobedience and
get arrested. What kind of response have you gotten from friends,
family, or members of your congregation?

For the most part everyone's been really positive. My wife is a professional environmental activist, so she thinks it's great (though she gets a bit jealous about how much easier it is for a minister to get publicity). People in the community notice because most of the religious political activism we've seen has come from the right, not the left. My congregation has been just terrific, some even helped organize the first big event at the Department of Energy in DC—and a half dozen people from my congregation were arrested [for civil disobedience, at the Religious Witness for the Earth action] with me!

I feel like we are having an effect in Unitarian Universalism nationally as well. In June of 2004 our General Assembly started a two-year study action initiative on climate—this generally leads to a resolution by the national association.

This sounds like it's all been well received.
Any unexpected obstacles along the way?

Well, not really. It's just . . . I guess I'm a little bit too idealistic, probably still a little naïve. I'm always shocked when people disagree with me—or don't jump right into the action! We need . . . how to put this . . . the fearlessness of the civil rights movement. And while we've had a little of that, nothing on a mass scale. Environmental issues are too broad, too diffuse, not so immediate. Or, when they are, they tend to be affecting Native Americans or African Americans—the people with the least power in our society.

You know, the young have less to fear, less to lose. And sad to say, this is as true about me as anyone else. I'd really like to be the Gandhi or the King for the environmental movement, but I probably won't be. I've got a daughter now, and I believe fathers should take as much responsibility for child raising as mothers. I can't go out and save the world while my wife does everything at home. In her environmental job she's saving the world, too. We've both got to be part-time parents and part-time world savers! I've got to earn a living as a minister. I just can't do this full time.

Tell me a little about your spiritual life.

I meditate every day. I began with the kind of focus on awareness that I learned from studying with Thich Nhat Hanh. More recently I've used the form of meditation taught by Eknath Easwaran, which holds my attention better in the face of distractions and planning. I memorize and silently recite passages from the *Tao Te Ching*, the *Gita*, the Prayer of Saint Francis, and the Bible. They help me in daily life, they helped me when I was in jail.

Fred, what sustains you during difficult times?

The idea of making everything an offering to the divine: work, life, success, failure. It all goes to God. I try to consecrate what I do, but I give up ownership. Do my best, but not take it personally.

Day to day, I take comfort in being a parent and in nature. Of course, we can't count on wilderness any longer. There is no place we can go that hasn't been contaminated. The hills are no longer "everlasting." But even if they are no longer timeless and unchanging, they can still open my heart and make me weep.

∾

Are we being drawn into an economic culture that abandons the poor and even condemns the poor as victims of human sacrifice to the false idols of elite greed, power and arrogance?

Are we being drawn into a culture of death that rapes our beautiful natural world of hills and hollers, and poisons our pristine streams and wells?

How can we promote a culture of life? How can we cherish the Earth and defend its rivers and streams, its glens and forests, its animals and people? How can we work with poor people as we build just communities?

—Tena Willemsma, executive director, Commission on
Religion in Appalachia

We are writing to you as representatives of religious organizations to urge you to oppose HR 1592, the Regulatory Openness and Fairness Act of 1999. Our organizations and members are committed to heeding the call to protect God's creation and to seek justice for the most vulnerable people, especially children.

—Tena Willemsma, cochair, National Council of Churches Working
Group on Eco-justice, letter to Congress, at Methodist Church

The values of religious environmentalism pose a stark alternative to the reigning American way of life. Concern for all instead of looking out for number one, love of the land instead of the highest possible rate of return on investments, justice for everyone instead of endless increases in the gaps between rich and poor, between have-a-lot and don't-have-much. If these values are to have a visible public presence, an enormous amount of slow, difficult, and often frustrating work must be done. Organizations must be built—meeting by meeting, memo by memo, issue by issue, fund-raiser by fund-raiser. Coalitions must be formed among those of different faiths and no faith at all. National groups and professional activists must connect to local communities, including people who may initially be suspicious of outsiders, "activists," or "environmentalists."

Tena Willemsma is one of the people who has taken on this work. A Dutch immigrant who came to this country at the age of ten, she broke away from a constricting religious background to work as a VISTA volunteer in West Virginia. There she encountered rural poverty, radical political views, and serious environmental problems while working in the beautiful—but often ecologically devastated—landscape of Appalachia. Raised in the Dutch Reformed Church, she initially rejected but then found a home in Christianity. However, her membership in the Evangelical Lutheran Church of America, she told me, is only a part of a spiritual life that is much more about creating justice and loving the earth than it is about any one denomination or institution.

The center of Willemsma's work has been the Commission on Religion in Appalachia (CORA). In the face of widespread poverty, jobs eliminated by globalization, local ecologies devastated by strip mining and mountaintop removal, CORA's mission is to bring together people from different faith traditions, connect to community organizations, and fight for justice and long-term environmental sustainability. With work in groups throughout Appalachia, CORA unites a familiar focus on employment, health, and taxation issues (a central problem in an area where a single mining company can own most of a county's land), with a commitment to highlighting the struggles of women, minorities, and victims of environmental damage.

CORA has an annual budget of more than $500,000 and has sustained itself (since 1965) as one of the largest and longest-lived regional ecumenical groups in the United States. Seventeen different denominations take part, along with the National Council of Churches, nine state church councils, and dozens of community groups. Willemsma has been its director since 1994 and in that capacity also served as cochair of the National Council of Churches Working Group on Eco-justice (whose Earth Day prayer we encountered in chapter 6) and the National Environmental Justice Advisory Council, a group charged with advising the Environmental Protection Agency on environmental justice issues.

Clearly, none of these groups has "won": enormous problems persist, in some cases getting worse. But in every program—from creating a public policy network to protecting forests and streams from pollution and mountaintop removal, from helping Appalachian residents understand the inequities of our economy to helping create worker-safety networks—Willemsma's work reflects the core principles of religious environmentalism. The organizations she has helped build and maintain are vigorous and visible public voices for safeguarding the natural world, enhancing the lives of those whose communities and lands have suffered in the creation of a modern U.S. economy, and reminding everyone that this work is the very heart of religion. Addressing the first meeting of a regional association of small-town and rural congregations, she made it clear that even in the face of near overwhelming economic and social forces, "there are things congregations can do to make a witness in their communities. We can use natural resources to advance mercy, justice, and peace. Commit ourselves to a just society where all have access to food, natural resources, education, and health care. Use our land to plant gardens and demonstrate energy conservation for our communities." Above all, she emphasized, "the basis is to organize, and organizing gives people a voice."[6]

What sparked your commitment to connecting religion and social change?

The church was such a big part of my childhood—community, family, religion, they were all tied in together. But as I got older I got frustrated. It was the 1960s, all sorts of things were happening, and the church didn't seem to be able to link up justice and religion. Also, I came to understand something about my family history. My grandparents were poor peasants in Holland, always working for a wealthy landowner. For most of their lives they had practically nothing.

So I had to break away. I went to college for a while, but there was so much going on and I wanted to be part of it. I joined VISTA and went to live in a tiny town in West Virginia. Seeing the poverty, listening to the other volunteers and some political people, it seemed the church was just irrelevant to all this. I wanted to make a difference, and religion wasn't going to help.

Then I went back to college and a professor of mine said, "Tena, no matter what you say, your Christianity is still a big part of you. Why not put your faith and your politics together?"

He was right! Even though many of the church people couldn't deal with political ideas of the time, some could. And I decided I'd be part of them. I realized that faith and spirituality are not the same as institutions. It's how you live out your life. Faith and theology connected to the work, justice and religion together. That's what I found in CORA.

How did environmentalism become part of this?

I was living in Nora, Virginia. A coal mining town where The Company owned more than half the land. It was a single-economy community. People were poor, the tax base was low. There was no decent health care, no environmental protection. I began to see how economic and environmental justice interact and that who owns the resources shapes everything else that happens in the community. The companies were ripping the tops off mountains above our home, our sewage ran into the McClure River by our home. So many trees had been cut down that the "hundred-year floods" were coming every three to five years because there was nothing left on the mountain to hold the water in. And all the big decisions were made by people far away from the land. I saw that this system just made it impossible to maintain an environment worthy of the Creator.

I also learned a lot from the people of Appalachia: their love of the land and the outdoors, and how they resist getting caught up in consumerism.

How did people react to your mix of environmentalism and other political ideas?

Sometimes, I have to admit, there are some tensions between environmentalism and economics. If you try to keep the industry clean, they just ship the jobs somewhere else. It becomes a choice between decent jobs or a decent environment. And some folks thought "environmentalism" was some liberal thing they couldn't relate to. But if you go across this region in practically every community you'll also find dozens of little groups, working for clean water, or to protect the forest, or to clean up toxics. They live on this land. The water is their water. If the mountainsides erode, they suffer. Whatever you call it, they know protecting all these things is crucial for them if their communities are going to survive.

Tena, why are you a Christian?

Because I was brought up that way! And my life's journey made me realize how rooted I was in a gospel that tells us to do justice and love mercy and walk humbly. Because it has a vision of justice and peace—of a time, like it says in Isaiah [65:21], when "They will build houses and dwell in them; they will plant vineyards and eat their fruit." And that's our vision, too: to live in sustainable communities, to have people's needs met, to have meaningful work.

With all the groups you've been part of, what do you feel best about?

Oh, it's not really so much what I've done, but what we've learned together: that collaboration and partnership with community organizations is what makes for real change. We've learned how to build with others, that almost every institution has people that can help you move and get others involved in the work. We've learned to listen to people who live the daily struggle, and connect what they know with the broader issues and with our faith.

What's disappointed you along the way?

My sorrow has come with how long things take to change. In my work life I have dealt with a lot of churches at the local level, and change happens at such a slow pace. In communities, it's often a matter of persons in seats of power both in the church and in institutions impacting economic and environmental decisions that block change. Yet there are prophets in all faith traditions who use their power to work for change: through stockholders' resolutions, through boycotts, though peaceful resistance, often at great risk to their own livelihood and personal safety. They speak truth to power.

What keeps you going when things don't go well?

Well, you know, this work can get hard. It's lonely. There's still a lot of sexism around. There isn't much money, and some of the denominations I work with are pretty conservative. Sometimes I do get to thinking: "Why am I doing this?"

Then I remember the spirit of my grandparents. The way they fought against exploiting landowners. Their struggle of resistance and inclusion. When I do this work, I feel I'm honoring their memory.

And I remember Mother Jones: "Don't mourn, organize!" She said it to others, and I say it to myself! I've found that just when things are at their worst, something transcendent comes . . . and I realize . . . this *is* an incredible journey.

❧

> Environmental justice affirms the sacredness of Mother Earth, ecological unity and the interdependence of all species, and the right to be free from ecological destruction.
>
> —First Principle of Environmental Justice,
> cowritten by Charon Asetoyer

I was somewhat relieved that the voice on the telephone was gentle and unassuming, for my last interview subject of this chapter, Native American Charon Asetoyer, has accomplished so much and received so much recognition that I found myself a little in awe of her.

Asetoyer's route into environmentalism came from her identity as a Comanche and her groundbreaking work in Native American women's health education. On the Yankton Sioux Reservation in South Dakota she established the first Native American women's health education center on a reservation, which has worked on a host of issues, ranging from domestic violence and cancer prevention to AIDS awareness and reproductive justice.

Asetoyer's approach to women's health blends traditional holistic healing with contemporary knowledge and techniques. She believes that health concerns arise in a larger context of community advocacy, grassroots organizing for empowerment, environmental safety, and the preservation of Native American language and culture. Her commitment, experience, and knowledge have led her to be a board member or advisor to numerous regional, national, and governmental institutions. These include the U.S. National Advisory Council for Health and Human Services, the Center for Women's Policy Studies, and the National Women's Health Network. Among groups specifically focused on environmental issues, she has served (with Tena Willemsma) on the National Environmental Justice Advisory Committee for the EPA, the Indigenous Women's Network, and the Honor the Earth Campaign.

Beyond U.S. borders, Asetoyer has been active in the United Nations and other international organizations. In August 2001, she facilitated a working group for the High Commission on Human Rights on "The Current Status of Health of the World's Indigenous Peoples," and from Nairobi and Beijing to Havana and Rio she has met with people working on women's health, human rights, and development.

For her work, Asetoyer has received a host of honors from a striking variety of sources, including the Ms. Foundation, the United Nations, and the Center for Women's Policy Studies. Most recently, Women's E-News selected her as one of 2005's Leaders for the 21st Century. For her leadership, grassroots organizing, and innovation in environmental justice work, she was given the "Bread and Roses" Award during the Second National People of Color Environmental Leadership Summit. In 1991, she was a key participant at the first Summit and helped write several of its principles, including Principle 1, which demands that we recognize the "sacredness" of Mother Earth.

*Charon, what does the word "sacred" add to the
environmental justice movement?*

It wasn't so easy to get the word in there! There were a lot of indigenous people involved in drafting those principles and it was a struggle to make our point clear—that First Peoples respect the earth and what she is capable of. It was a challenge to get other people to understand our relation to the earth. But people did come to understand and respect what we believe and what we know.

For me, "sacred" is the most special definition you can put on a situation, the highest form of respect. To say Mother Earth is sacred says that our relationship with her has to do with who we are, where we come from, and where we end up. And when we talk about the earth, what we are talking about encompasses not only human beings, but ties us all together—the two-legged, the four-legged, the finned, and those that fly. We all have to have a clean earth to survive, to be healthy.

Can you tell me some more about how your spiritual life and your environmentalism go together?

For me, you just can't separate them—because for Native American women, it's inherent in our understanding of who we are. Our spiritual identity and our care for the earth are always together. We are taught to respect where you came from, to respect Mother Earth. We see her as our mother. And we know she needs certain things to be healthy. She needs water and sun and wind—and if she is healthy then she will provide for us.

Was there anything in particular that led you to realize that we are in trouble environmentally?

When the eagles were declared endangered because of DDT. It thinned the eggshell, made them fracture. It was going to prevent another generation from being born. For me that was a real eye-opener. I saw so clearly how vulnerable the earth is, the environment is, and that what you put on the earth will affect all the beings—people and birds and fish, every aspect of life. I think of our water sources, how vulnerable they are and how polluted they've become. It's frightening! If all our water is polluted and all the animals in the water cannot survive—how will we survive?

Do you ever feel a personal or political conflict between love of nature and love of people?

Oh yes. You see it in communities that are dealing with encroachment of multinationals. They are after all the resources we have—minerals, timber, coal, oil—and they create high-paying jobs for some local people. And yes, people have to make a living and provide for their families. But how will we suffer for it? How will we pay for it down the line? What is the real cost to the next generation, to the next seven generations? The impact is devastating. We don't know if Mother Earth will ever recuperate. She is so damaged, so scarred. Our people are really vulnerable and have been taken advantage of. We get promises that the industries will respect the integrity of the environment, but that never works out. We end up losing all the way around. Years ago, our tribal leadership trusted what they were told, but that is no longer the story.

Have you faced any unexpected obstacles to your work?

There are always obstacles. The corporations challenge people all the time. We try to maintain pristine land, and they bring in housing developments, threats to wildlife, high-intensity chemical farming that pollutes our land and water. We see an increase in illness—cancer, birth defects, and many other things.

It is so hard to get people to understand that something as innocent-sounding as a landfill, a place to put your garbage, can hurt the land, pollute groundwater, contain cancer-causing illness and cause birth defects. People don't get the relationships. I'm not talking about Indian people, it's the non-Indian people around us. There was a major struggle over a regional landfill here at the Yankton Sioux Reservation. Twenty-six counties wanted to put a landfill within our boundaries. We tried to get people to understand that it was bad not only for Native Americans but for everyone. Due to the location of the landfill it would pose a danger to the drinking water for several counties.

But they wouldn't think long term. They just knew they needed a place to put their garbage and they didn't want it in their community. There was an absence of concern by the non-Indian community over the impact the landfill would have on the environment and how that would impact our health and well-being. The case went to court and the tribe lost. This kind of environmental degradation happens because they only want to deal with "right now" and don't look at the long-term impact, or think about the next generation. People don't think about that until after the disaster—when they can't drink the water anymore.

Have you ever felt that white environmental groups don't take the interests of people of color seriously?

What's done in the environmental movement is the same as everywhere else. Dominant groups want to set the stage, control the decision making, and not pay much attention to the environmental leadership within indigenous communities. They do not have much understanding of treaty law and what impact that has within "Indian Country." This disrespect is not only felt within our communities but also felt in other communities of color. That's why we organized the First National People of Color Environmental Leadership Summit. The Principles of Environmental Justice were a result of the Summit. It laid out principles which guide the movement and those working with and within our communities.

Now that the Principles are in place, there is an organized movement of people of color, including Native Americans. The Principles lay down a set of strong guidelines for everyone to follow. They are a checklist that respects people, our communities, and the environment. Still, a lot of mainstream organizations want to make decisions for us—and that is just not acceptable. They don't understand our relationship with Mother Earth, what we consider degradation of Mother Earth. We don't think the way they do, because we live off the land, and raise our children on it. And we are being directly bombarded by development, mining, logging, chemical farming. Our communities feel it first and we know firsthand how it affects our children, fish, wildlife, and water.

Have your attitudes and beliefs about religious
environmentalism evolved over the years?

In our community, we have a direct understanding of the impact of the factors that pollute our lands. A lot of committed people are working on environmentalism and they understand the complexity of the attacks and the long-term ramifications of what is going on. We come from the land, we raise our families here, we know if the water, land, air, and wildlife are polluted and how it will affect us. We still live off the land in many of our communities. We hunt and fish the wild game and harvest the wild fruits and vegetables. It is important to keep the land and waterways clean so our food will be healthy for our children. It is so hard when we see the dead areas—the rivers, lakes, and streams where nothing lives anymore. They are a source of death for those that once lived in them and a source of illness for our communities.

Charon, with all you've done, what are you proudest of?

The fact that I've been involved in helping maintain our values, our relationships, our understanding to the earth. Without that, we really have nothing. That is very, very important—to take care of Mother Earth and to protect our native lifeways. We don't own the earth, we just borrow it from the next generation. What we do or don't do is their legacy, the condition we leave the land in for the next generation. So I do what I can to take care of our lands and to help support people that take care of the lands they live on.

What sustains you during difficult times?

I have to always remind myself: what would this community be like, what would the world be like, if we didn't do what we do? If we didn't try to hold them back . . . we would not exist. I can keep going because I know that we are holding them back, and that what we are doing is right. I have an understanding that the work we do is protecting who we are, our culture, and Mother Earth. Knowing that is so powerful and so life giving, that it means the small advances we make are worth it. To protect where we come from, so there is another generation that can share in the joy in our native lifeways.

And in the end, our spirituality is not separate from the work we do; it is the work we do.

CHAPTER 8

OBSTACLES, PROSPECTS, HOPE

If consumer society has one Achilles' heel, it's not that it is going to
destroy the earth—it is, but that's not the Achilles' heel. The Achilles'
heel is that consumer society doesn't make us unbelievably happy.

—Bill McKibben, quoted in Jay Walljasper and Jon Spayde,
Visionaries: People and Ideas to Change Your Life

What we must do is incorporate the other people . . . the creeping people, and the standing people, and the flying people and the swimming
people . . . into the councils of government.

—Gary Snyder, quoted in Jim Nollman, *The Man Who Talks to
Whales: The Art of Interspecies Communication*

Religious environmentalism is a diverse, vibrant, global movement, a rich
source of new ideas, institutional commitment, political activism, and spiritual inspiration. Yet, despite the actions and commitments of the entire international environmental movement, the present world situation is, in many
ways, quite bleak. Although progress has been made on some fronts, human
beings continue to extinguish species, pollute, heat up the planet, cut down
forests, overfish the oceans, and destroy the fertility of the soil. Equally distressing, in a post-9/11 world many people find environmental concerns less
pressing than whether or not a suicide bomber will blow up a building, the
United States invade another foreign land, or countries be wracked by religious and ethnic conflict. Political violence, world poverty, AIDS in Africa,
the promises and threats of technology, and the clamors of fundamentalism
seem to crowd religious environmentalism in particular and environmentalism in general off an already crowded world stage.

Therefore, it makes a good deal of sense to ask: Even if religious environmentalism is as fine a thing as this book has claimed it is, can it make any
real difference in the world? What are the obstacles to its growth and positive

impact? To suggest (tentative!) answers to these questions, I examine the larger contexts in which religious environmentalism functions. In sketching these contexts, we will find many reasons to despair but also some grounds for hope. In a world as complex as ours, it should not surprise us that things can be pretty bad, and in some ways pretty good, at the very same time.

∾

Although there may be some exceptions to this rule, I believe that in the main, religious environmentalism must take its place in the broad tradition of progressive political movements, those that have historically fought for an expanded sense of democratic participation (for racial minorities, women, or colonized peoples), an enlarged arena of public concern (social welfare programs, public health), and limits on the undemocratic powers of either corporations or the state. It is no accident that antienvironmentalists lump the green movement with liberals, radicals, and feminists, as, for the most part, that is where we belong. This grouping is marked by a broad and activist commitment to democracy, human rights, pluralism, and community. If religious environmentalism is to function, it must be within that commitment.

In this chapter, I focus on three features of modern life that threaten that commitment. Consumerism, fundamentalism, and globalization are dominant forces in the world's culture, politics, and economics. If religious environmentalism is to "save the earth"—or at least make things a little better—it must come to grips with these forces. I conclude with some reflections on the political form—a vital sense of "ecological democracy"—in which this alternative response may unfold.

∾

It may shock some of us, but it is (unfortunately) not all that surprising that the United States has twice as many malls as high schools, that the average American consumes 120 pounds *per day* of manufactured or extracted materials, or that the rising number of "new consumers" in the emerging Asian powerhouses of India and China already outnumber high-level consumers in Western Europe.[1] From the late nineteenth century, when department stores brought a wide range of hitherto separated goods under one roof, through the explosive growth of advertising from the 1920s on, to the current media assault, consumerism has become an enormously powerful social and psychic presence. This daunting juggernaut challenges religious environmentalism in two distinct ways. First, it provides a critical barrier to any kind of *environmentalism*. Second, it threatens the integrity and significance of *religion*.

Consumerism, we should be clear, is not simply about buying a lot, though it certainly includes that. All through history people have wanted their basic needs met, and that small group with extra cash on hand made a point of getting a good deal more than that. The shape taken by consumerism in the modern world, however, involves not just the multiplication of what you *get*, but the endless expansion of what you *want*. Consumerism teaches that the central goal of human existence is the satisfaction of an ever growing, ever changing array of personal desires. To be a consumer, in this sense, is always to be wanting something else: the newest, fastest, largest (or smallest), best, prettiest, or most impressive. If the superlatives in these categories are restricted to the truly wealthy, the goal will be to get the best knock-offs one can afford. In this sense, consumerism is a quasi-addictive pattern, made up of unending cycles of the stimulation of desire—the satisfaction of desire (buying)—and the stimulation of new desires. Like any other addiction, we feel a rush of craving, a brief moment of contentment, the inevitable letdown—and then a new craving. (In case you think I am making all this up, consider the message promoting a new woman's clothing store: "Fashion is addictive.")

Besides the intrinsic power of any addictive process, consumerism has a profound *extrinsic* appeal in the way it connects deeply important personal characteristics, states of mind, or relationships to stuff that must be bought.[2] For the right price we can get sexual excitement, allure, and performance (from cars, perfume, or Viagra), a meaningful life (from the right "life style"), the virtuous satisfaction of being a responsible mother (from the proper bathroom cleanser or the tastiest cookie mix), good health (from food supplements or workout equipment), good looks (diet products, fashions, makeup), and entertainment (HDTVs, iPods, Playstations). If we want memories, we had better have the right digital camera. If we want to connect emotionally, we should look into the "family and friends" telephone plan. If we are to show affection at Christmas time, it must be through what we buy. This association of critically important human virtues and relationships with shopping further embeds the addictive process. If we cannot express love without buying, if we cannot *be* very much of anything without things, then how can we stop? Pride in work, devotion to God, emotional intimacy, and community spirit all are replaced by—or identified with—consumption.[3]

As many people have observed, a consumerist personality is at odds with any kind of serious environmental concern. Addicts do not take kindly to losing their fix, whether it is the junkie who runs out of cocaine or an American public that cannot conceive of ever limiting its shopping. As the first President Bush said at Kyoto, when he made clear the strict limits of U.S. participation in efforts to control global warming, "The American way of life is not up for negotiation." What he meant was not Democracy and the Bill of Rights, but a standard of living associated with unlimited consumption. Threats as distant and delayed as global warming, rising cancer rates, or desertification of farmland do not stack up against immediately felt addictive urges. Without a program of recovery, addicts put what they are addicted to above everything: their own health, the well-being of their children, the fate of the earth.

This personal identification with consumption as the source of pleasure, value, and love crowds out what Stephanie Kaza and David Loy call the "ecological self."[4] Our natural attraction to the rest of life and vision of ourselves as situated in a world of other living beings are submerged in obsessive self-concern and attachment to things. Like all addictive processes, addiction to consumption is profoundly narcissistic. As Bill McKibben observed, having studied one day's programming, including all those advertisements, on 140 cable TV stations, the one message that is repeated over and over is that you are the most important person on earth.[5] If "the good life" means consumption, then an environmentalism that aims at anything beyond our most immediate concerns (smog, polluted beaches) will be hard-pressed to get support.

Despite this bleak picture, there is some hope. In particular, we should realize that of all forms of ecological concern, religious environmentalism is perhaps the best equipped to respond to consumerism. There is, for a start, the religious traditions themselves. Despite the very real differences among the world's faiths, they pretty much all agree that a good life requires some mixture of holiness, moral living, religious virtue, devotion, and service to the wider community.[6] To the extent that religion still retains legitimacy, what it says about all this matters. If its legitimacy is less than it used to be— and this is partly because of religions' own hypocrisy and inconsistency on money matters—it still exists. Indeed, it is clear that in many places in the world, much to the surprise of those who thought that modernity would usher religion off the social stage, religion still retains billions of devoted followers.

More important, it is within the power of religions not only to preach alternatives to consumerism but to demonstrate that the best things in life (or at least some of them) are indeed free. Peace of mind, a caring community, and the fruits of enduring wisdom are resources that religions, and not the mall or Amazon.com, can provide. The prospect of spiritual fulfillment rather than self-denial or guilt is perhaps the most attractive aspect of what religious environmentalism offers.

Within this larger context religious environmentalism is a particularly strong counter to consumerism. It depicts the practical consequences of an economy based in thoughtless and unending expansion, not only in terms of traditional religious virtues like thrift, but as measured by ecological consequences like global warming. It shows how consumerism is destructive as well as childish and self-indulgent. It also offers real alternative sources of pleasure: reconnecting with earth community can provide a kind of deep joy that makes yet another trip to the mall seem pretty pale.

Of course, neither religion in general nor religious environmentalism can compete directly with the flashy, simple-minded, and essentially *easy* pleasures of consumerism. Religious fulfillment lacks the burning thrills of addiction. Sustaining a community, getting to know and love an ecosystem—or just a little patch of wetland—takes time, focused attention, energy, and patience. The addictions of consumption, by contrast, provide immediate pleasure at a seemingly small price, one measured only in money. The cost to the environment, community, and individual character will usually be paid later. That is why consumerism has such appeal and why religious images and stories—of goodness and compassion, wisdom and humility—provide a critically important window to another world of meaning. For as much as the consumerist messages prevail, they are not the only ones to be heard.

Yet the religious alternative to consumerism is itself threatened, not just because it confronts consumerism as an enemy, but because religion itself can succumb to the pressures of consumerism and become very much like that which it should oppose. When this happens, the distinctive self-discipline and satisfaction of religious virtues become impossible, because religion itself has become consumerist.

On one level, this development is to be expected. In a patriarchal or racist culture, religion will (sadly) have its patriarchal or racist aspects. Let a country's pastors find their nation at war and "Love your enemies" will be quickly replaced by "God grant us victory on the battlefield."[7] Nevertheless, it is dispiriting to see religious life falling prey to consumerism, for when this happens its claim to moral seriousness and its potential as a counter to destructive patterns of life simply evaporate.

When religion becomes consumerist its practices and beliefs are detached from the historical contexts and living communities that give them meaning. In this separation, the profound connections between religion, ethical action, and the earth itself are lost. If the world's wisdom can be purchased for $17.95 at Borders or learned in a weekend workshop, then achieving that wisdom through arduous study and a relentless struggle with the ego seems unattractive, unnecessary, and, well, just "old school." If religious teachers are to be measured by the size of their audience or their church's endowment, by how slick their Web site is or how hyped their bios, then religious leadership becomes a kind of celebrity and holiness can be gauged by numbers. If we look at life's choices as consumers, waiting for our sovereign preferences to be satisfied, then religion had better be "new and improved," make few real demands, and give us what we want. When the task of sustaining a personal spiritual vocation or a local congregation becomes difficult, we will simply move to another, more pleasant setting. It's all about choice.

In short, when religion gets colored by consumerism, everything it stands for becomes as temporary and trivial as most of what is listed on last month's MasterCard bill. This daunting prospect is made more real because the kind of liberal, progressive, or tolerant faith that is usually the context of religious environmentalism bears some affinity to consumerist religion.[8] Powerful currents in modern religious life say, after all, that it is up to us to pick and choose from tradition, that we may alter that choice as we see fit, and that modern life requires constructive change rather than blind adherence to the past.

Although these attitudes *can* give rise to self-centered superficiality, to a superficial pastiche, they don't have to. For the difference between the freedom of liberal religion and the emptiness of consumerism is in the moral and spiritual discipline that the former, but not the latter, requires. The alternative to a fundamentalist orthodoxy is not the freedom to do anything, any way, any time. In direct opposition to the lesson McKibben learned from two thousand hours of contemporary television, religious environmentalism tells us that what is most important is the whole, the community of life, the world (as Native Americans put it) of "all my relations." If my particular church, or aspects of my theology, or my religious practice, need to change to sustain me in a disciplined commitment to that sense of importance, so be it. Such change is still very far removed from a consumerist addiction to endless new desires or an inability to face a challenge. If anything, religious environmentalism is more demanding than many traditional faiths. It may be ecumenically open and willing to criticize its own history, but it takes on the responsibility of saving the world! This is hardly the mind-set of someone browsing the latest Brookstone catalog, searching out gadgets to promote a "lifestyle."

Further, many of religious environmentalism's teachings explicitly contradict the basic attitudes of consumerism. For one thing, because consumerism requires that we constantly move on from desire to desire, object to object, it must neglect any real connection to this town or village, a particular pond or forest. If we love our place and seek to protect it, by contrast, we reject the idea that it is always better to replace something old with something new, or that land that doesn't make money is worthless. If a new mall and the taxes and jobs the mall promises threaten this place, we may well decide that the place takes precedence, that in the scheme of things more money does not always trump every other concern.

Everything in consumerism directs us to immediate gratification. The glossy catalogues, the smiling FedEx man who brings the package to your door, the ease of "one-click" ordering on Amazon—all these whisper that there is no need to think about what the production of all this stuff does to other people or the earth. Religious environmentalism, by contrast, says quite plainly that it is our *religious* duty to find out how much energy it took to produce it, what happens to it when we're finished with it, and what the working conditions are of those who make it; that is, we must examine the consequences of our acts.

Like all addictions, consumerism contracts and narrows us: we lose sight of yesterday, tomorrow, and other people. We can think only of the glittering object of desire, the excitement of indecision, the climactic moment of purchase. Religious environmentalism, on the other hand, relying on a vocabulary of love, duty, God, wisdom, and enlightenment, asks us to see the effects of this form of life for other beings and ourselves.

Of course, this goal in no way distinguishes religious environmentalists from secular ones. Every serious environmental organization knows that consumerism is part of the problem. But once it lists the ecological damage involved, secular liberalism may be hard put to say what exactly is wrong with consumerism. A religious voice, however, can say quite clearly that this is not how we have been instructed to live, not how our saints, prophets, and gurus have lived, not what God wants of us—and not anything that will make us truly happy in the long run. When these words are spoken *within* a functioning religious community, for whom these saints and teachings and ideas are known, they have a force that secular cautions do not.

∾

If consumerism poses the danger that religion, like pretty much all else, will become trivial, then fundamentalism creates the possibility that in a narrow and constricted sense, religion will become *too* important, that it will create an endless cycle of religiously inspired separation, hatred, and violence and be much too preoccupied with defensive hostility to attend to the fate of earth.

The threat of fundamentalism is particularly acute because, as Martin Marty bleakly observes, "Today, nowhere around the globe do religious groups that promote tolerance or reconciliation outpace or out-attract groups that erect barriers against others, and in which the belongers are hostile to religious strangers."[9] This pattern is manifest not only in religions such as Islam, which has never really modernized, but also in such denominations as Protestantism and Catholicism, which, at least to some extent, have. There is a rising tide of socially conservative elements in religions that previously had experienced something of a liberalization process. Most conspicuously, Catholicism in Africa, Latin America, and even the United States has seen growing resistance to the reforms of Vatican II.[10] Mainline Protestant groups—the leading voices of religious environmentalism—have been losing ground to politically conservative evangelical groups who usually do not take environmental issues seriously and who reject other "liberal" ideas such as women's equality.

With countless variations involving (at least) hundreds of millions of people, there is no easy summary of fundamentalism. Yet we can identify a number of key elements.[11] Perhaps most important, fundamentalism arises when people are threatened by dramatic and seemingly uncontrollable change. Undermined by secularism, women's rights, technology, consumerism, and increased encounters with people of different cultures, the fundamentalist cannot accept a world in which all traditions, including his own, have become a matter of choice. Facing forces that diminish his meaning, status, and social power, the fundamentalist grasps at a vision of an eternally fixed and universally true source of authority to stem the tide. When (in the United States, for example) bizarre, decadent, or blasphemous values come to permeate the media or the schools, or (as in much of the Muslim world) the state begins to intrude on family relationships and education, fundamentalist movements rise up to demand that they, too, have a place in the public sphere. As politics seems to threaten religion, family, and traditional values, so the threatened communities have responded by contesting for power in the realm of politics.

A key part of that response is an idealized version of religious belief. Creating an imagined past of purity and homogeneous faith, fundamentalists claim access to the way religion was and should be again. Commentators point out, however, that this past is largely invented. Because fundamentalism is a reaction to the distinctly modern threats of competing religions, secularism, the modern state, and science, it cannot be the same as a tradition that dominated the cultural landscape and faced few, if any, alternatives. Traditional religion was pretty much the only game in town. Fundamentalism faces a pervasive tension, then, in trying to convince others (and itself) that the vision it offers now is really a faithful return to something that existed in the past. Conversely, however, fundamentalism's attempt to impose its own limited vision of religion in the present ignores the conflicts and dissenting tendencies that have always existed *within* religious traditions themselves. The "golden age" was never as homogeneous as it is pictured. Yet it must be pictured so, because it is precisely heterogeneity and difference that are fundamentalism's biggest enemies.

The central tension between liberals and fundamentalists, we should be clear, is not some amorphous value called "tolerance." In the end, a progressive like me is no more tolerant than Jerry Falwell or al Qaeda. Rather, it is a matter of different values, which the progressive religious community, one hopes, holds just as strongly as fundamentalists do theirs. Progressives, for example, are not "tolerant" of misogyny, repression of those who have different holy books, or terrorism. We don't think those things are acceptable, and we are not willing to compromise about it. Thus, the choice between fundamentalism and progressive religion is a substantial choice between women's equality, valuing diversity, using tradition as a basis for reaching out to others rather than constructing our own homogeneous world—or their opposites.[12]

Facing a social and political world that endangers so much of what they hold dear and is rife with a confusing and bewildering array of ideas and behaviors, fundamentalists use religion to make the society comprehensible and controllable. Symbolic struggles and mythical narratives that fill scriptures—from God's promise of divine judgment to Rama's struggles to rescue his kidnapped wife—are seen as analogues to current events: 9/11 becomes the judgment of God on a nation that tolerates feminists, abortion, homosexuals, and pornography; crashing airplanes into buildings is seen as an immediate ticket to heaven, for it is carrying out Allah's will.

Finally, dogmatic and blindly literal readings of the Bible, the Qur'an, or the Vedas are adapted to the most contemporary of purposes and represented as timeless authority. Scriptures' contradictions are wished away, their metaphors ignored. Attachment to these texts, which are taken to be both absolutely true and the source of everything we need to know in the modern world, becomes an emblem of authentic faith.[13] Using holy books selectively, as they must to make any sense of them whatsoever, fundamentalists claim that they are simply following them word by word.

Ironically, there is some common ground between environmentalism and fundamentalism. They are both critical of unrestrained consumption, unqualified acceptance of science and technology, and the privileging of global economic power over community. And both share the conviction that a purely secular world will not fulfill human needs. Both feel that the abstract and impersonal sources of order and authority that tend to shape life in modern society—banking and credit cards, transnational trade networks, and faceless bureaucracy—create a world without real human contact, authentic moral passion, and much chance at holiness.[14]

Overall, however, religious environmentalism and fundamentalism will always be in opposition. Fundamentalism's sense of religious identity is typically anthropocentric in the extreme, treasuring the most human-centered, scriptural, or culturally based aspects of a faith. Fundamentalists tend to move in a purely human world, ignoring any possibility that the rest of the earth has important connections to us, or that the way we live out those connections is a moral issue. Where religious environmentalism seeks to learn from other traditions and proposes an enlarged democracy to include every (human and nonhuman) group affected by industrial civilization, fundamentalism is confident it has all the truth it needs within itself, and tends to prefer that the power of government, if used at all, be instrumental in imposing that truth on the rest of the world. When a fundamentalist group is also defined by a national struggle—as it is for Indian Hindus, for example—the focus is on human-centered conflict: which group will end up with state power and which will not.

Also, fundamentalists are often fixated on sexuality and gender. Their near universal misogyny holds biological processes, typically identified with women, in contempt, or at least as always needing male direction and control. For example, more than half of the statutes of the Iranian constitution after the Islamic revolution involved sexuality.[15] Similarly, responses to abortion, gay marriage, and pornography often have pride of place in the public stance of American fundamentalist Christians.[16]

In the end, fundamentalism typically is just not that interested in *this* world, or in the fate of beings in this world who are not part of their narrowly

construed group, to make a great deal of common cause with serious environmentalism. Or, when it focuses on this world, it does so in a reactive, self-
protective, sectarian way. The believers, or the members of the national/
ethnic group, count; others do not. Even when it is concerned with the sacredness of the land (as are Jewish settlers in the West Bank), it is the land
conceived of as religious possession, not a living community with its own
destiny.

The anxieties about modernity that drive fundamentalism lead its adherents toward rigidity, strict hierarchy, and suppression of theological disagreement. Religious environmentalism, by contrast, seeks to overcome the impersonal—and ecologically destructive—powers of modernity with a more
inclusive community, reaching beyond their own culture, religion, nationality,
and even species. Fundamentalists are attempting to recreate a past that
never was, inventing narratives about a mythical Golden Age of Faith that
their coercive moralizing might bring back. Religious environmentalists are
telling new stories in which the Other is listened to and learned from.[17]

Of course, when fundamentalists achieve political power, they, like every
other government in the world, may be forced into thinking at least somewhat ecologically. Interestingly, along with all its strictures on sexuality, the
Iranian constitution had room for the following: "The preservation of the
environment, in which the present as well as the future generations have a
right to flourishing social existence, is regarded as a public duty in the Islamic
Republic. Economic and other activities that inevitably involve pollution of
the environment or cause irreparable damage to it are therefore forbidden."[18]
As we saw in the example of wildlife conservation in Saudi Arabia, environmental concern tends to arise whatever the religious or political orientation
of the ruling group.

Yet, where fundamentalism is for the most part an opposition movement,
as it is in the West, it will generally remain estranged from environmentalism.
Dealing with threats to cultural continuity and patriarchy, the fate of the
forest, or even of their own water supply, is usually the last thing on the
minds of fundamentalists. For many fundamentalist Christians, ecological
disasters are simply part of the God-created coming crisis that marks the
"last days" described in the book of Revelations. Alternatively, fundamentalists often simply deny that any serious environmental problems exist.[19] The
George W. Bush administration has given us an unfortunate taste of the
political expression of both responses. "Values" are limited to sexuality, gender, capital punishment, welfare, immigration, and the like, while the treatment of wilderness and pollution becomes simply a matter of "economic
sense." The social values of conservative Christianity are combined with economic service to the corporate elite.

Given the steadily increasing worldwide power of fundamentalism, all this
does not bode well for religious environmentalism. How can the public pres-

tige and influence of religion be brought to bear on the environmental crisis if religion becomes increasingly dominated by fundamentalism?

The encounter with fundamentalism is about the meaning of religion in the modern age. As religious people, what do we care about? What gets our attention, and what really doesn't matter very much? Even if religious faith is *personal*, the answers to these questions cannot be purely *private*. Because of the collective nature of modern life—the way our government, economic activity, and media have effects far beyond our own communities—these are questions that will get collective answers whether we like it or not. And these answers will often have little room for compromise. Just as we cannot simultaneously make pornography or abortion legal and illegal, so we cannot both take our relationship with the rest of the earth with moral seriousness and treat the environment as a dumping ground. Either caring for the earth—and for humans who are hurt when we don't care for the earth—is a central part of devotion to God or Spiritual Truth or it is not. Either we take bold steps to deal with global warming or we sit back and watch the temperature rise.

Although conflicts over the religious importance of environmentalism, like a host of other deep disagreements, are likely to continue into the foreseeable future, I believe that fundamentalism's present advance, at least in the West, will eventually peak and decline. What is authentic in it—the rejection of spiritless secularism, moral decadence, and a cheapened attitude toward sexuality in particular and human life in general—will be retained. Its national and religious chauvinism, sexism, and blindness to ecological issues will be increasingly questioned. As with all repressive forms of thought, internal struggle will eventually reveal the intolerable harshness of this set of ideas for what they are. The endless sense of external threat and victimization by the "liberal elite" or "secular humanists" will lose its attraction as people come to realize that the basic cultural and political freedoms of secular liberalism are in fact precious achievements, not optional arrangements to be dismissed or taken for granted. Throughout the world as a whole, people will see where fundamentalism leads. It will be revealed that if Muslims start by suicide bombings against Israeli civilians, they will eventually do the same thing, as Sunnis have been doing to Shi'ites in Iraq, to Muslims. If Israeli settlers "serve God" by terrorizing Arabs in the West Bank, they will soon be terrorizing other Israelis who, they think, are too supportive of Arabs. If Christian fundamentalism begins by attacking secular humanists, it will end up (as it already has) attacking Christians who are "not Christian enough"—and then move on to attack other fundamentalists for not being fundamental enough. Because the movement is a response to a perceived and encompassing threat, its inexorable logic always tends toward anger and schism.

As this process unfolds, we can hope that more people will opt for freedom rather than cultural coercion, though it may take some time before these people see that this is the choice they must make. Struggles over the soul of religion and community will then erupt everywhere. Conservative Protestants, Muslims, and Hindus will offer a less harsh, defensive, and violent self-definition.[20] Some will simply abandon the faith; others will proclaim that their faith is fully compatible with pluralism, women's rights, and care for the earth.

My hope, then, is that eventually fundamentalism will be rejected, or at least significantly modified, because people will see the damage it does. Indeed, no understanding of contemporary social life can retain even a shred of hope if it does not presume that people can realize when they have been misled.

This hope presupposes that human beings will come to cherish moral freedom and can learn from their mistakes, a presupposition certainly more doubtful than most of us would wish. "Has mankind learned the lessons of Auschwitz?" Elie Wiesel once asked, and answered, "No. For details consult your daily newspaper."[21] Yet, despite Wiesel's understandable pessimism, certain genuine accomplishments have been made over the past centuries. We have learned that human beings should not be slaves and that it is worthwhile to try to work together to keep the peace. Real strides have been made toward democratic political order, human rights, and women's social equality. Many believe there is no reason different religions cannot peacefully coexist. There is a worldwide environmental movement, with agencies and NGOs functioning in virtually every country, and more than three hundred international agreements on environmental issues, none of which existed before 1970.[22] If the world still has a long way to go, it is clear that Germany, for example, learned something (though only after unbearable cost to itself and the world) from its experiment in fascism, and that the Eastern bloc learned something from its experiment in totalitarian communism. If there is no guarantee that all these lessons are permanent, neither can we deny that many that were unthinkable three centuries ago have indeed taken root. All this offers some promise that people will come to see fundamentalism for what it is.

Alternatively, we should not forget that because fundamentalists also get cancer, breathe, and have to face the consequences of global warming, they may simply be forced to widen their worldview to include an ecological sensibility. Denial, avoidance, and just plain wishful thinking can last only so long. It will become obvious that the environmental crisis compels a kind of universal concern and that ecological problems simply cannot be kept at bay by national, religious, or ethnic boundaries. "We" will suffer from what "they" do just as much as they suffer from what we do. If we do not learn to think beyond those boundaries, we will be powerless to solve the problems.

But I suspect that once people begin to think ecologically, they will no longer think as fundamentalists. There is a basic contradiction between ecological holism and the partiality of a love restricted only to true believers. This contradiction can be overcome somewhat by making one's own society and government as homogeneous as possible. Yet, even if Saudi Arabia presumes that the Qur'an alone can guide its national wildlife preservation policies, it will still have to deal with non-Islamic cultures if it is to confront global climate change or pollution in the Arabian Sea. Ironically, then, the most powerful ally religious environmentalism has in confronting fundamentalism it also its greatest enemy: the environmental crisis itself.

In cases where fundamentalism actually does take state power, it will be held accountable for the environmental conditions of the people it governs. Ignoring those conditions might make a kind of twisted religious sense, but will also undermine political legitimacy in a hurry. This is especially true because so many of the people likely to be governed by a fully fundamentalist regime will be highly dependent on their direct connections to land, water, forests, and oceans. Ecological degradation will affect them immediately and powerfully. When this happens, a ruling fundamentalist group will have to find justification for a rational environmental policy in traditional texts. The only alternative to this recovery effort will be to admit that their authoritative texts do *not* contain all the wisdom needed for the contemporary world, and that indeed their own movement needs to learn some of what is missing from secular or religious environmentalists. This admission would contradict too much of their own purported source of power, and so they will have to undertake the recovery effort themselves.

However, even if all these positive possibilities become real, there is a very good chance that they will not do so until after a great deal of damage has been done. As with other forms of social learning, we may learn what we need to know only after incalculable human—and natural—trauma.

∽

The greatest threat to religious environmentalism and to any kind of environmentalism may not stem from the changing shape of religion or a commodified culture, but from a much greater power: the current form taken by economic and political globalization. If globalization cannot take a different shape from its present one, then whatever happens with immediate questions (who governs Iraq, whether Democrats or Republicans control the Senate, how to conquer AIDS in Africa), we are all headed for increasing global economic inequality, a deteriorating environment, eroded communities, democracies overridden by "market forces," and more widespread addictive consumerist technoculture (where people aren't starving, that is).

Globalization is a complex phenomenon, showing different faces in different parts of the globe and embodying an unprecedented combination of economic, political, and cultural factors.[23] Yet we can at least list its central features: the universal reduction of human beings to consumers and the replacement of subsistence labor by the production of commodities for sale on the global market; the lessening of local or even national political authority in favor of transnational economic (mammoth multinational corporations) and political (World Bank, NAFTA, World Trade Organization) institutions; and the treatment of all of nature as commodities, as in the genetic engineering of new life-forms and the privatization of community resources such as water. Underlying these political and economic developments is the worldwide spread of a culture that cherishes the global marketplace, diminishes community, isolates families, and projects the successful consumer as the model human being. Ultimately, globalization is the moral logic of Western, especially U.S., consumerism written on the earth.

At first glance, of course, one might think that globalization is a good thing: each country or people liberated to exchange the fruits of their labor on the world's markets; each culture free to learn from all the others; more buying and selling, higher standards of living, and modernity; less poverty and backwardness. In practice, however, much of globalization tends to promote an extremely selective, and often quite destructive and unjust, distribution of power and wealth. It supports certain cultures and communities and eliminates others. Its successes tend to be measured by the simplest and least humane of economic measures—more economic activity, more "wealth" understood purely as purchasing power—while its crushing human and ecological effects are ignored. Above all, globalization's transformations of the way people work, live, and raise families are not democratically chosen, but created and managed by political and economic elites.

To get a sense of globalization's dark side, consider an example of the international production of energy involving Enron in the Indian state of Maharastra. Enron contracted to build power plants there, and Maharastra agreed to pay hundreds of millions of dollars in return. Because the resulting facilities produced electricity that was between two and seven times more expensive than previously existing Indian plants, a new state government attempted to break the disastrous agreement. Pressure was applied by the U.S. ambassador (who soon retired from government service to become an Enron director), and soon a new contract was signed that was even more expensive. Millions of dollars of bribes to local officials secured the contract, threats from U.S and other global institutions solidified Enron's position, and Enron made billions in profits.[24] An already poverty-stricken area of a third world country became poorer, but economic activity measured as the exchange of funds increased. National boundaries, and to some extent national sovereignty, were diminished. Some people did quite well out of the deal, but many more suffered.

Similar outcomes arise when oil is developed for export: giant oil companies and their affiliates and friends reap the benefits while natives have their local ecology ruined by oil spills, waste products, and the intrusion of culturally foreign workers. A two-decades long development of oil-exporting facilities in Nigeria has seen the country's foreign debt increase 400 percent, and the Ogoni peninsula, where the oil wells are, has been acutely damaged ecologically and socially. Resistance by local residents has led to violent state repression and prayers (as we saw at the end of chapter 6) that no more oil be found.

Another harmful impact of globalization arises when subsistence farming is replaced by huge plantations growing a single export crop, and peasants who used to support themselves on the land move to already overcrowded cities with high unemployment. In such cases, people who had been living a reasonably secure existence, with access to land and food, get turned into consumers who must pay for everything they need. Economic activity increases, more money circulates, but the loss of access to their own fields, forests, or coastlines is not registered as a monetary loss, and because the ensuing poverty involves more cash flow, it can be seen as a "better life." Similarly, when traditional foods or herbal medicines are patented by multinational seed or drug companies and the labor spent cultivating and breeding these communally used plants is appropriated for a profit-oriented foreign corporation, despair and suicide wrack peasant communities. As Indian antiglobalization activist Vandana Shiva writes, "Economic globalization is leading to a concentration of the seed industry, the increased use of pesticides, and, finally, increased debt. Capital-intensive, corporate-controlled agriculture is being spread into regions where peasants are poor but, until now, have been self-sufficient in food. In the regions where industrial agriculture has been introduced through globalization, higher costs are making it virtually impossible for small farmers to survive."[25] In this process, indigenous attitudes toward the land in particular must be completely eradicated. Nothing could be farther from globalization's favored practice of the unrestricted exploitation of nature.

Thus, for many people, a great deal of economic data indicate, globalization is an economic disaster. Often, average standards of living decline even when the gross national product rises, tens of millions of refugees from economic "development" are dislocated by the commodification of agriculture, and fundamental ecological resources (forests, rivers, wetlands, mangrove swamps, water resources) are polluted and depleted. The combination of these factors can be devastating. Wangari Maathai, Kenya's Nobel Peace Prize–winner who founded a remarkably effective tree-planting campaign, comments about the joint effects of logged-out forests and commercial agriculture: "In the mid-1970s . . . I found myself talking to rural women about the problems they were facing. One of the issues was not enough energy— energy from firewood. Another was a lack of clean drinking water. We all know where water comes from, from forested mountains. Another problem was malnutrition—a lot of farmers had switched from producing food for household consumption to producing cash crops like coffee and tea to sell in the international market."[26]

All this may coexist with the creation of a sizable middle class of new consumers, or with the local political and economic elite doing quite well.

Economic activity as a whole may dramatically increase, while the quality of life deteriorates. Enormous loans may stimulate economic activity, but the activity may be ecologically destructive and plunge poor nations into a spiral of indebtedness that cripples their economy for decades. And, of course, "countries devastated by debt simply cannot afford to act in an environmentally responsible way."[27] They cannot protect their wilderness, develop long-term sustainable patterns of fishing or logging, or monitor pollution coming from mines and factories.

Justifications of globalization often rest on systematic denial of the social disruption and ecological damage that accompanies the rise in economic activity. The major principle is that all resources should be *privatized* and integrated in the global marketplace, and the human and ecological effects of the production of wealth should be paid for by *society*. Social dislocation, poverty, cultural despair, and ecological damage are all to be handled by the state, for any limitation on what can be produced or sold would be interference in "free trade." But because the world's governments are increasingly coming under a kind of monetary discipline that insists on lower social welfare services, there is literally no one to pay the price of globalization.[28] And crucial areas of the economy are dominated by firms so global that they can dictate economic conditions, tax breaks, and other forms of support from local governments.[29] The stranglehold on economic life of concentrated private interests often means that people must defer to corporations if they are to eat at all.

As a result, essential economic and ecological relationships that support communities and cultures are lost. With the rapid rise of commodification, subsistence labor—work that connects us to enduring communities, roots us in the welfare of people at least some of whom we know, in a land that we hope will be there for our great grandchildren—is replaced. Subsistence labor is oriented to local needs rather than distant ones, tends to be environmentally sustainable rather than destructive (because it is performed by people tied to the place where the labor is being performed), and organized by small groups rather than controlled by mammoth multinational corporations. The cheerleaders of globalization would have us believe that progress means the virtual elimination of subsistence labor and the movement of everyone into the lifestyles of North America, Western Europe, and Japan.

Yet in many cases, just the opposite occurs. For in the developing world, the goal cannot be to reproduce the American standard of living, where subsistence labor has been reduced to a minimum and everything from food preparation to the care of elders is increasingly done for pay. Such a goal is culturally questionable—and would be an unmitigated ecological disaster. Therefore, our goal should not be a nine-room house, three cars, and four computers per family, but security of work and basic necessities for everyone. Besides the ecological consequences, it is also the case that money, education, or prestige, in and of themselves, do not make for collective happiness. What is needed, rather, is the integration of labor into an economic and social system of exchange oriented toward the social good of a particular human and ecological community rather than profit for corporations that are essentially rootless. Simultaneously, local communities need to preserve some political control over their conditions of life.[30] This control, religious antiglobalization activists generally insist, needs to be democratically organized, informed by human rights, protective of indigenous peoples, and include just recompense for labor.[31]

When religious environmentalists take part in the transnational struggles against dam projects that would eliminate the land of tribal peoples and subsistence farmers, or challenge the World Trade Organization's rulings that prohibit member nations from refusing to accept unecological products, or argue at international meetings that compelling poor nations to sell off their ecological wealth to repay debts to the World Bank is unjust and irrational, they are confronting globalization. In this confrontation it becomes clear that the values of ecology directly oppose the transformation of all the earth into commodities and of people into makers and buyers of commodities.[32]

Of course, the world is not likely to return to simple community life. Just as every fundamentalist religious leader has his cell phone and his Internet hook-up, so even the most isolated of peasant villages or indigenous tribes now know they live in a wider world. And this is not always a bad thing. As rooted in subsistence labor and traditional community as the older cultures were, they often had their own versions of gender, racial, ethnic, or class hierarchy.

If we are to find a way out of the current quandaries of globalization, it will not be through a forced choice between the moral narrowness of traditional culture and a life based solely on buying and selling. For example, the women of as yet undeveloped countries should have a third option besides domination in a sexist hierarchy and working for 40 cents a day in a Nike factory. Nor do we want to exchange traditional superstition and customs (some of which are terribly oppressive) for a groundless faith in the wisdom of the market. In any case, as globalization in some form seems to be inevitable, what all 6 billion of us are trying to decide is what shape that globalization will take. Will it be the globalization of greed or of concern? The imposition of the worst—and long transcended in much of the West—features of competitive capitalism on the entire world, or a spread of democracy, human rights, and the accumulated wisdom that will allow for the preservation of human and natural diversity? As we confront this decision, environmentalism's message of concern for *all* of life is a distinct alternative to the modern marketplace's repeated insistence that the meaning of human existence is nonstop economic growth. Religious environmentalism roots the general environmental message in a spiritual framework, one that—among the dynamiting fishermen of Madagascar, Buddhists struggling over modernization in Sri Lanka, Catholics dealing with industrial pollution in Kenya or the destruction of the rain forest in Brazil—can have a powerful appeal.

Yet this appeal comes at a price: the recognition that effective environmental change requires a change in the living standards of the middle and upper classes in the developed world. Religious environmentalism has stressed the *interconnection* of all of life, but it has not fully acknowledged how much that interconnection is marked by profound *inequality*. The U.S. contribution to global warming will impact people throughout the world, as well as in the United States. But our enormous wealth will shield us from many of its worst effects in ways that will not be true for others. If Brazil cuts down all of the rain forests to produce beef for McDonald's, the world's climate will suffer, but the peasants who have lived in the rain forest will see their homes and their culture immediately destroyed. As John Cobb and Paul Santmire have observed, the liberal Protestant churches in the United States have made many resolutions about the importance of ecological values, but few have clearly stated that the United States should no longer pursue a policy of uninterrupted economic growth.[33]

Globalization will not be slowed without a worldwide pattern of resistance, but to create such a movement, religious environmentalists must take seriously what divides us as well as what we share. This will not be easy. The demand for a coordinated response to globalization—necessary because the agents of globalization are themselves both coordinated and enormously powerful—runs up against the fundamental differences among those who oppose it. There must be cooperation among middle-class lawyers in the United States and environmental activists in China, tribal people threatened by dams in India and consumer groups in Europe, Latin American peasants whose fields have been taken to grow bananas or coffee and those of us who are used to getting bananas and coffee for pennies.

To some degree, religious environmentalism has prepared for this encounter. The lessons learned from the environmental justice movement—a movement, we might remember, nurtured by parts of the religious community—are as applicable in global contexts as they are in national ones. Thus, it is not surprising that, for example, the U.S. Methodist Church has taken an active role in supporting fair trade coffee, working with farmers and cooperatives in Central America and Africa to promote organic, shade-grown, coffee that is bought directly from the farmers themselves.[34] Or that the World Council of Churches has been a vocal critic of the "structural adjustment" policies of the major economic institutions of globalization.

Yet such actions, as positive as they are, remain extremely limited when compared to the sheer scope of, say, Chinese industrialization or the clearing of land in the Amazon. Like the outcome of religious environmentalism's struggles with fundamentalism, the future of antiglobalization work does not look terribly hopeful at the moment. Still, just as people may learn important lessons about fundamentalism, so they may see that uncontrolled domination by private wealth is not desirable for human beings and the rest of the planet. There is a worldwide movement, composed of countless large and small organizations, parties, and theorists, that seeks to derail the runaway locomotive of globalization. Religious environmentalism takes its role in this struggle, the outcome of which is still in doubt.

∾

Politics is the arena in which fundamentalism, consumerism, and globalization can be opposed. Books (including this one!) may pave the way, prayers can keep us going when things look bleak, but only if the values of religious environmentalism get embodied in popular political movements will the necessary institutional changes stand a chance of happening. We obviously cannot love the earth or other people very well if we live in a society whose economic life is predicated on damaging both of them; thus, a newly found love of the earth moves us toward public life.

What shape should the politics of religious environmentalism take? There are, after all, an enormous range of possible forms of political action, from the minimal activity of voting for sympathetic political candidates to the high drama of civil disobedience. And there are a host of long-term political strategies and short-range tactics, from trying to convince businesses to become greener to seeking to expose their polluting activities, from grassroots organizing of affected communities to centralized lobbying efforts in the capital.

Underlying such differences are not only diverse beliefs about how to respond to the environmental crisis, but very different life situations from which environmental activism proceeds. Ecological care may be a central *value*: we love nature and see the earth as God's creation or as sacred in its own right. Or environmental activism can spring from a direct response to the *degradation of life*, to the countless particular ways the world is dirtier and more dangerous, to the elimination of species and ecosystems, and to the seemingly inexorable procession of global warming, dwindling biodiversity, and increasing cancer rates. Third, environmentalism may arise because the devastation of the environment is the destruction of my *immediate source of life*: cut down the forest, make the seals toxic, dam the rivers, cut the mangroves, and in a very short time I will starve, get buried in a mudslide, be poisoned by the foods I traditionally eat, find that my village is underwater, or get swept away by high tide.

Of course, some combination of all three orientations may exist for an individual or a group. The point is that the global environmental movement includes people in very different situations. The tribal groups being displaced, the middle-class American whose heart breaks for the birds choking on pesticides, the cancer activist enraged by refusals to ban dioxins—how are all these to work together? Mapped onto global society, the environmental crisis affects us all. Yet because of our varying positions within that society—our divisions of gender and race, nationality and social class, religion and political orientation—we do not come to environmental issues with the same expectations, powers, hopes, or fears.

If religious environmentalism is to play a significant role in global environmental politics, it must rise to this challenge—a challenge, we might note, that has faced virtually every progressive movement of the past 150 years. In the United States alone we have seen debilitating splits or failures of solidarity between native and immigrant workers, whites and African Americans, men and women, straight women and lesbians. The emphasis on diversity within liberal to radical movements, the serious (some might say obsessive) concern with acknowledging and balancing the interests of diverse groups, reflects these experiences. When religious environmentalism enters the political realm it has much to learn from this broader story. In particular, it needs to take diversity with absolute seriousness, yet also not succumb to the centrifugal tendencies that can turn a progressive political movement, religious or not, into little more than a collection of disjointed, politically correct splinters. There will always be a tension between the need to acknowledge and the need to ignore real social differences within the environmental movement. Balancing those opposing needs will require tact, intelligence, and judgment.

Clearly, religious environmentalism in particular and environmentalism in general *has* to some extent risen to face this challenge in the past fifteen years or so. The environmental justice movement has catalyzed the need for an understanding and policy that reflects our social position. And, as we have seen, there have been significant efforts at cooperation among environmentalists representing widely different communities.

Yet, for all the inclusiveness of religious environmentalism, and the wide variety of forms and places in which it exists, it will at times *not* see eye to eye with other environmental groups. Agreement *in general* on goals such as sustainability or wildlife protection in no way guarantees that in a *particular* situation different environmental activists will define short-term goals, tactics, or public demands in the same way. Cobb and Santmire's pointed criticism of American Protestantism's failure to confront America's need to restrict its economic excess is a case in point. Another example is the religious antipathy to socialism, which at times makes religious environmentalism reticent to confront the deep structures of capitalism and thus to join forces with ecosocialists. For an even more extreme example, one need only imagine how hard it would be for an Islamic environmental group to work with an ecofeminist one.

In a global environmental movement fraught with differences, what distinctive role can religious environmentalism play? Well, if nothing else, religious environmentalism can offer a kind of legitimacy for the movement as a whole, a new (or rather, old!) vocabulary in which to make environmental demands. Pointing out to Jews that God has commanded us not to waste may ultimately not mean much more than "Let's recycle, cut down on wasteful packaging, and turn down the air conditioner." Yet the religious injunction surrounds these practical measures with a distinct meaning. Appeals to act for the sake of God or Spiritual Truth carry a special intensity.

There is, however, more that can be asked. As religious environmentalism sees itself as the source of a kind of universal care, so it can do more than invoke God in support of particular policies. It can also contribute to what political theorist Douglas Torgerson calls the "green public sphere."[35]

For Torgerson, the task of environmentalism is not just to create a coherent and effective political movement aiming at specific goals. In a more encompassing sense, it is to sustain a public arena in which the widest possible variety of environmentalists encounter each others' values, experiences, and strategies for change. Torgerson's stress on the importance of a green public sphere, alongside that of more familiar concerns with building organizations and changing laws, reflects two critical political realities: the range of differences among environmentalists and a profound distrust of expertise.

As a number of theorists have argued, one source of the environmental crisis in particular and much contemporary injustice in general is the essentially undemocratic belief that administrative expertise—of the engineer or the doctor, the "highly trained economist" or the "authority on education"—can be trusted to organize social life rationally.[36] We have critically examined this position in chapter 2, indicating a few of the ways even scientific research must be in dialogue with democratic debate if it is not to surreptitiously serve interests counter to those of society as a whole. Numerous examples from the past two hundred years confirm this suspicion in virtually every field of human endeavor. These include the way communist totalitarianism was buttressed by the idea that The Party had scientific expertise to create a perfect society. From a contrasting political setting, we have the World Bank criticizing its own failures of expertise in supporting large dam projects that, though technologically impressive, were ecological, social, and economic disasters constructed with no input from the native people most affected.[37]

Thus, thinking of environmental politics simply as an "instrument," a tool to achieve goals decided on elsewhere by environmental "experts," forecloses debate, creates monolithic organizations, and leaves power in the hands of administrators. Even if these administrators are committed environmentalists working for the Sierra Club or Greenpeace, this will not do. As we saw in our discussion of the growth of the environmental justice movement, even the best-intentioned environmental groups can end up serving a too narrow conception of environmentalism. As well, environmental organizations, not surprisingly, are subject to the "iron law of oligarchy," in which leaders of political parties or focused organizations—just because they are the leaders—

develop interests at odd with the mass of people the organizations purport to represent.[38] They can become committed to the organization rather than the cause, and their own place within the organization above all.

There is nothing in the history of the environmental movement, or of society in general, that would lead us to uncritically trust in *anyone's* "expertise." Too many personal interests (such as those of a particular organization or career) and too many limitations of perspective (based on class, nationality, or race) can be at work. That is why, ultimately, the environmental community, as well as society as a whole, must have a place in formulating basic environmental concepts and goals.

A green public sphere, then, is a place in which fundamental differences can be aired, long- and short-term goals can be evaluated, and each person affected by the environmental crisis (which would seem to include us all!) can be heard. The green public sphere is "practical" only in the longest range of senses: to support a collective culture of environmental awareness and action and to foster the capacity for ecological self-examination by individuals, communities, and nations.

This means that along with maintaining a particular group (the National Council of Churches Task Force on Ecojustice, for example) or pursuing important concrete goals (recycling paper, stopping dams, or electing sympathetic public officials), we also need a sustained commitment to creating a cultural space in which a green culture can be nourished and green values explored. In this space our goal is not to worry about who is or who is not a "real environmentalist" (debates that have frequently wracked the Green Party in the United States and Germany and that have erupted in the U.S. Sierra Club over immigration); nor is it to decide on definitive policy recommendations (how many miles per gallon we should require automobiles to get, how much money should be spent on energy conservation as opposed to renewable sources). It is a place where the dominant themes of environmentalism—namely, its profound challenges to the unself-conscious confidence of industrial society—can be explored and where the emotional and moral strains of living as an environmentally aware person in a wasteful and polluting society can be shared.

The idea of a green public sphere is particularly relevant to religion. Religious environmentalism is, after all, only one part of the overall environmental community. It has its distinct ways of thinking, range of membership, and organizational concerns. It should not ever think of itself as defining environmentalism for everyone else, if for no other reason than that many people find religion alien and even threatening. The green public sphere is the place where all environmentalists can meet, exchange perspectives, learn from each other, and take some comfort that they are not alone. It can exist in publications or conferences, community meetings or casual conversations at the office. It arises in any place and time people take environmental questions seriously.

Religion's experiences of ecumenism are particularly relevant to the creation of a green public sphere. Modern, liberally oriented religions, and even some of the more conservative varieties, have tried to find common ground with members of other faiths, devising ways to communicate across significant theological and moral divides. These experiences can be enormously valuable if environmentalists who think that passing new laws is crucial wish to communicate with those who emphasize raising consciousness at the grassroots level, or if those whose passion is saving the whales are to work with those facing pollution in an urban neighborhood.

Ultimately, the most difficult question that will arise in a green public sphere is how to resolve tensions between useful but limited ecological *reforms* and the kind of necessary, but seemingly out of reach, ecological *revolution* that the environmental crisis may in fact demand. The increasingly professionalized environmental bureaucrats and administrators of the 1980s came to define the movement in terms of mainstream respectability, lobbying efforts, and compromise. From a scientific or holistically ecological focus, mainstream environmentalism turned to an economic one, necessarily accepting the reigning structure of society.[39] During this time, many of the more politically radical environmentalists complain, the dominant environmental organizations became flabby and professionalized, in tone, style, and ultimate goals not much different from the government officials and lobbyists for large companies with whom they are in daily contact. Connections with grassroots environmental concerns were often minimal, as the dominant and well-heeled environmental organizations came under the sway of the conservative corporate, bureaucratic, and foundation culture.[40] While acknowledging the truth of some of their critics' points, especially around the issues of environmental racism, the larger groups responded with the time-honored point that all the radical posturing in the world won't save a single tree or eliminate one drop of acid rain. In a comparatively conservative political climate, environmentalists must adapt, pursue reforms, and make deals. They might also have pointed out that it is quite common for popular movements to emerge out of public passion, and then, as the passion fades, to become embodied in more bureaucratic organizations.[41] In this debate, as in countless others over the past two hundred years, epithets of "sell out" and "impractical and ineffective" were exchanged, with each side having some justifications for its position.

Religious environmentalists, as spread out along the ideological spectrum as their secular counterparts, will not identify solely with either side. Yet, as with the problems of racial, gender, and class differences in progressive political movements, environmentalists can learn something from history here. In particular, they can be sensitive to the enormously destructive pattern of conflict within groups whose common interests should have led to compromise, humility about their own knowledge of "the truth," and simple courtesy. The unrestrained anger that frequently permeates activist political circles is understandable given what we are fighting for. Yet, once turned against comrades who are not what we want them to be (class-conscious, sensitive to race and gender, truly radical, cautious and "realistic," etc.), we open ourselves to a Pandora's box of destructive infighting. This pattern, perhaps as human as it is explicitly political, has crippled progressive movements for more than a century. It is a pattern we cannot afford to reproduce in environmental circles. Because every environmentalist needs every other environmentalist, it is almost always better to err on the side of inclusiveness, acceptance, and openness than in any of the reverse ways.

Religious environmentalists may have some distinct resources with which to further communication and soothe ruffled feathers when these conflicts arise. For one thing, people of faith can model the ability to take the long view. Believing that there is Something or Someone in the universe that is sympathetic to justice and love, that a residue of value will be retained no matter what happens, they can help resist the panic, desperation, and consequent bickering and disrespect that often plague activist political circles. A deep-seated spiritual outlook can support a calmer psychology, which in turn can lead to more effective politics.[42]

If nothing else, religious environmentalists, reaching deep into the moral foundations of their spiritual life, can show comradely respect for people with whom they are in near complete strategic or tactical disagreement. Any movement that questions the massively entrenched economic, political, and cultural forces creating the environmental crisis had better sustain its own members, and that includes promoting a humane, emotionally encouraging, and compassionate internal culture. This is far from trivial, for environmentalists, whatever their view of God, nature, ecosystems, government, state policy, or sustainable farming, are also human beings who work better when they receive respect from their fellows. If, as Aldo Leopold put it, "to have an ecological education is to walk alone in a world of wounds," then when wounded environmentalists gather together, they should be kind to one another.[43]

∾

Religious environmentalism's vision of universal care requires a truly ecological democracy that does not stop at the boundaries of our species. This is partly because environmentalism in general begins with a rich sense that democracy involves much more than simply adding up everyone's wants and seeing who comes out on top.[44] It is, rather, about facilitating communication among everyone within a society, so that we can hear each other's reasons, empathize with each other's points of view, and see if it is possible to respond to each other's real concerns. On this view, democracy rejects inherited political power, violations of human rights, and restriction of speech or religion not just because these keep us from getting what we want, but also because they keep us from saying what we need to say—from living freely in all the many dimensions in which humans are capable of expressing themselves.

Environmentalism expands this rich sense of democracy to include the nonhuman, suggesting that democracy cannot be restricted to human beings, for human beings are not the only members of the community whose voices need to be heard. Clearly, this realization requires that democracy, just like ecological religion, shift in its own self-understanding. The vitality of democratic modernity, after all, arose as a widespread challenge to tradition, social hierarchy, and inherited privilege. Yet, with that same modernity we also found ourselves in a desacrilized world, where "nature's tongue is taken away."[45] This silence is what we now seek to change. As philosopher John Dryzak puts it, "Humans . . . need to cultivate a new ability to hear nature's voice."[46]

Clearly, an expansion to ecological democracy would require a fundamental shift on the level of basic principles. For example, as conventional democracy cannot function successfully without some bedrock acceptance that all citizens share a kind of fundamental freedom and equality, so ecological democracy presupposes that nature has an independent destiny not defined solely by its instrumental value, and that close attention can put humans and nonhumans in communicative connection. It will assume that just as all humans deserve to be heard, so do all species.

A metaphoric but vital sense of nature as something with which we might communicate, as opposed to merely something we might manage more rationally, pervades religious environmentalism. Larry Rasmussen talks of "earth community"; John Cobb of the "liberation of life"; Norman Wirzba interprets "tending the garden" (Gen. 2:15) as an imperative to learn from nature in the contemporary movement of biomimicry; Mary Evelyn Tucker celebrates kinship "with all life-forms"; and Thomas Berry criticizes human "autism" in relation to nature.[47]

Despite these metaphors, of course, a fully expanded ecological democracy will not take place in a human language, nor proceed on the basis of extended arguments about rights or truth.[48] Something else will have to be exchanged besides words. And some new skills will have to be developed.

We can get some idea of what this might mean by way of analogy: if our democratic discussions are to work, participants must possess, if only in rudimentary ways, some basic capabilities. They must be able to offer reasons in support of their position when others disagree, understand basic mathematical concepts (such as "more" and "less," "increase" and "decrease") to comprehend policy proposals, have some sense of the effects of their actions on others, and grasp the idea of the "public good." One way to understand an *ecological* democracy, then, is to see that it requires a dramatic expansion of our democratic capabilities. If we are unaware of the nature that surrounds and sustains us, have never had intimate contact with a particular ecosystem, don't know what ecological degradation looks like, have never tried to grow food, never had extensive contact with animals, then we lack the basic knowledge to be informed participants in ecological democracy. An attunement to nature is part of our proper citizenship just as much as being aware of cultural differences among human beings.

This attunement cannot be developed by talking with oak trees or ravens. But verbal conversation is not the only way humans communicate. We can connect to each other with a touch, a smile, movements of shoulders or eyes. We also have relationships with infants, the severely handicapped, and people with Alzheimer's. These skills and capacities, and many others besides, will be brought to bear as we connect to nature. In the context of the natural world, attunement might come from partnering with domesticated animals or a truly sustainable agriculture that leaves the soil healthier than before we used it. It will be found in the knowledge of wildlife biologists, children, native hunters, and experienced conservationists. Surely it will arise in interspecies communication: reciprocal encounters between humans and animals such as whales singing with human musicians or dolphins swimming along with people.[49] By interspecies communication, I do not mean putting apes in cages and teaching them sign language, for such a context is not true communication but a training in which only one side gets to determine the terms of the interaction. As Jim Nollman puts it, "If it is truly to be considered communication, then it should also be based upon mutual respect. It must develop as an open-ended dialogue where both participants have the equal power to direct the course and subject matter of the learning experience."[50] These encounters must for a time replace the relentless drive to control with an open-minded (and open-hearted) sense of inquiry. We will be searching for communion, reciprocity, and understanding, not compulsively and tyrannically demanding or reshaping.

Alternatively, we may attune to nature by becoming aware of the consequences of our collective *lack* of attunement. If we look long and hard at the way frogs are "succumbing to parasites, to pesticides, to increases in ultraviolet radiation [from the hole in the ozone layer], to global warming," we will see that "frogs are telling us a lot."[51] We can read the growth rings of trees and see how their health has been diminished by changes in the soil caused by acid rain.[52] We can hear the silence of the extinguished species, the way the mechanical throb of a dam replaces the whoosh of a running river, or the enormous thud of a chunk of Arctic ice breaking off from global warming. These phenomena tell us that our society is not functioning as a democracy should. This is similar to the way we know purely human democracy is not working if large numbers of people are outside the educational or economic system, if leaders don't care for the common good, if the economy is not sustainable, or if people by and large do not trust the government.

Engaging in this attunement to the Natural Other will not, I suspect, be particularly furthered by talk of nature's "rights." We will, after all, continue to eat, use, and compete with nature, trampling on insects and uprooting plants in ways that would not be morally acceptable if done to people. But we can honor the reciprocity of our relationship with the earth, learn to limit our use to that which makes moral and spiritual sense, and try to take in (rather than avoid or deny) the consequences of what we do to it. If we love what we use, we are not so likely to use it all up; if we attune ourselves to that with which we compete, we may look—hard—for ways to coexist rather than to obliterate. Ecological democracy is right now only a hope, a distant possibility, for an industrial civilization that will never return to hunting and gathering or live in small tribes guided by shamans. What form it would take if we truly tried to practice it can only be guessed at. But surely this is true for all religious visions. Are we really further from an ecological democracy attuned to nature than from a society guided by the Golden Rule?

Rooted in this perspective, religious environmentalism *necessarily* calls on us to see political legitimacy—our sense of ourselves as constructing a just society—as requiring respect, care, stewardship, and sustainability aimed as nature as well as people. The "we" of the democratic community, in other words, includes the natural as well as the social. In this way, religious environmentalism is not, as philosopher Charles Taylor would have it, purely "modern." For, Taylor argues, it is the hallmark of modern politics to see the social order as founded purely on human action, rather than on some event and force that is out of time, some transcendent Power or Personality. In the modern mind, he says, political legitimacy depends only on ourselves.[53] Ecological democracy rejects this anthropocentric understanding, basing itself in the recognition that human society rests on—and within!—a more-than-human world. This world is one with which we have a reciprocal moral relationship, not just instrumental connections of usefulness or pleasure. If this is not literally a "transcendental condition" in Taylor's sense, it is not a purely human one either.

A commitment to include nature in our calculations of justice and care sets religious environmentalism off from modern liberalism, modern secular radicalism, and conservatively oriented fundamentalism. The vision of an ecological democracy both furthers and transcends even the broadest conceptions of progressive democracy. It is a crucial part of religious environmentalism's contribution to contemporary social life and a vital source of connection to the secular environmental community.

❧

The outcome of religious environmentalism's confrontations with consumerism, fundamentalism, and globalization will be determined by an extremely complicated dynamic in which culture, politics, technology, and economics interact. Estimating the eventual outcome resembles gazing into a crystal ball rather than reasonably assessing possibilities, for there are simply too many unknowns, each one of which affects all the others. Worsening environmental conditions could give rise to violent conflict over scarcer resources or to serious international cooperation. Fundamentalism could triumph everywhere, or be opposed by a kind of new traditionalism that seeks to fuse moral values and political freedom. Religious environmentalism could more fully integrate into secular environmental movements, or become marginalized in the face of an increasing divide between religion and modernity.

Social forecasting is a risky business in any event. No end of commentators, sure or this or that future outcome, have seen their predictions founder on shores of that most basic of human characteristics, unpredictability.

In any case, knowledge of the future is not really the point. We know enough *now* to know that every living thing on earth is threatened by the current environmental havoc. And those of us who understand the havoc in religious, spiritual, or moral terms—as well as scientifically, politically, and culturally—have no choice but to combine our religion and our environmentalism. In a sense, we are long past the point when they *can* be combined, for they simply no longer exist as separate. Loving the earth just is an element of our religion, and seeing care for the earth as in some sense a sacred task just is part of our environmentalism.

Yet, although we cannot have *knowledge*, or probably even very good guesses, about the future, few of us are so enlightened as not to worry about it. Indeed, a good deal of what motivates environmentalists is fear for the future, and much of what pains us emotionally is that we are never sure that we have made the future better, or better enough.

In the absence of any rational comfort, where is a religious environmentalist to turn? How are we to understand what we are doing?

Well, if nothing else, we can take some comfort in marginal gains. If we help clean up one river, reduce the air pollution in one medium-size city, or slow down the pace of globalization even a little, we have done something. After all, when our sun turns into a nova a few billions years from now, all life on the planet will be ended. Nothing that we cherish, nothing on this earth, is forever. So our task is not to guarantee eternal safety, but to make things a little better and healthier right now.

This is not a small thing—or if it is small, it is certainly not insignificant. And religions often comfort by telling us that the small matters. The *Bhagavad Gita* advises followers of Krishna to fulfill their responsibilities and detach from results. The Protestant philosopher Kierkegaard argued that our ethical task is not to Make History but to devote ourselves to acting rightly—all the while realizing that God, not us, is in charge of the Big Picture.[54]

This delicate balance of commitment and religious detachment is not passivity. It demands action, but seeks a way out of both obsession and despair. Given the severity of the environmental crisis and how dark the future sometimes seems, it may be the sanest posture that an environmental activist can take. It is also not without its own joys, ones proclaimed in the deeper teachings of virtually every religion. For the most authentic forms of religious life are not bound by a drab sense of responsibility, but are permeated by the joy of serving God in each moment. Ultimately, we meditate, or feed the poor, or pray, or follow our faith's moral teaching because this seems to us the most vibrant and fulfilling way to live each day. As the Talmud tells us, the best reason for performing a *mitzvah* (a righteous act, a religious obligation, a good deed) is simply having the opportunity to perform it, and the highest reward for doing it is the chance to do it again![55]

And so it goes. As religious environmentalists, we want to save the world, but right now we do what we do because we wish to be the kind of person who lives like this: who honors God's creation, feels and responds to the sacredness of the earth, and tries to love all of our neighbors as ourselves. Ultimately, perhaps, we are religious environmentalists because we just cannot live any other way. In that necessity, and in the answering call that we sense from both Spirit and Earth, lies the only surety that religious environmentalists will ever have.

It is, and for some time it will have to be, enough.

NOTES

Introduction

1. For two presentations of the Bad News, see Sandra Steingraber, *Living Downstream: An Ecologist Looks at Cancer and the Environment* (Reading, MA: Addison-Wesley, 1997); Jerome Groopman, "The Thirty Years' War: Have We Been Fighting Cancer the Wrong Way?" *The New Yorker*, June 4, 2001.
2. Frederic Buell, *From Apocalypse to Way of Life* (New York: Routledge, 2004).
3. Many believed the opposite: that the earth was under God's judgment as a sign of God's displeasure with human sin. Mark Wallace pointed this out to me.
4. Anne Frank, *The Diary of a Young Girl* (Garden City, NY: Doubleday, 1972), p. 172.
5. Eric Valli, "Golden Harvest of the Raji," *National Geographic*, June 1998.
6. C. S. Lewis, *A Grief Observed* (San Francisco: HarperSanFrancisco, 2001).
7. Dave Hunt, *Ecology, Shamanism, Science, and Christianity Part 3,* quoted at Ankerberg Theological Research Institute, http://www.ankerberg.com/Articles/new-age/NA0502W2.htm.
8. Moses Maimonides, *Guide to the Perplexed*, part 3, chapter 13, quoted in *Judaism and Ecology: A Hadassah Study Guide* (New York: Hadassah, 1993), p. 110.
9. Social critics like Thoreau, visionary poets like William Blake and Walt Whitman, disaffected political or cultural radicals like Max Horkheimer, Theodor Adorno, and Martin Heidegger, or vaguely spiritual nature lovers like John Muir.
10. References to many books, articles, and Web sites follow. Special mention must be made of the single most important Web site for this subject, that of the Forum on Religion and Ecology, which offers a breathtaking collection of statements, articles, links, and bibliographies. There is no better place to begin further study: http://environment.harvard.edu/religion/.
11. For an extensive discussion of the effect of denial and avoidance on spiritual life, see chapter 2 of Roger S. Gottlieb, *A Spirituality of Resistance: Finding a Peaceful Heart and Protecting the Earth* (Lanham, MD: Rowman and Littlefield, 2003).
12. Joanna Macy, *World as Lover, World as Self* (Berkeley: Parallax Press, 1991).
13. See her excerpt from *Poison Fire, Poison Earth: Testimonies, Lectures, Conclusions. The World Uranium Hearings, Salzburg 1992,* pp. 256–258, Nuclear Guardianship Project, http://www.ratical.org/radiation/WorldUraniumHearing/JoannaMacy.html.
14. United Methodist Church, General Board of Church and Society, quoted at Earth Ministry, http://www.earthministry.org/.
15. The NCC Earth Day service is discussed in greater detail in chapter 6.
16. The "Caring for Creation: Vision, Hope, Justice," social statement was adopted

by a more than two-thirds majority of the Evangelical Lutheran Church in America, Churchwide Assembly on August 28, 1993. ELCA Environment Task Force, "Basis for our Caring," in *This Sacred Earth: Religion, Nature, Environment*, 2nd ed., ed. Roger S. Gottlieb (New York: Routledge, 2004), p. 221.

17. Quoted in Trebbe Johnson, "The Sacred Creation," *Sierra* (November/December 1998).

18. Robin Broad and John Cavanagh, *Plundering Paradise: The Struggle for the Environment in the Philippines* (Berkeley: University of California Press, 1993).

19. Mary John Mananzan, "Globalization and the Perennial Question of Justice," in *Spiritual Question for the Twenty-First Century*, ed. Mary Hembrow Snyder (Maryknoll, NY: Orbis Books, 2001), p. 157.

20. Quoted in Roger S. Gottlieb, ed., *This Sacred Earth: Religion, Nature, Environment* (New York: Routledge, 1996), p. 182.

21. National Religious Partnership for the Environment, http://www.nrpe.org/.

22. *Tikkun*, www.tikkun.org.

23. Michael Lerner, *Spirit Matters* (Hampton Roads, VA: Hampton Roads Publishing, 2002).

24. For a detailed account of religion's participation in progressive political movements, see Roger S. Gottlieb, *Joining Hands: Politics and Religion Together for Social Change* (Cambridge, MA: Westview Press, 2002), and Roger S. Gottlieb, ed., *Liberating Faith: Religious Voices for Justice, Peace, and Ecological Responsibility* (Lanham, MD: Rowman and Littlefield, 2003).

25. This is the basic theme of Gottlieb, *A Spirituality of Resistance*, particularly chapter 5.

26. Aldo Leopold, *Round River* (New York: Oxford University Press, 1993), p. 165.

27. The relationship between spirituality and resistance is the center of Gottlieb, *A Spirituality of Resistance*. For a rather different way of approaching the same general point, see Dorothy Soelle, *The Silent Cry: Mysticism and Resistance* (Minneapolis, MN: Augsburg Fortress, 2001). Michael Lerner (in *Spirit Matters*, as well as in the pages of *Tikkun*)—and other people in a variety of vocabularies—stress that "God" is a way to refer to the power of healing and transformation in the universe.

28. This is one of those quotes that I remember clearly but for which I cannot find the reference!

Chapter 1

1. I use "ecotheologians" rather loosely to refer to religious thinkers from all faith traditions, and to nondenominational spiritual writers as well.

2. Daniel Maguire, *The Moral Core of Judaism and Christianity: Reclaiming the Revolution* (Minneapolis: Fortress, 1993), p. 5. The widely respected Protestant Jurgen Moltmann said that the environmental crisis signals "the beginning of a life and death struggle for life on earth." *God in Creation: An Ecological Doctrine of Creation* (London: SCM, 1985), p. xi.

3. Steven Bouma-Prediger, *For the Beauty of the Earth: A Christian Vision for Creation Care* (Grand Rapids, MI: Baker Academic, 2001), p. 40.

4. Thomas Berry, *Dream of the Earth* (San Francisco: Sierra Club Books, 1988), p. 77.

5. Peter Harrison, *The Bible, Protestantism, and the Rise of Natural Science* (New

York: Cambridge University Press, 1998), p. 205. See also the excellent discussion
in Bronislaw Szerszynksi, *Nature, Technology and the Sacred: Religion and Spirituality in the Modern World* (Malden, MA: Blackwell, 2005).

6. On Native Americans, see N. Scott Momaday, "A First American Views His Land," in *At Home on the Earth*, ed. David Landis Barnhill (Berkeley: University of California Press, 1991).

7. I encountered this image, then applied to science in particular and knowledge in general, in the work of W. V. O. Quine, who borrowed it from mathematician Paul Ramsey.

8. Islamic intellectual Ibrahim Ozdemir summarizes: "Environmentalists claim that there is a strong and direct relationship between environmental problems and our modern understanding of nature," especially an understanding in which "the only value that nature can have is instrumental value." "Environmental Ethics from a Qur'anic Perspective," in *Islam and Ecology: A Bestowed Trust*, ed. Richard Foltz, Frederick M Denny, and Azizian Bahruddin (Cambridge, MA: Harvard University Press/Center for the Study of World Religions, 2003), p. 5.

9. Lynn White, "The Historical Roots of Our Ecological Crisis," *Science* 155, no. 3767 (March 10, 1967), reprinted in *This Sacred Earth: Religion, Nature, Environment*, ed. Roger S. Gottlieb (New York: Routledge, 1996; 2nd ed. 2004).

10. Steven C. Rockefeller, "Faith and Community in an Ecological Age," in *Spirit and Nature: Why the Environment Is a Religious Issue*, ed. Steven C. Rockefeller and John C. Elder (Boston: Beacon Press, 1992), p. 142.

11. Norman Wirzba, *The Paradise of God: Renewing Religion in an Ecological Age* (New York: Oxford University Press, 2003), p. 172.

12. Daniel Swartz, "Jews, Jewish Texts, and Nature: A Brief History," in Gottlieb, *This Sacred Earth*, 2nd ed., pp. 94–95.

13. For a summary of this position in the tradition, consider the following from a widely respected nineteenth-century German rabbi:

> "Do not destroy anything" is the first and most general call of God. . . . If you should now raise your hand to play a childish game, to indulge in senseless rage, wishing to destroy that which you should only use, wishing to exterminate that which you should only exploit, if you should regard the beings beneath you as objects without rights, not perceiving God Who created them, and therefore desire that they feel the might of your presumptuous mood, instead of using them only as the means of wise human activity—then God's call proclaims to you, "Do not destroy anything! Be a *mentsh [responsible person]*! Only if you use the things around you for wise human purposes, sanctified by the word of My teaching, only then are you a *mentsh* and have the right over them which I have given you as a human. However, if you destroy, if you ruin, at that moment you are not a human but an animal and have no right to the things around you. I lent them to you for wise use only; never forget that I lent them to you. As soon as you use them unwisely, be it the greatest or the smallest, you commit treachery against My world, you commit murder and robbery against My property, you sin against Me!"

Samson Raphael Hirsch, *Horeb*, chapter 56, paragraph 398, citing Talmud Shabbat 105b, quoted in article on "Bal Taschit," at Coalition on the Environment and Jewish Life, http://www.coejl.org/learn/je_tashchit.shtml. For an important earlier source, see Maimonides, *Mishneh Torah*, Laws of Kings 6:10.

14. For an overview, see Jeremy Cohen, "On Classical Judaism and the Environ-

mental Crisis," in *Judaism and Environmental Ethics: A Reader*, ed. Martin Yaffe (Lanham, MD: Lexington Books, 2001).

15. As John B. Cobb Jr. observed: "One can find within the Bible excellent grounds for overcoming anthropocentrism and for care for the earth. But Christians did not do so until the insights of persons outside the church led to accusations against them." *Reclaiming the Church* (Louisville, KY: Westminster John Knox Press, 1997), p. 64. See also remarks on the role of secular, scientifically oriented environmentalism in prompting ecological action in the National Council of Churches in Dieter Hessel, "The Church's Eco-Justice Journey," in *Eco-Justice: The Unfinished Journey*, ed. William E. Gibson (Albany: State University of New York Press, 2004).

16. Harrison, *The Bible, Protestantism, and the Rise of Natural Science*.

17. Cohen, "On Classical Judaism."

18. For example, Richard L. Fern, *Nature, God and Humanity: Envisioning an Ethics of Nature* (Cambridge, UK: Cambridge University Press, 2002).

19. Lawrence Troster, "Created in the Image of God," in Yaffe, *Judaism and Environmental Ethics*.

20. Theodore Hiebert claims that there is a powerfully ecological strand running throughout the critical first five books of the Bible, what scholars often refer to as the "J" voice: *The Yahwists' Landscape* (New York: Oxford University Press, 1996).

21. Though the theological commitments of later interpreters led to different translations of the exact same Hebrew!

22. That is, for those who wish to find it.

23. See the eloquent account in Wendell Berry, "The Gift of Good Land," in Wendell Berry, *The Gift of Good Land: Further Essays Cultural and Agricultural* (San Francisco: North Point Press, 1981), pp. 267–281.

24. Deuteronomy 20:19–20; 22:6–7; 25:4.

25. Andrew Linzey, *Animal Theology* (Chicago: University of Illinois Press, 1995), p. 108.

26. Sallie McFague argues that in early Christianity, redemption and creation, the natural and the moral/psychological, were closely interwoven. *Life Abundant: Rethinking Theology and Economy for a Planet in Peril* (Minneapolis: Fortress Press, 2001), p. 167. For the relation between Christ and the rest of creation, see Romans 8:19–21: "The creation waits in eager expectation for the sons of God to be revealed. For the creation was subjected to frustration, not by its own choice, but by the will of the one who subjected it, in hope that the creation itself will be liberated from its bondage to decay and brought into the glorious freedom of the children of God." Also Colossians 1:17: "He is before all things, and in him all things hold together."

27. Keith Warner, "Was St. Francis a Deep Ecologist?" in *Embracing Earth: Catholic Approaches to Ecology*, ed. Albert LaChance and John E. Carroll (Maryknoll, NY: Orbis Books, 1994). Francis also had his contradictory moments: "Every creature proclaims: 'God made me for your sake, O man.'" Quoted in John Passmore, *Man's Responsibility for Nature* (New York: Charles Scribner's Sons, 1974), p. 112.

28. H. Paul Santmire, *The Travail of Nature: The Ambiguous Ecological Promise of Christian Theology* (Philadelphia: Fortress Press, 1985).

29. Christopher Manes, *Other Creations* (New York: Doubleday, 1997).

30. For postbiblical (Talmudic, Midrashic, Chasidic, and modern) Jewish resources,

see David E. Stein, ed., *A Garden of Choice Fruit: 200 Classic Jewish Quotes on Human Beings and the Environment* (Wyncote, PA: Shomrei Adamah, 1991). For example, from Abraham Isaac Kook (chief rabbi of Palestine in the 1920s): "Every part of the vegetable world is singing a song and breathing forth a secret of the divine mystery of the Creation" (p. 69). Or from eighteenth-century Reb Nachman, "If a person kills a tree before its time, it is like having murdered a soul" (p. 97).

31. Basic Buddhism is developed in countless books. For example, Peter Harvey, *An Introduction to Buddhism: Teachings, History, and Practices* (New York: Cambridge University Press, 1990).
32. *Avatamsake Sutra*, book 1, at Buddhist Information, http://www.buddhist information.com/ida_b_wells_memorial_sutra_library/avatamsaka_sutra.htm.
33. William LaFleur, "Enlightenment for Plants and Trees," in *Dharma Rain: Sources of Buddhist Environmentalism*, ed. Stephanie Kaza and Kenneth Kraft (Boston: Shambhala, 2000), p. 111. Although Mahayana Buddhism stresses this point more than Theravada, it can be found in the latter as well.
34. See Stephanie Kaza, "To Save All Beings: Buddhist Environmental Activism," in Gottlieb, *Liberating Faith*.
35. For a development of the position that it is Buddhist conceptions of virtues rather than specific attitudes toward nature that are the key to Buddhist environmentalism, see David Cooper and Simon James, *Buddhism, Virtue and the Environment* (Aldershot, UK: Ashgate, 2005).
36. Myoe, "Letter to the Island," in Kaza and Kraft, *Dharma Rain*, p. 63.
37. Quoted in Gary Snyder, "Blue Mountains Constantly Walking," in Kaza and Kraft, *Dharma Rain*, p. 132.
38. Caroline A. F. Rhys Davids, *Stories of the Buddha: Being Selections from the Jataka* (New York: Dover, 1989).
39. LaFleur, "Enlightenment for Plants and Trees."
40. Such ideas, though immensely valuable, are not in themselves adequate to our situation. For example, Kenneth Kraft values the traditional Zen Buddhist idea that nothing is "waste" and therefore nothing should be "wasted." Yet "no premodern forms of waste were toxic in the ways that nuclear waste is. . . . Dealing with the waste produced by a monastery is one thing; dealing with tens of thousands of tons of atomic waste generated by nuclear reactors and weapons plants is a problem on a different scale. . . . We also notice a discrepancy between the focus on individual action in the Zen example and the highly complex collective action required for the production and prospective containment of nuclear waste." "Nuclear Energy and Engaged Buddhism," in *Buddhism and Ecology: The Interconnection of Dharma and Deeds*, ed. Mary Evelyn Tucker and Duncan Ryjken Williams (Cambridge, MA: Harvard University Center for the Study of World Religions, 1997), p. 280.
41. Iqtidar H. Zaidi, "On the Ethics of Man's Interaction with the Environment: An Islamic Approach," *Environmental Ethics* 3 (1981): 41.
42. Ozdemir, "Environmental Ethics from a Qur'anic Perspective."
43. J. Baird Callicott, *Earth's Insights: A Multicultural Survey of Ecological Ethics from the Mediterranean Basin to the Australian Outback* (Berkeley: University of California Press, 1994).
44. Bill McKibben, *The End of Nature* (New York: Anchor, 1997).
45. James A. Nash, *Loving Nature: Ecological Integrity and Christian Responsibility* (Nashville, TN: Abingdon Press: 1991), p. 72, emphasis added.

46. Anna Peterson, "In and Of the Worlds: Christian Theological Anthropology and Environmental Ethics," in Gottlieb, *This Sacred Earth*, 2nd ed., p. 116.

47. It is not hard to see how this religious image mirrors the strict and complicated social hierarchy of both the ancient world and Europe's Middle Ages, reflecting in theology the hierarchical relations of kings, aristocracy, merchants, and peasants, as well as men and women. Although Judaism never carried the soul-body division that Christianity did, it mirrored its offspring's separation between humans and nature with a frequent and profound anthropocentrism: as the critically important eleventh-century Talmudic scholar Moses Nachmanides (known as the Ramban) states, biblical "mastery" means God "gave them power and dominion over the earth to do as they wish with the cattle, the reptiles, and all that crawl in the dust, and to build ... and from its hills to dig copper, and other similar things." *Commentary on the Torah, Genesis* (New York: Shilo, 1989), p. 55. A modern Orthodox commentary on Genesis echoes this perspective: "In a sense, the universe is like a machine that was built for a specific purpose. . . . The universe was brought into existence as the means by which to carry out the Torah. Remove the Torah and there is no need for the universe." *The Family Chumash: Breishis*, Overviews by Rabbi Nosson Scherman (New York: Mesorah, 1989), p. ix.

48. Leonardo Boff, *Cry of the Earth, Cry of the Poor* (Maryknoll, NY: Orbis, 1997), p. 189.

49. Ibid., pp. 69–70.

50. Mark Stoll, *Protestantism, Capitalism, and Nature in America* (Albuquerque: University of New Mexico Press, 1997), p. 70.

51. "Bourgeois society is ruled by equivalence. It makes the dissimilar comparable by reducing it to abstract quantities. To the Enlightenment, that which does not reduce to numbers, and ultimately to the one, becomes illusion; modern positivism writes it off as literature." Max Horkheimer and Theodor Adorno, *Dialectic of Enlightenment* (New York: Seabury, 1974), p. 7.

52. Martin Heidegger, in *The Question Concerning Technology and Other Essays* (New York: Perennial, 1982), argues that modern technology is distinguished by its ability to shape, alter, and use the powers of nature, rather than simply taking advantage of what can be found. Nuclear power and genetic engineering would be two of the most dramatic examples.

53. This historical process, argues Bronislaw Szerszynski in *Nature, Technology and the Sacred*, leads to the "sacred" returning as the human self, whose technical mastery of the world renders him God-like; to the awe-inspiring products of modern technology; and to nature.

54. To take one example: pioneering Catholic ecotheologian Sean McDonagh, whose turn to environmentalism was prompted by firsthand experience of ecological degradation in Africa, had to wait three years to find a publisher for his groundbreaking book *To Care for the Earth* (London: Chapman and Sons, 1985), in which he argued that the church should pay as much attention to creation as to redemption. Garry W. Trompf, "Sean McDonagh," in *Encyclopedia of Religion and Nature*, ed. Bron Taylor (London: Continuum, 2005).

55. See Stoll, *Protestantism, Capitalism, and Nature in America*, for an account of the role of liberal Protestantism in nineteenth-century conservationism.

56. John Hart, *What Are They Saying about Environmental Theology?* (New York: Paulist Press, 2004), pp. 7–9.

57. John B. Cobb Jr., "Protestant Theology and Deep Ecology," in Gottlieb, *This*

Sacred Earth, 2nd ed., pp. 248–249. Originally published in David Barnhill and Roger S. Gottlieb, eds., *Deep Ecology and World Religion* (Albany: State University of New York Press, 2001).

58. Patricia Hunt-Perry and Lyn Fine, "All Buddhism Is Engaged: Thich Nhat Hanh and the Order of Interbeing," in *Engaged Buddhism in the West*, ed. Christopher S. Queen (Boston: Wisdom, 2000).

59. In the nineteenth century, Swami Dayananda Sarasvati created the Arya Samaj, a Hindu reform movement, which was in part oriented away from rigid ritual (including the caste system and child marriages) and which incorporated social justice as one of its principles. In chapter 5 we will see an example of contemporary ecological social action led by Hindu Baba Amte. Strong statements on ecological values by Hindu religious leaders can be found in Martin Palmer, *Faith in Conservation: New Approaches to Religions and the Environment* (Washington, DC: World Bank, 2003), pp. 91–96. For a comprehensive bibliography on the subject, see the Forum on Religion and Ecology's section on Hinduism, http://environment.harvard.edu/religion/religion/hinduism/bibliography.html.

60. Norman C. Habel, *Seven Songs of Creation: Liturgies for Celebration and Healing the Earth* (Cleveland, OH: Pilgrim Press, 2004), p. 12.

61. Arthur Waskow, "Global Scorching and Pharaoh's Advisors," Shalom Center, http://www.shalomctr.org/index.cfm/action/read/section/Oiloholic/article/article 731.html.

62. Arthur Waskow, "What Is Eco-Kosher?" in Gottlieb, *This Sacred Earth*, 1st ed., pp. 297–298. Kenneth Kraft has fashioned a similar environmental rethinking of a traditional concept for Buddhism: "eco-karma." Kraft, "Nuclear Ecology and Engaged Buddhism," pp. 277–280.

63. Arthur Green, "Vegetarianism: A Kashrut for Our Age," in Gottlieb, *This Sacred Earth*, 1st ed., pp. 301, 302, emphasis in original.

64. McFague, *Life Abundant*, p. 145.

65. Mark I. Wallace, *Finding God in the Singing River: Christianity, Spirit, Nature* (Minneapolis: Fortress Press, 2005), p. 125, emphasis added.

66. Mark Wallace, building on Jurgen Moltmann's concept of the "wounded God," echoes this theme: "Earth Spirit is the wounded God who daily suffers the environmental violence wrought by humankind's unremitting ecocidal attitudes and habits." Wallace, *Finding God*, p. 134.

67. Of course, the science-religion relationship remains complex and troubled, as we shall see in chapter 2.

68. Theologian Larry L. Rasmussen tells us, "We simply will not allow our experiences to dissipate in purely private sentiments. We insist that the larger meanings of life and their implications of behavior find a public and institutional form, become the material of conscious socialization. . . . We are incorrigibly cosmic storytellers and without cosmologies we literally would no know what to do." "Cosmology and Ethics," in *Worldviews and Ecology: Religion, Philosophy and the Environment*, ed. Mary Evelyn Tucker and John Grim (Maryknoll, NY: Orbis Books, 1994), p. 178.

69. T. Berry, *Dream of the Earth*, 120.

70. Quoted in ibid., p. 79. However, Aquinas, like much of the rest of the Western tradition, contains a variety of positions. He also argues that nature was created simply for the use of human beings and that we have no moral responsibilities toward the nonhuman. He approvingly quotes Augustine: "When we hear it said, 'Thou shalt not kill,' we do not take it as referring to trees, for they have no

sense, nor to irrational animals, because they have no fellowship with us. Hence it follows that the words, 'Thou shalt not kill' refer to the killing of a man." Aquinas, *Summa Theologica*, IIa–IIae, q. 64.

71. T. Berry, *Dream of the Earth*, 130.
72. See Jeffrey Stout, *Democracy and Tradition* (Princeton, NJ: Princeton University Press, 2003), for an account of arguments whose form is essentially: "Look at this!"
73. Marc Bekoff, *Minding Animals* (New York: Oxford University Press, 2002).
74. Jay McDaniel, "Comments on Mark Bekoff," paper presented at The American Academy of Religion conference, November 20, 2004.
75. Holmes Rolston, "God and Endangered Species," in *Ethics, Religion and Biodiversity: Relations between Conservation and Cultural Values*, ed. Lawrence S. Hamilton (Cambridge, UK: White Horse Press, 1993). Rolston adds, "Laws are important in natural systems, but natural law is not the complete explanatory category for nature, any more than is randomness and change. In nature, beyond the laws is grace. There is creativity by which more comes out of less" (p. 56).
76. Lisa H. Sideris, *Environmental Ethics, Ecological Theology and Natural Selection* (New York: Columbia University Press, 2003). Or as theologian Karen Baker-Fletcher puts it, sometimes "far from having an ecstatic, transcendent experience of nature . . . we realize simply that we compete with nature more than we sometimes like to admit." *Sisters of Dust, Sisters of Spirit: Womanist Wording on God and Creation* (Minneapolis: Fortress Press, 1998), p. 33.
77. The most extreme version of this is the belief of some Christian ecotheologians that nature, as well as human beings, will be redeemed and made whole by Christ and thus reach a stage beyond competition, conflict, or violence. One cannot disprove such a vision, but one can say that this is not nature as it exists now.
78. Snyder, "Blue Mountains Constantly Walking," p. 136.
79. Rosemary Radford Ruether, "Ecofeminism: Symbolic and Social Connections of the Oppression of Women and the Domination of Nature," in Gottlieb, *This Sacred Earth*, 2nd ed., p. 397.
80. Quoted in Linda Lear, *Rachel Carson: Witness for Nature* (New York: Holt, 1997), p. 86; Rachel Carson, *The Sense of Wonder* (New York: HarperHarper, 1965).
81. Especially a God who is absent now. Without miracles and direct revelation, nature is all most of us have.
82. Personal communication from Rabbi Dovid Gottlieb (author's brother) many years ago.
83. David Abram, *The Spell of the Sensuous: Perception and Language in a More-than-Human World* (New York: Vintage, 1996).
84. Shalom Rosenberg, "Concepts of Torah and Nature in Jewish Thought," in *Judaism and Ecology*, ed. Hava Tirosh-Samuelson (Cambridge, MA: Harvard University Press, 2002).
85. "Ecosystem people all over the world have viewed themselves as members of a community of beings, in coexistence with fellow creatures be they trees, birds, streams, or rocks. Many of these are revered and protected as sacred." Madhav Gadgil and Ramachandra Guha, *Ecology and Equity: The Use and Abuse of Nature in Contemporary India* (London: Routledge, 1995), p. 91.
86. Joanna Macy, address to American Academy of Religion, San Francisco, 2000. The works of Paul Shepard are particularly important on the human-animal link. See, for example, *The Tender Carnivore and the Sacred Game* (Athens: Univer-

sity of Georgia Press, 1998) and *Nature and Madness* (Athens: University of Georgia Press, 1998).

87. When certain trees (willows and maples were tested) are subjected to extreme defoliation, neighboring trees will increase production of the defensive chemicals in their leaves, as if having been "warned" by the defoliated ones. Jack C. Shultz, "Tree Tactics," *Natural History* 92 (May 1983). On the rat adopting the rabbits, see Jeffrey Moussaieff Masson, *When Elephants Weep: The Emotional Lives of Animals* (New York: Delacorte, 1995). Another astounding example concerns a species of small river fish in Latin America: pairs of the fish will swim to a new area to see if it is safe for feeding. If one holds back, thereby lessening danger to itself, its partner will shun contact with it when they return to the group. This and other examples of animal reciprocity are from Lee Dugatkin, *Cheating Monkeys and Citizen Bees: The Nature of Cooperation in Animals and Humans* (New York: Free Press, 1999).

88. Some of these will be discussed in chapter 6.

89. John McPhee, *Encounters with the Archdruid* (New York: Farrar, Straus and Giroux, 1997).

90. John B. Cobb, *Is It Too Late? A Theology of Ecology* (Beverly Hills, CA: Bruce, 1972); Rosemary Radford Ruether, *Sexism and God Talk: Toward a Feminist Theology* (Boston: Beacon Press, 1983).

91. James Martin-Schramm and Robert Stivers, *Christian Environmental Ethics: A Case Method Approach* (Maryknoll, NY: Orbis, 2003).

92. Ecojustice Ministries, www.eco-justice.org.

93. As with the tendency of the new ecotheology to embrace—while giving its own meaning to—current scientific work in cosmology and ecology.

94. Ivone Gabara, "The Trinity and Human Experience: An Ecofeminist Approach," in Gottlieb, *This Sacred Earth*, 2nd ed., p. 405.

95. Herman Daly and John Cobb Jr., *For the Common Good: Redirecting the Economy toward Community, the Environment, and a Sustainable Future* (Boston: Beacon Press, 1989).

96. Soelle, *The Silent Cry*, especially pp. 191–207.

97. For example: "The structural institutions and systemic forms separating the haves and the have-nots in our time, [we must]...name them for what they are: evil. They are the collective forms of 'our sin.' They are the institutions, laws, and international bodies of market capitalism." McFague, *Life Abundant*, p. 176. More remarkably, there is the following statement by Catholic bishops from Canada:

> Over the years, Albertans have lived as if the abundant forests, minerals, oil, gas and coal deposits, fertile prairie topsoil and clean air and water extended without limit.... However, times have changed. Our stewardship of this abundance is now being questioned. Our *economic model of maximizing profit* in an increasingly *global market* is unsustainable.... The issue of global climate change being pushed by rising fossil fuel consumption and deforestation goes to the heart of Alberta's *economic priorities*.
>
> The move to *large-scale corporate agriculture* in search of greater *economic efficiencies* runs the risk of destroying the agricultural foundations of fertile topsoil, clean air and water as well as the social ecology of vibrant rural human communities.

> The rapid, *widespread harvesting* of the boreal forest is testing the
> limits of ecosystem integrity and risks the future of what should be a
> renewable resource for future generations.

"Celebrate Life: Care for Creation. The Alberta Bishops' Letter on Ecology for October 4, 1998," at *Western Catholic Reporter*, http://www.wcr.ab.ca/bin/eco -lett.htm emphasis added.

98. Nawal H. Ammar, "An Islamic Response to the Manifest Ecological Crisis: Issues of Justice," in Gottlieb, *This Sacred Earth*, 2nd ed., pp. 296, 287–288.

99. Of the now enormous literature on environmental racism and environmental justice, one might start with Robert D. Bullard, *Unequal Protection: Environmental Protection and Communities of Color* (San Francisco: Sierra Club Books, 1994), and James Lester, David Allen, and Kelly Hill, *Environmental Injustice in the United States: Myths and Realities* (Boulder, CO: Westview Press, 2001). In an excellent treatment of these issues in India, Gadgil and Guha, in *Ecology and Equity* (p. 95), observe that how we treat nature is typically a question of access to it: in the third world, who will get to use natural resources. In the developed world, quite often, the question is who will get to pollute it.

100. Deeohn Ferris and David Hahn-Baker, "Environmentalists and Environmental Justice Policy," in *Environmental Justice: Issues, Policies, and Solutions*, ed. Bunyan Bryant (Washington, DC: Island Press, 1995). I discuss this connection further in chapter 4.

101. Larry Rasmussen, *Earth Community, Earth Ethics* (Maryknoll, NY: Orbis Books, 1996).

102. Karen Baker-Fletcher, "Something or Nothing: An Eco-Womanist Essay on God, Creation and Indispensability," in Gottlieb, *This Sacred Earth*, 2nd ed., p. 436.

103. Thomas White Wolf Fassett, "Where Do We Go from Here?" in *Defending Mother Earth: Native American Perspectives on Environmental Justice*, ed. Jace Weaver (Maryknoll, NY: Orbis Books, 1997), p. 199.

104. For a useful overview of the by now large ecofeminist literature, see Victoria Dayton, "Ecofeminism," in *A Companion to Environmental Philosophy*, ed. Dale Jamieson (London: Blackwell, 2001). For studies of seventeen religious ecofeminists from around the world, see Rosemary Radford Ruether, *Integrating Ecofeminism, Globalization, and World Religions* (Lanham, MD: Rowman and Littlefield, 2004).

105. See the discussion in Peter Wenz, *Environmental Ethics Today* (New York: Oxford University Press, 2001), pp. 200–208. Also see Vandana Shiva, *The Violence of the Green Revolution* (Atlantic Highland, NJ: Zed Books, 1991).

106. Vandana Shiva, *Staying Alive: Women, Ecology, and Development* (London: Zed Books, 1989).

107. Denise Ackermann and Tahira Joyner, "Earth-Healing in South Africa," in *Women Healing Earth: Third World Women on Ecology, Feminism, and Religion*, ed. Rosemary Radford Ruether (Maryknoll, NY: Orbis Books, 1996), p. 122.

108. Gabriele Dietrich, "The World as the Body of God: Feminists' Perspective on Ecology and Social Justice," in Ruether, *Women Healing Earth*, p. 95.

109. Sulak Sivaraksa, "The Religion of Consumerism," in Kaza and Kraft, *Dharma Rain*, pp. 178–179.

110. Introductory statement in *Religion and Ecology: Can the Climate Change?* Special issue, *Daedalus* 130, no. 4 (Fall 2001): 1.

111. Abraham Joshua Heschel, *The Sabbath: Its Meaning for Modern Man* (New York: Farrar, Straus and Giroux, 1951), p. 12.

112. Stephanie Kaza, "Overcoming the Grip of Consumerism," *Buddhist Christian Studies* 20 (2000).
113. The exception is the way that many people treat pets better than they treat other humans. This complicating case does not refute the general point, however.
114. On pigs in Hawaii, see Patrick G. Derr and Edward M. McNamara, *Case Studies in Environmental Ethics* (Lanham, MD: Rowman and Littlefield, 2003), pp. 139–146. On the immigration debate, see *Sierra* (Fall 2004).
115. Sideris, *Environmental Ethics*; Fern, *Nature, God and Humanity*.
116. Nash, *Loving Nature*, pp. 176–186. Nash's discussion of this issue is extremely sophisticated and valuable.
117. I was prompted by John Sanbonmatsu to address this point.
118. In the environmentally progressive Brazilian city of Curitiba, for example, one simply is not allowed to cut down a tree, any tree, without prior permission. You must have very good reasons to do so and must in almost every case plant two new ones in its place. Bill McKibben, *Hope Human and Wild: True Stories of Living Lightly on the Earth* (St. Paul, MN: Ruminator Books, 1997).
119. Jeanne Kay, "Concepts of Nature in the Hebrew Bible," in Yaffe, *Judaism and Environmental Ethics*.
120. Louke Van Wensveen, *Dirty Virtues: The Emergence of Ecological Virtue Ethics* (Buffalo, NY: Humanity Books, 1999). This approach is valuable, but cannot remove all difficulties. For surely a good life is one in which what is valuable is treated as such. And we cannot know what is in fact valuable without some general principles of value.
121. John B. Cobb Jr., *Sustainability: Economics, Ecology, and Justice* (Maryknoll, NY: Orbis Books, 1997), p. 85.
122. Abdul Aziz Said and Nathan C. Funk, "Peace in Islam: An Ecology of the Spirit," in Foltz et al., *Islam and Ecology*, p. 165, emphasis added.

Chapter 2

1. John Rawls, *Political Liberalism* (New York: Columbia University Press, 1993), pp. xxxix–xl.
2. Ellen Willis, "Freedom from Religion," *The Nation*, February 9, 2001, emphasis added.
3. Robert Edgar, interview, December 10, 2004. For numerous examples of religious contributions to human rights struggles, see Peter Ackerman and Jack Duvall, *A Force More Powerful: A Century of Nonviolent Conflict* (New York: St. Martin's, 2000).
4. Timothy S. Shah, "Making the Christian World Safe for Liberalism: From Grotius to Rawls," in *Religion and Democracy*, ed. David Marquand and Ronald L. Netter (Oxford: Blackwell, 2000), p. 126. I am indebted to Shah's excellent article.
5. William Penn, *Collected Works*, ed. Joseph Bess, 1726, vol. 2, quoted in George Corey, "Tolerating Religion," in *The Politics of Toleration in Modern Life*, ed. Susan Mendus (Durham, NC: Duke University Press, 2000), p. 50.
6. Søren Kierkegaard, *Concluding Unscientific Postscript* (Princeton, NJ: Princeton University Press, 1974), pp. 179–180.
7. The fundamentally different attitude toward verbal theology in Eastern religions makes this problem rather different there.

8. Robert Wuthnow, *After Heaven: Spirituality in America Since the 1950s* (Berkeley: University of California Press, 2000).

9. Glenn Tinder, "Faith, Doubt, and Public Dialogue," in *A Nation under God? Essays on the Fate of Religion in American Public Life*, ed. R. Bruce Douglass and Joshua Mitchell (Lanham, MD: Rowman and Littlefield, 2000).

10. Jim Wallis, *The Soul of Politics: Beyond "Religious Right" and "Secular Left"* (New York: Harcourt Brace, 1995), pp. 39–40.

11. Corey, "Tolerating Religion," p. 60.

12. Paul Weithman, "Why Should Christians Endorse Human Rights?" in *Religion in the Liberal Polity*, ed. Terence Cuneo (South Bend, IN: University of Notre Dame Press, 2005).

13. This view is found in countless writers. One classic formulation was that of H. Richard Niebuhr, who distinguished between "Christ," or the essential-but-never-fully-or-finally-found heart of Christianity, and "culture," which is the historically and socially relative way Christianity is practiced at a particular time. It is our task, said Niebuhr, always to beware of thinking that the former had been encompassed by the latter (*Christ and Culture* [New York: Harper, 1951]). See also the works of Reinhold Niebuhr. This theme is developed throughout the work of Amanda Porterfield, who refers to a late twentieth-century "awakening to the social and psychological construction of religion." *The Transformation of American Religion: The Story of a Late-Twentieth Century Awakening* (New York: Oxford University Press, 2001), p. 230.

14. Stephen Toulmin, *An Examination of the Place of Reason in Ethics* (Cambridge, UK: Cambridge University Press, 1961).

15. Robert Audi, "Liberal Democracy and the Place of Religion in Politics," in *Religion in the Public Square: The Place of Religious Convictions in Public Debate*, ed. Robert Audi and Nicholas Wolterstorff (Lanham, MD: Rowman and Littlefield, 1996), p. 25.

16. See, for instance, his 48,000-word encyclical *Evangelium vitae*, at Vatican, http://www.vatican.va/holy_father/john_paul_ii/encyclicals/documents/hf_jp-ii_enc _25031995_evangelium-vitae_en.html. His argument is based on the idea that because humans were made in God's image, we should act with the same loving spirit He does. This would rule out violence, including abortion.

17. Some, in fact, argue that the secular ideal of human rights derives from, and even makes little sense without, the idea of each person being created in the image of God. See Michael J. Perry, *The Idea of Human Rights: Four Inquiries* (New York: Oxford University Press, 1998).

18. Mary C. Segers and Ted. G. Jelen, *Wall of Separation? Debating the Public Role of Religion* (Lanham, MD: Rowman and Littlefield, 1997).

19. See the extensive discussion of this point in Christopher Eberle, *Religious Conviction in Liberal Politics* (New York: Cambridge University Press, 2002).

20. As philosopher William Galston observes, respect is rooted not in agreement, but in thoughtful honesty: "We show others respect when we offer them, as explanations, what we take to be our truest and best reasons for acting as we do." *Liberal Purposes: Goods, Virtues, and Diversity in the Liberal State* (New York: Cambridge University Press, 1991), p. 109.

22. Rawls, *Political Liberalism*.

22. A related but distinct failure haunts the efforts of another famous philosopher, Richard Rorty. Unlike Rawls, Rorty doesn't believe that any universal rules can be found. The liberal belief in autonomy, freedom, natural science, and rights is

just one more ethnocentric habit, no more "rational" than fundamentalist Islam or alchemy. The best we can hope for is that we'll all tolerate each other's idiosyncratic beliefs, while trying to develop some compassion for each other's suffering. We won't try to convince each other of our truths, we'll share our stories. Religion, like art or extreme forms of any philosophical belief, will simply be part of our personal self-development. Yet Rorty, no less than Rawls, wants to keep religious (and philosophical) passion private. See Richard Rorty, *Contingency, Irony, and Solidarity* (New York: Cambridge University Press, 1989). Rorty's inconsistencies here are pointed out very well by J. Judd Owen, *Religion and the Demise of Liberal Rationalism: The Foundational Crisis of the Separation of Church and State* (Chicago: University of Chicago Press, 2001). For some of Rorty's interesting speculations about spiritual life, including his claim that moving away from metaphysical religious belief signals a movement away from power and toward love, see Richard Rorty and Gianni Vattimo, *The Future of Religion* (New York: Columbia University Press, 2005).

23. The term is Rawls's. It is these views that he seeks to eliminate from public conversation.

24. Michael Sandel, *Democracy's Discontent: America in Search of a Public Philosophy* (London: Belknap Press, 1998).

25. I am indebted to Jeffrey Stout's original and highly intelligent perspective here in *Democracy and Tradition*. In general, the past thirty years of political philosophy has shown a tremendously increased stress on conversation—on being allowed to speak and being heard—as essential to all aspects, even to the very definition, of justice. Perhaps the most important exponent of this view is Jürgen Habermas, *A Theory of Communicative Action*, 2 vols. (Boston: Beacon Press, 1981).

26. Segers and Jelen, *Wall of Separation?* The point is also developed in Sidney Verba, Kay Schlozman, and Henry E. Brady, *Voice and Equality: Civic Voluntarism in American Politics* (Cambridge, MA: Harvard University Press, 1995).

27. Allen Hertzke, *Representing God in Washington: The Role of Religious Lobbies in the American Polity* (Knoxville: University of Tennessee Press, 1988).

28. This position was developed by early nineteenth-century philosopher Ludwig Feurbach and was a starting point for Marx.

29. This approach to religious belief was beautifully articulated by John Wisdom, "Gods," in *Classical and Contemporary Readings in Philosophy and Religion*, ed. John Hick (Upper Saddle River, NJ: Prentice-Hall, 1989).

30. Carolyn Merchant, *The Death of Nature: Women, Ecology and the Scientific Revolution* (San Francisco: Harper SanFrancisco, 1990).

31. Here religious environmentalists join hands with what is sometimes called "postempiricist" philosophy of science. The overall trend of this widely varied movement is to point out that the actual practice of science depends on and thus expresses social relationships.

32. Zillah Eisenstein, *Manmade Breast Cancers* (Ithaca, NY: Cornell University Press, 2001); Janette D. Sherman, *Life's Delicate Balance: Causes and Prevention of Breast Cancer* (New York: Taylor and Francis, 2000); Steingraber, *Living Downstream*.

33. Sherman, *Life's Delicate Balance*, p. 207.

34. Sheldon Krimsky, *Science in the Private Interest: Has the Lure of Profits Corrupted Biomedical Research?* (Lanham, MD: Rowman and Littlefield, 2003), pp. 179–180. Equally serious, in a 2002 survey of 3,247 scientists, nearly 16 per-

cent said they had changed the design, methods, or results of a study "in response to pressure from a funding source." Malcolm Ritter, "Survey: Scientific Misbehavior is Common," *Free New Mexican*, http://www.freenewmexican .com/news/28863.html. Similar situations were reported in the United Kingdom. See Melissa Jackston, "Sponsors 'Manipulate' Scientists," BBC News, http:// news.bbc.co.uk/1/hi/education/4379457.stm.

35. Robert Proctor, *Cancer Wars: How Politics Shapes What We Know and Don't Know about Cancer* (New York: Basic Books, 1995), p. 266, citing Peter Chowka, "The National Cancer Institute and the Fifty-Year Cover-Up," *East-West* (January 1978): 22–27; Ralph Moss, *The Cancer Industry* (New York: Paragon House, 1991).

36. Proctor, *Cancer Wars*, p. 266. See also Sharon Batt and Liza Gross, "Cancer, INC." *Sierra* (September–October 1999).

37. This point was well developed by Catriona Sandilands, "Opinionated Natures: Towards a Green Public Culture," in *Democracy and the Claims of Nature: Critical Perspectives for a New Century*, ed. Bob Minteer and Bob Pepperman Taylor (Lanham, MD: Rowman and Littlefield, 2002).

38. On Thailand, see Bruce Rich, *Mortgaging the Earth: The World Bank, Environmental Impoverishment, and the Crisis of Development* (Boston: Beacon Press, 1994), pp. 19–20. On the fishing disaster, see Susan Pollack, "The Last Fish," *Sierra* (August 1995), and Dick Russell, "Vacuuming the Seas," *E Magazine* 7, no 4 (July/August 1996).

39. Meera Nanda, *Prophets Facing Backward: Postmodern Critiques of Science and Hindu Nationalism in India* (Piscataway, NJ: Rutgers University Press, 2003).

40. There are many writers who identify with both science and spirit, including professional scientists who view their subject matter in spiritual terms. One spiritually oriented ecology text by a biology professor and researcher is Christopher Uhl's *Developing Ecological Consciousness: Path to a Sustainable World* (Lanham, MD: Rowman and Littlefield, 2004).

41. Some of these points were developed in Gottlieb, *Joining Hands*.

42. Stanley Hauerwas, "September 11, 2001: A Pacifist Response," *South Atlantic Quarterly* 101, no. 2 (Spring 2002); Stanley M. Hauerwas, *Wilderness Wanderings: Probing Twentieth Century Theology and Philosophy* (Cambridge, MA: Westview Press, 1997), p. 9; Stanley Hauerwas and William H. Willmon, *Resident Aliens: Life in the Christian Colony* (Nashville, TN: Abingdon, 1989); Stanley Hauerwas, *The Hauerwas Reader* (Durham, NC: Duke University Press, 2001).

43. Reinhold Niebuhr, *Moral Man and Immoral Society* (New York: Scribner's, 1953), pp. 276–277, emphasis added.

44. Hannah Arendt, *Eichman in Jerusalem: A Report on the Banality of Evil* (New York: Viking, 1964); Gottlieb, *A Spirituality of Resistance*, chapter 3.

45. Thomas Merton (1962), quoted in Murray Polner, *Disarmed and Dangerous: The Radical Life and Times of Daniel and Philip Berrigan* (Boulder, CO: Westview, 1997), p. 107.

46. For a discussion of such a project, see Rich, *Mortgaging the Earth*.

47. Charles Cummings, "Fruit of the Earth, Fruit of the Vine," in LaChance and Carroll, *Embracing Earth*, p. 156.

48. Gustav Gutierrez, *Theology of Liberation* (Maryknoll, NY: Orbis Books, 1988), p. 116.

49. This section and the next are based on arguments developed in much greater length in Gottlieb, *Joining Hands*.

50. Steve Bruce, *Religion in the Modern World: From Cathedrals to Cults* (Oxford: Oxford University Press, 1996).
51. As in Oscar Wilde's definition of a cynic.
52. Wilhelm Reich, "What Is Class Consciousness," in *Sex-Pol* (New York: Vintage, 1972).
53. Criticisms of the identification of "reason" with limited, instrumental rationality are at the heart of the Frankfurt School of anticommunist neo-Marxist theory. See Horkheimer and Adorno, *Dialectic of Enlightenment*; Jürgen Habermas, *Knowledge and Human Interests* (Boston: Beacon Press, 1968).
54. Paul H. Ray and Sherry Ruth Anderson, *The Cultural Creatives* (New York: Harmony Books, 2000).

Chapter 3

1. There is a strain in social thought that emphasizes the power of norms to shape behavior, as opposed to interests and desires. An interesting version is Christian Smith, *Moral Believing Animals* (New York: Oxford University Press, 2003).
2. According to a major World Bank study, "Poor people trust religious organizations more than any other organizations except their own social institutions." Palmer, *Faith in Conservation*, p. 25.
3. "Address of His Holiness Ecumenical Patriarch Bartholomew at the Environmental Symposium, Santa Barbara, CA, November 8, 1997," in Gottlieb, *This Sacred Earth*, 2nd ed., pp. 229–230.
4. This position reverberates throughout a good deal of Orthodox Christianity. Most Reverend Metropolitan John of Pergamon, a theologian and church leader, points the finger at Christians as well as humanity in general: "The ecological crisis is the most serious contemporary problem facing us. To some extent the Christian tradition bears responsibility for causing it." John Pergamon, "Orthodoxy and the Ecological Problems: A Theological Approach," at Ecumenical Patriarchate of Constantinople, http://www.patriarchate.org/. For an overview of Orthodoxy and nature, see John Chryssavgis, "The Earth as Sacrament: Insights from Orthodox Christian Theology and Spirituality," in *The Oxford Handbook on Religion and Ecology*, ed. Roger S. Gottlieb (New York: Oxford University Press, 2006).
5. Evangelical Declaration, in Gottlieb, *This Sacred Earth*, 2nd ed.
6. "For the Health of the Nation: An Evangelical Call to Civic Responsibility," at National Association of Evangelicals, http://www.nae.net/images/civic_respon sibility2.pdf. See also Laurie Goodstein, "Evangelical Leaders Swing Influence behind Effort to Combat Global Warming," *New York Times*, March 10, 2005; Blaine Harden, "The Greening of Evangelicals: Christian Right Turns, Sometimes Warily, to Environmentalism," *Washington Post*, February 6, 2005.
7. Ismar Schorsch, "Tending to Our Cosmic Oasis," *Melton Journal* (Spring 1991), at Luminaries, http://learn.jtsa.edu/topics/luminaries/monograph/tendingto.shtml.
8. The following discussion of Catholicism is indebted to conversations with Thomas A. Shannon and John Hart. For a concise summary of much of this history, see Pontifical Council for Justice and Peace, *From Stockholm to Johannesburg: An Historical Overview of the Concern of the Holy See for the Environment, 1972–2002* (Rome: Vatican Press, 2002).

9. *Rerum Novarum*, in *Catholic Social Thought: The Documentary Heritage*, ed. David O'Brian and Thomas A. Shannon (Maryknoll, NY: Orbis Books, 1995). The Vatican Web site has most encyclicals: http://www.vatican.va/holy_father/.

10. Starting with Locke, those who justify the human benefits of agricultural expansion and industrial development require—but typically do not offer—some way to assess when development and production become damaging to human beings or simply wasteful.

11. *Redemptor hominis*. Available at the Vatican Web site: http://www.vatican.va/edocs/ENG0218/_INDEX.HTM.

12. Charles M. Murphy, *At Home on Earth: Foundations for a Catholic Ethic of the Environment* (New York: Crossroad, 1989).

13. *Sollicitudo Rei Socialis* (Concern for social matters). Available at the Vatican Web site: http://www.vatican.va/edocs/ENG0223/_INDEX.HTM.

14. Ibid., emphasis added.

15. John Paul II, "Message of Pope John Paul II for the Celebration of the World Day of Peace, January 1, 1990," emphasis added. Available at the Vatican Web site: http://www.vatican.va/holy_father/john_paul_ii/messages/peace/documents/hf_jp-ii_mes_20031216_xxxvii-world-day-for-peace_en.html.

16. Interview with Anthony Judt, *Frontline*, http://www.pbs.org/wgbh/pages/frontline/shows/pope/interviews/judt.html.

17. Jürgen Habermas, *Theory and Practice* (Boston: Beacon Press, 1971), p. 282.

18. There is also his criminal neglect of any serious response to the sex abuse scandal.

19. John Paul II, "Message of Pope John Paul II for the Celebration of the World Day of Peace, January 1, 1990."

20. John Paul II, General Audience, January 26, 2000, quoted at Catholic Conservation, http://conservation.catholic.org/pope_john_paul_ii.htm, emphasis added.

21. Thomas Aquinas, *Summa Theologiae* (New York: Bensiger Bros., 1947), 1.47.1.

22. William French, "Christianity: Roman Catholicism," in Taylor, *Encyclopedia of Religion and Nature.*

23. Possibly (as Elisabeth Johnson suggests) because Galileo's treatment by the church scared people. "Losing and Finding Creation in the Christian Tradition," in *Christianity and Ecology: Seeking the Well-Being of Earth and Humans*, ed. Rosemary Ruether and Dieter Hessel (Cambridge, MA: Harvard University Press, 2000).

24. Deuteronomy 12:2: "You shall surely destroy all the places where the nations whom you shall dispossess served their gods, on the high mountains and on the hills and under every green tree."

25. Bishops of the Philippines, "What Is Happening to Our Beautiful Land?" in *"And God Saw That It Was Good": Catholic Theology and the Environment*, ed. Drew Christiansen and Walter Grazer (Washington, DC: United States Catholic Conference, 1996), pp. 309–310. Along with some excellent essays, this volume also reprints several statements, including those from John Paul II and bishops' groups from different countries. On the Web, "What Is Happening?" is linked to the Forum on Religion and Ecology Web site (which has links to dozens of other statements as well): http://environment.harvard.edu/religion/religion/christianity/statements/index.html.

26. "What Is Happening?" pp. 312, 313.

27. Twenty years later, the Appalachian bishops issued a report evaluating successes, changes, and developments in the ensuing two decades. See "At Home in the

Web of Life," published by the Catholic Committee of Appalachia, 1995, at Professor John Willetts of DePaul University, http://condor.depaul.edu/~jwillets/aeseminar/At%20Home%20in%20the%20Web%20of%20Life.doc.

28. From U.S. Council of Catholic Bishops, http://www.usccb.org/sdwp/ejp/bishops statement.htm, emphasis added.

29. In 1998 the bishops of Alberta, Canada, echoing this thought, taught Catholics to see creation in a sacramental way: "The abundance and beauty of God's creation reveals to us something of the generosity of the Creator. God is present and speaks in the dynamic life forces of our universe and planet as well as in our own lives. Respect for life needs to include all creation." "Celebrate Life: Care for Creation," the Alberta bishops' letter on ecology for October 4, 1998, at *Western Catholic Reporter*, http://www.wcr.ab.ca/bin/eco-lett.htm.

30. For a concise history of this pattern of development, see Hart, *What Are They Saying about Environmental Theology?*

31. For significant activities of local priests and congregations resisting serious industrial pollution in Thika town, Kenya, see Samson Gitau, "Christian Environmentalism in Kenya," in Taylor, *Encyclopedia of Religion and Nature*. For the USCCB task force on pollution and children's health, see USCCB, http://www.usccb.org/sdwp/ejp/case/todo.shtml.

32. See, e.g., USCCB, "Let the Earth Bless the Lord: God's Creation and Our Responsibility: A Catholic Approach to the Environment," USCCB, first edition 1996. Available at http://www.usccb.org.

33. Walt Grazer, interview with author, July 15, 2004.

34. For a useful compendium drawn from a wide array of his writings, see "His Holiness, the 14th Dalai Lama on the Environment," at Peace Jam, www.peacejam.org/lama/enviro01.html#3. He has also strongly criticized the Chinese for their unecological practices since the occupation, especially their use of Tibet as a disposal area for nuclear wastes. See Kaza, "To Save All Beings," pp. 171–172.

35. Dalai Lama, foreword to *Dharma Gaia: A Harvest of Essays in Buddhism and Ecology*, ed. Allan Hunt Badiner (Berkeley: Parallax Press, 1990).

36. This point is developed in "The Sun My Heart," in Kaza and Kraft, *Dharma Rain*.

37. Thich Nhat Hanh, "The Last Tree," in Badiner, *Dharma Gaia*, p. 218.

38. Thich Nhat Hanh, "Individual, Society, and Nature," in *The Path of Compassion: Writing on Socially Engaged Buddhism*, ed. Fred Eppisteiner (Berkeley: Parallax Press, 1988), p. 44.

39. Ibid., p. 43.

40. "Monks Discuss Religion's Role in Environmental Conservation," *Cambodia: The World Bank* 2, no. 6 (June 2004), at Alliance for Religion and Conservation, http://arcworld.org/projects.asp?projectID=232; http://siteresources.worldbank.org/INTCAMBODIA/newsletters/20221708/E.pdf.

41. From the World Bank, http://lnweb18.worldbank.org/essd/envext.nsf/48ByDoc Name/FaithsandEnvironmentFaithsandForestsInitiative.

42. Betsy Gaines, "Mongolian Buddhism and Taimen Conservation," in Taylor, *Encyclopedia of Religion and Nature*.

43. "Prime Minister of Mongolia to Be First International President of ARC," at Alliance of Religion and Conservation, http://www.arcworld.org/news.asp?page ID=6.

44. Palmer, *Faith in Conservation*; Alliance of Religion and Conservation, http://www.arcworld.org/projects.asp?projectID=100=.

45. Gaines, "Mongolian Buddhism and Taimen Conservation"; Tributary Fund (supporting the taimen project), http://www.thetributaryfund.org/mongolia.htm; Joan Hines, "Quammen to Restore Mongolian Monastery, Watershed," *Bozeman Daily Chronicle* (Montana), August 20, 2004, http://www.bozemandailychronicle .com/articles/2004/08/20/news/mongoliabzbigs.txt.

46. The problem was stated clearly by a noted economist more than twenty-five years ago. Robert Riddell argued that "development" tended to benefit already wealthy nations and caused poverty, excess resource use, and other social problems in poorer ones (*Ecodevelopment* [Westmead, England: Gower, 1981]).

47. All these tactics (and more) are described in Sharon Beder, *Global Spin: The Corporate Assault on Environmentalism* (White River Junction, VT: Chelsea Green, 1998). The particular tactic of corporations representing themselves as green when they are not is the subject of Jed Greer and Kenny Bruno, *Greenwash: The Reality behind Corporate Environmentalism* (Croton-on-Hudson, NY: Apex Press, 1996). For a detailed study of Exxon-Mobil's attempts to discredit assertions of global warming (to the tune of some $8 million), see Chris Mooney, "Some Like It Hot," *Mother Jones* (May/June 2005). A study of how timber companies use rhetoric about trees ("Plant a tree—save the world," etc.) as a way to avoid serious environmental issues is Shaul E. Cohen, *Planting Nature: Trees and the Manipulation of Environmental Stewardship in America* (Berkeley: University of California Press, 2004).

48. The meaning of terms like communist, socialist, and Marxist are themselves subject to an enormous amount of debate. For my understanding of these issues, see Roger S. Gottlieb, *History and Subjectivity: The Transformation of Marxist Theory* (Philadelphia: Temple University Press, 1987), and *Marxism 1844–1990: Origins, Betrayal, Rebirth* (New York: Routledge, 1994).

49. Fernando Funes, Luis García, and Martin Bourque, *Sustainable Agriculture and Resistance: Transforming Food Production in Cuba* (Oakland, CA: Food First Books, 2002); John S. Dryzek, *Green States and Social Movements: Environmentalism in the United States, United Kingdom, Germany, and Norway* (New York: Oxford University Press, 2003).

50. Joseph Romm, *Cool Companies: How the Best Businesses Boost Profits and Productivity by Cutting Greenhouse Gas Emissions* (Washington, DC: Island Press, 1999). In these cases, there are typically large-scale economic benefits to the companies.

51. See Stanley Manahan, *Industrial Ecology* (New York: CRC Press, 1999). The newly built plants that escape U.S. regulations have been described in many places. See, for example, Julie Light, "La Linea: NAFTA, Justice, and the U.S.-Mexico Border," *Corporate Watch*, June 30, 1999, http://www.globalpolicy.org/globaliz/special/lalinea.htm.

52. There are many comprehensive ecosocialist oriented critiques of capitalism. For example, Joel Kovel, *The Enemy of Nature: The End of Capitalism or the End of the World?* (Thetford, VT: Glad Day Books, 2002); see also the journal (of which I am an editor) *Capitalism, Nature, Socialism: A Journal of Socialist Ecology*, http://www.tandf.co.uk/journals/titles/10455752.asp.

53. This is similar to the way corporations move to countries where unions are illegal and repressed.

54. And that in any case, the reforms took place only because of a mobilized popular movement. The following claim is focused on Latin America but has wide global relevance: "Governing groups have rarely promoted reforms to benefit the pop-

ular sectors or to protect natural resources, without being subjected first to heavy pressure." David Kaimowitz, "Social Pressure for Environmental Reform," in *Green Guerrillas: Environmental Conflicts and Initiatives in Latin America and the Caribbean*, ed. Helen Collinson (London: Latin American Bureau, 1996), p. 21.

55. The case against the Bush administration's treatment of science is made in Chris Clark, "Bush's Bizarre Science," *Earth Island Journal* 18, no. 2 (Summer 2003). The *Lancet*, Britain's premiere medical journal, editorialized on the administration's packing of supposedly scientific panels: "Members of expert panels need to be impartial and credible, and free of partisan conflicts of interest, especially in industry links or in right-wing or religious ideology. Any further right-wing incursions on expert panels' membership will cause a terminal decline in public trust in the advice of scientists" (*Lancet*, November 14, 2002). For an overview of the administration's disastrous environmental policy, see Carl Pope, *Strategic Ignorance: Why the Bush Administration Is Recklessly Destroying a Century of Environmental Progress* (San Francisco: Sierra Club Books, 2004).

56. Such positions usually include claims that the environmental crisis is vastly exaggerated by environmentalists. The most famous exposition of this position is Bjorn Lomborg, *The Skeptical Environmentalist* (Cambridge, UK: Cambridge University Press, 1997). See also Peter Huber, *Hard Green: Saving the Environment from the Environmentalists: A Conservative Manifesto* (New York: Basic Books, 2000). For a more technical version of the argument, the authors of which have serious environmental credentials, see Paul Hawken, Amory B. Lovins, and L. Hunter Lovins, *Natural Capitalism: Creating the Next Industrial Revolution* (Boston: Little, Brown, 1999).

57. Cornwall Declaration, at Interfaith Council for Environmental Stewardship, http://www.stewards.net/CornwallDeclaration.htm.

58. World Council of Churches, http://www.wcc-coe.org/wcc/who/index-e.html.

59. World Council of Churches, http://www2.wcc-coe.org/pressReleasesen.nsf/09c9d22d54ad7a37c1256d0a004ebd7d/c0cc4cb160ebf5b6c1256da40051b72f?Open Document.

60. World Council of Churches, press release, November 14, 2000, http://www.wcc-coe.org/wcc/news/press/00/34pre.html.

61. The WCC representatives flatly stated, "Wealthy polluting countries should not be allowed to buy their way out of the problem [of global climate change and emissions] through paying for projects in other countries." Press release, November 14, 2000, http://www.wcc-coe.org/wcc/news/press/00/34pre.html.

62. World Council of Churches, http://www.wcc-coe.org/wcc/what/jpc/cop6-e.html, emphasis added.

63. I have dealt with this issue at much greater length in Gottlieb, *Joining Hands*.

64. I have examined this moral situation in some detail in chapter 4 of Gottlieb, *A Spirituality of Resistance*.

Chapter 4

1. Jan Nunley and Jerry Hames, "Episcopalians Join Protest against Drilling in Arctic Refuge," Episcopalian News Service, May 14, 2001; Massachusetts Conference Edition, *United Church News*, "Four Conference Clergy Members Arrested at

Protest," June 2001; "22 Arrested in Peaceful Civil Disobedience at Dept. of Energy: Religious Leaders Pray for Arctic Refuge," *Arctic Truth*, May 3, 2001. Information and links to news stories at Religious Witness for the Earth, http://www.religiouswitness.org/.

2. Margaret Bullitt-Jonas, "Conversion to Eco-Justice: Reflections on the Inner Journey," based on remarks given at the Costas Consultation in Global Mission 2002–2003, "Earth-Keeping as a Dimension of Christian Mission," February 28–March 1, 2003, unpublished ms.

3. From Shin Shalom, twentieth-century Jewish poet: "On Tu B'Shvat . . . an Angel descends, ledger in hand, and enters each bud, each twig, each tree, and all our garden flowers. . . . When the ledger will be full, of trees and blossom and shrubs, when the desert is turned into a meadow and all our land is a watered garden, the Messiah will appear." In Stein, *A Garden of Choice Fruit*, p. 65.

4. Letter to Charles Hurwitz from Naomi Steinberg for Children of the Earth, reproduced at Green Yes, http://greenyes.grrn.org/1997/0248.html.

5. Seth Zuckerman, "Redwood Rabbis," *Sierra* (November/December 1998); Margaret Holub, "Redwoods and Torah," *Tikkun* (May/June 1999).

6. Religious Witness for the Earth, http://www.religiouswitness.org/.

7. Andrea Ayvazian, interview with author, October 14, 2004.

8. Shalom Center, http://www.shalomctr.org/index.cfm/action/read/section/about us/article/article711.html.

9. COEJL, www.coejl.org.

10. Hadar Susskind, interview with author, May 31, 2005. COEJL's Israel program is the Jewish Global Environmental Network.

11. Palmer, *Faith in Conservation*, p. 3.

12. Dwarka, India—A few weeks ago, the crew of an Indian fishing boat in the Arabian Sea thought they had the biggest catch of their lives. A 40-foot-long unsuspecting whale shark had entered their nets on a still night. But instead of killing the creature, known as the gentle ocean giant, the captain called the boat owner who promptly told him to let it go. "I may have lost a lot of money. But I'm happy that I could play a role in saving the protected fish," Kamlesh Chamadia, the boat owner said. Two years ago, Chamadia, like hundreds of other fishermen along the Saurashtra coast of India's western Gujarat state, would have had little hesitation in killing whale sharks. But a lively campaign by a wildlife group and a popular religious leader has helped reduce the killing. . . . The whale shark protection campaign in Gujarat has also got a religious flavor to it after Murari Bapu, a popular Hindu preacher, agreed to be its brand ambassador.

Bapu, who holds his audience spell-bound with his narration of the stories from the Hindu epic Ramayana, likens the migration of the whale shark to pregnant daughters coming to their parental home for the delivery. "Would you ever think of any harm to your daughters, let alone killing them. Whale sharks are your daughters and you should take good care of them," Bapu told a gathering of hundreds of fishermen in Dwarka, a coastal pilgrimage city said to be founded by Lord Krishna. Activists have also staged a street drama depicting a pregnant daughter pleading with her fisherman father not to kill a whale shark trapped in his net. The play, which has been performed in towns across the Saurashtra coast, strikes an emotional chord with the fishermen and four towns have adopted the shark as their mascot.

Thomas Kutty Abraham, "Whale Shark Finds New Friends in Indian Fishermen," Reuters, December 10, 2004. Thanks to Cynthia Read for bringing this story to my attention.

13. Alliance for Religion and Conservation, www.arcworld.org/projects.asp?project ID=173.
14. National Commission for Conservation, http://www.saudinf.com/main/a63.htm.
15. Alliance for Religion and Conservation and the Khalsa environmental project, www.khalsaenvironmentproject.org/project_environment.htm.
16. Martinus L. Daneel, *African Earthkeepers: Wholistic Interfaith Mission* (Maryknoll, NY: Orbis Books, 2001), p. 185. African Independent Churches "are all-African churches founded *by* Africans *for* Africans, and have emerged during the twentieth century as thoroughly inculturated movements throughout Africa, south of the Sahara, representing more than half of African Christianity in Zimbabwe and South Africa." This quote is from Martinus L. Daneel, "African Initiated Churches as Vehicles of Earth-care in Africa," in *The Oxford Handbook on Religion and Ecology*, ed. Roger S. Gottlieb (New York: Oxford University Press, forthcoming).
17. Daneel, *African Earthkeepers*, p. 15.
18. M. L. Daneel, "African Earthkeeping Churches," in Taylor, *Encyclopedia of Religion and Nature.* To get an idea of what this number of trees means, the Green Belt Movement of Kenya, whose leader, Wangari Maathai, won the 2004 Nobel Peace Prize, planted approximately 30 million trees over a much longer period of time.
19. Daneel, *African Earthkeepers*, p. 55. "Instead of withdrawing from the traditionalist practitioners of ancestor veneration to demonstrate its rejection of 'heathenism,' the prophetic earthkeeping church underscored at least ecological solidarity with its traditionalist counterparts in the green struggle" (Daneel, "African Initiated Churches").
20. Daneel, *African Earthkeepers*, p. 155.
21. Bruce Byers, "Mhondoro: Spirit Lions and Sacred Forests," *Camas* (Fall 2002), reprinted in Gottlieb, *This Sacred Earth*, 2nd ed., p. 659.
22. Daneel, *African Earthkeepers*, p. 104.
23. Ibid., p. 151.
24. Ernst Conradi, Charity Majiza, Jim Cochrane, Weliel T. Sigabi, Victor Molobi, and David Field, "Seeking Eco-Justice in the South African Context," in *Earth Habitat: Eco-Injustice and the Church's Response*, ed. Dieter Hessel and Larry Rasmussen (Minneapolis: Fortress, 2001). The essay lists other interesting projects, including the Catholic-based "Planters of the Home," which focuses on urban agriculture and greening, and the Methodist-based Khanya Program, which joins sustainable agriculture, appropriate housing, and micro-industries (Khanya program, http://gbgm-umc.org/umcor/stories/khanya.stm).
25. See comments by Geoff Davies at NECCSA, http://www.neccsa.org.za/Issues -Toll%20road.htm. Also see Save the Coast Campaign, http://www.wildlife society.org.za/SWC%20press%20Bishop.htm.
26. "The Earth Belongs to God:Some African Church Perspectives on the World Summit on Sustainable Development (WSSD) 2002 and Beyond," statement adopted at the African Regional Consultation on Environment and Sustainabil-

ity, Machakos, Kenya, May 6–10, 2002, at Network of Earthkeeping Christian Communities in South Africa, http://www.neccsa.org.za/Documents-Earth%20belongs%20to%20God.htm. Ernst Conradie brought the Network to my attention.

27. Quoted at http://www.uspg.org.uk/news2004/newsaut2.htm. For a detailed history of activities in the province, I was fortunate to consult Andrew Warmback, "The Diocese of Umzimbuvu," chapter 4 of *The Household of God: The Environment, Poverty and the Church in South Africa*, unpublished doctoral dissertation.

28. Tovis Page, "Reflections on the 6th International Sisters of Earth Conference July 15–18, 2004," unpublished ms.

29. EarthLinks, www.EarthLinks-Colorado.org.

30. These remarkable women were brought to my attention by the immensely valuable research of Sarah Macfarland Taylor. See Sarah Taylor, "Reinhabiting Religion: Green Sisters, Ecological Renewal, and the Biogeography of Religious Landscape," in Gottlieb, *This Sacred Earth*, 2nd ed.

31. Carol Coston, interview with author, September 23, 2004.

32. See S. Taylor, "Reinhabiting Religion," and Web sites of EarthLinks, Genesis Farm (www.genesisfarm.org/), Crystal Spring Earth Learning Center (http://home.comcast.net/~cryspr/), Santuario Farm (http://www.sisterfarm.org/), and Sisters of Earth (http://www.sistersofearth.org/).

33. Santuario Sisterfarm, http://www.sisterfarm.org/.

34. S. Taylor, "Reinhabiting Religion," p. 618.

35. MacGillis interview.

36. Rosemary Radford Ruether, "Sisters for [*sic*, should be "of"] Earth," Faith in Place, http://www.faithinplace.org/sisters-for-earth.php.

37. S. Taylor, "Reinhabiting Religion," p. 613.

38. Ruether, "Sisters."

39. Coston interview.

40. Given the pace of recent industrialization in India and even more in China, in a decade or so this may be somewhat less true.

41. Ross Gelbspan, "Slow Death by Global Warming," *Amnesty International* (Fall 2004): 6. See also *Time* magazine's September 2004 issue on global warming in Alaska. For a concentrated picture of global events, see Max Seabaugh, "Feeling the Burn," *Mother Jones* (May–June 2005): 46–47.

42. Andrew Simms, "Farewell Tuvalu," *The Guardian* (Manchester, UK), October 29, 2001; Michael Grunwald, "Bizarre Weather Ravages Africans' Crops: Some See Link to Worldwide Warming Trend," *Washington Post*, January 7, 2003, http://www.massclimateaction.org/African_crops_WashPost010703.htm.

43. David G. Hallman, "Climate Change and Ecumenical Work for Sustainable Community," in Hessel and Rasmussen, *Earth Habitat.*

44. For a compressed account of this history, see Hessel, "The Church's Eco-Justice Journey."

45. Hallman, "Climate Change," p. 126.

46. World Council of Churches, http://www.wcc-coe.org/wcc/what/jpc/economy.html.

47. World Council of Churches, http://www.wcc-coe.org/wcc/what/jpc/cop6-e.html.

48. Web of Creation, http://www.webofcreation.org/ncc/climate.html.

49. Web of Creation, www.webofcreation.org.

50. See an account of this development and the statement itself in Mary Evelyn Tucker, *Worldly Wonder: Religions Enter Their Ecological Phase* (Chicago: Open Court, 2003), pp. 116–123.
51. National Religious Partnership for the Environment, http://www.nrpe.org/.
52. What Would Jesus Drive?, http://www.whatwouldjesusdrive.org/tour/intro.php.
53. My account of Tzu-Chi is indebted to Wan-Li Ho, "Environmental Protection as Religious Action: The Case of Taiwanese Buddhist Women," in *Ecofeminism and Globalization: Exploring Culture, Context, and Religion*, ed. Heather Eaton and Lois Ann Lorentzen (Lanham, MD: Rowman and Littlefield, 2003). On Taiwanese environmentalism in general, see Hsin-Huang Michael Hsiao, "Environmental Movements in Taiwan," in *Asia's Environmental Movements: Comparative Perspectives*, ed. Tok-shiu F. Lee and Alvin Y. So (Armonk, NY: M. E. Sharpe, 1999).
54. Tzu-Chi, July 2, 2004, http://www.tzuchi.org/global/news/articles/20040602.html.
55. Tzu-Chi, http://www.tzuchi.org/global/about/index.html.
56. Cheng Yen, "Let's Do It Together: Environmental Protection for Mind, Health, and the Great Earth." Tzu-Chi, http://www.taipei.tzuchi.org.tw/tzquart/96winter/qw96-2.htm.
57. Tzu-Chi, http://www.tzuchi.org/global/about/missions/culture/index.html#tagstay.
58. Chang Shun-yen, "Environmental Protection at the Abode of Still Thoughts," *Tzu-Chi Quarterly* (Summer 1997), Tzu-Chi, http://taipei.tzuchi.org.tw/tzquart/97summer/97summer.htm.
59. Ho, "Environmental Protection," p. 132.
60. Sarvodaya, http://sarvodaya.org/Introduction/sarvodayaover.html.
61. Quoted in George D. Bond, *Buddhism at Work: Community Development, Social Empowerment, and the Sarvodaya Movement* (Bloomfield, CT: Kumarian Press, 2004), p. 16.
62. Detlef Kantowsky, *Sarvodaya: The Other Development* (New Delhi: Vikas Publishing House, 1980), p. 166.
63. Sarvodaya, http://sarvodaya.org/Introduction/sarvodayaphilos.html.
64. Sarvodaya, http://sarvodaya.org/Library/Overview96/Paurushodaya.htm.
65. Quoted in Bond, *Buddhism at Work*, pp. 50, 33.
66. Quoted in ibid., p. 50.
67. "Justice and Witness Ministries board members witness in opposition to a U.S. Army plan to incinerate tons of neutralized nerve gas near East St. Louis, Illinois." United Church of Christ, http://www.ncccusa.org/.
68. Dollie Burwell, "Reminiscences from Warren County, North Carolina," in *Proceedings of the First National People of Color Environmental Leadership Summit*, ed. Charles Lee (New York: United Church of Christ Commission for Racial Justice, 1992). Earlier studies had documented the existence of racial or class imbalances in this area, starting with an article in *Science* in 1970 and including a General Accounting Office study in 1983. See Robert J. Brulle, *Agency, Democracy, and Nature: The U.S. Environmental Movement from a Critical Theory Perspective* (Cambridge, MA: MIT Press, 2000), pp. 210–213. For a survey of the history of the attempt to connect environmental and other political issues, see Robert Gottlieb, *Forcing the Spring: The Transformation of the American Environmental Movement* (Washington, DC: Island Press, 1993), pp. 235–269.
69. Commission for Racial Justice, *Toxic Wastes and Race in the United States* (New York: United Church of Christ, 1987), pp. xiii–xiv.

70. Ibid., p. xii.
71. Lee, *Proceedings*, p. 85.
72. Ibid., pp. xiii–xiv; the Principles are also in Gottlieb, *This Sacred Earth*, 1st and 2nd eds.
73. Letters initiated by the Southwest Organizing Project and the Gulf Tenants Association. See Dana Alston, "Moving beyond the Barriers," in Lee, *Proceedings.*
74. The Sierra Club, for instance, adopted an environmental justice policy in 1993 and created a specific environmental justice program. For an overview of its campaigns since then and interviews with some of its staffers, see Jennifer Hattam, "Why Race Matters in the Fight for a Healthy Planet," *Sierra* (May–June 2004). On the other hand, relative to other environmental concerns, the environmental justice movement is woefully underfunded. See Daniel Faber and Deborah McCarthy, *Green of Another Color: Building Effective Partnerships between Foundations and the Environmental Justice Movement*, a research report initiated by Nonprofit Sector Research Fund of the Aspen Institute, April 2001, available at Northeastern University, http://www.casdn.neu.edu/~socant/misc/Another%20Color%20Final%20Report.pdf.
75. Robert Bullard, "Solid Waste Sites and the Black Houston Community," *Sociological Inquiry* 53 (Spring 1983).
76. Robert Bullard, *Environmental Justice Project* (Washington, DC: Lawyers' Committee for Civil Rights Under the Law, 1993). For a brief but effective account of the history of environmental justice, see Target Earth, http://www.targetearth.org/about/human_rights.html. For a description of the emergence and importance of the movement, see Gottlieb, *Forcing the Spring*, 1993; 2nd ed., 2005.
77. *Rachel's Environmental & Health Weekly* 595 (April 23, 1998), http://www.rachel.org/bulletin/index.cfm?St=4. The United States has been joined in this dubious distinction by Afghanistan and Haiti. See Basel Convention, http://www.basel.int/ratif/frsetmain.php.
78. U.S. Forest Service, http://www.fs.fed.us/land/envjust.html.
79. Conclusions critical of implementation of the policy, including the Bush administration's stated policy of redefining "environmental justice" to apply to "everyone," are contained in a report from the inspector general of the Environmental Protection Agency: "EPA Needs to Consistently Implement the Intent of the Executive Order on Environmental Justice," Office of the Inspector General, U.S. Environmental Protection Agency, March 1, 2004. See "Reverse Environmental Justice by Bush EPA," Greenwatch, http://www.bushgreenwatch.org/mt_archives/000070.php. A detailed analysis, and criticism, of the policy implementation is also given by the U.S. Civil Rights Commission report *Not in My Backyard: Executive Order 12,898 and Title VI as Tools for Achieving Environmental Justice*, October 2003, U.S. Civil Rights Commission, http://www.usccr.gov/pubs/envjust/main.htm.
80. Mishra was identified as one of seven "Heroes of the Planet" by *Time* magazine for his work in protecting the fresh waterways of the earth. See Sankat Mochan, http://members.tripod.com/sankatmochan/index.htm.
81. Franklin Rothman and Pamela Oliver, "From Local to Global: The Anti-Dam Movement in Southern Brazil, 1979–1992," in *Globalization and Resistance: Transnational Dimensions of Social Movements*, ed. Jackie Smith and Hank Johnston (Lanham, MD: Rowman and Littlefield, 2002), pp. 119–123.

82. William A. Shutkin, *The Land That Could Be: Environmentalism and Democracy in the Twenty-First Century* (Cambridge, MA: MIT Press, 2000). See also Gottlieb, *Forcing the Spring*; Dewitt John, *Civic Environmentalism: Alternatives to Regulation in States and Communities* (Washington, DC: Congressional Quarterly Press, 1994).

83. Raymond Bonner, *At the Hand of Man: Peril and Hope for Africa's Wildlife* (New York: Knopf, 1993).

84. Lori Goodman, interview with author, September 28, 2004. See also Winona LaDuke, *All Our Relations: Native Struggles for Land and Life* (Boston: South End Press, 1999). This book and *The Winona LaDuke Reader* (Stillwater, MN: Voyageur Press, 2002) were major sources for this section. See also the large number of links on the Web site of the Indigenous Environmental Network, www.ienearth.org/.

85. Gail Small, "The Search for Environmental Justice in Indian Country," *Amicus Journal* (March 1994).

86. Diné CARE, http://dinecare.indigenousnative.org/.

87. *Ernie Atencio*, "After a Heavy Harvest and a Death, Navajo Forestry Realigns with Culture," *Western Roundup*, October 31, 1994.

88. Goodman interview.

89. An aptly titled and wide-ranging anthology making reference to more than twenty geographical contexts is Mario Blaser, H. A. Feit, and G. McRae, eds., *In the Way of Development: Indigenous Peoples, Life Projects and Globalization* (London: Zed Press, 2004).

90. "Since the 1950s, the U.S. has tested hundreds of nuclear weapons on Western Shoshone homelands and disposed of thousands of metric tons of radioactive waste in unlined trenches at the Nevada Test Site. Currently Congress has passed legislation to dump all of the nuclear industry's high-level nuclear waste at Yucca Mountain." Western Shoshone Defense Project, http://www.wsdp.org/index.htm.

91. Winona LaDuke, "Native Environmentalism," *Earth Island Journal* 8, no 3 (Summer 1993).

92. For example, Szerszynksi, *Nature, Technology and the Sacred*.

93. Donald D. Jackson, *Custer's Gold: The United States Cavalry Expedition of 1874* (New Haven: Yale University Press, 1966), pp. 8–9.

94. Matthew Glass, "Law, Religion, and Native American Lands," in B. Taylor, *Encyclopedia of Religion and Nature*. I found the newspaper quote in Glass's excellent article.

95. Central Land Council of Aborigines of Australia, *Our Land, Our Life* (Alice Springs, Northern Territory, Australia: Central and Northern Land Councils, 1991), quoted in Fabienne Bayet, "Overturning the Doctrine: Indigenous People and the Wilderness—Being Aboriginal in the Environmental Movement," in *The Great New Wilderness Debate*, ed. J. Baird Callicott and Michael P. Nelson (Athens: University of Georgia Press, 1998), p. 319. Compare this quote from Paula Gunn Allen: "We are the land. To the best of my understanding, that is the fundamental idea that permeates American Indian life; the land (Mother) and the people (mothers) are the same.... The earth is the source and being of the people and we are equally the being of the earth. The land is not really a place separate from ourselves.... Rather for the American Indians ... the earth *is* being, as all creatures are also being: aware, palpable, intelligent, alive" (*The Sacred*

Hoop: Recovering the Feminine in the American Indian Traditions [Boston: Beacon Press, 1989], pp. 60, 119). See also John A. Grim, "Indigenous Traditions: Religion and Ecology," in Gottlieb, *Oxford Handbook*; Kenneth M. Morrison, "The Cosmos as Intersubjective: Native American Other-than-human Person," in *Indigenous Religions: A Companion*, ed. Graham Harvey (London: Cassell, 2000); J. Baird Callicott, "American Indian Land Wisdom? Sorting Out the Issues," in *In Defense of the Land Ethic: Essays in Environmental Philosophy* (Albany: State University of New York Press, 1989).

96. "Native Traditions and Land Use," in B. Taylor, *Encyclopedia of Religion and Nature*.

97. Paula Rogers Huff and Marshall Pecore, "Case Study: Menominee Tribal Enterprises," Menominee, http://www.menominee.edu/sdi/csstdy.htm#A.

98. On the buffalo massacre, see Momaday, "A First American Views His Land." On megafauna extinctions, see Ted Steinberg, *Down to Earth: Nature's Role in American History* (New York: Oxford University Press, 2002), pp. 126–127.

99. Commenting on the sources of Native American knowledge, John A. Grim observes: "These forms of interactive knowledge may not be scientific as that term describes Western modes of empirical, falsifiable, experimental investigation, but indigenous knowledge has its own modes of empirical observation, acquisition through lived experience, and testing in the context of one's community." Grim, "Indigenous Traditions."

100. Dave Foreman, "Wilderness Areas for Real," in Callicott and Nelson, *The New Wilderness Debate*, p. 402.

101. For a highly detailed account of traditional native management practices in a specific region, see M. K. Anderson, *Tending the Wild: Native American Knowledge and the Management of California's Natural Resources* (Berkeley: University of California Press, 2005).

102. Goodman interview.

103. Melanie Griffin, Sierra Club, interview with author, October 4, 2004; Bob Edgar, National Council of Churches, interview with author, December 10, 2004.

104. There are many accounts of this struggle. Two are Friends of the Narmada, http://www.narmada.org/, and Arundhati Roy, *Power Politics* (Boston: South End Press, 2001).

105. International Rivers Network, http://www.irn.org/index.asp?id=/basics/damqa .html; see report on large dams.

106. Baba Amte biography, at Maharogi Sewa Samiti, http://mss.niya.org/people/ baba_amte.php.

107. For a thoughtful account of the different dimensions of the resistance to Narmada, see William E. Fisher, "Sacred Rivers, Sacred Dams: Competing Visions of Social Justice and Sustainable Development along the Narmada," in Gottlieb, *This Sacred Earth*, 2nd ed. There are many other internationally oriented efforts, including those that focus on the Brazilian rain forest and stopping the James Bay dam project in Canada.

Chapter 5

1. Quoted in Laura Barandes, December 23, 1999, Court TV, http://www.courttv .com/.

2. Bonner, *At the Hand of Man.*

3. For accounts of Hamilton and Pinchot, see (of many possible sources) Gottlieb, *Forcing the Spring.*

4. Wuthnow, *After Heaven.*

5. Edward Conze, *Buddhism: Its Essence and Development* (New York: Harper, 1951).

6. Henry David Thoreau, "Walking," The Thoreau Reader, http://eserver.org/thoreau/walking3.html.

7. John Muir, *My First Summer in the Sierras,* in *John Muir: The Eight Wilderness Books* (Seattle: The Mountaineers, 1992), p. 211.

8. Sigurd Olson, "Why Wilderness?" in Callicott and Nelson, *The Great New Wilderness Debate,* p. 101.

9. John Burroughs, *Leaf and Tendril,* Ecotopia, http://www.ecotopia.org/ehof/burroughs/index.html.

10. The Project Gutenberg EBook of *The Writings of John Burroughs,* by John Burroughs, vol. 5, http://www.gutenberg.org/dirs/etext05/pepac10.txt.

11. Michael P. Nelson, "An Amalgamation of Wilderness Preservation Arguments," in Callicott and Nelson, *The Great New Wilderness Debate,* p. 168.

12. John Muir, *The Yosemite* (San Francisco: Sierra Club Books, 1988), pp. 196–197. Ironically, supporters of the dam also used religious reasons, keyed to the familiar biblical idea of humanity's right to master the earth. See Stoll, *Protestantism, Capitalism and Nature in America,* pp. 166–168.

13. Quoted in James M. Glover, *A Wilderness Original: The Life of Bob Marshall* (Seattle: The Mountaineers, 1986); James M. Glover, "Robert Marshall," in B. Taylor, *The Encyclopedia of Religion and Nature.*

14. Some of the results from these seminars are forthcoming in H. Ken Cordell, John C. Bergstrom, and J. Michael Bowker, eds., *The Multiple Values of Wilderness* (State College, PA: Venture Publishing).

15. Charlene Spretnak, "Ecofeminism: Our Roots and Flowering," in *Reweaving the World: The Emergence of Ecofeminism,* ed. Irene Diamond and Gloria Freman Orenstein (San Francisco: Sierra Club Books, 1990), p. 8.

16. Ralph Waldo Emerson, "Nature," in Gottlieb, *This Sacred Earth,* 2nd ed., p. 33.

17. Martin Buber, *I and Thou* (New York: Free Press, 1971).

18. Quoted in Karen Gridley, *Man of the Trees: Selected Writings of Richard St. Barbe Baker* (Willis, CA: Ecology Action, 1989), p. 25.

19. Edward Abbey, *Desert Solitaire* (New York: Ballantine, 1985), p. 190.

20. Howard Zahniser, "The Need for Wilderness," quoted at Wilderness Society, http://www.wilderness.org/.

21. David Iverson, interview with author, October 15, 2004; Forest Service Employees for Environmental Ethics, http://www.fseee.org/, emphasis added.

22. Dale Iverson, review of B. L. Driver, Daniel Dustin, Tony Baltic, Gary Elsner, and George Peterson, eds., *Nature and the Human Spirit: Toward An Expanded Land Management Ethic* (State College, PA: Venture, 1996). Available at the U.S. Forest Service Web site: http://www.fs.fed.us/eco/eco-watch/ew970401.htm.

23. Robert Perschel, interview with author, October 22, 2004.

24. Robert Perschel, "Work, Worship, and the Natural World: A Challenge for the Land Use Professions," in *The Good in Nature and Humanity: Connecting Science, Religion, and Spiritual with the Natural World,* ed. Stephen R. Kellert and Timothy J. Farnham (Washington, DC: Island Press, 2002).

25. Brock Evans, interview with author, June 21, 2005.

26. William Cronon, "The Trouble with Wilderness," in Callicott and Nelson, *The Great New Wilderness Debate*, p. 483.
27. Steinberg, *Down to Earth*.
28. Ramachandra Guha, "Radical Environmentalism and Wilderness Preservation: A Third World Critique" and "Deep Ecology Revisited," both in Callicott and Nelson, *The New Wilderness Debate*.
29. Indeed, we might say that *every* human value—love and justice no less than God or nature—is interpreted in varying ways throughout history. This variation does not invalidate the attempt to realize any of these values, for if we wait for a value that is not historical, we will be left with no values at all.
30. Martin Luther King Jr., "Letter from a Birmingham Jail," in Gottlieb, *Liberating Faith*, p. 178.
31. History Matters, http://historymatters.gmu.edu/d/5090/.
32. Barry Commoner, *The Closing Circle: Nature, Man, and Technology* (New York: Knopf, 1971), p. 33. Although Muir talked similarly, the attitude is not reflected in his environmental policies or goals.
33. Daniel Botkin sees Thoreau (of all people) as someone more at home in the human-inhabited suburbs than as a dweller in the wilderness. He argues that Thoreau's experience of coexistence with nature can be instructive for us today. *No Man's Garden: Thoreau and a New Vision for Civilization and Nature* (Washington, DC: Island Press, 2001). For a moving account of an attempt to live out environmental and spiritual values in the inner city, see Melody Chavis, *Altars in the Street: A Neighborhood Fights to Survive* (New York: Bell Tower, 1998).
34. Iverson interview.
35. Starhawk, "Power, Authority and Mystery: Ecofeminism and Earth-Based Spirituality" in Diamond and Orenstein, *Reweaving the World*, p. 73.
36. Aldo Leopold, *Sand County Almanac*, quoted in Steinberg, *Down to Earth*, p. 242.
37. Liberty Hyde Bailey, *The Holy Earth* (New York: New York College of Agriculture, 1980), p. 35.
38. Edward Abbey, *The Journey Home: Some Words in Defense of the American West* (New York: Plume, 1981), p. 229.
39. Howard Zahniser, "The Need for Wilderness Areas," *Living Wilderness*, no. 59 (Winter–Spring 1956–1957), quoted at National Park Service, "Wilderness Quotations," http://planning.nps.gov/wilderness/document/Wilderness%20Quotations .pdf.
40. Barry Lopez, *Crossing Open Ground* (New York: Vintage, 1989), p. 71. We might also note here the emerging discipline of ecopsychology, part of the focus of which is the negative psychological effects of contemporary society's alienation from nature.
41. See E. O. Wilson, *Biophilia* (Cambridge, MA: Harvard University Press, 1986); Bill McKibben, *The Age of Missing Information* (New York: Plume, 1993).
42. Thomas R. Dunlap, *Faith in Nature: Environmentalism as Religious Quest* (Seattle: University of Washington Press, 2004), p. 42.
43. John Burroughs, *The Gospel of Nature* (Bedford, MA: Applewood, n.d.), p. 32.
44. Quoted in Dunlap, *Faith in Nature*, p. 26.
45. Dunlap, *Faith in Nature*, pp. 142–143.
46. I have struggled with these tensions at greater length in chapter 4 of Gottlieb, *A Spirituality of Resistance*.
47. This theme runs through much of both religious and secular environmental

ethics. It is particularly strong in ecofeminism. For a survey of ecofeminist think-
ers, see Ruether, *Integrating Ecofeminism, Globalization, and World Religions*.
For some interesting case studies of activist groups, see Eaton and Lorentzen,
Ecofeminism and Globalization.

48. *Ethics of the Fathers*, 2:16.
49. This phraseology is basic to Michael Lerner's writings. See *Spirit Matters*.
50. Rachel Carson, *Sense of Wonder*, quoted in Dunlap, *Faith in Nature*, p. 16.
51. David Brower, *Let the Mountains Talk, Let the Rivers Run* (Gabriola Island, Canada: New Society Publishers, 2000), p. 176.
52. Ibid.
53. This can be an issue even if they are generally supportive of environmentalism.
For instance, Norman C. Habel, author of an often eloquent set of liturgies for
"healing creation," makes it clear that the liturgies are not concerned with "making Earth the theme of worship [but] to create a way of worshipping with Earth
and . . . with all living creatures to worship and celebrate our God" (*Seven Songs
of Creation*, p. 9). Similarly, a quite strong Evangelical Lutheran Church statement on environmental issues emphasizes that "*The world is good, but it is not
God*" and that it is wrong to make "a God of nature itself" (ELCA Environment
Task Force, "Basis for Our Caring," in Gottlieb, *This Sacred Earth*, 2nd ed.,
pp. 216, 221).
54. The distinction surely does not hold for indigenous religions, to which spiritual
environmentalism often bears a real similarity (at times having served as its
partial example and inspiration).
55. Another one of those quotes that I've been familiar with for a long time, but I
can't remember the source.
56. Elie Wiesel, "Yom Kippur," in *Thinking the Unthinkable: Meanings of the Holocaust*, ed. Roger S. Gottlieb (Mahwah, NJ: Paulist Press, 1990), p. 205.
57. I do not want to argue here (though perhaps I might somewhere else) that this
nonconsequentialist attitude toward morality is uniquely religious or spiritual.
Clearly, someone might say "This is the kind of person I wish to be" and "It just
is the right thing to do" without having a spiritual temperament. However, I
believe (and could provide a fair number of examples to support the belief) that
purely secular approaches do tend toward utilitarian calculations of consequences, and that the idea of committed action without attachment to results
generally originates in religious contexts. In any case, when it does arise among
religious or spiritual people, it is closely connected to beliefs in the ultimate
nature of existence, rather than being simply limited (as it was for Kant, say) to
beliefs about people alone.
58. Barry Lopez, *Arctic Dreams: Imagination and Desire in a Northern Landscape*
(New York: Scribner's, 1986), p. xx.
59. Paul Wapner, *Environmental Activism and World Civic Politics* (Albany: State
University of New York Press, 1996), p. 50.
60. Shundahai Network, http://www.shundahai.org/index.html.
61. Peter Litster, interview with author, October 30, 2004.
62. An interesting (and too lengthy for this book) discussion might be had as to
whether religion and politics were also fused in the civil rights movement. I
would say they were not, as the goal of the movement, though completely legitimate, could be separated from its religious dimension. Rights for a particular
disadvantaged group are not the same as the kind of universal care that is inherent in at least some forms of environmentalism.
63. Hauerwas and Willimon, *Resident Aliens*.

64. Any history of progressive movements will substantiate this point. For my own account, see Gottlieb, *History and Subjectivity.*
65. This point was raised to me by David L. Barnhill.
66. For one account of this development, which is the subject matter of many books, see Leslie Paul Thiele, *Environmentalism for a New Millennium: The Challenge of Coevolution* (New York: Oxford University Press, 1999). For a convergence of radical politics in the same direction, see John Sanbonmatsu, *The Postmodern Prince: Critical Theory, Left Strategy, and the Making of a New Political Subject* (New York: Monthly Review Press, 2004), chapter 7.
67. Petra Kelley, *Thinking Green: Essays on Feminism, Environmentalism and Nonviolence* (Berkeley: Parallax Press, 1964), p. 37.
68. Barrie Brusila, "Of Whose Health Do We Speak?" *Distant Thunder: Journal of the Forests Stewards Guild*, no. 16 (Fall 2003): 2.
69. Southwest Organizing Project, http://www.swop.net/ej.htm.
70. Elisabeth Wyrick, Southwest Organizing Project staff, interview with author, October 29, 2004.
71. Greenpeace International, http://www.greenpeace.org/international_en/extra/?item_id=4265&language_id=en.
72. Clark Stevens, Greenpeace, interview with author, October 28, 2004.
73. National Resources Defense Council, http://www.nrdc.org/about/.
74. Friends of the Earth International, http://www.foei.org/about/faq.html#3.
75. Lisa Grob, publications manager, National Resource Defense Council, interview with author, October 29, 2004.
76. David Kinsley, *Ecology and Religion: Ecological Spirituality in Cross-cultural Perspective* (Englewood Cliffs, NJ: Prentice Hall, 1995), p. 6.

Chapter 6

1. Quoted in Elizabeth Roberts, ed., *Earth Prayers from around the World: 365 Prayers, Poems, and Invocations for Honoring the Earth* (San Francisco: Harper SanFrancisco, 1991), p. 46.
2. Nachman of Bratslav, quoted in Stein, *A Garden of Choice Fruit*, p. 69.
3. See "America the Noisy," Environmental News Service, January 5, 2005, at EarthLinks, http://home.earthlink.net/~cevent/1-4-05_america_the_noisy.html.
4. Arthur Waskow, "And the Earth Is Filled with the Breath of Life," Shalom Center, http://www.shalomctr.org/.
5. United Methodist Church, General Board of Church and Society, Earth Ministry, www.earthministry.org/earthday.htm.
6. "Fact Sheet on the Ogoni Struggle," Ratical.com, http://www.ratical.org/corporations/OgoniFactS.html.
7. Quoted in Leslie Fields, *Friends of the Earth* 33, no. 3 (Fall 2003).
8. Wendell Berry, in Roberts, *Earth Prayers*, p. 76.
9. Thich Nhat Hanh, "Earth Verses," in Kaza and Kraft, *Dharma Rain*, pp. 446–447.
10. Robert Aitkin, "Verses for Environmental Practice" in Kaza and Kraft, *Dharma Rain*, p. 472.
11. Tenshin Reb Anderson, "Dedication for Buddha's Birthday at the Gate of the Nevada Nuclear Test Site," April 10, 1994, cited in Kraft, "Nuclear Ecology and Engaged Buddhism," p. 395.

12. For a much more extended account of what valuable resources religion can offer political activism, see Gottlieb, *Joining Hands*, chapter 4.
13. David Cockrell and EcoSpirit New England, Appendix B, in "The Seventh Principle Project," in *Green Sanctuary: Eco-Spirituality for Liberal Religious Congregations*, The Seventh Principle Project, www.uuaspp.org.
14. Pipog Udomittipong, "Thailand's Ecology Monks," in Kaza and Kraft, *Dharma Rain*.
15. Rainforest Information, http://www.rainforestinfo.org.au/deep-eco/welcome.htm.
16. Macy, *World as Lover*, p. 200.
17. Ibid., pp. 198, 205.
18. Part of the traditional text of the Haggadah.
19. "The Cosmic Walk," Rainforest Information, http://www.rainforestinfo.org.au/deep-eco/welcome.htm.
20. Elias Amidon, "Mall Mindfulness," in Kaza and Kraft, *Dharma Rain*.
21. This account of my plant journal exercise is taken from Roger S. Gottlieb, "Earth 101," *Worldviews: Environment, Culture, Religion* 8, nos. 2–3 (2004).
22. Paul Tillich, *Dynamics of Faith* (New York: Harper & Row, 1957).
23. Roy Rappaport, *Ritual and Religion in the Making of Humanity* (New York: Cambridge University Press, 1999).
24. Abram, *The Spell of the Sensuous*. For a brilliant and unique treatment of this theme in European culture, see Hans Peter Duerr, *Dreamtime: Concerning the Boundary between Wilderness and Civilization* (London: Blackwell, 1987).
25. Buell, *From Apocalypse to Way of Life*.

Chapter 7

1. The material that follows is based on interviews with subjects and biographical information they provided.
2. For instance, Calvin B. DeWitt, *Earth-Wise: A Biblical Response to Environmental Issues* (Grand Rapids, MI: CRC Publications, 1994). See also the Au Sable Institute Web site, http://www.ausable.org/or.resources.mailorder.cfm#books.
3. Shalom Center, http://www.shalomctr.org/index.cfm/action/about/.
4. Arthur Waskow, *Down to Earth Judaism: Food, Money, Sex, and the Rest of Life* (New York: William Morrow, 1995); Ari Elon, Naomi Hyman, and Arthur Waskow, eds., *Trees, Earth and Torah: A Tu B'Shvat Anthology* (Philadelphia: Jewish Publication Society, 1999); Arthur Waskow, ed., *Torah of the Earth: Exploring 4,000 Years of Ecology in Jewish Thought*, 2 vols. (Woodstock, VT: Jewish Lights Publishing, 2000).
5. Mordechai Liebling and Dvora Bartnoff.
6. "ELCA STaR Ministry Alliance Forms at First Annual Meeting," ELCA News Service, July 7, 2004, at Worldwide Faith News archives, www.wfn.org.

Chapter 8

1. Stephanie Kaza, introduction to *Hooked! Buddhist Writings on Greed, Desire, and the Urge to Consume*, ed. Stephanie Kaza (Boston: Shambhala, 2005), p. 3.

Also see Norman Myers and Jennifer Ken, *The New Consumers* (Washington, DC: Island Press, 2004), for accounts of the spread of consumerism in the developing world.

2. Karl Marx, "On Money," in *Economic and Philosophical Manuscripts of 1844,* in *The Marx-Engels Reader,* ed. Robert Tucker (New York: Norton, 1978).

3. "In the earlier phases of capitalism, work, that is work in paid employment roles, formed the core of many people's identity.... Now, it is consumer goods and household patterns of consumption which play an important part in the social and cultural construction of identities for men, women, and children" (Robert Bocock, *Consumption* [New York: Routledge, 1993], p. 109).

4. Kaza, introduction to *Hooked!*; David Loy, "The Religion of the Market," *Journal of the American Academy of Religion* 65, no. 2 (Summer 1997).

5. McKibben, *The Age of Missing Information.*

6. Even this generalization, as essentially correct as it may be, must recognize the phenomenon of the "prosperity churches" which teach that wealth (best displayed quite conspicuously) is a sign of God's favor.

7. For a survey of some current images of Jesus (the "muscular Jesus," the "manly Jesus," etc.), see Chris Suellentrop, "Jesus Christ: Choose Your Own Savior," *Slate,* April 9, 2004, http://slate.msn.com/id/2098553/#ContinueArticle.

8. Much of my analysis here is indebted to Vincent Miller's excellent *Consuming Religion: Christian Faith and Practice in a Consumer Culture* (London: Continuum, 2003). See also Kaza, *Hooked!* This point, however, is one that Miller missed and weakens his otherwise valuable book.

9. Martin E. Marty, *When Faiths Collide* (Malden, MA: Blackwell, 2005), p. 83.

10. Tim Padgett, "Bible-Belt Catholics," *Time,* February 14, 2005.

11. My treatment of fundamentalism is indebted to Mark Juergensmeyer, *Terror in the Mind of God: The Global Rise of Religious Violence* (Berkeley: University of California Press, 2001); Malise Ruthven, *Fundamentalism: The Search for Meaning* (Oxford: Oxford University Press, 2004); Karen Armstrong, *The Battle for God: Fundamentalism in Judaism, Christianity and Islam* (New York: HarperCollins, 2000); Martin Riesebrodt, *Pious Passion: The Emergence of Modern Fundamentalism in the United States and Iran* (Berkeley: University of California Press, 1993).

12. Charles Kimball identifies absolute truth claims, holy war, blind obedience, and an "end justifies the means" mentality as symptoms of religions gone wrong. I agree with all but the first, which I think is characteristic of anyone with any religious or ethical stance whatsoever (*When Religion Becomes Evil: Five Warning Signs* [San Francisco: Harper SanFrancisco, 2002]).

13. It is taken for granted by many fundamentalist groups in the United States that the Bible is the direct and inerrant word of God. Many Hindu fundamentalists have claimed that the ancient Hindu scriptures (suitably read, of course) contain the basis for key developments in modern science.

14. Anthony Giddens, *The Consequences of Modernity* (Stanford: Stanford University Press, 1990).

15. Armstrong, *Battle for God,* p. 103.

16. On the Christian Coalition's Web site, http://www.cc.org/mission.cfm, seven out of eighteen agenda items for the 109th Congress focus on this area. None concern environmental issues.

17. Marty, *When Faiths Collide,* p. 157.

18. Article 50. This ministry has been headed by M. Ebkatar, the woman who rose

to fame as the spokeswoman for the students who held American hostages in the embassy in Tehran from 1979 to 1981.

19. For a source that does both at the same time, see Bible Believers, http://www .biblebelievers.com/EarthDay1996.html:

> The future is dismal and foreboding according to many passages in the Holy Bible. The "last days" will be cataclysmic, destructive, fatal, disastrous, catastrophic, fateful, calamitous, and ruinous. Even the environment will be affected in many, many ways. How does this relate to the view we espouse which questions the "doom-and-gloomers" of the Left? Well, we hold that the world-wide, futureevents foretold in the Bible will be Supernatural in origin and NOT a result of Western Civilization's existence. Yes, man has made a mess of things, but not in a way characterized by those out in left-field.

20. For a fascinating account of a struggle along these lines in the American Muslim community, see Asra Q. Nomani, "Pulpit Bullies," *America Prospect* 16, no. 3 (March 2005). In March 2005, Nomani initiated a Women's Freedom Tour throughout the United States emphasizing women's *Islamic* rights to personal, public, and religious equality. As an example of the kind of progressive rereading of tradition that is and will continue to occur, see Asma Barlas, *"Believing Women" in Islam: Unreading Patriarchal Interpretations of the Qur'an* (Austin: University of Texas Press, 2002).

21. Elie Wiesel, *A Jew Today* (New York: Vintage, 1979), p. 12.

22. Kirkpatrick Sale, *The Green Revolution: The American Environmental Movement 1962–1992* (New York: Hill and Wang, 1993).

23. The following account of globalization draws on Manfred B. Steger, *Globalism: The New Market Ideology* (Lanham, MD: Rowman and Littlefield, 2001); Vernonia Bennholdt-Thomsen, Nicholas Faraclas, and Claudia Von Werlhof, eds., *There Is an Alternative: Subsistence and Worldwide Resistance to Corporate Globalization* (London: Zed Books, 2001); Smith and Johnston, *Globalization and Resistance*; William F. Fisher and Thomas Ponniah, eds., *Another World Is Possible: Popular Alternatives to Globalization at the World Social Forum* (London: Zed Books, 2003); International Forum on Globalization, *Alternatives to Economic Globalization: A Better World Is Possible* (San Francisco: Berrett-Koehler Publishers, 2002).

24. Roy, *Power Politics.*

25. Vandana Shiva, "Globalization and Poverty," *Resurgence* 202 (September–October 2000), http://resurgence.gn.apc.org/issues/shiva202.htm.

26. Quoted in Mia MacDonald, "Something Wonderful Happens When You Plant a Seed," *Sierra* (March/April 2005): 10. As Madhav Gadgil and Ramachandra Guha observe, this process dates back at least to the nineteenth century. In India, English colonialism took control of forests, altered social relationships in the village, and expanded the power of the state (*Ecology and Equity*, pp. 90–98).

27. Noreena Hertz, "The Air We Breathe," *Tikkun* (January–February 2005): 21. For a full treatment of this issue, see Hertz's *The Debt Threat* (New York: HarperCollins, 2004).

28. Just the physical process of moving all these goods and people from one place to another has enormous environmental effects in everything from land taken over by roads to ocean pollution from oil tankers to urban noise pollution.

29. "*The Economist* recently reported that in the consumer durables, automotive,

airline, aerospace, electronic components, electrical and electronics, and steel industries the top five firms control more than 50% of the global market, placing them clearly in the category of monopolistic industries. In the oil, personal computers and media industries the top five firms control more than 40% of sales, which indicates strong monopolistic tendencies" (David Korten, "Taming the Giants," *Resurgence Online*, http://resurgence.gn.apc.org/articles/korten.htm).

30. Roy, *Power Politics*; Bennholdt-Thomsen et al., *There Is an Alternative*.

31. See, for instance, the antiglobalization writings of the spiritual ecofeminist Starhawk, *Webs of Power: Notes from the Global Uprising* (Gabriola Island, Canada: New Society Publishers, 2002), pp. 237–241.

32. It is also the case that globalization and fundamentalism are sometimes related, as the social dislocations of globalization often provoke the hostile cultural defensiveness that is one of fundamentalism's chief characteristics.

33. H. Paul Santmire and John B. Cobb Jr., "The World of Nature According to the Protestant Tradition," in Gottlieb, *Oxford Handbook*.

34. See the Web site of the United Methodist Committee on Relief: http://gbgm -umc.org/umcor/hunger/coffee.cfm.

35. Douglas Torgerson, *The Promise of Green Politics: Environmentalism and the Public Sphere* (Durham, NC: Duke University Press, 1999).

36. The notion that knowledge is affected by social structure goes far back, at least to Marx.

37. For an account of communism's relation to the issue of expertise, see Gottlieb, *Marxism 1844–1990*. On the World Bank and dams, see International Rivers, http://www.irn.org/.

38. This general point was first made by sociologist Robert Michels when the world's socialist parties were unable to resist their nations' descent into the militarism of World War I. The phenomenon has arisen in trade unions, groups representing women and ethnic minorities, left political parties, and elsewhere. See Robert Michels, *Political Parties: A Sociological Study of the Oligarchical Tendencies of Modern Democracy*, available at electronic text resource, University of Virginia Library, http://etext.lib.virginia.edu/toc/modeng/public/MicPoli .html.

39. See Steven Bernstein, *The Compromise of Liberal Environmentalism* (New York: Columbia University Press, 2002).

40. For a particularly self-righteous version of this critique, see Jeffrey St. Clair, *Been Brown So Long It Looks Like Green to Me: The Politics of Nature* (Monroe, MN: Common Courage Press, 2004).

41. One can certainly read the history of the labor, women's, and racial equality movements in this way. For an interesting, though philosophically very abstract, account of this pattern (derived from study of the French Revolution), see Jean-Paul Sartre, *Critique of Dialectical Reason* (London: Verso, 2004).

42. This position is developed at length in Gottlieb, *Joining Hands*.

43. Leopold, *Round River*, p. 165.

44. See the discussion by John S. Dryzek, "Political and Ecological Communication," in *Ecology and Democracy*, ed. Freya Mathews (London: Frank Cass, 1996). This excellent essay crystallizes many important themes.

45. "Once it was the endeavor of art, literature, and philosophy to express the meaning of things and of life, to be voice of all that is dumb, to endow nature with an organ for making known her sufferings.... Today nature's tongue is taken away. Once it was thought that each utterance, word, cry, or gesture had an

intrinsic meaning; today it is merely an occurrence" (Max Horkheimer, *Eclipse of Reason* [New York: Seabury, 1947], p. 101).

46. Dryzek, "Political and Ecological Communication," pp. 226–227. See also Carolyn Merchant's work on "partnership (between humans and nature) ethics," for example, *Reinventing Eden: The Fate of Nature in Western Culture* (New York: Routledge, 2003).
47. Rasmussen, *Earth Community, Earth Ethics*; Charles Birch and John B. Cobb Jr., *The Liberation of Life: From the Cell to the Community* (New York: Cambridge University Press, 1981); Wirzba, *The Paradise of God*; M. Tucker, *Worldly Wonder*, p. 11; T. Berry, *Dream of the Earth*, p. 17.
48. Which some writers in the Marxist tradition think are essential. See Steven Vogel, *Against Nature: The Concept of Nature in Critical Theory* (Albany: State University of New York Press, 1996).
49. Musician Jim Nollman outfitted a boat so that he could amplify the sound of his guitar underwater. From time to time whales would gather round, and he and they would exchange riffs. Ironically, he was at times forbidden to interact with them because some were members of "endangered species," and the only people who could legally interact with them were scientists studying them! Nollman, *The Man Who Talks to Whales: The Art of Interspecies Communication* (Boulder, CO: Sentient Publications, 2002), and *The Charged Border: Where Whales and Humans Meet* (New York: Henry Holt, 1999).
50. Nollman, *Man Who Talks to Whales*, p. 11.
51. William Souder, *A Plague of Frogs: Unraveling an Environmental Mystery* (Minneapolis: University of Minnesota Press, 2000), p. 287.
52. Uhl, *Developing Ecological Consciousness*, pp. 127–131.
53. Charles Taylor, *Modern Social Imaginaries* (Durham, NC: Duke University Press, 2004).
54. Kierkegaard, *Concluding Unscientific Postscript.*
55. *Ethics of the Fathers* 4:2.

INDEX